Marthe

TRANSLATED FROM THE FRENCH BY
DONALD M. FRAME

INTRODUCTION BY FREDERICK BROWN

A Helen and Kurt Wolff Book

Harcourt Brace Jovanovich, Publishers

San Diego   New York   London

Marthe

Library of Congress Cataloging in Publication Data
Marthe. English.
    Marthe.
    "A Helen and Kurt Wolff book."
    1. Young women—France—Normandy—Social conditions—
Case studies. 2. Young women—France—Normandy—Sexual
behavior—Case studies. 3. Family—France—Normandy—
History—19th century—Case studies. 4. Normandy (France)
—Social life and customs—Case studies. 5. Normandy
(France)—Nobility—History—19th century—Case studies.
6. Normandy (France)—Moral conditions—Case studies.
I. Frame, Donald Murdoch, 1911-   . II. Title.
HQ1619.N67M3713   1984   306.8'5'0924   84-10921
ISBN 0-15-157550-9

Designed by Dalia Hartman

Printed in the United States of America

First edition

A B C D E

Foreword

Marthe consists of letters discovered a decade or so ago in the attic of a French château. Written between 1892 and 1902, they are remarkable for the tale that unfolds in them and for the extraordinarily vivid picture they draw of the *petite noblesse,* the landed gentry who maintained themselves as a distinct class until World War I swept away almost everything on which their existence had been based.

When the story opens, Marthe de Montbourg is twenty, unmarried, and several months shy of bearing a child by a servant or farmhand on the family estate in Normandy. From this predicament a series of calamities follows, which Marthe's widowed mother, Émilie de Montbourg, describes in detail to her brother, Charles de Cerilley, himself a prolific letter writer. The titular heroine seldom appears onstage. What we see of Marthe are mostly images projected by the people in whose hands her fate lies: her mother, guardian, uncle, and later, husband.

To avoid scandal, Émilie leaves Normandy with her two daughters (the elder a shadowy, neurasthenic figure who has renounced marriage) and seeks the anonymity of Paris. There Marthe spends the last months of her confinement in a home for pregnant girls. Once the child is born, they settle in Grasse, near Nice, and undertake to find a man who will legitimize Marthe's son and satisfy her lusty nature. Émilie enlists the help of priests and relatives. Personal ads are placed and answered. Minute inquiries are made to verify the credentials of suitors for whom the burden Marthe brings is outweighed by the handsome dowry that comes with her. After two years, during which a pharmacist, a postal functionary, and two stationmasters receive consideration, the search ends with a local man, Robert Caron d'Aillot, who has demonstrated no perceptible talent at earning a livelihood—quite the contrary—but who enjoys in Émilie's eyes the inestimable advantage of possessing, like Marthe, a noble patronymic.

The marriage almost immediately proves disastrous. Letters flying among the concerned parties omit nothing of the quarrels that rage between Marthe and Robert. With his mother and maiden sisters, Robert tyrannizes Marthe in the name of moral rehabilitation. "A good husband who took on his painful task with patience and perseverance to make this girl, a poor lost girl . . . full of vices and defects, into a nice wife able to take her place in a salon," Robert calls himself. Marthe becomes a virtual prisoner, employing ruses to let the outside world know how things really stand while feigning happiness and contrition in letters written under her husband's scrutiny. Did the Napoleonic Code not declare that obedience was what every wife owed her husband in return for protection? And obedience was something he could legally enforce *manu militari,* if need be.

Several years pass before Marthe musters the courage to run away. She has been hindered from doing so by a sexual bond to which she freely admits, by the knowledge that her family—at least its head, Charles de Cerilley, whose opinions usually prevail—fear her freedom more than they deplore her enslavement, and finally by the evidence of a tainted past, which would undermine any action she might bring against her husband in a court of law. Halfway through the correspondence we learn from Robert that Marthe's pregnancy was not, as he had been told, the result of a single lapse but of sexual adventures begun at age fourteen and tolerated by her mother. Émilie was the more disposed to turn a blind eye to her daughter's promiscuity because she has a secret of her own to conceal. This secret, when Robert suddenly bares it, introduces the family ghost, Émilie's deceased husband Armand de Montbourg. If we may believe Robert or his informant Marthe, Armand de Montbourg contracted syphilis during a youthful affair with a dancer in Caen and later transmitted it to his wife. The fact that Marthe has had periodic skin eruptions since the age of nine persuades Robert that she was born diseased. Heredity enters the picture in its pseudoscientific, nineteenth-century role as a stand-in for original sin. Begotten by a fallen father—a *père déchu* Émilie calls him—the fallen woman was born to fall.

Marthe does not flee until her husband, believing that she has cuckolded him with a valet during one of his sojourns in Marseille, threatens to murder her. Before long, divorce proceedings begin. Under close examination by lawyers hired to represent Marthe, witnesses to her alleged indiscretion turn against Robert, who had apparently bullied them into perjuring themselves. Robert capitulates, a sum of money is settled on him, and he disappears from Marthe's life. Free at last to assume the responsibilities of motherhood, Marthe retrieves her four-year-old son, Georges, from the nurse with whom he has lived since birth.

No sooner are we convinced that justice has won out when information reaching Charles de Cerilley persuades him that Robert's allegations about Marthe and the valet are true. "What the devil, I'll agree that hysteria is an invincible passion," exclaims the uncle, "but it renders us oblivious to our acts only during *crises,* and in anticipation of such crises the honest soul appeals for protection. Did she? No. When she hasn't been cynical with her mother she has put on shows of every kind, lying out of self-interest or fear, shrewdly imitating candor. . . ."

Once the drama has concluded, the personae are dispatched in quick succession. Marthe's child, sister, and mother all die of what is diagnosed as acute dysentery. Marthe herself retires with a female companion to a cottage outside Millau in the Aveyron and exchanges warm letters with her relatives, who in correspondence among themselves dwell upon her duplicitous nature. After several years, Marthe begins to ail. Her symptoms indicate a respiratory disorder. Several visits to the spa at Mont-Dore for hydrotherapy have no effect, and she dies in 1902 at the age of thirty.

There is nothing more poignant about *Marthe* than the dilemma of Émilie de Montbourg shopping in a matrimonial bargain basement for the man who would "save" her daughter while still doing her utmost to look grand. Indeed, Émilie grew more and more fastidious in her concern with appearances as the prospect of coming down in the world was borne home by the humble applications her daughter received. "I myself feel incapable of resolving the difficulty of such a mismatch, which negates the principles of my whole life," she declared when the candidate for Marthe's hand was a small-town stationmaster. "Because of my nephews and nieces and the people we know, wouldn't there be a way, for the sake of appearances, to pay the government for authorization to add the name of *de Beauvoisin* to his? The family comes from Pont de Beauvoisin in Dauphiné." This strategy (fashionable among newly enriched bourgeois) did not inhibit her, several years later, from telling one of those nephews on whose account she had been tempted to employ it that he was right in scoring the aristocratic class for violating its honor, "because then it lacks its fundamental virtue." The ease with which Émilie could give the slip to her venal, calculating self and voice opinions worthy of Corneille's Chimène would have provided excellent material for a tragicomic role in *Remembrance of Things Past.* What strikes one as Proustian about her is the hysterical piety she lavished on forms that hid the real circumstances of her life. Aristocracy had become snob theater and the gentlewoman a character forever reinventing herself.

Her moral investment in conventional appearances, ceremonies, and façades went together with the feeling that, in her daughter, her honorable self was bonded to a wild woman and subject to acts over which she had no control. Here she exemplified a state of mind not at all uncommon among the upper classes. We need only consult books on domestic management, which proliferated during the late nineteenth century, to see how often the maid figured as one such threat. A manual read by girls in high school asserts that it is no easy task "mastering these untutored or degenerate natures" who, left to their own devices, would subvert home life.

Even before she compromised herself, this intimate outsider stood accused of opening the family to public view, of absconding with its secrets and introducing, in her own person, a morbid element. Although material theft may have been widespread, the vigilance wives and mothers were urged to maintain bespoke a fear that embraced the whole issue of social identity. The maid-thief came from the underworld. There lurked in her a lower species (with all that connoted in the way of coarse language, moral obtuseness, criminal physiognomy, disease) and a primitive past against which the combined agencies of church and state were thought to offer inadequate protection. Being sexually dangerous, she would, if let loose upon the husband or son, rob the family of a future by contaminating its offspring with her own degenerate nature.

Even more sinister than the maid was the ex-maid who, after leaving or being expelled from the domestic ranks, descended to the street and became a prostitute, like Edmond de Goncourt's fictional heroine in *La Fille Élisa*. Indoors she had had, in her mistress, a mother substitute; outside no moral influence could touch her. Measures by which the government tried to sanitize prostitution did little to dispel the fears of ladies and gentlemen who pictured the prostitute as a fifth-columnist in a civil war that would either save or doom the family order. Prostitution "saps the family little by little, without one's being aware of it, much the way rats undermine a house unknown to its tenants," warned Dumas *fils* in his long preface to *Camille,* which describes with alarm the mongrel species resulting from intermarriage between upright sons and fallen women. The power of infiltration conferred upon the prostitute lost nothing of its supernatural quality when, after 1878, researchers discovered the bacilli responsible for gonorrhea and syphilis. She was evil, a bearer of evil, and those who preached against her understood hell on earth to be the rotting away of posterity it was her mission to accomplish: The havoc socialists would wreak by political means she would sow in bed.

As the century wore on, this vision, which was profoundly related to the mass hysteria that beset France during the Dreyfus Affair (the Jew being another subversive bacillus), gained converts among men who ordinarily prided themselves on their skeptical demeanor. "Though it was not for some time apparent, a terrible anguish began to grip the medical profession," writes Professor Alain Corbin. "In that milieu, the conviction took hold that the prostitute was preparing or rather accelerating the destruction of the bourgeois classes. The two major phantasms of the age intersected here—fear of regression and fear of degeneration. The venal woman was indeed considered a model of regression." It is paradoxical that a society so baleful in its view of things to come should otherwise have set store by the idea of progress. Or perhaps the idea of progress was inherently bound up with this terror of regression that found a scientific rationale in theories of heredity and a genetic villain in the whore. At any rate, time no longer held indefinite promise for those whom it had once favored. It was seen more and more to hold buried secrets the revelation of which would kill, maim, or stunt the innocent.

What could be hidden from sight now would in due course, when "time ran out," produce a generation of hostages. Émilie de Montbourg's letters articulate the sense that time had indeed run out, that matrimony was more likely to visit ghosts upon the future than to create something greater or better. Thrown into a world abounding in secrets, Émilie is at once the sleuth for whom venality lurks everywhere and the fugitive with nowhere to go. "Really, when a young man has had a stormy life, does he reveal anything about it except what he cannot hide? If all young people confessed to the families of their intended how many marriages would take place?" she asks her brother. We know how Ibsen or Zola would have answered her. *Ghosts* and the novels that make up the Rougon-Macquart series evoke a haunted world where the dead force the living to pay heavy tribute.

Such a tributary was Marthe, in whom her relatives saw the features so often cited as belonging to the pathological condition of womankind (she is "incomplete," "unraveled," "hysterical," "fickle," "duplicitous") and others as well that set her apart. "You know very well that [should she divorce] the material consequence for her will be *the street*—you understand me clearly—*the street,* as long as age hasn't *utterly* cooled off her morbid ardor," proclaimed Charles de Cerilley. Had she been a man, "morbid ardor" might have been called "slumming it" or passed off as inverted snobbery of the kind that had become fashionable in Paris, where the upper crust affected street slang and made forays into "Apache territory." As it was, there seemed no proper explanation for her affinity to men beneath her in social rank except the hereditary one, which had it that Armand de Montbourg's sins came home to roost in Marthe. "What then is this nature?" lamented Émilie, who, though not always unaware of the rage and shame from which Marthe's will to self-debasement sprang, felt genuinely baffled when told that her latest inamorato was an omnibus driver. Life had played Émilie dirty. For all her suffering motherhood, it had given her an aristocratic whore for a daughter, a *fille-mère* in whose freakish constitution nothing squared with the social norms of the day. Robert Caron d'Aillot boasted that he had "made of that little monstrosity that you knew a woman like other women," but even the penitential regime of marriage failed to correct nature's wrong.

Nature's wrong for some was nature's due for others, or so one gathers from the Larousse *Grand Dictionnaire* where it is categorically stated that her sexual appetite makes the average woman the equal of two and a half men. No matter. In Charles de Cerilley's eyes, Marthe remained aberrant until the last, and when she died he forbade obituary notices to be published. Without an official announcement of its conclusion, her life would be as if it had never been. "She lied all her life; play-acting came naturally to her" was how he dismissed her in 1902, long after the Church had given up denying actresses burial in consecrated ground.

This indictment could have been served up against the indicter, but by and large a country whose civil code did not acknowledge the existence of the "natural family" found ostracism beyond the grave appropriate punishment for female renegades, including above all *fille-mères*. Even feminist groups eschewed the unwed mother lest they discredit themselves and some actually scolded her in public. The most hospitable opinion was expressed by a contributor to *La Française* in 1913: "A woman who gives herself outside marriage is guilty. But there exists no proportion between the nature of the error and the judgment with which the world scourges it. What makes still more odious the shame inflicted on natural mothers and children is the absolution granted the father." As for lawfully wedded women, their husbands would continue to be the arbiters of their personal conduct and their correspondence until 1938, when a socialist government revised the matrimonial code.

If Charles de Cerilley was so determined to consign Marthe to oblivion, why did he preserve these letters, which have made her a celebrity in France eighty years after her unpublished death? He himself answers the question toward the end, in a note to Marthe that shows nothing of his characteristic phlegm: "I've finished sorting out the papers. Lord, what correspondence, throbbing with painful interest!!! And how important it is to preserve it well! That's your protection." Before the curtain had quite rung down on the drama in which he played an important role as Marthe's protector, he managed to gain distance from it and review its episodes as an enthusiastic spectator. What unexpectedly got the better of him was that huge nineteenth-century appetite for the intricately plotted story on which newspapers traded with the serial novel and lending libraries with the "three-decker." Tucked away in Burgundy, this squire, about whom one surmises that he usually applied himself to serious matters such as agronomy and law, had been kept in suspense during the previous seven years by the twists and turns of his unpredictable niece.

De Cerilley's absorption calls to mind an essay entitled "Literary Memories" in which Paul Valéry wrote that at theaters and concert halls he would often imagine "an all-powerful sultan" surrounding the crowd and compelling every member of it to relate the strangest thing he had ever seen, heard, or experienced. "What a catch! What an abundance of impressions!" he exclaimed. Squeezed like a sponge, "the public would see its personal past, its singular experiences stream before it. For the public itself is that sultan who sits bored upon his treasures. A writer, be he poet or storyteller, is just another man bold enough to have broken the general silence and taken the floor." In *Marthe* we find characters who broke the silence unintentionally and wrote their tale with none of the self-consciousness that often afflicts those who take the floor. They turned out to have been authors in need of an editor for the first-rate epistolary novel Zola and the naturalists never brought forth.

—Frederick Brown

Principal Characters

(The ages given are those either of 1892 or of the date of the character's first appearance in the correspondence.)

MARTHE DE MONTBOURG, age 20; at the beginning, uses the pseudonym MARIE ROUGEMONT.[1]

ÉMILIE DE MONTBOURG, age 68, née de Cerilley, mother of Marthe, widow of Armand de Montbourg.

ÉLÉONORE DE MONTBOURG, age 24, older sister of Marthe.

ÉMILE DE MONTBOURG, older brother of Éléonore and Marthe, died in 1891 at age 28.

CHARLES DE CERILLEY, age 66, brother of Émilie, uncle of Marthe.

MADELEINE DE CERILLEY, wife of Charles, mother of Henri.

HENRI DE CERILLEY, age 30, son of Charles, cousin of Marthe.

ADÈLE DE CERILLEY, wife of Henri, mother of several children.

ROBERT CARON D'AILLOT, age 33, husband of Marthe.[2]

SOPHIE DE MONTBOURG, age 60, née de Cerilley, sister of Émilie and Charles, wife of Honoré de Montbourg.

MONSIEUR DE SAINT-RENÉ, age about 70, distant uncle and quondam tutor of Éléonore and Marthe de Montbourg.

SUMMARY FAMILY TREE

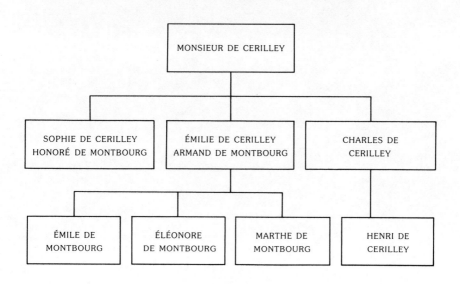

The Château de Saint-Savin[3] is located in Normandy, that of Sangy in Burgundy. Labastide and the Château des Clues are situated in the Alpes-Maritimes. The other place names are familiar.

Since money will often be an issue in the following letters, a few basic facts have been brought together so the reader can estimate, if only approximately, the value of the sums cited:

1. *Wages and salaries* (all per month). Chambermaid (with food, lodging, and laundry): 30 francs. Cook: 50 francs. Pension of a retired customs officer (captain): 100 francs. Salary of a small-town tax-collector: 330 francs.

2. *Food.* One Bresse chicken: 4 francs. One partridge: 2.50 francs. One two-kilo pâté: 10 francs. One kilo of pastry-shop biscuits: 6 francs.

3. *Miscellaneous.* Hyères-Cannes rail fare, one way (about 65 miles): 10.55 francs. A fine hunting rifle: 180 francs. Selling price of a cow: 300 to 500 francs.

Obviously, the coefficient for changing figures of the period (1890s) into current (1982) figures is quite variable, according to the object in question, multiplying by anything from 10 to 50.

To conclude this preamble, note that the Montbourgs' fortune in 1892 may be estimated at at least 500,000 francs of that time—between 5 and 25 million of our present-day francs (between approximately $600,-000 and $3 million at current rates).

Marthe

Correspondence
1892

ÉMILIE DE MONTBOURG
TO CHARLES DE CERILLEY
Paris, August 22, 1892

Dear Charles,

I'm heartbroken about the letter that Marie [Marthe] has written you and that those ladies[4] have sent me opened, to be sure I took note of it. A cult! And she sends you to pray at the tomb of her father, who would kill that odious scoundrel! What thoughtlessness! Believe me, her spells of melancholy and her deep despair come simply from the fact that she can't continue the frightful little game she's been playing. Her madness is not diminishing. She is calmer physically, but she has no sense, and even less feeling. You have no idea of her selfishness toward poor Madame Berteau, whom she sends out to get whatever it comes into her head to eat, and toward us, whom she wears out with errands and expenses, without ever inquiring about our fatigue and our means. And she would like to marry a penniless workman! The agent gave us an estimate on Saint-Savin. Here is his summary:

Château and 3 hectares of park as far as the road . . . . 50,000 [francs]
Reserve: 17 hectares 60 ares. 50,000
Farm: 46 hectares 25 ares 165,000
Total 265,000

I've told you that the twenty-one-year term will not expire until May 17, 1893. That gives us some time to sell, but we'll soon have to get busy. I beg you to tell that poor creature in no uncertain terms that she's the one making it necessary for us to sell, and to strangers, too, for no one in the family will want to put up with the mud splashed by her misdeed. And for her sister, for me, for herself, staying in the region is impossible! How can she not feel how painful this sale is for us—for me, who had so much work done on the place, who have suffered so much so that my children might benefit, and whom she puts in the position of seeing strangers profit by it? I myself am becoming a wanderer in my last years, unable to take advantage of what is mine, and lacking everything I enjoyed at home! My poor Éléonore, uprooted just as she is feeling the urge to settle down, ashamed to live in the same part of the world as her sister! And filled with terror for the troubles the infamous creature can still cause her! . . . If God has me live until she is twenty-five, dear brother, I'll sail for America, where it might be hard to find me to get a consent I shall *never* give! Honor forbids crowning the most horrible of crimes! The curate of Tourette[5] writes me that in so many words. Send my enclosed letter to the agent.

Very affectionately, your sister,

Émilie

Be sure to tell M. it's her conduct that's causing the sale of Saint-Savin: she holds me responsible and bears me quite a grudge for that.

ÉMILIE DE MONTBOURG
TO CHARLES DE CERILLEY
Paris, August 23, 1892

Dear Charles,

Marie has really been carrying on lately! She was given a bottle of Málaga wine with cinchona and went at it too fast; her whirling head led her to seek the support of the priests from the Midi for her rebellion against the family. Those ladies have sent me her letters. I must explain the situation. I hope these two priests will give her wise advice, and have asked them to send me their answer. She had already tried to incite her table-mates against the nuns, who acted wisely by locking Marie in her room, alone. I told her to stop behaving like that, with such pure ingratitude; they do everything they can for her. All her culinary fancies are satisfied; the nuns and we ourselves bring her everything she asks for. I warned her seriously that if she continued I'd tell Monsieur de Saint-René about it, and he would have her transferred to some place where she'd be worse off. She says so many stupid, nasty things that the nuns, as well as her companions, always call her *the lunatic.* A long bath would have eased her lower back. She was to take one on Monday; but on Sunday, while reciting to me the fine phrases she had written to the curate of Tourette for me to comment on, she flew into a rage, refused the bath, and declared that she doesn't want to see me for a week. But I am still to ask them for the little dishes she likes. During that week she hopes to receive a reply that will put her in the right, against us, so as to defy me a little more arrogantly. She'll get caught at it, no doubt. . . . We'll see the effect of this first reply. I have the letter she wrote this morning to the other priest, whom I must inform of her mental condition and of the situation she's dreaming about for the future. Public opinion has more influence on her than our opinion. Here she took a dislike to the daughters of the nobility, who are outraged at how unrepentant and ungrateful she is— they, who don't know how to ask pardon enough of their families, though their families certainly would not have chased after them to give them a fresh start; and she throws herself in the arms of the daughters of the people who flatter her, and to whom she gives all her things. She doesn't care a bit about the kind deeds of the Father,[6] who amuses her, says she! I assure you, you mustn't think that after the delivery we'll be able to take her in with us. We'll have to put her into another institution until she is twenty-five—a Bon Pasteur [Good Shepherd],[7] for example, where she will be kept as she is here.

Many fond greetings to you and Madeleine. It's been pouring since this morning.

Your affectionate sister,

Émilie

ÉMILIE DE MONTBOURG
TO CHARLES DE CERILLEY
Paris, August 26, 1892

Dear Charles,

From Saint-Omer I've been offered a match for Marie. I'm going to reply that a carriage accident left her with a condition of the spinal cord, and that at this point we cannot think of seeing her married.

Monsieur de Saint-René came to see us yesterday; he's well and leaving for the country. We agreed that since Marie will not reach age twenty until May 17, 1893, we have plenty of time to sell Saint-Savin.

The rain has come at last to lower the temperature, from which we were suffering badly. The *complete* analysis of Marie's urine showed that she lacks phosphate and that there are *vibrions* [bacilli]. What are they? Animals, or microbes?

We went to the Jardin des Plantes,[8] which was *roasting* in the sun. Éléonore enjoyed seeing the animals; we'll go again. The trolley runs along the boulevard beside us and goes straight there.

Little by little I'll show her Paris. Alas, you understand that I can't enjoy anything and that all this is a chore for me. Yet I have to appear interested, for Éléonore is perceptive, and wouldn't want to go out any more.

Marie is calmer, but she doesn't want to see me these days, because I don't appreciate her ideas. She gave Éléonore a better welcome—out of egoism, of course! I'm going to give some artificial flowers to the nuns' chapel, to make them better disposed to put up with M.'s bad character. The good curate of Tourette has answered me that obviously our honor cannot allow a marriage to crown such wretched conduct. I'm sure the doyen de Coursegoules[9] will be of the same opinion. These gentlemen of the active clergy are in a better position to judge such things than are monks (that chaplain Marie makes fun of, for instance).

We'll see the effect produced by these two priests on the poor child, who imagined that out of *conscience* I'd be led to give my consent.

Since there is still more than a year before she reaches twenty-one, there are six before she turns twenty-five. Until then how much do we still have to put up with?

If she stays calm, we won't have to worry about a Good Shepherd except for after the delivery. In any case, they don't accept girls in her condition there. She really must have caught something, to be isolated for her meals.

Today I'll go find out what the doctor thinks of the result of M.'s urinalysis. In spite of all the trouble she gives me, I mustn't ever have to reproach myself for not having done everything for her.

You shouldn't wait for the harvest to send the bag of potatoes. It would be better if that could be done right away. You'll have to address them to Madame Moreau and pay the freight charge. See if that can be done right away, for poor Madame Berteau, who does all the errands, is worn out. My heartfelt greetings, my kind brother.

Your shattered sister,

Émilie

Dear Charles,

Please mail the enclosed letter to Adrienne: the dear child is always thirsty for our affection, and the anniversary of her engagement would be painful without a friendly word from us. Alas! My poor heart suffers from these relationships, and God must take a hand in them if I am not to fall ill. But Marie's contrition makes me feel better.

Her good intentions persist not to marry the good-for-nothing. But . . . the hysteria also persists, and after the ordeal I'll have to look around seriously for a husband. The sentence in your letter that she rereads with pleasure, "It would be better to make a poor but honest man happy," has made her hark back to the sight she had in Vence of that young man of eighteen, son of the justice of the peace, personally attractive, a nice boy, but without a secured position or money, or special education; his half-brother, a son by the first marriage, is a tax collector. The justice of the peace, once a schoolmaster without property, took the daughter of a small —very small—landowner as his second wife, and they had three children, this one and two younger ones. It was her regret at leaving Vence just as a violent passion bloomed that brought on the famous attack. I'm sorry she's thinking about him again, for she needs a more mature guide and support, who would fully comprehend the gravity of an act of adoption —who would not repent of it later and make his wife repent. Gratitude is not enough to bind men, as experience often shows! She understands that after she is back on her feet, if God permits that, she will have to be protected from herself in some religious institution until she marries. Yesterday Éléonore and I went to Clamart. Besides the fifty healthy children we saw in a real, well-shaded park, there are, in a little house attached to it, two girl-mothers bringing up their children, under the surveillance of one of the nuns at all times. Marie cannot do even that: someone else's milk would be better for the child. To bring him up simply, we would need a woman who was accustomed to such things, yet it is not prudent to let her get near anyone but the nuns. So I think we'll have to put the child out to nurse, arranging for his trace and ours to be lost, for I fear someone may blackmail us if we are discovered carrying out this odious scheme. Unfortunately, Clamart is very cold in winter. I beg you, help us to find a husband who is attractive in person, in health, and in character. Marie will have 6,000 francs right away. I dare not promise more; though after I am gone, there will be perhaps another 6,000, and Éléonore will not do wrong by her nephews and nieces if they are nice to her. When we sell Saint-Savin, we'll save her some linen and silverware. I leave you now so I can go out with Éléonore, who is getting a headache. Good-bye, my dear brother.

My most affectionate greetings,

Émilie

ÉMILIE DE MONTBOURG
TO CHARLES DE CERILLEY
Paris, September 10, 1892

Dear Charles,

The grapes arrived yesterday evening in excellent condition. They are quite as handsome and good as those that sell here at 8 sous a pound.

Marie is suffering from hemorrhoids, both internal and external; apart from that, her general condition seems better; that is to say, she no longer suffers head and lower-back pain. But since her legs are weakening and she is getting thin, having no more appetite though all her dietary fancies are satisfied, I sent a piece of flannel to Bordeaux.[10] As soon as his reply arrives, Éléonore and I will go to Vence to move out. The landlady is having us pay half the rent, as compensation. That's better than the whole thing! Moreover, here we make do without a lot of things, especially warm blankets, and, since we must move out, we'll bring along everything that will be useful to us here and address the rest to the Sangy station in your name. You won't mind, will you, seeing that they are dropped off at the Minster?[11] For us the future is the unknown. . . . The problem is getting through the winter without suffering too much from the cold or falling ill.

We shall probably leave next Wednesday or Thursday, to make a round trip. What a pity that circumstances prevent us from stopping at Sangy. We'll be away eight to ten days, which is too long for Marie; she needs to have someone fix her something to eat every day, for the cooking there is detestable, and when you already have no appetite, it's out of the question. Yesterday, while we were out gathering information for our trip, we bought her a partridge for 2 francs 50. It's a good one, and in our remote district there aren't any. The poor child is beginning to appreciate our being near and our devotedness in comparison with the others, and though she is in pain, she knows very well that she would be in even greater pain if we were not there. So we must cut the trip as short as possible, for I'll not be able to leave her fresh food for ten days. Éléonore is happy to be traveling. For me it's another matter, but I have no choice.

Éléonore cannot go so far away by herself—I'd be too worried. So don't write to me *here*. Good-bye, dear Charles, my very fond greetings. The sale of the livestock will not take place until October 2. If you want one more batch of butter, I'll make a note of it.

Your very affectionate sister,

Émilie

ÉLÉONORE DE MONTBOURG
TO CHARLES DE CERILLEY
Paris, September 10, 1892

Dear Uncle,

I'm asking Mama for a little space into which to slip my very heartfelt thanks, which I send both to you and to my aunt, for the splendid grapes you sent us. We got them yesterday evening, and Mama immediately spread out those beautiful bunches on towels, so that thanks to you we have before us a little reminder of the vintage. You know about the fortunate change that has taken place in our Marie; it's a great consolation, and even as we continue to take precautions, we can hope that Notre-Dame-des-Victoires[12] will grant us this consolation in full. Mama goes there twice a day, and Madame B. was telling me yesterday that Marie wants these visits so much that she is always ready to go to the parlor. What a mercy to have found this excellent lady! She calls herself everyone's grandma, and all the boarders regard her as such.

We're going to go to Vence and move out, taking advantage of the last days of summer. Marie is no longer suffering from those headaches that were worrying the doctor, and Mama will leave her a good supply of pleasant and nourishing goodies.

Dear uncle, please share with my dear aunt my very affectionate gratitude,

Éléonore

ÉMILIE DE MONTBOURG
TO CHARLES DE CERILLEY
Paris, September 20, 1982

Dear Charles,

We arrived yesterday evening, very tired but safe and sound. You will receive by freight: one case, one bag, one big crate that I will ask you to have forwarded to the Minster, plus three bundles of bedding and padding to be put on the table and chairs that will be assembled. The bag of linens, too. All this to accommodate us until we can settle somewhere.

Back there [in Vence] I learned of the death of the justice of the peace: on a spree at a wedding, he fell downstairs and landed on his head. He leaves many debts, and not a sou to pay them. He has run through half his wife's estate, which was not much. There are four children. Those by the first wife have nothing from their parents. Nevertheless, the second wife wants the children by the first wife to pay half of the debts. The oldest is starting as a tax collector; the second, who had so strongly impressed Marie and who was unsuccessful in his studies, is strolling around, cane in hand. They say he's going to try the military school at Saint-Maixent and that if he fails he will try to get a tax-collectorship. All that has greatly distressed M., but she understands that that dream is beyond realization, and she's getting used to it.

The good curate of Tourette, on whom we called in his mountain retreat, is going to check up on a young man in his parish for Marie. Age twenty-three or twenty-four. Has one more year of military service. Good family, coat of arms and motto. No noble particle before his name, Italian style. Little money. [One of] four children, the son and three daughters. The son, personally attractive, a good lad, intelligent, did very well at the Collège Stanislas,[13] in Cannes, I think. Has his degree. While he was waiting for his military service, his father put him to work helping him at the record office of the justice of the peace of Grasse; the father occupies the position of justice, which he would like to leave his son. But if the thing should work out, Marie would prefer the railroads.

The doctor is taking care of M. Her health is better at last. It was possible to combine the counsels from Bordeaux with those from here, and the effects are apparent in her improved morale. Lord help us! I'm also going to send a few strands of Éléonore's hair, which fell out when she was combing it; there's no other way to get any, but I am assured that this will be enough. But would that she were willing to follow this advice! It's their father's obstinacy, I find it in them all, and to their misfortune, in a different way in each! In the last seven days, 2,200 kilometers, a climb under the burning sun, and the move—that's a lot for the two of us! It was time we settled down. They're making great preparations for the 22nd.[14] We'll probably rest up. Good-bye, dear Charles.

A thousand fond wishes from your distressed sister,

Émilie

Dear Charles,

A thousand thanks for the memorial service you dedicated to the memory of my son. I feel that he's well off in heaven, but nevertheless, you'll have an anniversary service performed in my name next October 17. I owe it to the region. Should I have one ordered at Saint-Savin? I'd just as soon not, for that would mean calling the public's attention to us. There's quite enough of that from the sale of our livestock October 2. What do you think? A service, in that region, requires written announcements, the same way as for a death—a number of priests, bread to the poor, and problems! In your opinion, what should I do? What would you do in my place? People think I'm at Sangy. I had several hundred Masses said for my poor Armand during the year, and I didn't have any service performed at the end of the year. So that won't astonish anyone! Especially since the tomb is at Sangy.

Marie offered some of your grapes, which we greatly enjoyed, and for which she asks me to thank you very much.

The death of her dog, who must have swallowed some poison when he ran away, is driving my poor daughter to despair; he was a concern that kept her occupied, for she gets very bored among the staff, in spite of my two long visits a day. She would like to have another six-month-old dog, and the nuns are letting her wheedle them into it. The midwife, who is alarmed at the condition she finds Marie in, is going to speak about it to the Father, the director of the house. I'm waiting a few days before getting involved, for she may make up her mind to do without one, which would be best. But if she falls ill, I'll have to make a decision; now Madame Moreau is becoming so authoritarian, so curt, that the boarders are full of complaints and would walk out if it weren't for the kindness of Madame Berteau. Unfortunately, we must not put pressure on Madame Berteau, for the Father and the directress together make her very unhappy, and what is more, her kind heart suffers from everything her two superiors make the people around her endure.

I had ordered the second parcel of butter sent, at the same time as the first. Haven't you received it? The one I ordered just lately is the third.

If health and circumstances allow a marriage for M., people will say quite simply "a marriage of inclination."

I'm very sorry about Madeleine's pimples. It's not serious, but it is annoying.

I'm sending you the program for the celebrations, which aroused curiosity, but no enthusiasm: there was not one shout of "Long live the Republic!" The windows are still decorated.

Send me the 700 francs, in the name of Rougemont, *here*. In small bills if you can. Don't worry, I keep only business letters. All the others are burned.

You must be pleased about your young vines.

I send all my sisterly sadness,

Émilie

ÉMILIE DE MONTBOURG
TO CHARLES DE CERILLEY
Paris, September 28, 1892

Dear Charles,

I received very punctually the 700 francs you addressed to me on the 25th, also the three packages of grapes, one of them for Marie. Everything arrives safe and sound, as you see. The bag of potatoes will give great pleasure, for there are at least thirty-two mouths to feed in the house, and the poor cook has a lot of trouble satisfying everyone with the amount they give her for cooking. I'll send you back your empty bag along with your two pretty baskets, and if it's still under five kilos, I'll put in an empty bag of ours, so as to have another bag of potatoes later. M. is making up her mind to get along without a dog. She sees perfectly well that she arouses jealousy because of the favors they grant her, though these are necessary for her health. My presence allows these favors, for the nuns know I am there to take care of her. Besides, I reduce their trouble and expenses by paying 150 francs a month, and the little gifts keep up their friendship.

The curate of Tourette will not speak to the family he has in mind until he returns from the retreat he began last Monday, the 25th, in Nice. Since he will return to his parish next Saturday, he will not be able to speak to them until the beginning of next week. By the end of the week we will know whether the first overture is accepted by the parents. Our visit made too great a stir in the little village. Out of prudence the curate had to wait till after his trip, to put people off the track.

From Bordeaux I learn that Éléonore does not have any damaged organs. All her troubles come from weakness. Her diet absolutely must be changed, but she stubbornly resists my entreaties: eat fresh food, lots of grapes to avoid pimples, and leave the brandy alone.

I'll be sure not to write to my old Norman curate, which would be an admission that I have no one else to confide in about the dismal situation. I have had no Masses said at Saint-Savin, and I shall certainly not have any said except by monks. And instead of giving bread to the poor of Saint-Savin, I'll give clothes to the children of Saint-Raphaël. That will be a profitable charity for us and will avoid arousing the malicious gossips back there.

Good-bye, dear Charles; affectionate greetings to you, and my congratulations on the prospect of becoming a grandfather.

Your ever-distressed sister,

Émilie

M. is going to do an oil painting of a bouquet of dahlias for Saint-Raphaël, as an altarpiece, and then one for the Holy Virgin. Éléonore is preparing the flowers on velvet for her.

ÉMILIE DE MONTBOURG
TO CHARLES DE CERILLEY
Paris, October 1, 1892

Dear Charles,

A cold in my eyes has kept me from thanking you right away for sending us the grapes, which have given us great pleasure. Éléonore is eating them with gusto; the French ones are better than the American. Sophie has offered me some Sainte-Apolline pears.[15] I'll wait until the summer cholera has started to pass. In these last few days there were three cases on this street, one of them next door to us. All are cured or in the hospital, but one must be prudent; still, I'm grateful for the offer. Alas! Our fine fruit from Saint-Savin has mostly been stolen, or else is selling for very little, and my children get little good out of it.

The good curate of Tourette comes back from his retreat today and will test the ground. He wrote as much to M.; God grant that it works!

Please forward the letters enclosed in the envelope right away. Some of them are very urgent.

The great heat spells are over, and now we'll have to reckon with the weather before going outside. However, Éléonore is badly in need of air and exercise; but we must be careful about her neuralgia.

M. has stopped having fainting spells, thanks to the broth prescribed by Bordeaux.

Good-bye, dear Charles, I must run to the butcher's: I've got to make her something for dinner, since the food they serve apparently kills one's appetite.

When you can, please send the potatoes. I send my fondest gratitude. Your afflicted sister,

Émilie

ÉMILIE DE MONTBOURG
TO CHARLES DE CERILLEY
Paris, October 5, 1892

Dear Charles,

Madame Moreau has granted us permission to buy a dog for Marie. We'll put up a doghouse for him in the courtyard, and Marie will have him in the garden every day. He will supposedly belong to me; and if the others want the same favor, they'll be told: "Have your parents do the same." This concession is an unheard-of thing coming from the directress, but, then, she has never had a boarder like Marie. I pay them with a promptness equaled only by our constant gracious favors. I'm going to buy them a carpet for the stairs, which the girls keep falling on, though they insist on waxing them just the same.

Among the boarders is one girl who is very well behaved, very calm, and in very good health, who will set herself up as a wet nurse after her delivery, to make some money so she can marry her child's father. She comes from 100 leagues from here, and her young man, too.

To occupy the heart, time, and imagination of Marie, it might perhaps be good to let her bring up her child with a wet nurse, in the Clamart house, under Madame Moreau's aegis, while we stay as close as possible. What do you think about that?

I'm waiting to hear from the curate of Tourette how the overture was received. If God wills that the poor child comes out of it well, she'll need time to recover.

Oh, now she appreciates the good fortune of having kind family attentions, for she has a lot to endure in her contact with the common girls who rub elbows with her. Her room is a refuge. Madame Berteau, as a real good angel, spares her all the pain she can. But even some of the nuns are narrow, low, and stupid, and they make Madame Berteau *and* the directress suffer. The Father is such an ascetic, he stupefies these poor girls. One of them is sick in her head. She sets herself up to spy on everyone, both mistresses and boarders, for the greater glory of God; so she is detested by everyone.

When they send the potatoes (as soon as possible), have them put in some mediums to fill the empty spaces left by the big ones. When I return the bag, I'll fill one of the little grape baskets with some hyacinth and tulip bulbs that we had in Vence and I brought back for my Émile's tomb.

Do tell the curate of Sangy that I'm asking for a solemn service, and of course I'm paying. Thanks for being willing to feed these gentlemen of the cloth. Have Madeleine get some poultry from my farmers. I think you finally got the third batch of butter I ordered sent. Our man forgot the second, and I'm very sorry about it.

Madame Gardet[16] has written me that we left too precipitately, that *if there were still time for it* I would do well to take a trip to Normandy, but with my daughters! I'm answering her that the malice of Norman tongues is well known, that we will not undertake such a tiring trip just because of gossip, that no doubt we should have asked the public's permission to leave *quickly* when we're called away *quickly*. That probably people would say we're ruined because the apportionment of the estate might well bring on the sale of Saint-Savin. But that, without asking permission, in this matter we would follow the guidance of the surrogate guardian, who wants equal incomes for the two sisters, which is not possible because the château is now included in one of the shares. That as for me, since the death of my son, I feel that I can no longer live there. Since she's a gossipmonger, she'll be delighted to have that reason to give: no one ever dreamed that we would have the idea of selling Saint-Savin, where they thought they could go on bleeding us to the end. The presence of the surrogate guardian in the necessary apportionment is a good reason to put forward, don't you think? My letter will show her that I absolve her from telling me what the public is thinking, and that we'll regard as gossip whatever people may say.

Good-bye, dear Charles. Sympathize with me for the role I must play. But it's getting easy for me, because I've let no one in Normandy see my distress.

Your afflicted sister,

Émilie

ÉMILIE DE MONTBOURG
TO CHARLES DE CERILLEY
Paris, October 7, 1892

Dear Charles,

The sale of the supplies stocks on hand was not too bad, even though it has been a bad year for hay, which brought down the price of the livestock so badly. Everything sold briskly; the bailiff is even more delighted than I am, for after all the 500-franc cows did sell for 300 francs, and the tools and equipment did sell, though for very little. There's 5,900 francs, from which many expenses must be deducted. Approximately 5,500 will be left, and these in large part belong to me, I gather from what the notary told me, because all that comes out of my administration since my husband's death. Alas! The whole thing was to belong to my Émile, as an investment of his income. I was counting on leaving the storehouse fully stocked, as you know! But it's not paid for in cash, and there may well prove to be gaps in the bill.

The poor child is in so much pain that I don't want to refuse her anything. I'm going to write to Bordeaux, for there are persistent colics that the midwife and doctor don't know how to account for, and white [leucorrhea], yellow, even pink discharges, very abundant, and unusual in her condition. I'm worried . . . and quite vexed not to be able to take care of her myself, the more so because nobody takes responsibility for her, and she often lacks the strength and courage to attend to the small things that might alleviate her sufferings. Oh, I assure you, she's atoning, in spite of everything I can do for her! Her room is damp; I can hardly wait till she can have a wood fire. But they're waiting for the chimney sweeps, as are we. The foot muff is very useful to her, likewise the hot-water cylinder and an alcohol lamp.

They sent home a boarder just recently, a paying one, who was stirring up the others and wouldn't follow the regulations of the house. I think they wanted to set an example. Although M. isn't always easy to handle, her kind heart and my presents make sure she's tolerated; still, one mustn't stretch the cord too tight, for I've been given to understand that this establishment was meant primarily for the poor. You see, they have all the work done by the poor girls, even the maintenance of the Clamart orphanage, and you can't require it of those who are paying 5 francs a day and are fed for the most part by their family, like Marie. The cuisine is lamentable, it seems. The nuns don't look very well, except Madame Berteau, who is the good angel of the house.

Yes to the two bags of potatoes.

Good-bye, good-bye, let me have news of you. I'm going out for a doghouse and a dog.

Most affectionately, your forlorn sister,

Émilie

Dear good Uncle,

    I can at last write you without fearing to disturb you, and thank you for the delicious grapes you were kind enough to send me. Thanks to the ineffable goodness of Madame Berteau, I'm less unsociable, and I'm getting more or less used to Saint-Raphaël. I made an altarpiece in oil on velvet. All the nuns considered it a real success, which has encouraged me to make one soon for the altar of the Holy Virgin. I am extremely grateful to you, my kind uncle, for allowing me to keep my child near me, which will be a great consolation to me. I hope Monsieur de Saint-René won't oppose that. I surely have the right to keep my child; it's quite enough to deprive him of his father without depriving him of his mother. Mama has no doubt talked to you about the plan of the good curate of Tourette? That kind man is willing to take an interest in me, for which I am very grateful. However, I'm not getting any illusions. I have become very hard to place; I don't know who will be willing to adopt the child, for without that no marriage is possible. I insist on having the poor little fellow treated as well as possible; if it were to happen otherwise, I'd put up a real fight. I'd have the right, as a mother has the right and the duty to protect her child. Furthermore, I haven't yet received the definitive answer from the good curate. I hope it will be good, for, though I don't look it, I'm terrified about the future: I cannot go on without support, and the child without a father, and, besides, people are so cruelly caustic. There's no use struggling against them, for they always wind up crushing you pitilessly. If I were alone, that wouldn't matter so much—but my child. Oh, no, I won't abandon him to this howling world; I'll keep him with me. Yet I'm only a woman. I know that the child will need a defender. You who are so kind to me, guide me, advise me. I have—alas!—let myself be guided all too much by my own mind, which has led me into misfortune. Your letters, which I have treasured, once in a while restore my morale, which is often very low. If Mama didn't come to see me, I think I'd end up falling into a melancholy spell, but fortunately she does. So—and it will be especially for her sake that I'll do it—I'll let myself be married. As long as the child is happy, I care little about anything else. Let me hear from you as often as possible, dear kind uncle, for your letters always give me much pleasure and do me much good. You are the only one who has shown me kindness, so I'm both attached and grateful to you.

Please accept, dear kind uncle, this assurance of my profound and respectful affection.

Marie Rougemont

ÉMILIE DE MONTBOURG
TO CHARLES DE CERILLEY
Paris, October 17, 1892[17]

Dear Charles,

You see that her good intentions continue, but the poor child doesn't tell you that she's suffering cruelly and that we are constantly afraid she will have an accident. Nor does she tell you that Madame Moreau shows not the slightest sympathy for her sufferings; that, in spite of the 5 francs a day that we pay, she is very badly cared for; that this heartless lady thinks I come see her too often; that they refuse to let me go up to her room when pains nail her to her bed; that they let her freeze in her damp room in spite of the wood and all the fireplace implements I've supplied for her; that they sometimes forget to give her what I have brought for her to eat, to supplement the abominable cooking. In short, I'm very displeased, and I'm looking elsewhere. When I've found something, I'll lay down my ultimatum. I've learned from the chaplain of the maternity hospital that we were badly directed! The Saint-Raphaël where we are is indeed the cradle of the operation. Madame Moreau used to be a subordinate here, like Madame Berteau. The directress had been in charge for twenty-five years when Madame Moreau, by her intrigues, managed to supplant her and drive her out. That directress went and founded another Saint-Raphaël asylum on the Rue de l'Abbé-Groult in the Vaugirard section [of Paris]. I'm going there right now, in a carriage, to see what it's like. They say that that directress is very distinguished and the midwife very knowledgeable, a primary concern in a maternity case. Madame Moreau is just an ingrate, an autocrat without mercy. I can't bear the torment of knowing that my daughter is suffering without relief and growing desperate all alone. That is intolerable, and it shall change! I'll let you know what happens today, which may perhaps have a decisive effect on our stay.

October 18

Madame Moreau capitulated when she learned that I had sought and found another Saint-Raphaël, where I would be allowed to see and tend to my daughter when she needed it. So we stay here; but she is warned that if she goes back on our agreements, we leave immediately. Kind Madame Berteau was the linchpin of Providence. The two bags of potatoes, which arrived this morning, made the whole household realize that an exceptional boarder deserves special consideration. The nuns and the boarders all indicated to M. their joy at seeing her stay. I think Madame Moreau saw the wrong she would be doing the house by denying me permission to take care of my daughter personally. When she saw that my mind was made up, she deigned to reread the house regulation where it is stated that "The mother, sister, or other person who brought the boarder may go up to her room if the boarder cannot come down to the parlor." So it is understood that when M. feels ill by day or night, they'll come and get me and if I can I'll see her once a day for two hours when she's well, and two or even three times if she is disturbed in her mind; I'll spend the night in her room if that suits me. I cannot ask any more.

My very affectionate wishes, dear Charles.

Your distressed sister,

Émilie

MADAME GUIBERT DE KERLECH
TO ÉMILIE DE MONTBOURG
Saint-Lô, October 19, 1892

Dear Madame,

Your younger daughter's future is at issue today, and I know that for any mother that is the subject of the gravest concern and the most fervent prayers. Who knows whether right now I may not be the instrument of Providence in coming to propose for her a certain young man of about thirty-five who belongs to one of the best families in Saint-Lô. His father was for a long time the manager of direct taxation here and left behind the most honorable memories. His grandfather was mayor of Saint-Lô at a time when the king's choice placed the sash of office only in good hands. My protégé, although shy, is very intelligent. He has read a great deal and made good use of his reading; he knows several languages, he has been a cuirassier, has always had a taste for horses, used to know them well, and rode them remarkably well, in the opinion of experts.

He knows your daughter, has heard a lot about her, likes her, and writes me that he would be only too happy if she were willing to accept him.

His mother, who was a saintly and worthy woman, died last winter

17

of influenza, and two or three days after her death the poor boy slipped in the snow on his way home and broke his leg. The doctor who gave him first aid judged right away how hard it would be for the invalid to endure a long illness without having any other care than that of a more or less faithful housekeeper. So the doctor set him up right away in a nice room in the hospital, where, thanks to a good income, he has enjoyed all the comfort he could wish. That is where Providence was waiting for him. He divided his free time during his long convalescence between study and wise reflections. He learned or perfected two or three languages. He made good resolutions, returning to religious practices that he had neglected a bit before, I think. He is becoming a serious man, determined to make himself a home and live in it as a good husband, pleasing the woman willing to be his mate. A good family life in the country will make him happy and suit his tastes perfectly. If, like many young men, he has had his lapses, he is the first to recognize it and regret it. Should we not be grateful to him for his frankness and take into account his good intentions? The good sisters at the hospital, greatly touched by him, never run out of praise for their patient.

His father and mother, who were our intimate friends, have always praised the gentleness of his character, which lacked only a little energy to gain him a fine position. He has retained the most affectionate memory of his parents, and furthermore has only to recall the example of his father to be an excellent husband.

As for his means, it seems to me I heard talk of 2,000 francs in income.

I'm praying for the success of this step of mine, the more urgently because in fulfilling the wishes of my protégé, I am convinced I will be making your daughter and you happy at the same time. Moreover, dear madame, I am entirely at your disposal to give you all the details and all the information that your maternal solicitude might still desire.

Very sincerely, etc.

E. Guibert de Kerlech

ÉLÉONORE DE MONTBOURG
TO CHARLES DE CERILLEY
[Paris, c. October 19–20, 1892]

Dear Uncle,

As I finish copying these two letters that Mama is submitting for your wise counsel, allow me to thank you for your most affectionate solicitude toward us and our *enfant terrible*. She was very happy today because

Mama bought her a dog. This young puppy is playing thousands of monkeyshines on us this evening; he's delirious with joy at seeing himself free. I would certainly like to be able to walk as fast as he does, but my sprained foot is still not completely healed, and all the Parisians with experience of this streetcar ailment do nothing but preach patience. Fortunately, Mama has not caught bronchitis again, and since we have just about all the shops we need on this street, she will not have to make any long trips on foot (we're in between two streetcar stops). The other day Marie had us get some canned goods so we don't have to go out, and a fur boa for Mama. It was all selected very well, and you can see she's really changed for the better. No doubt you know that we came close to leaving this house, but the directress, who would have lost her boarder, consented to everything Mama was asking; so maybe we'll stay. Dear uncle, let me express my very affectionate gratitude.

Your niece and goddaughter,

Éléonore

MONSIEUR LEBERNIER
TO ÉMILIE DE MONTBOURG
Saint-Lô, October 20, 1892

Dear Baroness,

Yesterday Madame Guibert brought me the letter you will find enclosed; she wanted me to address it to you myself, so that you would know I am acquainted with her plans, and so that I, too, might give you information about the young man, whom I have known for ages and whose family, one of the most honorable in Saint-Lô, I knew well. The young man is exactly like the picture drawn in the letter; I may add that he is very good and is of noble ancestry, though he has never done anything but enlist in the pontifical zouaves some fifteen years ago.

Very sincerely yours, etc.

I. Lebernier

MARIE ROUGEMONT
TO CHARLES DE CERILLEY
Saint-Raphaël, October 22, 1892

Dear kind Uncle,

I'm very worried about your silence; I fear you may be ill. Please give me, and have my aunt give me, news of you, so that I'll stop worrying.

I'm pretty well for the moment, but bored with being shut away. Still, I've only got what I deserve. I'm so fearful of the future, there are days when I give myself up to despair. I'm suffering from this disastrous situation. It is true that on leaving here I'm going to Clamart to bring up my child there, and that I'll stay there a year or more, if Madame Moreau allows me to. What's especially annoying for me is not living under the same roof as Mama any more. Éléonore has become more eccentric than ever, making scenes with Mama about my having stayed here instead of going elsewhere. My word, here I am, here I stay; I've had enough trouble making my niche here, but she hasn't understood that; in short, she's like an angry cat; she'd better not come around reproaching me, for I'd let her have it. Madame Moreau is letting me have another dog. Mama will go get him on Sunday at the dog market, which takes place at noon. At last I'll be able to leave my room—I've shut myself up in it since the death of my poor Doune. I'd be very grateful if you'd send Mama my two issues of *Chasseur Français,* [18] which you must have received, for I'm missing the September and October ones. As soon as I have a definite answer from the curate of Tourette, I'll let you know.

Dear uncle, I send my deep and respectful affection.

Marie Rougemont

ÉMILIE DE MONTBOURG
TO CHARLES DE CERILLEY
Paris, October 22, 1892

Dear Charles,

This morning a wreath for the tomb of my dear Émile is being sent, addressed to you at the Sangy station. Have it placed as well as possible; I got one made entirely of beads because they're more durable. Oh, my brother, how unhappy I am! That child was my life, my happiness! I loved him dearly; he had cost me so many sleepless nights, so many fits of anguish; and God snatched him from me just as I was saying to myself, "At last, here he is!" The present, the future, everything vanished with him. Alas, Marthe *would* not understand that she could, she should, replace him! She didn't love her elders, and she made herself a life outside her family, concealing it with a subtlety one would not have thought her capable of, given the bluntness of her character. Just think: she has only halfhearted remorse for her misdeed, and that only because it prevents her from establishing herself in the family's line! In spite of all my advice, even my prayers, she will not change a thing in the unpleasant way of life she has adopted! What can anyone do about it? The curate of Tourette doesn't write me a thing; I'm worried.

Today I'm sending you back the two cases, the three baskets, and the two empty bags, postage due, for I don't know what all the packing will cost. It's over the five-kilo regulation limit. Please just charge the postage to my account. Thank you, thank you for all you've sent us. Madame Berteau is very grateful for the potatoes, but they're for the house. Her birthday is coming, and we'll have to find something *personal* to get her.

Éléonore sprained her right foot getting off a streetcar. Thinking it wouldn't be anything, she insisted on walking, her ankle swelled up, and the pain finally obliged her to stay still. She is better, however. But she's so unhappy about the situations M. has put herself in, and the coolness she shows in spite of all Éléonore's devotion, that she will pine away, especially as regards her diet, no matter what I do. Oh, my dear, I'm very, very unhappy! And I cannot do anything about the emptyheadedness of these children. I've suffered much from this without complaining. I've done what I could without talking about it. People cannot know it, and I'll be blamed to the hilt. That's the way life goes, alas! People hand out blame right and left; I go ahead with God's help, with a will to do good, without expecting anything for myself; if He does not enlighten me further, that's His affair!

The cold is getting bitter; we are glad to warm ourselves. M. has all she needs, too. So don't worry about us on that score. In the little case that closes with hooks, you'll find the flower bulbs I brought from Vence for the tomb of my Émile. His fiancée enjoyed their flowers last winter. There is also the little hammer and the little tongs you said you'd like in Paris; I bought them for you on the boulevard, which is very convenient.

Good-bye, dear Charles. My very affectionate greetings to you, also to Madeleine. Take care of yourself for her, for us, for your dear children.

Your broken-hearted sister,

Émilie

ÉMILIE DE MONTBOURG
TO CHARLES DE CERILLEY
Paris, October 23, 1892

Dear Charles,

I've just received a letter from Saint-Lô that you sent me and that Éléonore is copying for you.

Madame Guibert de Kerlech is a very distinguished woman of the highest society! If she takes an interest in the gentleman, it means she thinks well of him. But I'm going to find out from Monsieur Lebernier whether he drinks or gambles, what his property consists of, and whether he has a house somewhere along the Channel. We'll also need his photograph. Please send me back the one of Marthe that I sent. If his lapses are only youthful follies, one might pass over them, as long as he has no debts. But, then, as for M., how to proceed? I don't know whether Monsieur de Saint-René will be willing to take a hand in it, but it seems to me that a man of the family might get his confession better than I could— a confession that, according to Madame G.'s letter, is not hard to get. If the facts are acceptable, then, after pointing out the advantages of Marie's social and pecuniary position, one might make known the great *But* if one judged one was dealing with a man of honor who could keep such a secret. What do you think? Perhaps Monsieur de Saint-René might be too harsh in his assessment of Marthe's character? I'd have more confidence in you to carry the thing off successfully.

I'm writing to Monsieur Lebernier by this same mail to get more details, and to Madame G. to thank her and ask her for additional information.

M. still has three and a half months before the great moment. It may not be appropriate to be concerned with marriage at this point, especially since she will probably be a long time recovering. What do you think about that? I wouldn't want to jeopardize her life in trying to settle her future. Really, I'm most perplexed. She'll be very hard to place. Advise me. I'm going to ask Monsieur de S. to come read Madame G.'s letter. Did you get the wreath for Émile, your baskets, and your bags? Good-bye, my dear brother. My heartfelt fond wishes. Éléonore's foot still hurts.

Your most affectionate sister,

Émilie

ÉMILIE DE MONTBOURG
TO CHARLES DE CERILLEY
Paris, November 2, 1892

Dear Charles,

I've just received the two letters you sent me. Oh, Lord, I'd certainly like to be able to snap all these threads that enmesh us when we'd like to isolate ourselves. This sad anniversary brings me condolences that would seem sweet to me in other circumstances. I've received nothing from Saint-Lô, and I give you full authority to open the letters that come to me from there, so that you can advise me as you send them to me, thus saving time.

Éléonore did not copy for you all the preliminaries of the letter. The lady said that maybe she was a manifestation, an instrument, of Providence; that her gentleman had heard a lot about M. Does that mean that people know about the concession that has to be made? It's vague! And, in any case, I oughtn't to accept a son-in-law who has a taste for gambling and drink, and who has debts. I asked the questions very squarely. Madame G. must have forwarded my letter. The gentleman, put on the spot, may perhaps withdraw on his own. I hope so, considering the place and time we're in. May God come to our aid!

Here the house is filling up more and more! An officer of the Legion of Honor, with his ribbon in his buttonhole, has just been escorted across the courtyard by Madame Moreau. This sight of the misfortune of others comforts Éléonore, who sees that we aren't the only unhappy ones.

M. is still maintaining her good intentions. Madame Moreau has allowed her to make her confession to another priest. She needs the sacraments badly if she is to improve. The girl chosen for a wet nurse gave birth last night. When she has recovered, she will go and nurse her child at Clamart; we'll pay 2 francs a day for her food, plus 15 francs a month to compensate for what she won't be earning. Madame Moreau considered this arrangement equitable. Finally, when she takes M.'s child, she'll be paid 40 francs a month. Since she'll be paying 25 francs for a nurse for her own child, you see she'll have 15 francs left. In short, we'll have her three months in advance, but she's a good girl, healthy, with a good character, presentable, in no hurry to marry a brute, and she's not a stranger with one more family to inform in full about our miseries. What do you think?

Take care of your cold. I've had good results from syrup of tolu balsam.

Your unhappy sister,

Émilie

ÉMILIE DE MONTBOURG
TO CHARLES DE CERILLEY
Paris, November 4, 1892

Dear Charles,

I'm sending you a copy of the letters I've just received. One is from Madame G., the other from the gentleman, who wrote to Madame G.

Equipped with his name, I shall be able to ask for information. I'm writing to Monsieur de Saint-René, keeping the photograph to show it to him. Since it's eighteen years old, I'm asking for an up-to-date one. The one they sent me, M. doesn't like, but in eighteen years the gentleman may very well have changed. Yet he's an adventurous spirit, not to say an adventurer, and I'd be afraid that Saint-Savin might be converted into capital and ventured, too. I also greatly dislike his need to drown his sorrows in wine. In short, the time is badly chosen; we'd have to make him wait perhaps a year. Can one tell how M. will make out? If you and Monsieur de Saint-René are in agreement with me, I'll reply that since the family council has resolved that Saint-Savin must be sold to balance the shares, M.'s husband will have to have a career if he has no property to manage to occupy his time. All in all, that is indeed the necessity in which she has placed herself.

But so that I may have nothing to regret, I'm going to try to get some information before I reply, and I'll do that only after learning your opinion. I'm quite sure that Sophie and Honoré could not accept a match in their own region. That might perhaps cause serious disadvantages, even if they went away temporarily, for Normans always come back to their burrow.

M. doesn't feel well and is obliged to stay in bed. She is enormous, and yet the child is very small. The midwife says there is much fat on the mother; much liquid around the child, says the clairvoyant: he moves a lot, and his movements hurt her a lot, which would indicate an unusual case. We're going to try a series of sitz baths. In short, as you see, we're very uneasy, and we could have done without the G. episode.

My very fond tender wishes. Your unhappy sister,

Émilie

MADAME GUIBERT DE KERLECH
TO ÉMILIE DE MONTBOURG
Saint-Lô, October 31, 1892

Dear Madame,

My protégé's name is Louis Veuillot de Bois-Guillaume. I have been a little slow to give you the information you were asking for, because I wanted to be clearer and surer about it; I have questioned the young man himself, since no one could assure me better than he of the sincerity of his feelings, and I'm sending you what he calls his general confession. In it you will see, madame, that his lapses are forgivable and his frankness is the surest guarantee of his good intentions. Of debts he has none—and his father, although from a very good family, left him only a small inheritance.

He's not the one to tell you that he's a big handsome man, and that the gentleness of his character is certainly a serious guarantee of happiness in family life.

In the discussions I've been having with him for some time now, he has reiterated to me that he had long noticed your daughter, he has heard much about her, he knows her tastes, her way of life, he likes her, and if he were fortunate enough to be accepted, he would devote himself to making her happy.

I hope, madame, that your reflections will be favorable to Monsieur V. and that it will be granted him to find in your family the same affection that his excellent parents had for him; I'm fully convinced that he, for his part, will respond to it. He understands the full gravity of an act such as marriage and is preparing for it with the best of resolutions.

I'm sending you, madame, a photograph he had had taken while he was at the École du Pin. For the moment, I have no other at hand. It will give you an idea of his features, keeping in mind, however, the difference between a young man of seventeen and the same person at thirty-five.

I hope, madame, that I've calmed your maternal anxieties, which I understand so well, and answered your questions in a way that makes you share the confidence inspired in me by the honesty and good resolutions of my protégé.

With cordial regards, I am sincerely yours,

E. Guibert de Kerlech

LOUIS VEUILLOT DE BOIS-GUILLAUME
TO MADAME GUIBERT DE KERLECH
[no place or date given]

Dear Madame,

Since I would never, in an affair as serious as an offer of marriage, deceive the mother of a family, I'm going to make you a general confession which may help you inform Baroness de Montbourg completely about me.

I did have some lapses in my early youth, but no one can reproach me with the slightest offense against honor.

My first error was leaving the École du Pin just as I was about to become a stud-farm officer. By way of excuse I will state merely that I was only seventeen at the time.

My second lapse—more serious, it is true, for I had more experience —was undertaking some travels in South America that, incidentally, as a result of unforeseen circumstances, did not turn out well for me. Not only am I not a gambler, but I don't even know how to gamble. Though I have occasionally taken a drink, that was at times when I thought I could drown my sorrows.

I enjoy very good health. As for the accident I was in, the doctors have certified to me that after a certain period of time I will not suffer even the slightest limp.

Having stayed rather a long time away from Saint-Lô, I have very few friends there, but those I have are among the most honorable citizens.

My great-grandfather Antoine Veuillot, before the Revolution, was advocate at the Parlement of Normandy and at the Audit Office (Cour de Comptes).

After offering to defend the king before the bar of the Convention, he came back to Saint-Lô, was named mayor, and, when the Committee of Public Safety came to Saint-Lô, managed, by his energy, to prevent a recurrence of the Nantes massacres.

As for myself, *the trial I have just undergone, a trial perhaps inflicted by God to punish me for my past stupidities,* has given me ballast.

I am fully resolved henceforth to walk the straight and narrow, which will be made easier for me by the experience I have already acquired.

Respectfully yours,

Louis Veuillot de Bois-Guillaume

ÉMILIE DE MONTBOURG
TO CHARLES DE CERILLEY
Paris, November 4, 1892

Dear Charles,

I wrote you this morning, but I'll take this opportunity to tell you that M., with whom I had a long chat after writing you, would not be averse to marrying a reformed sinner like herself so that he should not be able to cast reproaches upon her for the past. She is coming around to reason, says she! Would you believe it? Now she wants us always to live together! Being obliged to spend long hours alone in her room, she keeps thinking. She is preoccupied with her child's future, she is reproaching herself bitterly and recognizing all the wrong she's done. Now that she understands clearly that Normandy is no longer possible, she's searching for any indication of properties in Brittany.

Two gentlemen have gone to Saint-Savin. Whether it is to buy, or whether it is the gentleman presented by Madame G. with a friend, I don't know. The good condition of the buildings will do the sale no harm, likewise the fine state of the crops. Alas, I was doing all that for my children, not for strangers!

The future wet nurse will have milk, it seems. I gave her a fur-lined coat for the baptism; she's very happy with it.

Good-bye, dear Charles; I'm short of time. I'm going to make some broth to take to M. and spend some more time with her. All my fondest wishes.

Your most affectionate sister,

Émilie

MONSIEUR LEBERNIER
TO ÉMILIE DE MONTBOURG
Saint-Lô, November 7, 1892

Dear Baroness,

I thought that the latest letters from Monsieur V. and Madame G. might inform you about the young man's past and his family. I can probably only repeat to you what they have told you.

His fortune would amount to 50,000 francs at least; that's more than Madame G. told you, which means he has taken little out of his capital, for his father had declared to one of his boyhood friends, not long before he died, that he was leaving his wife and son only the 60,000 francs he had saved up. It's on the income from these 50,000 francs that the son is living.

His mother, née de Clairvaut, had no fortune but belonged to one of the most honorable families in the region, and his father had very little from his family (a few thousand francs, though the family was also one of the most honorable). When the young man was at Saint-Lô, he rode horseback every day; later he traveled widely. Having little money, he must not have drunk much; moreover, all his friends were very sober. He was not a gambler, and I have never known him to have a mistress at Saint-Lô; as for character, I don't think any better can be found. I do not know his political opinions, but his friends were conservatives, and he was reformed since he fractured his leg—that is to say, without pressure, for his sainted mother was dead, as well as his father. I think, madame, that you can trust the confession he has made to you, and I also think you can have confidence in the promises he will make to you, for according to his friends he is a very honest and good fellow. As for the family, it has been, and is still today, one of the finest and most esteemed in the region.

Respectfully yours, etc.

I. Lebernier

ÉMILIE DE MONTBOURG
TO CHARLES DE CERILLEY
Paris, November 8, 1892

Dear Charles,

Monsieur de Saint-René came yesterday to talk about the matter that is preoccupying us, and he asked me to assure you of his complete sympathy and of the confidence he has in your judgment.

He does not reject the thing in principle; but he wants us to take our time, getting more detailed information than the explanations given so far. He says, with reason, that nothing could be decided before the great ordeal; that from the letters, he thinks they don't know anything, and that we must say nothing until we know how that will turn out. When we have received the current photograph, I'll send it to you and submit it to Monsieur de Saint-René with your reflections, on which he sets great store. If the photograph suits everyone, beginning with the one most concerned, I'll write to the lady who presented the young man that the opinion of the family is that we must settle all the questions of inheritance and guardianship of my children before anything else, and that my daughter is too close to coming of age to be emancipated.

Nevertheless, I'll ask him what made him leave the stud farm of Le Pin just when he was to become a stud-farm officer. Also the motive and purpose of the trips to South America, and where in America. Finally, we must know positively what the little bit of property he has left consists of.

It would be very nice of you to write to the inspector-general of the stud farm of Le Pin, near the town of Saint-Léonard, to find out from that side why Monsieur V. had to leave the stud farm suddenly at age seventeen; it's probably not the same inspector, but the young man's file remains, and perhaps we'll learn the truth about his departure. I remember that at that time or thereabouts, young V. had so thoroughly disappeared that his despairing parents were having a search made for him in the river at Saint-Lô, fearing he might have drowned. A good many days later, it was learned that the young man, having left—on foot or otherwise—to join the Carlists[19] in Spain, had fallen among a band of Spanish republicans who wanted to have him shot the next day. His youth saved his life, but to punish him for his temerity before sending him back to France, they had him pass between two rows of soldiers, who did not spare him blows with the flat of their sabers. You saw that our agent said he had been a pontifical zouave. Monsieur de Saint-René, judging by his letter, finds that he is still childish, that he may have good sense but he's no genius. . . .

M. has at the moment a neuralgic condition that needs to be treated. The nuns are glad that I am caring for it, and they no longer create difficulties. I make use of their good will, but without abusing it; that's not in my nature! Thank God, there's nothing serious in her condition. Sister Thérèse gives very good advice, which we follow to our advantage. I don't recall whether I told you that the girl we were counting on for a wet nurse has no milk. If the child is strong enough, we'll try him on the bottle. Éléonore's foot is better, but the other one is weak, too. That should prove to her that she's not getting blood to her extremities, and should make her resolve to improve her diet. Oh, what stubbornness, and what vexation for me.

Sympathize with me, dear brother. Your unhappy sister,

Émilie

ÉMILIE DE MONTBOURG
TO CHARLES DE CERILLEY
Paris, November 12, 1892

Dear Charles,

I received the leases to sign for the Saint-Lô house, and at the same time an answer from our agent containing the information on the gentleman in question. I've copied it out for you. He tells me, furthermore, that the people interested in the property want to inspect all the bedrooms. Now, ours are still in some disorder; we can't take the time to tidy up everything, as you know, and I see that we'll have to go there as soon as M. is well enough to be left alone for a few days. Until then, I will keep looking for information, as well as the up-to-date photograph. It occurred to me that our doctor at Saint-Lô—very discreet, very serious, and very fond of M.—might well, if I asked him, take the responsibility for explaining the immense concession that has to be made. He must know the young man. Perhaps he was his family's doctor. I think I can count on the delicacy and discretion of this doctor. Since he never leaves Saint-Lô, we hadn't been able to consult him for Émile. He's the doctor for the hospitals, of the asylums, and the aristocratic clientèle of the town—in other words, there is plenty for him to do.

So, if you agree, I'll fill him in on the dismal situation; he's the only person I can count on. In any case, if the young man doesn't withdraw, there still could not be a conclusion until next September, and we'll advance the date for settling the apportionment.

What do you think? You see that God gives me the courage to drink the cup down to the dregs! M. is happy to see herself restored by our mercies!

Her neuralgic condition still needs attention, but it's moving in the right direction. Éléonore's foot is better, and she enjoys getting around. The fog does not deter her sufficiently; I'm always afraid she'll get sick, but she's so irritated at our dismal situation that there's not much to say to her.

A thousand fond wishes, my good brother.

Your sad sister,

Émilie

ÉMILIE DE MONTBOURG
TO CHARLES DE CERILLEY
Paris, November 18, 1892

Dear Charles,

I'm writing you on my knees while M. is asleep. Yesterday she had an attack that lasted three and a half hours and has left her shattered. The doctor who had taken care of her at first is ill. They found the one who looks after the sisters on the Rue Cassini, who specializes in the ailments we're treating at this moment. He advised two grams of bromide for three days, after which he'll come back. Absolute bed rest. The child is very small, but these attacks, which he considers hysterical, might advance the dénouement; I no longer leave her day or night. They are going to give us a bigger room. Will we be better off? Monsieur de Saint-René and Sophie came yesterday. They thought the photograph was very good, and we'd accept the gentleman on the basis of the latest information. Did I copy it out for you? M. has been so sick, I don't know where I am. But when all is set forth and discussed, Monsieur de Saint-René's ultimate advice is that we must wait for the child and use as pretext the need to settle matters among my children, which depends on the sale of Saint-Savin. I must postpone things for three months, while giving assurance that until then we will make no other commitment. If the gentleman learns something during that time, he can withdraw on his own.

If the outcome of the nine months is good, we'll have to make up our minds to let him know the situation; for that we'll employ a canon of the Paris cathedral who has come to hear Marthe's confession and has taken quite a liking to her. This is the plan for the moment. My only concern is that for fear of missing out on this match, the gentleman may want an engagement right away and begin paying his court. What do we do then? Use the canon right away, and rely on his honor? May God help us. Read my letter to Madame G. before putting it in the mail. Who can tell how that's going to turn out?

My poor Éléonore has neuralgia of the stomach from all this, and I can't be with her! Fortunately, she is in the habit of taking care of herself in her own way, and she insists on it. But she's quite alone, since I'm not leaving M. any more. . . . Éléonore brings us our meals when one of the nuns can't replace me. At the moment several are ill.

Affectionately, your unhappy sister,

Émilie

SOPHIE DE MONTBOURG
TO CHARLES DE CERILLEY
Paris, November 25, 1892

Dear Charles,

As soon as it was possible for me, I came to see our poor Émilie. I'm devoting almost all my time to her. We've talked a lot, as you can imagine, and she has brought me up to date on all the information about Monsieur V. The photograph indicates a gentle nature. The information thus far is satisfactory. His income of 2,000 francs is all he has, now or in the future. He saw Marie last year; she must not have seemed unattractive to him, since he's asking for her hand. That is certain and very important. But it's also absolutely certain that he knows nothing about her health right now, or that, if gossip has got around, nothing has confirmed it, and consequently his first impression has not been shaken. It remains to be seen whether any unhappy result remains from his youthful follies, in America or Spain. Monsieur de Saint-René tells us that it is virtually impossible to clear that up through the consulates. All that is left is the most recent years, which he has spent in Saint-Lô, and Émilie has enough connections there to have him dissected.

We've studied the problem with our cousin from every angle. Does the match offer guarantees or not? If it does, as we all wish: he must be informed of the situation and about the sale of Saint-Savin, which perhaps he wants for a home. By whom? We think that a canon who lives here, a kindhearted man, would be the most independent intermediary. Would he be willing? Émilie will sound him out on this subject. Would he if necessary make the trip to Saint-Lô? Monsieur de Saint-René considers it impossible to have the gentleman himself come to be filled in on the liquidation of the estate. He advised taking plenty of time, on the head of the liquidation, until M. is fully recovered. I've seen her once. She's become very pale, which is not astonishing. For the past two weeks she's been having little bouts of fever that keep her in bed. How will it all turn out? God only knows. All the devotion of her near and dear ones is needed. The thought of marriage sustains her morale. God grant that she may not suffer a great disillusionment and that all will come out for the best! Éléonore is quite ill and no longer eats anything but a little porridge with milk. Her mother sits up night after night. I'm always afraid she'll fall.

Our farming this year is not much. We must persevere and reduce our expenses as much as possible to be able to give our dowries without delay. Let's hope next year will be better.

Don't leave me without news of you, please. As for me, I'm getting old fast. It seems to me that I'm a hundred. Honoré, too, is getting a bit slow-witted, and he tires easily. May God help us all. Good-bye, my good brother; my fondest wishes.

Your very affectionate sister,

Sophie

ÉMILIE DE MONTBOURG
TO CHARLES DE CERILLEY
Paris, November 29, 1892

Dear Charles,

The director's letter is so clear and so hard on Monsieur V. that it seems to me necessary to clear up the two principal questions as soon as possible. Read my letter to Monsieur Lebernier. If you find in it anything to criticize or to change, make the correction and send it back to me. I'd like to consult the doctor in Saint-Lô whom I spoke to you about. He'll tell me the truth, I hope, for he's very fond of M. and of us all. Trust that I will not give out anything confidential on our side! If there is any tie abroad, the marriage is impossible. As soon as I know the names of the countries where the gentleman stayed, I'll inquire of the consuls. Monsieur de Saint-René may perhaps be very useful to us in that.

Sophie's visit, which was perfect, and M.'s demands on my time have made me forget to acknowledge to you my receipt of the 400 francs. Forgive me. I have indeed received the letter from the stud farm, and I am and shall be absolutely discreet. M. has felt such sharp pains that the doctor came; he prescribed two grams a day of potassium bromide, one at a time, to combat hyst[eria], and the pains stopped as if by magic; he recommended absolute bed rest. I'm expecting him this morning. I can't wait till she can get up a bit to divert the blood from her head. Just think: it's about twenty days that she's been staying in her room and in bed, and she still has six or seven weeks to go.

I remember that in 1875 or 1876 there was an English or American circus at Saint-Lô. Perhaps Monsieur V. was charmed by the equestriennes and followed them? However that may be, I don't like that adventurer's life one bit. And yet I know that M. has made it necessary to offer concessions. If there was an affair without a legal marriage, or a legal marriage and widowhood, do you think we should still do it? In any case, drunkenness would be an insuperable obstacle, for M., as you have pointed out, needs a calm, sure, and firm guide. I'll communicate to Monsieur de Saint-René the letter from the stud farm, with the response of Monsieur Lebernier and others. I cannot ask him to visit us too often. A thousand fond greetings, my most devoted brother.

Your afflicted sister,

Émilie

I'm going to send to Sangy the dahlias, the gladioli, and some cuttings I've made. Your gardener will save us a few for next spring; at Clamart we will surely have a garden. Éléonore needs flowers. Here she stops happily in front of flower-decked shopwindows, but we may not have growing plants on our window sills: it's forbidden by the lease.

ÉLÉONORE DE MONTBOURG
TO CHARLES DE CERILLEY
Paris, November 21, 1892

My very dear Uncle,

Mama is answering you today, but I want to thank you myself for your kind thoughtfulness. I don't know if Mama acknowledged receipt of the 400 francs, for she may perhaps not have written you since, but I'm the one, as a rule, who is there to receive the mail, and I gave her that letter like all the rest. Poor Mama: the letter from the stud farm of Le Pin upset her completely, and with good reason, one must admit. They sent for another doctor for M.; Madame Berteau questioned him in private, and he assured her that he finds nothing serious. If he had spoken only to Mama, you might perhaps not believe him. Since the patient was suffering from neuralgic pains, he prescribed antipyrine[20] instead of quinine, and now she's much better. Mama has a cold. She can sleep a little better now, and they put her mattress on M.'s chaise longue, which can serve as a day bed. The nuns behave so harshly among themselves, it's hardly edifying. Of course they dare not act that way toward the boarders, but the spirit of false perfection is always there. Our poor Madame Berteau is exhausted. They take advantage of her kindness in every way.

Mama has asked for fuller information about Monsieur V. The important thing would, no doubt, be to know where in America he stayed, so we could inquire of the consulate. From Paris, that's easy. Please note, uncle, that the letter from Le Pin is the only one that mentions anything so serious. I doubt whether one can clear up these most important points at Saint-Lô. It might perhaps be preferable if you would be so kind as to ask that gentleman who wrote you for the name of the country in America and more precise details.

We could go back to the sources and see if he was led astray; in any case, he certainly has a right to perfect confidentiality.

My dear uncle, I send you my very respectful and affectionate greetings,

Éléonore

SOPHIE DE MONTBOURG
TO CHARLES DE CERILLEY
Sainte-Apolline, Thursday

Dear Charles,

As I was finishing my letter to you from Paris, Émilie asked me to go up secretly to M.'s room. I came back heartsick and upset! That attic . . . with a horrible dog . . . the material and moral disorder . . . have the effect on me of those novels that one doesn't read. She is plunged in material sensations; and I fear that in her mother the nurse prevails over any other feeling. Él.'s position there is absolutely abnormal. She devotes herself completely to M., running back and forth, bringing her meals. She's eccentric about her health; but her shame is only too natural, and anything that might reduce it would corrode her morals. Her education was not as solidly based as most, and what if some day, when she is in better health, her imagination should get the better of her . . . ? It's hard for me to accept the idea that at Saint-Lô people have anything but suspicions. Madame Gardet wrote to Émilie that she would do well to come back to the region, even if only for a few days, with her two daughters (underlined). Which means that there's a rumor to shoot down. — As far as Monsieur V. is concerned, there's a redoubtable unknown. Would you believe it? Émilie and Marthe would have wanted a marriage right away! For Émilie that's incredible! Even as an idea. I'm sending your letter to Hon., who has to pass through Saint-Lô again, and I'm asking him to get some more information, even though I fear that Émilie (if the information is not good) may be angry with us for breaking off this lone branch she has to cling to for salvation. Anyway, your letter may perhaps put her a bit on her guard. All we'd need now would be a case of bigamy! To be sure, one can't afford to be hard to please . . . but the remedy must not be a poison, and she must *be able to stick to it.* I'm sorry it comes from Saint-Lô. If that doesn't work, she'll look far afield, that's certain.

M. declares that she will love the child more than her husband (that's her animal nature, and no comment). And that if she doesn't get married, she doesn't want to be under the same roof as Él. She accepts Éléonore's care, but detests her just as much as ever. Whatever will happen? The potential buyers demand to see the inside of the house at Saint-Savin. Ém. can't go there and won't trust us with the keys. For two weeks now, M. has been having painful attacks that keep her in bed. One of the nuns whispered in my ear that the doctor thinks the baby may come sooner than expected. I'm on red-hot coals! If misfortune were to strike the mother, we must be in agreement as to the illness she died of. What do you think? It's essential that we come to an understanding. *Meningitis,* like Émile, would be logical. Diphtheria? Or peritonitis? Those are also violent illnesses, and since births are recorded summarily in Paris, that would work. She would have come back there from the Midi for the apportion-ment. You understand that I couldn't talk about that eventuality to the poor mother. And I forgot to bring it up with Monsieur de Saint-René.

Léon is delighted with his garrison duty at Saint-Lô. His father will introduce him to society there. You can judge how painful for us any confirmation of the gossip there would be. He might hear whispers. You can't do anything about that. Ém.'s intention would be to use the sale of the land to buy a little something for M., in the depths of Brittany. But the sale has not been made. I pray God with all my strength to come to their aid—and to ours, too.

Good-bye, my kind brother. I want my letter to go out right away; I have left only the time to send you my very fond wishes.

Your affectionate sister,

Sophie

MONSIEUR DE SAINT-RENÉ
TO CHARLES DE CERILLEY
Paris, November 28, 1892

Dear Friend,

On each of my visits to the Rue Saint-Jacques I have occasion to speak of you, and each time I am confronted with an opinion to give, a decision to make, I give your sister the responsibility of referring it first to you, because I know and appreciate your sincerity and your clear-sightedness. So I was delighted to learn from your letter that we are in agreement in the dismal affair we have on our hands.

It is not possible for us to repair the damage already done, but we can seek ways to attenuate its dread consequences. For the moment, it seems to me that we should do nothing, absolutely nothing. Not even to concern ourselves with this overture of marriage, which appeared in such complicated circumstances and such strange conditions. I am even more hesitant than you are to believe that Monsieur V. has a fairly precise knowledge of the situation. Yet, if such a supposition is allowed, one must nevertheless recognize that nothing in the letters addressed to your sister makes even a remote allusion to it or makes one feel that Monsieur V. has any intention of taking advantage of the family's problems.

I lean still further toward seeing things this way because, I will not conceal from you, if the contrary were true I would form the most dismal assumptions about Monsieur V.'s character and morality. As a consequence, his marriage to M. would worry me a good deal.

I would greatly mistrust a *social outcast* who on his own initiative would go looking for such a dubious situation and who would hope his success would bring him only a living to ensure repose for his laziness and incapacity.

I would rather, as you indicate, it were possible to come upon an unknown, a hard-working man, one who would accept, on reflection, a situation the dangers of which he would have understood even better than its advantages.

But there is one element we must keep in mind in our deliberations. We must think of that unfortunate child, who has such dull wits and feelings, who is almost unaware of her own self, and incapable of tracing out a line of conduct in advance and following it.

In these conditions, it is a very delicate matter to assume the responsibility for making a choice for her but without her.

Marthe has only one aim: to assure freedom of action for herself. How will she use it? That's a problem.

However that may be, considering the state the poor child is in, there must be no thought of following up Monsieur V.'s overture for three more months. That would be impossible.

The anticipated outcome may give rise to new complications. So we must await events.

I do not even think we should continue, at least for the present, to seek information about Monsieur V. We will have the right to dig into his life only if we decide to follow up the overture of marriage he has made, and nothing is less sure as yet. Your observations will then weigh very heavily—they are so just and well founded—in the decisions to be made.

This is also true, but to a lesser degree, of what you say about hereditary diseases.[21] It is useless to try to foresee troubles from so far off.

As you suppose, the unborn child will have to be registered at birth on the rolls of the Office of Civil Status [État Civil] with the mother's name and the notation "father unknown." But what you seem not to know is a certain legal arrangement by which *any gentleman whatever* may *always* claim to be the child's father. All one must do to fulfill this formality is to present oneself at the town hall with two witnesses and make an *ad hoc* declaration. Should it be contested later, the *any gentleman whatever* has only to establish by rather easy proofs that he has had somewhat mysterious relations with the mother.

Conclusion: the sword of Damocles still hangs overhead. How many people, in our region, if they knew this law, would run a steeplechase to get there first?

Your coachman is a stout fellow who doesn't shrink from anything; he's at the same time victor and victim, and I have no doubt that today he bitterly regrets his triumph.

Come when you can; your presence comforts your sister. She is bearing up with marvelous energy under the misfortunes she is victim of. Her courage and resignation are worthy of the greatest respect.

I would very much like to have your trip coincide with the time of the dénouement. It's at that moment that everyone's advice will be valuable to your sister, and yours especially so.

As for me, dear friend, have no doubt of the pleasure I shall take in seeing you again and shaking your hand.

Yours as ever,

Monsieur de Saint-René

This isn't a letter, it's a chat with you.

SOPHIE DE MONTBOURG
TO CHARLES DE CERILLEY
Sainte-Apolline, Sunday

Dear Charles,

Your letter about the information on V. frightened me so that I sent it to Honoré with the request, since he was to go to Saint-Lô, that he try to get people to talk about the gentleman in question. Émilie did not entrust this job to us, though we live in the region. That must mean that she does not have confidence in us, for one thing; or, for another, that she wants so badly to get M. married that she does not want to be completely informed. So you're the one to whom I write the result of my personal request to Honoré. He has introduced Léon into the most staid and substantial households in Saint-Lô. At one of these he was able to slip in the name in question and ask what kind of man he is; here is the reply, verbatim: *"He's a wretch!* His father was an honorable man, but he himself has plunged into filth and is still wallowing in it. He's been turned away everywhere. I wouldn't put anything past him." About the supposition that he might have got married somewhere? "It's quite possible. I wouldn't put anything past him." Besides, he *drinks like a fish.* Émilie reproached me for not having given her enough warning in time about M., but she wouldn't have believed me and took no account of my advice. I am sure it would be the same this time, yet I can't keep such information for us alone. That would be a second dishonor and an even more complete disaster. She wrote me a few lines on receiving your letter, telling me that she considers the director of the stud farm to be too severe and asks for confirmation. I urged her to get information herself at Saint-Lô. Good Lord! Horrors! Try to get Ém. to give up this dismal match and switch her hopes to the multiple listings of matrimonial agencies. She'll find no worse among them than this one, and a poor but honorable one might just be found for whom the concession will be less exorbitant outside his home region.

Don't use our name if you can help it, for fear of making her balk, since she has given us no authorization to act. I was the first to be fooled by the letters of the matchmaker, for I wanted this marriage as a providential rescue. How much one can be deceived—I shudder at the thought!

Good-bye, my dear kind brother; my fondest wishes to you.

Your devoted sister,

Sophie

HONORÉ DE MONTBOURG
TO CHARLES DE CERILLEY
Sunday evening

Dear Charles,

The other day, coming back from Saint-Lô, I let Sophie write you the result of my investigations while I myself wrote to Monsieur de Saint-René. I'm glad, by the way, that my information is in agreement with yours. It is all the more certain in that I collected it personally, not in writing *(verba volant)*, so it compromises no one. Moreover, I have it from someone who holds perhaps the highest rank in Saint-Lô society.

Monsieur de Saint-René wrote me this morning that he has communicated the information to the mother without naming its author, just as you yourself did, according to a letter of Émilie's enclosed in that of Monsieur de Saint-René. I thank you for that, although I wholeheartedly assume responsibility for my investigations and for what I write. If we had written it, either Sophie or I, we wouldn't have been believed, or would at least have been charged with exaggeration. The matter is buried, adds the cousin, and I'm delighted! That would have been one more scandal in our region.

The mother had written to several persons at Saint-Lô who did not answer, and for good reason *(scripta manent,* this time). This would serve to confirm *our hearsay* if need be.

In all this I don't particularly understand the role of the *woman friend* proposing this squalid match. It's one of two things: either she knows nothing about the situation, in which case she's worse than a practical joker, or she knows everything and so does the gentleman, and that's a scandalous piece of blackmail and a bad favor to do, plunging the two people in question still further into the gutter. Above all, M. must get out of the region, Saint-Savin must be sold, and we must have done with it!

Monsieur de Saint-René seems to have a very great influence on the mother, and that's most fortunate! She tells him in her letter that she will consult him on everything and for everything.

Sophie has come back from Paris, *heartsick* to see her older sister, the one who brought her up, in such a sad situation, both morally and materially speaking. What a fall! What a thing to happen at the end of one's life.

I was told in Saint-Lô, however, that this Madame Guibert is estimable, and I've been urged to introduce my son to her at her home; he is in garrison at Saint-Lô, as you know. But, seeing that, Sophie writes me to do nothing about it until further notice, which is prudent.

What do you think about that pretty Panama business?[22] Such muck! And we poor but *honest people* are swindled!

Devotedly yours,

Honoré de Montbourg

ÉMILIE DE MONTBOURG
TO CHARLES DE CERILLEY
Paris, December 2, 1892

Dear Charles,

Your letter, which I got yesterday morning, was followed that same evening by a letter from Monsieur de Saint-René saying that he, too, had received some very bad information and that we should call the whole thing off. At the same time you enclosed a letter from the gentleman himself saying he is blissful at the hope that Madame Guibert gives him, that he hopes to take the place for me of the son I've lost, etc. I'm waiting for Monsieur de Saint-René to draw up the letter breaking off negotiations without compromising anyone.

I am thinking of writing to Madame Guibert that, all things considered, it is impossible for my daughter, with her dowry and Monsieur V.'s modest means, to run a household in the conditions necessary for her; that since Monsieur V. is too old to receive special training for a career, the family has decided that this plan could not be realized and must be considered as absolutely broken off. That's the gist of it. Monsieur de Saint-René will find the expressions to be used in such a case.

I'm astonished that Monsieur Lebernier hasn't answered me! Could he be that gentleman who wrote to Monsieur de S. and to you, instead of answering me? Why don't you tell me your source? I'd be grateful to him and would never mention his name. Then I'd be better informed on the degree of trust I might place in him. Really, you're wrong not to let me know who he is.

Here, I hope, is better news of M.: she's in less pain, though she must stay in bed as much as possible. Fortunately, she has a fine big bed in this new room. I'll take advantage of the improved situation to go to Clamart and see the apartment lined up for her for the month of April, accompanied by the baby and the nurse, for she's determined to try it. Since she will not be able to accept the house's rules, she will have to do her own housekeeping with the maid. If she were more reasonable, it would of course be advantageous to rent one apartment for us all, with a garden, but I dare not undertake to look after her. Anyway, we'll see how the great trial will be passed. I think it will take her a good two months to recover here; one of these days I'll find out what they're going to charge us to lodge the maid and the child. We'll feed all of them: if the nuns do allow this maid—their boarder who was to breast-feed but has had no milk—to return to their house, they will not allow her to communicate with the other boarders. Here everything requires special permissions which must be acknowledged by us with money. Oh, my dear, we would be in debt if we didn't reduce ourselves to the bare necessities. The Midi, the fire, the consequences of the misfortune that keeps us here, all burden us with heavy expenses, but we shall not have to borrow since we have taken the plunge and given up our servants.

My very fond wishes to you, dear Charles. Don't do anything rash in your diet, and keep out of the cold. They are still to send to Sangy some cuttings and some cyclamens. We'll share what remains after the winter: my Émile's tomb and Éléonore need flowers.

Your very affectionate sister,

Émilie

A million thanks for getting the information *yourself.* It's a great lesson: I'll know from now on that one does not tell the truth to the parties most interested.

ÉMILIE DE MONTBOURG
TO CHARLES DE CERILLEY
Paris, December 9, 1892

Dear Charles,

I've been waiting for the potatoes to arrive before writing to you, but I've heard nothing about them. Monsieur de Saint-René, who was supposed to come, has not notified me as he promised to, and I begrudge the time because it is urgent to stop Monsieur V.'s hope: he will be more disgruntled the more he has lingered in it. Note that he wrote me that he is happy in his hope. Tell me whether the motive offered for breaking it off will adequately hide the basis for the refusal. We must not compromise anyone. My old doctor answered me in general terms that M. wouldn't be happy with a husband who didn't have the moral qualities she needs, and Monsieur V., they say, is not reasonable in anything.

Monsieur Lebernier hasn't answered me; perhaps it was he who made up his mind to inform you? I repeat, I can hardly wait for the whole thing to be over, and I curse the snow, which keeps Monsieur de S. from coming.

This snow has caused Éléonore neuralgic pains in her stomach. For M. it came in the head and the abdomen, and very severely. The doctor prescribed quinine for six days. Her head is better, and elsewhere the pains are letting up. Oh, the poor child is really biting her fists [with impatience].

December 10

Madame Berteau had not thought to tell me: the potatoes arrived in good condition the day before yesterday. They emptied the bags right away. I'm going to ask for them, and when the weather is better I'll take them to the railroad office. You'll find inside a book of Émile's dealing with matters in India. I brought it back from Vence with you in mind. At the same time I'll send you for your desserts a box of the kind of chocolate creams that Éléonore often nibbles during the day. I keep a box on hand for her permanently, within reach. We're near the factory.

We're much better off in the big room, and it's understood not only that M. will undergo her great trial here, but also that another room, right next door and communicating, will be at our disposal for the child and the maid. M. wants to try the bottle.

The canon who comes here for morning Mass has consented to represent the curate of Tourette for sponsorship. That's better than the sexton. As for me, I'll take care not to appear in all this.

To tend to M. we'll have a sister who watches over deliveries to help me with the mother and train the maid for the child. The midwife and the doctor are booked; as you can see, she will not lack anything. This trial will bear some good fruits, we must hope! We are paying dearly for her return to better sentiments.

The need to stay shut up with the patient makes the temperature in the room seem southern to me. I'm coughing all the time, but no bronchitis.

I'm rejecting the claim of the miller, who deceived us completely about the quality of the flour he had supplied us with. Please put my letter in the mail.

A thousand fond wishes for you both.

Your ever-afflicted sister,

Émilie

ÉMILIE DE MONTBOURG
TO CHARLES DE CERILLEY
Paris, December 13, 1892

Dear Charles,

An attack of rheumatism in my wrists gives me pain and greatly restricts me. However, I want to tell you that while you're away I'll write to Normandy as little as possible. Oh, yes! M. will never be able to understand what a multitude of annoyances she causes.

The Bordeaux clairvoyant, whom I've consulted about my health and to whom I sent Monsieur V.'s letter, states that Monsieur V. doesn't know M.'s deplorable situation, that he's led a very checkered life but that now he's settled down and is thinking about raising a family, that that's the purpose of his request, and that consequently self-interest is not foreign to it—that for himself he would accept, for good reason, the situation that M. has got herself into, but that because of his family he would put up a fuss about it; that nevertheless the thing could be done, and that he would make his wife happy.

But the fuss she mentions should, in my opinion, be smoothed over by a bridge of gold that I cannot build, for as I recently said to Éléonore, who was grief-stricken over the sad situation that M. has created for her, "My poor child! It would be even sadder if you wanted to get married!" She replied to that sharply: "I'll get married when I want to, I'm not a nun; but at this moment, I have quite enough of family life." Now, however, she knows that there's a young man waiting for her, well connected, a good person, who refuses any other match. So from every point of view, I think it is urgent to break off as soon as possible with this Monsieur V.; I will not speak about age, though, for M. may well be obliged to make that concession with another man.

December 14

M. has suffered very sharp neuralgic pains in her head; antipyrine took care of them, but her eyes still hurt. Since I've been taking care of her, I've noticed that she often runs a fever. For several days the pains were coming at the same time of day, and the doctor prescribed quinine sulfate. This left her tired. Fortunately the Bordeaux clairvoyant, or anyway the doctor who employs her and whom Sophie told me about, sent me a prescription for pills in which quinine valerianate is combined with cinchona extract, and these pills do not cause her any distress. We've had to go back to broth, for the baby was exhausting our patient.

Still nothing from Monsieur de Saint-René or Monsieur Lebernier.

I hope in a few days to have the maid who is to try to nurse the child on the bottle. She will sleep near Éléonore, whose housekeeping she'll do, and she'll spend part of the day with Marie; that way I'll feel easier. But we must wait, for she's not yet recovered enough.

Madame Moreau is very grateful for the potatoes. As long as they last, that's a saving of a franc a day. Since it's Madame Berteau who manages the household here, she's the one who is really obliged. She richly deserves it, I assure you!

M.'s going to get up and try to come downstairs a bit, to be with the other boarders while I'm airing out her room. The good ladies do nothing but bring up wood for us. We're providing all M.'s food, for the house's diet does not suit her.

My affectionate wishes, my good brother, and your nieces send the same. Take good care of yourself. . . .

Your afflicted sister,

Émilie

ÉMILIE DE MONTBOURG
TO CHARLES DE CERILLEY
Paris, December 16, 1892

Dear Charles,

Monsieur de Saint-René came yesterday, and he was kind enough to bring me a draft of the breaking-off letter all ready to send to Madame Guibert. There were only a few things to change to make it, it seems to me, into a letter very well suited to the circumstances. Nobody in the world is compromised by the information given in it. The family council is a serried battalion that people do not dare confront, and the surrogate guardian has also joined its ranks. Lack of a career, lack of funds—every day you see marriage plans founder because of that. Now, since the gentleman, at the age of thirty-five, could have had both if he had wanted to work, he can have no one to blame but himself. That matter's over and done with.

Now I have only to support Éléonore in the moral trial that distresses her so, and M. in the physical trial that's drawing near. We're following the advice of the midwife, the doctor here, and the Bordeaux one, seconded by the clairvoyant; I think we can do no more.

The girl M. chose as maid to bring the child up on the bottle still has a weakness in her leg that would have degenerated into phlebitis if she did not rest completely. During this time we haven't been paying her. She's taking care of herself. Yesterday they moved her into a room right next to M.'s. During the day she keeps M. company. I'm going to take advantage of that to take Éléonore out. Fortunately, the rheumatism that grips my arms and lower back isn't so nasty today, and M. is pretty well.

Your unhappy sister,

Émilie

Monsieur de Saint-René would favor putting the child out to nurse and having M. resume her place in our home at the same time as we make our return in society. But, my dear, given the temperament we know, isn't it better to let her stay in the shelter of an asylum and fulfill the duties of motherhood? That alone often straightens out natures in which some good sentiments remain, and, thank God, she still has stuff in her. We have time to see, but first we must get over the worst step.

MONSIEUR DE SAINT-RENÉ
TO CHARLES DE CERILLEY
December 23, 1892

Dear Friend,

I much appreciated the kind words you were good enough to send me along with your New Year's greeting. I thank you, and assure you that, for my part, I have the same feelings of esteem and sympathy toward you. Please express to Madame de Cerilley my respectful and cordial New Year's wishes.

The overture from Monsieur Veuillot of Saint-Lô is buried for good and all. That is exactly what it deserved. The circumstance prompted an exchange of letters with your brother-in-law Honoré de Montbourg, and I was happy to be able to assure him of our full agreement.

I'm positive that poor Madame de Montbourg today recognizes deep inside her that, in spite of her intelligence and devotion, she has to a certain extent failed in bringing up her children.

Accordingly, since the collapse of that unhappy family, caused as much by tragic events as by the last catastrophe, I see that your sister wants to rely on our common opinions. She has the greatest confidence in you, and I know how much she can count on from you, from your heart and your resourcefulness.

I went to see her a few days ago and, in chatting about the various courses to follow at this moment and presently for M., I voiced the opinion that it would be well, *immediately after the delivery,* to put the child out to nurse in *any place whatever* near where Madame de Montbourg and her children might choose to live.

I was pointing out to her the advantages of settling the matter *right away*, explaining that the more they delayed the harder it would be, and that, besides, this was the *only* way to resume a situation in society without stirring up too many questions. I will not hide from you that I bumped up against some rather unexpected opposition, which I hope will not be permanent.

Your sister told me that M. would never consent to part with her child, that she would not even dare broach the question at this moment, so frightened was she about M.'s health and about the fits of hysterics, which could even put her life in danger. Your sister seems to believe—and Éléonore shares her opinion on this matter—that the only way to restore balance to M.'s character and conduct would be to let her keep her child.

I asked how one could reconcile such a determination with the indispensable resumption of social life. I see a new black spot there: M.'s inexperience on the one hand, and on the other the mother's weakness, abetted by the involuntary complicity of Éléonore, may create obstacles that the poor women do not suspect, and of which they would still be the victims.

Éléonore is getting tired and bored. The situation weighs on her more and more, I see, and I think she hasn't yet glimpsed the personal solution that *she* may be looking for. In her state of health, with her quaint ideas, the burden must seem too heavy for her to think of marriage.

For many reasons that we both know, *she is not marriageable,* and marriage is the last course I would advise her to follow if the idea occurred to her seriously. We're not yet at that point, are we, thank God?

I send you my best regards and wishes, my friend, and say to you *à bientôt,* for we're not finished with this lamentable affair.

Monsieur de Saint-René

ÉMILIE DE MONTBOURG
TO CHARLES DE CERILLEY
December 25, 1892

Dear Charles,

M. and my rheumatism in the wrists make correspondence very difficult. The pains she is suffering make one think the delivery is not far off, and then everything quiets down and you have to begin all over again. Oh, if she were ever, stupidly, to put herself in the way of another such trial, she would have to have lost her memory.

Talk about marriage would not be welcome to her at this moment. I am very worried about how it will go, for she's so nervous that one must fear eclampsia. The midwife and the doctor will be there, but I also want a nursing sister. God grant it all comes off well!

I'm sending off parcel post your two bags, enclosing a box of chocolates for Madeleine and you, a very special treat; also a box of Dijon *nonnettes*[23] that I ask you to have sent by express after paying the postage at Sangy.

As for the visiting cards, I'll wait till you return and enclose them in a parcel-post package for you.

It's been freezing since yesterday; we're using the heat.

Good-bye, my good brother. I send all my wishes for happiness for the year soon to begin. As for me, I close my eyes and, with my thoughts anticipating only pain and sadness, may God have pity on me at last!

Most affectionate wishes to you, and to Madeleine if she is with you.

Your unhappy sister,

Émilie

MARIE ROUGEMONT
TO C. AND M. DE CERILLEY
December 29, 1892

My good Uncle and my good Aunt and Godmother,

I don't want to let Mama's letter be sent without offering you my wishes for the year that is soon to begin, and thanking you for the sympathy you have been kind enough to show me. I am making a hard atonement for my misdeed, and it is truly in misfortune that we need our family's attentions; if Mama weren't there I would lack even the most basic of these, for people are not kind at Saint-Raphaël. I'm still a bit tired, but

47

I'm getting near the fateful moment, of which I am much afraid. I fully assure you, my good uncle, that I won't begin again: the experience I'm having is too harsh. I hope that you and my good aunt are not too severely tried by the Siberian cold that reigns everywhere, and that you are in good health. Mama is suffering cruelly from her rheumatism and Éléonore from her neuralgia. To please Mama, I'll put my child out to nurse. The doctor who's looking after me has found me one he will answer for. This woman is from the department of Yonne. She owns a cow and is fairly well off, so I hope she will take care of my little child. Besides, she has already brought up three in the same situation, which gives me a little confidence. That means that I shall not go to Clamart, which I do not regret. Dear kind uncle and aunt godmother, I send this assurance of my deep and respectful affection.

Your niece and goddaughter,

Marie Rougemont

ÉLÉONORE DE MONTBOURG
TO CHARLES DE CERILLEY
December 29, 1892

Dear Uncle and Godfather,

I would like to be the first of your goddaughters to offer you her wishes for happiness this year, I who have so much to thank you for. Truly, God has chosen you to show us that we must never despair completely under the cruelest trials; and I don't intend to forget it, either.

Mama is suffering from her rheumatism, which has affected her hands; she asks me to send her excuses for the unavoidable delay in answering my aunt's most affectionate letter. Please be sure, dear aunt, that her heart thanks you even before her pen can do so, and let me also express all my own gratitude for your kind sympathy.

Please accept, dear uncle, and share with my aunt, this assurance of the very grateful and respectful feelings of your niece,

Éléonore

1893

ÉLÉONORE DE MONTBOURG
TO CHARLES DE CERILLEY
Paris, February 20, 1893

Dear Uncle,

Mama is suffering so from the rheumatism in her hands that she entrusts me to be her secretary today. She received on schedule the 1,000 francs that you sent her. Mama thanks you for the details you gave her in your last letter and congratulates herself on the reserve she maintained in the one she wrote in response to Henri—a reserve that was not appreciated, it seems, since she still awaits the letter that her godson has always sent her for New Year's Day.

The worries, the sadness, and the extreme fatigue of these last days have kept Mama from sending you her sympathy on your painful anniversary, but she asks me to tell you that she keeps in her heart the memory of the two cousins who for a brief moment shared her maternal care.

M. continues to be as well as possible. Baby, a very pretty child and very strong, has left with his nurse. We got excellent news from them this morning. *He has been registered at the church and the town hall under complete incognito.* That advice was given, in the best interest of the child's future, by his godmother, who is very knowledgeable on what can be done in such cases. The godfather, who is the curate of Tourette, was represented by the priest who baptized the child in the godmother's parish, which is not the one we live in. The wet nurse was procured for us by the doctor, who has known her for many years. She is, he says, trustworthy in every respect, and has brought up many children without having the misfortune of losing a single one. She knows wonderfully well all the things babies need, and owns all the necessary equipment. She demands a high price, but there is absolute security. *She doesn't know our real name.*

As for Saint-Savin, we will not go back there, Mama and I, except to move out. That is the advice of Monsieur de Saint-René. He also advises us further to go to Sangy as soon as possible, and to ask you and my aunt to be good enough to take M. in during our absence, which we will keep to the minimum. Will you be so obliging?

Your niece and goddaughter,

Éléonore

ÉMILIE DE MONTBOURG
TO CHARLES DE CERILLEY
Paris, February 23, 1893

Dear Charles,

By dint of liniment, sedatives, and turpentine pills, my wrists are a little better; but I need absolute rest, which is impossible. The nurse who had served as midwife left us yesterday evening, but she will come back every morning up to the twenty-first day, for it is impossible for me to give M. the necessary care. Furthermore, there was a good girl we were hoping to keep as a domestic, but she has not been able to recover from the trial she's been through. Yesterday the doctor at last recognized an internal phlebitis, the result of poor care in childbirth. If M. did not have me with her, who knows how she would come out of this, for various methods are applied haphazardly, and in certain cases carelessness is shown.

Her milk is not much of a problem. So all goes well since the retention of urine has stopped. Nonetheless, her bladder is still painful, and I'm going to consult someone about that.

Éléonore must have told you that the child has a strong constitution and is pretty, and that the wet nurse who came on the basis of a letter should inspire complete confidence. We pay her 50 francs a month; that's expensive, but there is utter security. She does not and shall not know our real name. The child has been registered at the town hall and the church as born of a father and mother *unnamed,* on the advice of the directress of the other Saint-Raphaël asylum, who has a great deal of experience; sure enough, the midwife who did the registering did not have the slightest difficulty at the town hall. We did have much embarrassment at the baptism: just imagine, Madame Moreau did not even allow Madame Berteau to be *represented* even though the priest had permitted it and

Madame Berteau had promised to be there. So all we had left were the poor girls: the midwife for godmother and the beadle to represent the godfather, who is the curate of Tourette. Now, it was not fitting that these two persons should appear together on the church's rolls. I submitted the case to two ecclesiastics, who advised me to find a proper godmother. Where can you find one on such short notice? Note that they put off answering this until the eve of the event, so we had to act fast! I rushed to see the former directress, whom Madame Moreau had treated outrageously, and who had withdrawn with all her fellow workers to found a new asylum. When I told her of my problem, she spontaneously offered to be the godmother. Then I asked her to extend her generosity by looking for a priest who would be willing to represent the curate of Tourette. She asked that the baptism be held in her parish; this could be done because we are as it were in transit, and one of the vicars represented the godfather while giving the baptism. That didn't cause a ripple. I accompanied the child in a carriage with the wet nurse, who was holding him, and I was present, veiled, at the ceremony. The godmother distributed the honoraria we had agreed on, and very honorably. In recognition of her cordial helpfulness and her advice of complete incognito, I gave her 200 francs toward her good works. We are on the best of terms, believe me, and the ladies here cannot suspect the trick we played on them.

We'll keep our *nom de guerre* in Paris and we'll put inquiries off the track, if anyone were tempted to do any, for in the middle of next month we'll move to another quarter, where we'll take lodgings for three months, to give M. time to regain her figure.

During that time, Monsieur de Saint-René advises us to take a flying trip to Normandy to get the silverware, the china table service, and whatever we want to sell at the Hôtel Drouot,[24] to bring all the papers, and to draw up a liquidation of assets among us. He says it's necessary in order to conclude any sale of Saint-Savin. While I'm doing this, I'll entrust M. to the godmother, who offered to take her in. We'll say she stayed with her godmother at Sangy because traveling is costly and she could not be useful. We'll stay as short a time as possible, and will not unpack. We'll move out another time, and give the same reason. No one will dare say anything to our face.

Monsieur de Saint-René had thought you intended to come to Paris in the spring. He came yesterday; I related to him all we had done, our intention of going to another quarter as soon as possible. He seemed satisfied.

But, dear Charles, how do you suppose M. can think of marrying when she is still in pain from what she has gone through? We must give her time to forget or she will refuse the idea of marriage altogether.

Our need to get away from Normandy means that we'll settle in the Midi—that's why I don't want to get too far away from the influence of the curate of Tourette, which we will need. After waiting the length of time needed before I can present M. in public, we'll go to Sangy for two or three months, but then we'll have to go to the Midi. I've thought of the town of Grasse, which is near Tourette and must have resources of all kinds, since foreigners come there in winter. I'm going to ask the curate of Tourette to try to find us a house with a garden and enough rooms for us to settle there comfortably.

As for Saint-Savin, we'll never stay there again.

But it occurred to me that the heat will more than likely oblige us to return to Sangy during the summers, and that fruit trees would be appropriate in the garden. Since pear trees are planted too closely at Saint-Savin, I'd like to send some from there. Also there are grafts in nursery, and oaks that produce black truffles. They're quite young, these oaks. You'll take half of them. What do you think of my idea? Let me know.

Oh, if only I could count on a future for my daughters, I'd try to beautify my Minster, which deserves it. But! . . .

If you send me 500 francs, try to make it in small bills. You can write me here—the letters arrive quicker.

We'll use my rheumatism to explain our long stay at Sangy. Since we no longer have horses, we won't pay visits. A thousand thanks for being willing to take in M. when we go to move out of Saint-Savin, but we can't tell when.

Good-bye, dear Charles. I've put in half a day on this letter, because I have to stop every other moment to rest my hand; but I badly wanted to give you all these details, to bring you up to date on everything.

My most affectionate greetings. Oh, yes—have some wood prepared for us, please, that's essential.

Your distressed sister,

Émilie

I'm going to rest! . . .

SOPHIE DE MONTBOURG
TO CHARLES DE CERILLEY
Rambouillet, April 25, 1893

Dear Charles,

I've just come back from Paris, where I spent four days, staying at the Hôtel du Luxembourg. I found the arrangement there very unwise, and according to the letter from you that Ém. read me, I see that you are opposed to it with all your might. Monsieur de Saint-René likewise. Their doctor said so in front of me. M. is playing at her fits of hysterics and phlebitis at will, and the mother's weakness gives in to three-quarters of it, instead of laying down the law. The maidservant tried to blackmail her, of course. I arrived in the middle of one of M.'s scenes; she wanted to give right in, and was spouting angry things and absurdities that would make you shudder . . . warning us that she had informed the girl of her name . . . and that, besides, she could pick her own name perfectly well herself. Instead of cutting her short immediately as the doctor advises, her mother temporizes. . . . The maidservant has talked already, for the hotel steward who took down my trunk gave me a knowing look so different from the one on my arrival that it told me quite a bit. I warned Ém. of this; she is so trusting, in spite of her cruel experience, that she often leaves her suite at the same time as her older daughter, leaving M. with the maidservant. I'm afraid of *everything*, absolutely *everything*. The elder does not have the same temperament, it's true, but her complete absence of religion will leave her defenseless against other types of infatuations, and the Cape of Good Hope[25] is not behind her yet. The influence she exerts over her mother is not always a happy one, because she lacks the experience that creates foresight. And along with that, she systematically opposes every idea that comes from elsewhere. It's enough to make you weep, to see all this going on down in the depths without being able to do anything about it!

Still no buyer for Saint-Savin, it seems, and the farmer has them on short rations. I'm going to ask Hon. how he goes about bringing a suit when one of ours acts with such ill-will. It is certain that, for business, Ém. must go on a short trip to Saint-Lô. At the beginning of my stay, I had proposed to Ém. to come and take her place for two days, before I leave for Rambouillet.

But I see that it would be an *enormous* responsibility, and one in which the older sister would be rather an obstacle to me than a help. You would do better than I, because they would fear you. I haven't seen Monsieur de Saint-René. I haven't had time to; besides, our poor sister might perhaps think that I play some part in his decisions. You may pass him my letter if you wish. We have great confidence in him, and they certainly don't tell him everything.

As for the poor mother's health, it is sustained by some divine grace. Only her rheumatism, settled in her right arm and sometimes extending into the bronchi, makes her suffer.

Good-bye, my good brother, and very fond regards.

Your very affectionate sister,

Sophie

ÉMILIE DE MONTBOURG
TO CHARLES DE CERILLEY
Paris, May 25, 1893

Dear Charles,

The doctor has decided that we could leave as soon as M.'s period has resumed normally.

But now Éléonore is suffering from a sort of apoplexy in her hand, and, in her infernal stubbornness, she won't see a doctor.

I suffer more than you can imagine from the stubborn streaks of these two girls, which keep on growing with age. It's certainly the spirit of their father, who never would give up on a half-baked idea. They will be their own victims, and I won't be able to do anything about it, exhausting each day my stock of observations, orders, and prayers. It's hard for a devoted mother like me.

The doctor to whom I was confiding the ideas of marriage that have been sprouting in M.'s head has declared that it would be dangerous to her life for a few years, and forever dangerous to her happiness, because even the best of husbands would not fail, at some point or another, to reproach her for the past; since she is not a woman to bow her head, unhappy things might follow.

If, in years to come, she can meet a man perfect enough to accept the given situation honestly, without bringing it up, then she will have to decide, but it must be a man of mature years, who has suffered.

May God manifest one such when the time has come.

I don't think we can leave Paris before the end of June, so our health may not require medical treatment at Sangy. In the second half of June, if Éléonore is strong enough, we'll go to Saint-Savin to pick out and dispatch the furniture we need for the villa. I hope matters will be sufficiently settled by then so that everyone will have his allotted share. I must live surrounded by my own furniture and not my children's; I am fully determined to establish all my rights. The steep increase in pay your cook has asked for might well be a decent pretext for leaving you. Don't send that perfect coachman of yours to our little house at the Minster. When we get there, we'll manage with the woman you have engaged for us. You know what they used to say: We had a coachman so perfect that people had to look for his defects; well, he was a libertine, a drunkard, and a crook, who used his intelligence to hide his vices. I'm afraid of ostensible perfection. You don't tell me whether the bedroom wallpaper and the dining-room trim go well together.

Good-bye, dear Charles; my most affectionate wishes.
Your distressed sister,

Émilie

SOPHIE DE MONTBOURG
TO CHARLES DE CERILLEY
Sainte-Apolline, September 29, 1893

Dear Charles,
The weather has now turned into heavy rain. I hope it gets nice again for É.'s trip and her move. You're right, she must hurry and settle at Grasse. Alas, why didn't you urge her to go there a year ago? We learned recently that Stéphanie's sister-in-law, really adept in good works, knew of her presence in the Rue Saint-Jacques after two weeks! From this lady to the family of the girl that our Antoine was in love with was not very far, and so I understand the mother's absolute opposition to the marriage, even though her daughter returned his affection! The presence of É. and her older daughter had a striking effect. The directress must have advertised it. . . .

Thérèse is married; it's on our Antoine that the sad effect has fallen! Fortunately, he hasn't guessed it, poor child. It would have been horrible for him. He thought it was only the parents' great ambition for money. I sense all too well that their opposition had this reasonable side to it. You cannot conceive of the reprobation that such a stain brings on those who set honor above life. This severity is indispensable for maintaining noble Christian upbringings. Illness excuses nothing and is never invoked as a pretext.

Émilie is high in her praise of Adèle,[26] her goodness, her good judgment, her affection for you. I'm very happy about it, and I hope the future holds great joys for you through your good son. For my part, I'd like to see the future of our Léon happily settled before I die. God grant that oblivion may descend on what Antoine has so unjustly atoned for! There are days when I can hardly stand up and when the thought of heaven is, as it were, veiled by such cruel memories that my heart, my mind, all of me remains crushed!

Good-bye, my good brother; my fondest wishes to you and to all your dear family.
Your most affectionate sister,

Sophie

ÉMILIE DE MONTBOURG
TO CHARLES DE CERILLEY
Grasse, November 28, 1893

Dear Charles,

For a few days now, Marthe has been driving us mad, worse than ever, apropos of the Paris maidservant and her idea of living with her and with her own little one. Madame Clément thinks that yesterday, when she was permitted to put one letter in the mail, she actually put in two—in other words, one for this maidservant. I'm writing her to forbid her to reply. Sunday, while staying alone with Madame Clément for a moment, she found a way to get free, and when I came back, the lock on the letter box on our door, on the inside, had been tampered with. I wear the key to it hanging around my neck. Could she be waiting for other answers? She's so secretive!

The curate of Tourette is wasting his efforts trying to get her to change her mind: all day long, she keeps telling us she's waiting to be twenty-five to go off and get married as she pleases. While helping to arrange the books, she found a code. She's studying it and says that she's waiting for the right moment to tell me off, and the family, too. The curate of Tourette has taken several steps to sound out several clerks; but when he touches on *the thing,* they don't want to hear any more about it. I'm heartsick about all this, as is Éléonore. Dear kind Madame Clément is distressed and, you understand, we're all ill! I have time only to send fondest wishes, dear Charles, before mailing my letter.

Mail the one I'm sending you, after sealing it.

Your most unhappy sister,

Émilie

1894

ÉMILIE DE MONTBOURG
TO MONSIEUR DE SAINT-RENÉ
Grasse, February 3, 1894

Dear Cousin,

I am being badgered by M., who absolutely insists on getting herself married, and by the curate, who wants a decision. I'm falling back on the family council, with you at the head, for I myself feel incapable of resolving the difficulty of such a mismatch, which negates the principles of my whole life. Perhaps the mild and serious character of the young man would suit him better than someone else for home life with this terrible girl!

One might, no doubt, demand that his career be further advanced; that this candidate be placed in the Grasse station, which is more important than that of Tourette, while waiting until he has acquired enough experience in different services to be placed in the railroad *administration* at Nice. But that would still not give him either the name or the family that we would like to see, and as for means, we can count on nothing but his salary: his mother has only 1,500 francs in income, and there are three children!

Because of my nephews and nieces and the people we know, wouldn't there be a way, for the sake of appearances, to pay the government for authorization to add the name of *de Beauvoisin* to his? The family comes from Pont de Beauvoisin in Dauphiné. It would be a big favor to me, dear cousin, if you could find out about that as soon as possible, and obtain it without spending too much; for you understand that if the thing works out, all possible expenses will be charged to me.

The Paris doctor would have liked to see a longer rest for M., but he does not think there is any danger.

I shall make no decision without your assent, dear cousin, or without my brother's. I may perhaps have revealed to you too much concerning my personal reluctance, but I shall be able to sacrifice my feeling to duty if you see fit, so as to spare this miserable child nameless misfortunes into which the miserable temperament she gets from her father might still sweep her.

My poor Éléonore won't say what she thinks of all this, so as to avoid any responsibility, but she grows sadder as she feels the heavy weight of her cross.

I am better, but how can I be well when everything is so painfully trying to me?

Your affectionate cousin,

Baroness de Montbourg

Since the other brother of Monsieur Borderet[27] also works on the railroad and on the same line, mightn't one give as a reason the need to distinguish between the brothers by having one take on the place name?

MONSIEUR DE SAINT-RENÉ
TO CHARLES DE CERILLEY
Paris, February 7, 1894

Dear Friend,

Just as I received your last letter, Madame de Montbourg herself informed me of the overtures made to her for M. I did not want to reply to your sister until I had come to an agreement with you, but a few days ago, as a result of a new, very urgent letter, I thought I must write her immediately. I'm sending you this last letter to allow you to judge, in substance, the observations I submitted to your sister.

To begin with, since I was unwilling to make myself responsible, by expressing a decisive opinion, for events taking place so far from me, and about which I have only incomplete information, here is what I said to Madame de Montbourg: "I am no longer the tutor of your children; consequently, my opinion and my advice are now no more than secondary. They must give way before the advice that can be given you by the members of your family who are directly concerned with decisions that must be reached jointly."

I added that, nevertheless, I would not refuse to express my opinion to her, but that I feared I might add to her perplexities rather than show her the way to get out of the trouble.

Let's examine together, dear friend, the question before us now. I'm quite sure we shall be in agreement.

I think it is becoming more and more desirable to get M. married. Any other girl in her position might have and should have waited, perhaps for a few years. But this poor child, so morally and intellectually incomplete, is unconscious of her position. She obeys only instincts, as we know, almost animal ones. In these circumstances, she is always on the verge of repeating her dismal adventure. Besides, she is a perpetual source of worry and disappointment for your sister, whose household she fills with agitation and conflict. So it would be desirable to get rid—the word is not too strong—of this dangerous and compromising personality. But here's where the difficulty begins. It would be absolutely necessary, in my view, for M. to get married far from the residences of all members of the family. Now, the young man in question and his family live near the place chosen by Madame de Montbourg for her winter residence. Whence I conclude that she cannot easily escape certain relations that public opinion will more or less impose on her. If your sister had not signed a lease, she could have got her daughter married and moved away, thus avoiding the present situation and possible problems in the future.

It's not the young man's social position or his ordinariness that seem to me the most painful things to accept. What is sad about this affair, quite singularly so, is being, so to speak, at the mercy of a hussy who inflicts such painful times on her family. So all one may desire is that the young man be neither an adventurer nor an outcast—and not too much of a dowry-chaser.

He has resolutely accepted the *fait accompli,* they say he is decent, he has an earned position, and, I add, even an honorable one. But has he already seen M., has he been able to judge her character, her abnormal and violent nature, or won't there be either initial misunderstanding or serious disagreement after marriage? We can only ask ourselves these questions; we'd have to be on the spot to come up with probable answers. — One could make some other observations, but it would lead me far afield to talk to you about them.

You will note that in her letter Madame de Montbourg asks me if it would not be possible for the young man to add to his family name that of the locality where he was born, Beauvoisin. Your sister imagines that these additions to names are made routinely and cheaply, like sending a letter in the mail. She is wrong. To make such a scheme succeed, you have to go through an administrative investigation, submission of legal opinions, a judicial decision, revision of vital statistics, etc.

It's quite true that today, in society, a number of people sport titles or added names that do not belong to them. One may even add that the thing is done commonly without inconvenience and without penalty, for the vital-statistics officers themselves have become very accommodating on this subject; nevertheless, these usurpations are not always easy to regularize.

I admit to you that in the circumstances—for reasons that you will approve, I think—I am inclined only to supply Madame de Montbourg with information that she may perhaps use. I have always kept myself at her disposal, to do all in my power as tutor to her children, and I have a feeling of duty conscientiously and disinterestedly performed; I have no desire, however, to set out on a campaign for something that demands to be examined and studied close at hand.

The only way I may end this long letter is to give you renewed assurance that I will lend you my most devoted cooperation each time the fate and future of your nieces is at stake, although I have not found in my ex-pupils the unreserved affection I might have expected.

Please give my affectionate respects to Madame de Cerilley and have faith, dear friend, in my feelings of friendship.

Monsieur de Saint-René

ÉMILIE DE MONTBOURG
TO CHARLES DE CERILLEY
Grasse, February 17, 1894

Dear Charles,

I'm sending you the letters I have just received. I strongly suspect the husband of the Borderet lady of being a simple workman or day laborer. That penniless station at Tourette cannot suit M., and the thought that all family links with her will be broken pains me so much that I cannot bring myself to consent to such a match. From another direction, Madame Clément warns me that an omnibus driver has caught M.'s attention here, and that she is thinking about him. That's even worse! Oh, good Lord, what can you do with a nature like hers?

If we must absolutely get her married soon (and yet she knows that it is necessary for us to overcome her bad reputation locally) it will definitely be at her own risk and peril, for I will not give her a dowry if the candidate is unworthy of being fully accepted in view of the social rank of her family.

But I thought of a relative of Edwige[28] whose father ran through his fortune. Six years ago he was an employee in the railroad office at Mâcon. He must have moved up since then. Try to find that out. Oh, brother, how vexed I am! My poor Éléonore grows more and more sad, seeing the base egoism of her sister, who does not feel obliged to seek a suitable social circle for them both, and yet she is so devoted to her! But this creature thinks only of eating, drinking, and sensual amours! That is indeed the character and the temperament of the fallen father!

Probably, considering all this, the family will prefer for her to be married far away; but I reject marriage with a person of low degree, from a milieu incompatible with ours; if she insists on ruining herself by hurrying so, and if you judge that we must let her have her way with regard to this Monsieur Borderet, I'll undertake to pay for the child at nurse and for his upkeep, but that's all; I have no other way of protesting. It is doubtful that she will be accepted with the 2,000 francs of income that her share of her father's fortune will give her in my lifetime. But the omnibus driver would certainly accept her if she's crazy about him.

Two Paris churchmen have not succeeded in finding her a husband. It is fully understood that if no other member of the family will be present at her marriage, we shall not be present, either, and we will break with her completely too. I am disgusted with so much ingratitude and presumption.

She certainly intends to attach Madame Clément to herself, but if she has only her 2,000 francs, she won't be able to pay and feed her. I have had another, more general attack of rheumatism, and I am restricted to bed, unable to walk; I need the warmth of the bed and the dressing. Good-bye, my good brother. A thousand tender wishes.

Your affectionate sister,

Émilie

ÉMILIE DE MONTBOURG
TO CHARLES DE CERILLEY
Grasse, February 24, 1894

Dear Charles,

The Borderet scheme is canceled, thank God! M. herself has done it, absolutely refusing to live at the Tourette station. I'll tell you her reasons when we see each other; I can't entrust them to paper. In any case, the announcement of our families' resolution to snub the new household had greatly displeased those who thought, on the contrary, to use this marriage as a means to rise above their proper sphere.

I had indeed spoken of a change of railroad stations, but the curate who was handling it turned a deaf ear. Moreover, neither he nor the mayor of Pont de Beauvoisin was willing to make known the status or the profession of a husband who married without the consent of the girl's family. His brother has married the daughter of a carpenter, which is far too removed from our social rank! M. came to see what egalitarian vulgarity there is here, with the help of a respectable woman, sister-in-law of the hospital chaplain. That horrified her, thank God! She avoids such people, and dreads to meet their likes in the B. family. So that affair is buried. God grant that we find better! But, given M.'s headstrong nature, I'm uneasy. Fortunately Madame Clément is conscientious, and naturally needs to feel that she is in good society, since she is pained by anything wicked or vulgar.

I doubt that the curate of Tourette will seek a husband for M. at this point. Two have rejected her past; we are rejecting the third. Ultimately, Providence will provide; I can neither force M.'s will nor change the situation.

Here we are having violent winds and very cold nights. I hardly go out into the garden, and I must take good care of myself. I've now had three bouts of influenza, plus an abominable sciatica in my lower back and hip, all the way down to my left foot. I'm comfortable only in bed, and yet I can't spend my life there, for while I'm taking care of myself, M. is drinking more than she should and driving everybody crazy. Her health is better and her ideas improved at this moment—at least superficially, but I dare not trust her. Poor Éléonore would certainly like to have her sister marry so things would quiet down; but she also fears that might bring us other troubles.

Your affectionate sister,

Émilie

The curate writes me that the B. family will never accept being snubbed and will protest that sort of treatment. He had gone on about our fortune, and although the expenses I accepted responsibility for came to 3,000 francs, which made 5,000 with M.'s 2,000, they don't think that's enough. I flatly reject that, especially since before that letter, M. had decided against it, so that in refusing I am only conveying the decision of the person most directly concerned, even while thanking them cordially.

Dear Charles,

The Bordeaux doctor is the one who, with the help of his clairvoyant, guided us so happily during M.'s pregnancy, so he knows all about the situation. His wife is his clairvoyant; consulting for me this winter, she saw that M.'s future and present worry me enough to do serious harm to my health, and since she is very good, she *offered* to try to get her married. I must not refuse anyone's good will, reserving to myself all rights of serious examination. But I don't think a good catch would be willing to move or to make up his mind to take on the baggage of the past, and a change of place would be indispensable. A position with the railroads would be better for that, even though it would be less lucrative.

You understand that in withdrawing completely from the contract, I wanted to make the curate's plan fall through. That was the only way. I was able to go to Nice the day before yesterday to get a corset for M. and to have new photographs taken.

As we passed through T. we did not fail to look. The stationmaster is a man of really good appearance and very respectable dress; his mother came to the window, since the passing trains are the sole distraction in this desert! Oh, my friend, what a bitter face, with such rage against the human race! I know one doesn't marry the mother-in-law, but there are obligatory relationships, and with that one, the blood-sucker type (I could not get her to let go until I flatly withdrew all subsidies), there would have been plenty of unpleasantness for the couple. Moreover, that tiny station is really impossible as a place to live, and since it takes more than half an hour to find a living soul and a piece of bread, and only by climbing a mountain impossible for Madame Clément, that was one more difficulty. We would still, if absolutely necessary, have accepted this situation for *a limited time.* But the family connections, which you know—they could not be changed.

Besides, the curate of T., on whom we were counting as a neighbor, is leaving his parish on the 14th of this month to go to Nice as a chaplain. Nevertheless, the sight of the man, who is really attractive, gave M. regrets, and at Nice she nearly had an attack. Distraction and errands for her to do, thank God, diverted her attention.

If a marriage plan took on substance, it goes without saying that for this year I would let the burial-vault project go; but I would like to have that carried out as soon as possible. My heart still gives me trouble from maintaining the painful struggle against M. and the curate over the abandoned scheme, the rheumatism that has turned into sciatica and has spread so much could go to my heart, and I might be taken away in a short time; I want to be beside my Émile.

Good-bye, dear Charles; my fondest wishes.

Your affectionate sister,

Émilie

MARTHE DE MONTBOURG
TO CHARLES DE CERILLEY
Grasse, March 7, 1894

My good Uncle,

I thank you very much for your good advice, including what you told me at Sangy. Yes, the plan of a marriage to Monsieur Borderet is broken off: although he is a nice boy, I've refused him. I do indeed have some regrets about this now. But it was impossible. His mother, whom we saw Monday, March 5, on our way to Nice, looks more like a knitting machine than a woman. I might perhaps have passed over that if I had not had other, more serious, reasons for not living in the station at Tourette, reasons that it is impossible for me to describe in writing and that I will tell you about at Sangy when we go there in July. I hope, dear uncle, that you and my aunt are not suffering too much from the cold in Burgundy. Here the climate is fine, far preferable to that of Nice, which is so variable!

Dear uncle and aunt, I send assurances of my feelings of affectionate respect.

Marthe de Montbourg

ÉMILIE DE MONTBOURG
TO CHARLES DE CERILLEY
Grasse, March 10, 1894

Dear Charles, *For you alone.*

Since you recommended that I profit by all possible occasions to try to get M. married, I have had Madame Clément write to a gentleman of twenty-eight who advertised in the journal *Le Chasseur Français.* Here is his answer:

Dear Madame,

In reply to your letter, I have the honor of letting you know that I am a collector of direct taxes. My residence is Condé-sur-Ifs, arrondissement of Falaise (Calvados). I am a sincere Catholic. I have the most cordial relations with all the priests of my collecting district; moreover, Abbé Lefranc, curate of Condé-sur-Ifs, with whom I have the best of relations and who considers me a real friend, would, I dare say, be pleased to supply you with all the information you might consider useful on this point. As you see, belonging to a secret society does not figure among my ideas.

My family came originally from Haute-Marne, arrondissement of Langres. My parents live in Levallois, near Paris, 41 Rue Danton, and live from their income. They have two children, my sister and me. After my parents' death, I estimate that my share will amount to 30,000 to 35,000 francs.

I almost forgot to tell you that I have been attached to the Ministry of Finance since the age of twenty, that I was nominated to my present post, at 4,000 francs, two years ago, and that within a year from now, two years at the most, I hope to get a promotion. I was twenty-eight in November 1893. *I am in excellent health.* I have brown hair and I am 1 meter 68 tall [about five feet six].

There, madame, is *my situation honestly* expounded, and, hoping you will be willing to continue in your plan, I send my respectful greetings as Your Servant,

Édouard Granjean, Collector, Condé-sur-Ifs

I am having this reply sent by Madame Clément:

Dear Sir,

The girl I take an interest in comes from a very good family. She is assured of 5,000 francs as her total income, and, after the death of her mother, who is a widow, she will have 2,000 or 3,000 francs more in income. Her older sister does not want to marry, so she's a fine match, but . . . there is a one-year-old child to be *acknowledged.* You would also have to change your baptismal name, which recalls sad memories, and, finally, transfer to our collecting district, because the mother would not consent to move so far.

Consider, sir, whether you will accept these conditions, and answer me. The assets consist of landed property and government funds. The accounts for the guardianship are cleared.

If you accept the conditions, my young friend's mother will submit your case to the family, which is very close-knit.

Allow me, with that eventuality in mind, to keep your letter of the 25th, which I promise to return to you if you don't accept.

Sincerely, etc.

What do you think of the collector's position? I find it preferable to that of a petty stationmaster.

The transfer is essential: Calvados is quite impossible, though I'm not saying so.

They might have some information at the Ministry of Finance. I'll have the parents, at Levallois, investigated by a Paris priest; but for the ministry, if you have no one, we'll need Monsieur de Saint-René. I'll involve him *if the conditions are accepted:* no need to bother him pointlessly.

Éléonore is so sorely tried by her sister's excesses, her torments over marriage, and her whole personality that I can't wait to see a marriage concluded.

I send all my fondest wishes as a most affectionate sister,

Émilie

ÉDOUARD GRANJEAN
TO MADAME CLÉMENT
March 30, 1894

Dear Madame,

The question of my moving nearer the Midi is a very simple matter. I have friends at the Ministry of Finance who will make this change easy for me *whenever I want it.* Moreover, my personal tastes, if I had had to choose at the moment of my appointment, would have been for the land of the sun. As for changing my first name, that's a minor question that presents no difficulty.

But I wish to marry to make myself a home and have a mate to whom I will give all my affection; I would want that to be reciprocal; I would not want, in entering this marriage, to be merely a straw man. So I ask you, madame, to be good enough to tell me if the girl has a gentle and affectionate character and if her heart is now free of any other attachment, for, I repeat, my desire is to have a loving mate, with whom I'll be happy to share all my joys.

With this reservation, I accept all the conditions contained in your letter.

With the request that you give me as soon as possible some details about the girl, as well as about her family, I remain, madame,

Respectfully yours,

É. Granjean

ÉMILIE DE MONTBOURG
TO CHARLES DE CERILLEY
Grasse, April 2, 1894

Dear Charles,

Éléonore is copying for you Monsieur Granjean's letter, which we have just received. I'm writing to a very substantial abbé in Paris asking him to get information on the young man from the curate of Condé-sur-Ifs, and at the same time on the respectability of the father and mother. Madame Clément, who—alas!—is going to leave us because her cousin promises to leave her a good part of her fortune, promises me to look around in Levallois (she will be near there) for information on the family. I'm going to write to Monsieur de Saint-René. Madame Clément will continue the correspondence, so that our name will not be revealed unless the gentleman has to come here.

The remark about the secret society is simply a reply to my question. Considering the times we're living in, as soon as you go outside our society, it's a good thing to find out, for these affiliations are widespread, especially among civil servants.

We ask him to change his baptismal name, Édouard, because that's the name of the child's father.

If this plan succeeds, I'll be glad to have your approval of it; but, good Lord, how we're going to miss Madame Clément, especially M.! She hopes to persuade her cousin to come to Grasse, if the cousin can be moved: it seems she has an intestinal tumor. Madame Clément promises to come back to us if the cousin dies, or if she does not carry out her promise. The dear lady believes she cannot refuse because of her mother and sister. I agree with her; but she has given herself to us, and, once free, she fully counts on returning to us. Her family is not so close to her heart. Meanwhile, we are quite upset. I'm going to take on a housekeeper, a pious girl who will come in every day.

Your affectionate sister,

Émilie

I am having the answer sent that M. has a very affectionate, devoted, and energetic character, that she is lively but easily pleased, that in her gratitude for seeing her child adopted she will love twice as much the man willing to adopt him, that he can be easy about the past: there is no possible connection, and the family has moved far away.

Burn my letter.

ÉMILIE DE MONTBOURG
TO CHARLES DE CERILLEY
Grasse, April 6, 1894

Dear Charles,

I'm sending you the photograph of the gentleman with the copy of the letter that accompanied it, which explains the severity of his features. I won't send M.'s until we have the information requested, and will not send it at all if that is unsatisfactory.

M. claims that if Madame Clément cannot come with her, she doesn't want to get married. Madame Clément, now detained by her cousin, cannot leave her, so the gentleman would have to arrange to be appointed to Grasse. Is that possible? I would certainly offer to put up the young family until Madame Clément is free, but Éléonore is not anxious for it, and I must not cross her.

You see that things are getting complicated, and M.'s sickly willfulness makes it very perplexing. She is not enchanted by the photograph.

If by chance she changes her mind, it seems to me that the best thing would be for them to go to Paris to meet, and, if they get along and understand each other, to get married in Paris. First, though, he ought to have his appointment. I hope you would be willing to come for the contract and the wedding. Monsieur de Saint-René would be on the spot, and nothing would happen *here*. The acknowledgment could also take place there; what do you think about it? The parents are close to Paris, which would be one factor.

I know very well that this will cost me a lot, but what am I to do? There will be no celebrations.

Send me back the photograph, or else send it to Monsieur de Saint-René with the copy of the letter.

Your affectionate sister,

Émilie

SOPHIE DE MONTBOURG
TO ÉMILIE DE MONTBOURG
Sainte-Apolline, April 10, 1894

Dear Émilie,

Yesterday, on receiving your first letter, I promptly wrote to someone who has connections in the arrondissement of Falaise; and this morning Honoré put a gentleman he knows on the track of Monsieur Édouard Granjean. Condé-sur-Ifs is 18 kilometers from Falaise. It's only a little market town of 457 inhabitants, which makes it a village. I believe we will get sure information; but we need to be patient, for this will take, I think, two weeks. Honoré has not seen your second letter, having left before the postman came. When he comes back, he'll go and see the collector of direct taxes. Perhaps he knows him. But he doesn't know the present receiver general at all. He and I will see whether he couldn't get this information through an assessor he knows.

Obviously this course would be better than the first, socially speaking. I'll slip the moral question of character in among the questions about his civil service ratings. I've made a whole list of questions of my own: religious principles, conduct, reputation, education, character. I'll transmit the reply to you without changing anything in it. I'm also asking about his general appearance. He's rather on the short side, Honoré was told this morning. A 4,000-franc collectorship at age twenty-eight proves that he is recognized to be very intelligent, or that he has strong support, which will be necessary to obtain a transfer without a cut in pay.

This career is very good, and allows a man to live a long time in the country, which M. would prefer. There would be independence from the in-laws. In short, many good things, if the man is willing.

Madame Clément's leaving must be a great complication for you! And I wish all the more for M.'s marriage. I understand that she misses her, too; but be sure to tell M. that a husband ordinarily likes to have his wife depend solely on him and that it is often his direction which attaches him to her most strongly at first. So it is mainly for your sake, my poor sister, that I miss the presence of Madame Clément, because of all she would have helped you to do in these circumstances. Anyway, as you say, it was impossible to ask that she give up the bread of her old age by refusing to go to be with her cousin—who, moreover, needs her.

So you must resign yourself to her absence. But what have you found to replace her? The three of you can't live alone. I hope your bronchitis is now cured.

I'm beginning to suffer again as I did last summer and am without any strength at all. Perhaps it is the blood stirring in the spring. Here we are still threatened by drought; how shall we be paid?

It makes one desperate.

Your very affectionate sister,

Sophie

ÉMILIE DE MONTBOURG
TO CHARLES DE CERILLEY
Grasse, April 11, 1894

Dear Charles,

I had already written to Sophie, and I did so again when Monsieur de Saint-René replied to me that the only information he could obtain at the ministry was too superficial, and that we had to go, through Honoré, to the more immediate superiors in the hierarchy—namely, the superintendent of collections and the receiver general at Caen. I'm sending you Sophie's answer.

The photograph I sent you is frighteningly harsh. If the gentleman is like that, I could never have my daughter marry him: he would make her unhappy. If it is only a matter of a bad photograph, he would do well to have a better one to send. But we cannot broach this question until the information is received.

No reply has come from the curate of Condé to Madame Clément. The Paris priest I was counting on to write to the curate has declined, on the pretext that he had promised himself never to become involved in such matters. I have just asked a missionary in Marseille to do me that favor. I've asked Madame Clément to write the mayor of Condé-sur-Ifs, Calvados, but will he answer? It's very sad, and you see that I badly need Sophie and Honoré. Madame Clément was to get the information in Paris on the gentleman's family; it's a week now that we've had no letter from her, which worries us.

Madame de La Neuville[29] is proposing to me for M. a young count of twenty-nine who would accept the situation. I'm asking her for more complete information, but I fear some stain and am not dwelling much on this idea.

Your very affectionate sister,

Émilie

Dear Friend,

Since Madame de Montbourg has announced to you that she has written to me about the Granjean candidacy, she should have communicated to you the reply I made to her interrogations. Here is approximately what I told her: I have been unable to obtain at the Ministry of Finance anything but completely banal information; the gentleman's dossier seems to contain only documents relative to his service. It is true that I do not have at the Ministry of Finance the facilities I might perhaps have in other administrative offices to obtain fully *confidential* information.

But I think one could become well enough informed on the morality, the conduct, and the habits of Monsieur G. by addressing the superintendent of direct taxes in Calvados, the mayor, and the curate of the place where Monsieur G. lives. I think that Madame de Montbourg would get what it is important to her to know if she got the help of her brother-in-law and other trustworthy persons she knows at Saint-Lô. I indicate only the course to take in that event.

Now, even if the information were satisfactory, I think there would be a very great danger in rushing the outcome—that is to say, the marriage. It is an act of conscience and prudence to foresee as humanely as possible the catastrophes that might happen later. We must not, I believe, make a marriage that would be a risky venture, as might happen without sufficient precautions. There are already in an *affair of this nature* so many redoubtable risks that one must not add any more by being too hasty.

So my advice would be to instruct Monsieur G. to take at least a two-week leave, which he would spend near Madame de Montbourg (at the hotel, of course). But *where, when,* and *how*—all that would remain to be settled. I wouldn't say in Paris, because to move Madame de Montbourg and her children would cost too much if things did not work out. Besides, it's easier for a man to move about and make any sort of trip than for a family. A meeting place would have to be determined that would reconcile the interests at stake. For example, if Madame de Montbourg resumes her summer residence in Burgundy, mightn't one set Lyon as a meeting place? It is a big city about halfway between them. Or Marseille, which would permit us, after the first few interviews, to know whether we can come to an understanding, and go on with the plan in question.

That would constitute a first step of acceptance, and after a stay of twelve to fourteen days, either in Grasse or in Burgundy, Monsieur G. and

M. could be definitely committed. I don't go into all the details of this arrangement, which I leave to your sagacity.

To speak frankly, I have only slight confidence in the result of this affair. Like Pilate, I wash my hands of it. Neither of the principals interests me, and I wish quite simply that they'd leave me alone. I fear the girl may be nothing but a *high liver,* past, present, and future; as for the gentleman, he'd like to have me believe he's strictly honorable. Moreover, I see that in this, as in many other things, you and I are of the same opinion.

I think, lastly, that if there are sincere disclosures—and sufficiently circumstantial ones, as they must be if you want to prepare in advance for *discords in the household*—that will be the moment to shout "Beware the bomb," for there are things a prospective groom has a right to ask and that it is impossible to refuse him when one makes a compromise with his conscience as Monsieur G. is doing.

I understand that Madame de Montbourg is in a great hurry to be rid of an insubordinate daughter of equivocal conduct. I strongly urge her, in spite of everything, not to act precipitately. It is very regrettable that the gentleman lives in Normandy, almost the only region forbidden to M., and where, for another thing, it will be so easy for an indiscreet person to find out a lot about her. What interests me in all this is the mother and the family.

To sum up: retain of my letter only what you wish to. I persist in my recent advice to them so as not to cast the unfortunates into an abyss with their eyes closed. Communicate to Madame de Montbourg whatever part of my letter you see fit.

What remains for me to say to you relieves my heart and mind, for that consists in asking you to remember me fondly and send friendly greetings to you and Madame de Cerilley.

Monsieur de Saint-René

P.S. I'll send back the photograph.

ABBÉ LEFRANC
CURATE OF CONDÉ-SUR-IFS
TO MADAME DE MONTBOURG
Condé-sur-Ifs, April 12, 1894

Dear Madame,

I am happy to have the best of information to communicate to you about Monsieur Granjean, tax collector at Condé-sur-Ifs. He is an exceptionally amiable young man, tactful and of exquisite delicacy in his dealings, of irreproachable conduct, fully dedicated to the responsibilities of his position, which he handles with perfect order.

Gambling and debauchery are absolutely unknown to him. I only wish that all girls might find such husbands.

Respectfully yours,

Lefranc

ÉMILIE DE MONTBOURG
TO CHARLES DE CERILLEY
Grasse, April 15, 1894

Dear Charles,

I'm answering your letter of the 13th:

1. I have not received the photograph I sent you.

2. Inquiries are under way at Condé-sur-Ifs with the curate and the mayor.

3. Inquiries are also under way in Haute-Marne on the respectability of the family.

4. Honoré and Sophie are getting information at Condé, Falaise, and Caen. Let's wait for the answers.

5. To gain time and forestall the impatience of the young man, who would like to know his fate and have a photograph of the young person, I've had Madame Clément write that the severity that was so marked in him on his photograph made an unfortunate impression, and that he ought to have himself photographed by an experienced portraitist to destroy that impression. If the information is not suitable, we'll say the first impression cannot be erased.

6. One must say absolutely nothing about the past except the result; otherwise one would spoil everything. The distance is great, and the husband will be the very first interested party to veil the past. I think he is flattered to be marrying into the nobility.

Really, when a young man has had a stormy life, does he reveal anything about it except what he cannot hide? If all young people confessed to the families of their intended how many marriages would take place? Do you imagine, for example, that I would have married Armand if I had known he was capable of being infatuated with a dancing girl at Caen?

However, that's what happened, and even his family knew nothing about it.

Consequently, if you give me the great pleasure of coming to Paris, I entreat you to touch on no subject relating to conduct or health. The Bordeaux clairvoyant assures me that the marriage will be happy.

If the information is suitable, it seems to me the best thing to do is to stay at the Hôtel de Normandie, as on all our other trips. Madame Clément would write to this gentleman to introduce him to us, since it is she who has put herself forward for the negotiations (they will learn our name only if we suit one another); then, if the hotel wants too much money, we'll take a furnished apartment. And everything would take place in Paris, where the gentleman could make the most of his influence to obtain a collectorship around here. As a matter of fact, a collector (not the one for Grasse) who lives across from our villa is very ill.

I have just this moment received a letter from Madame Clément containing the curate of Condé's reply; you couldn't ask for better. God be praised. I enclose a copy. Madame Clément will come back to us. She doesn't like her cousin. I'm very glad she has compared the two situations and is returning of her own choice. But I'm going to ask her to be patient until we arrive in Paris. I have to collect all my financial resources for so many expenditures, and my strength for so many fatigues. Madame Clément will be very useful to me in Paris.

Éléonore is also very happy about the information we have received, for her sister's husband will be her brother! As for me, nothing will replace my Émile!

Your very affectionate sister,

Émilie

ÉMILIE DE MONTBOURG
TO CHARLES DE CERILLEY
Grasse, April 20, 1894

Dear Charles,

Honoré has gotten more circumstantial information from a gentleman who addressed himself to the curate. Here is a copy of his letter:

Dear Baron,

Not knowing the young man you tell me about well enough, I thought I could do no better than to inquire of the curate of Condé-sur-Ifs, who is a very worthy man. I'm sending you his letter. As for me, Baron, as municipal councilor of Vieux-Fumé I have several times had occasion to talk with Monsieur Granjean, whom I have always found fine in every respect. I noticed last year that he had quickly familiarized himself with his functions, and I found him congenial and well bred. Toward everyone, and in particular toward my family and myself, he has always been a man of exquisite politeness. I like to think that the fuller letter from the curate will inform you and satisfy you completely.

Here is that letter:

Very dear Sir,

I'm extremely sorry that a three-day absence prevented me from answering you by the first mail, the more so because I have the best of information to communicate to you about the conduct, the respectability, and the amiability of Monsieur Édouard Granjean, tax collector of Condé-sur-Ifs.

Entirely dedicated to the cares of his collectorship, he combines tact with devotion to duty in all his dealings; thus he is liked by the taxpayers, even the most recalcitrant, and he takes in all funds due.

I cannot tell you anything about his means, except that he furnished the deposit necessary to handle a collectorship paying 4,000 francs a year. Likewise, his family is completely unknown to me. The father is from the Vosges, the mother from the south of France. The parents, retired from the wine business, live in Levallois-Perret, I believe. I find it impossible to add the slightest piece of information that could be useful to you, for I do not know his parents.

To sum it all up, he is a young man combining all the qualities necessary to make a wife happy.

Respectfully yours, etc.

I think that if the parents had retired from business in bankruptcy, he wouldn't have got a collectorship. I also have an idea that if Monsieur G. had advanced republican opinions, he wouldn't show himself so desirous of marrying into the nobility, especially with the wretched means that M. brings. The poor boy is so afraid that the impression of severity in his photograph may spoil things that he has written what follows to Madame Clément.

Dear Madame,

I'm very sorry that my photograph produced the effect you describe to me. I assure you that I do not have that expression of harshness at all; *on the contrary,* my character is among the gentlest and the merriest. Moreover, madame, if you think it useful, I'll make the trip to Paris quite expressly to convince you of this, and when you have seen me, I beg you to plead warmly for me.

As for the question of a transfer, as I have told you, madame, I have influential friends in Finance itself who will continue to exert their good influence for me and will facilitate for me, *I'm certain,* my appointment, either in the Alpes-Maritimes or at least in the neighboring departments. As for being appointed in Grasse itself, which is first-class, I admit to you, madame, that I cannot think of it, but I am *sure* of being able to get my appointment to an equivalent position, if not a superior one, in the department itself or in the adjacent ones.

You, madame, know my situation, which I have exposed to you with the greatest sincerity and the greatest frankness. It's ten years now that I've been in Finance, and I think my superiors can provide nothing but good reports about me. The only thing I ask of you is not to talk to them about *a transfer;* you will, madame, understand this reservation. Thus, madame, I shall have the honor of presenting my respects to you on the day and hour you indicate to me, for I am very anxious to convince you that I am neither morose nor surly and that, on the contrary, my manner is cheery, I will even say sprightly.

Respectfully yours, etc.

Since M. is so eager for the plan to work that she would marry even the most hard-featured man, I think that trip is useless. To keep him patient, while we waited for information we sent the photograph of M. taken recently in Nice, which was a great success. It's very probable that he will like her. If the information continues to be good, I would like very much, for everyone's sake, that everything should take place in Paris. But Madame Clément has been laid low by the change in temperature; she knows that Éléonore and I are so delicate that we cannot change climates in this season with impunity. So the interview will have to take place in Marseille, where we'll spend several days. If we all suit one another on both sides, we must have him renew the promise to acknowledge the child, and we will reveal our name. From Marseille Monsieur G. will be able to study the collectorships in the Grasse area; there must be a roster, as there is for lawyers. Already we know that a collector for these areas around Grasse, who lives in the town itself, is very ill. Perhaps his collectorship is up for the taking. I had Madame Clément say that it would be in order to inquire at the ministry. I will not consent to the marriage until the position is set and agreed to by us. I think you will approve.

In writing to Honoré, I asked him if we could count on a Montbourg as a witness. He would be angry if I didn't ask, but I doubt that anyone will take the trouble for so ungratifying a marriage.

I'm coming back to what you said to me, that we should reveal details on health and on the past, because I must tell you that M. would be so unhappy at the collapse of this plan, which she is paying for with such a sincere return to the good, that I would not answer for her life or perhaps for her reason; consequently a disclosure that proved to be useless would be not just a mistake, but a frightful misfortune. So, I ask for your word as a gentleman, to soothe the poor child, who will—I have no doubt of it—be a faithful and devoted wife.

My very fond wishes to you and to Madeleine. What does she think of this marriage? Alas, you know well that it is not what I wanted for my daughters! God has taken delight in shattering all my hopes. I submit! After the death of my Émile, all is broken in me! . . .

Your affectionate sister,

Émilie

ÉMILIE DE MONTBOURG
TO CHARLES DE CERILLEY
Grasse, April 26, 1894

Dear Charles,

I'm answering the letter which you enclosed with Sophie's. I think it's pretty strong that she should tell you, M.'s uncle, things regarding a prospective husband for *my daughter* which must be of greater concern to a mother. Thus this much-vaunted character, this extreme amiability toward the taxpayers is translated into *sharp* words when *he*'s the one at fault; and several times in a row, this most precise civil servant—again according to the curate—is absent from his office, without any other good reasons to offer than *sharp* words? Well, that's a sign of bad character for the young man, and of a lie for the curate. And Sophie wasn't telling me! . . . Fortunately, the gentleman lied in saying that his parents were living from their income, and the curate lied in saying they had retired from business.

The shop, open and stocked with wines and liqueurs, was not finished, it seems, and Madame Clément went back to see the stock. Now, here is the description (I'm copying): the sign bears no name, it says simply "The Great Danton Cellars" (that's the name of the street, but that may also be the name of their party's hero). The main entrance topped by a big awning and, in big letters, WINE TASTING. Then on either side the sign,

"The Great Danton Cellars," and shopwindows containing fine wines and choice liqueurs. On the inside, six very cute little round tables and, opposite the door, a counter where there will certainly be people coming to have something. It's a new style, which would work well in the nice sections of Paris, and at Levallois there is not one like it. The son will be able to tell me whether it is indeed for his sister that they are setting up that business, for it might be that these people spent too much money for this place and want to get some of it back.

In any case, they are the ones who serve the customers. All the marks of retail trade are there; the gentleman cannot say that it's large-scale trade. So we mustn't think about it any more! Madame Clément is reclaiming the photograph and promised to send his back with the letters I kept to send to the family. You blame me for having sent M.'s picture. Alas! You don't know how eagerly one takes the good information, how much difficulty one has putting faith in the bad. She *wants* to get married, God help us. Yet she freely gave him up, confronted with the café and the lack of frankness of this individual who wrote, "I am a sincere Catholic," and who, we have learned, *does not even go to Mass.* He could not have found out our name. I forbade the photographer at Nice to tell it if he is asked. So rest easy. Madame Clément will be back soon; we're awaiting her impatiently. Good Lord, how tiring and distressing this hunt for a husband is, because you mustn't trust any report. I'll keep you posted on what comes to me from Bordeaux. If the information is good and M. refuses, I'll think of Adrienne.

All my fondest wishes, dear Charles.

Your most affectionate sister,

Émilie

Return the letter and photograph to me.

Like you, I am astonished that he accepts the big condition so easily! . . . Alas, the general moral level has sunk, it seems; if you only knew the theological latitude of the clergy—it's frightening.

ÉMILIE DE MONTBOURG
TO CHARLES DE CERILLEY
Grasse, May 5, 1894

Dear Charles,

Madame Clément has come back to us, as happy to be here as we are to receive her. I hope it's for always. She had two visits from Granjean, whom she finds very distinguished. He brought her a *notarized lease* for the wine shop his parents have opened at Levallois. The lease is for twelve years, beginning next July 15. They wanted to set up the shop and then rent it. Consequently, as of July 15 they will no longer be wine retailers. In fact, the father is a wholesale dealer in wine, in the Bercy warehouses, which would be more acceptable, although the son wrote that his parents *live from their income*. He didn't know, he says, that his parents had decided to set up this retail business to provide custom for their tenant, and Madame Granjean, not knowing her son's intentions, did not think she should confide in Madame Clément. Their daughter married a young man, son of a postmaster, who had promised a dowry that was swept away by the Panama scandal; after that Granjean the father was no longer willing to give his daughter's dowry. However, it seems that things will work out and that the parents will set the young people up as retail wine merchants. Here is the background on that side of the family.

Madame Granjean is from Aveyron. Madame Clément will ask for her family's name.

The mayor answered Madame Clément:

Dear Madame,
I must tell you that the Granjean family, originally from our commune, is a very honorable family which has always been reputed as the best there is from the area, and which at the time this family went to Paris enjoyed a rather large fortune.
Yours, etc.
The mayor's stamp was over the signature.

I've written to ask Sophie to get details on the one lady who has given negative information, too vague not to leave a vast field open to suppositions. The certainty that this wine retailing operation is only temporary changes matters on that score.

The father-in-law of the daughter is a deputy postmaster retired from the postal ministry. He also lives in Levallois.

M. doesn't want to hear about the marquis, so all I can do is give back his photograph and stop concerning myself with it.

And so this project is reviving while we await the completion of Sophie's information—if, like me, you accept the view that the notarized lease changes the situation. Now, to get to the practical side of the matter, if it were to take place, there would be one great obstacle. Monsieur Granjean thinks it will take about three months to get a transfer from the north to the Midi, and before making his application for a transfer, he would like to be assured that the marriage will take place. He doesn't know our name and thinks we are from the Midi. I'm not keen on long engagements. On the other hand, M. cannot go to Normandy. Shall I be obliged to spend the hottest months of the summer in Paris to allow the gentleman to make our acquaintance? In any case, if the marriage is to take place it will be in Paris, since the legitimation must precede the marriage and the declaration was made in Paris. During that time the arrangements for transfer can be taken; the wedding would not take place until after the appointment.

I'm waiting impatiently for the results of Sophie's investigations. My word, and I thought everything was off!

By the way, Monsieur Granjean already has a nice set of furniture for a bachelor. His cleaning woman is sixty. That's a good point of decorum. Tell me what you think of all this.

I send you fond greetings in haste, my good brother, because of the mail.

Your affectionate sister,

Émilie

CHARLES DE CERILLEY
TO HENRI DE CERILLEY
Sangy, June 28, 1894

Dear Henri,

All France is uttering one long cry of horror at the abominable assassination of President Carnot.[30] Humanity pays its instinctive and honorable debt, but the overly theoretical liberals can wear double mourning, for it is quite evident that the assassin is a member of an anarchistic group so numerous that all governments are going to find themselves obliged, in the face of this new crime, to pass more and more severe edicts. The most urgent thing is to muzzle the press and oppose all dubious opinions. For more than twenty years they have been allowing incitement to murder, to pillage; they have practically been protecting the strikers, and after that people wonder that overexcited young heads respond to propaganda with *action!* All the theoretical liberals are guilty and have themselves prepared the muzzle that I certainly hope will be put on the press.

What a sad journey Madame Carnot and her sons made to Lyon! How blind popular passion is, even when good feeling is at the heart of it! Are all Italians settled in France supposed to be responsible for their scoundrelly compatriot? Surely this crime is the result of a plot of the International.

If the good weather persists without interruption, I think I'll be free as of July 10. I have six reapers, seventeen tedders, men and women. There's a mass of hay.

The barometer is falling, despite a steady north wind, which worries me. Thank you for the details about the dear little children.

Good-bye, and see you soon.

Your affectionate father,

Charles de Cerilley

ÉMILIE DE MONTBOURG
TO CHARLES DE CERILLEY
Grasse, July 5, 1894

Dear Charles,

For some days I have been waiting for information to pass on to you; only a part of it has arrived, but I'm going to talk to you about it right away. Here it is: M. has noticed a young man in the post office at the money-order window. He's not handsome, but she likes him! So I had to get information. He's a Monsieur Pradet, native of Castellane, in the Basses-Alpes, about three hours from here by carriage. Castellane is the chief town of the arrondissement; there are 1,838 inhabitants. These details are important to the situation.

The letter comes from a well-to-do and well-regarded tradesman, a friend of the treasurer of the seminary at Grasse, who got information, without knowing us, on the request of the chaplain of the Order of the Visitation, my confessor. I am copying:

I hasten to respond with the information you request, and if I've delayed a few days, that was to be able to send it to you as precisely as possible. Monsieur Pradet the father, deceased about fifteen years ago, was chief road surveyor at Castellane, and he married a widow with one daughter. By this marriage he had three children, two girls and the boy about whom you are asking me for information. One of the daughters married a baker at Castellane. So the mother now lives with the younger daughter, and last winter they went and spent the bad cold days at Grasse, with the son.

The information on morality is very good, for the whole family.

As for means, the mother owns here at Castellane a rather pretty house with a value of 7,000 to 8,000 francs, plus a little garden and a property that together may be worth from 5,000 to 6,000 francs. Besides, she owns at Demandolx (a commune in our area) a fairly large open tract, on which there are farmers. I cannot give you the exact valuation of it, but it brings in a pretty good income.

The father's estate was divided into three portions, and after her death the mother's estate will be divided into four portions. The son has been a soldier, enlisted at eighteen in the Marine Light Infantry. He took part in the Tonkin campaigns. He is a nice boy and very quiet and has a certificate as an elementary-school teacher. He entered the postal service after his military enlistment expired.

In short, these are fine people, very honorable and enjoying very good health.

The first daughter, born of the first marriage, is excellently situated; she married a man of private means here at Castellane. Since this family is not originally from Castellane, I cannot give you any other information.

M.'s confessor has written to the curate of Castellane. Once he has the answer, he can, through his colleagues in the postal service, who did their studies with him and entered the postal administration, get details about the character, the cast of mind, and the habits of the gentleman. I hope to be able, through my chaplain, to find out if he has any future. The baker brother-in-law is a great drawback, although they don't have the same name. What do you think? If you approve, I'll have M.'s confessor feel out the terrain: he will ask the young man (without naming us) whether he would accept the situation and the condition, under the seal of a secret that it would be in his interest to keep. But I don't yet know what salary postal employees enjoy—one must be able to live comfortably!

I must also find out the mother's name, her origins, the name of her first husband (who was probably better off than the second, since his daughter is well situated).

At one time I had hoped for something else, but there was a misunderstanding; the thing is not possible.

These last few days, we made the pilgrimage to Laghet without accident or illness, thank God, and I took M. and Madame Clément around Monaco. É. wouldn't come: she stayed at the station by the sea at Monte Carlo, in the company of other ladies.

The prince's palace (which we visited), the gardens, and the chapel delighted them. M. never stops thanking me for this visit. Then, on the way back, all four of us went up to La Turbie on the funicular railway. The climb is frightening—you go just about straight up, pushed from behind by a locomotive—so I promised myself not to go back down by that perilous means. From La Turbie you go almost a league on foot to the chapel located in the monastery. We set out bravely, without knowing where we would be able to sleep, for the monastery does not admit women. On our way we met a large pilgrimage coming back with gigantic rosaries as belts for the women and decorative sugar hearts for the men. That's typical! At last we arrived, very tired, and Providence procured us two rooms with a widow and her daughter, also a widow. But what destitution! Without counting the fact that you see daylight through the roof and the windowpanes are broken! Finally, fatigue put us to sleep perforce; at five in the morning we were in the chapel, which is old and in very good taste, amid the cloisters that surround it. You would not believe *there* that humanity is losing faith; for faith and the most sincere piety are imprinted on the pilgrims' faces. The men make confession to the Carmelite Friars who officiate at the chapel, whose meditations are so edifying. I would have liked to get souvenirs for my whole family, but the pilgrimage of the day before emptied the only store, which is in the hands of a Carmelite Father.

Were you as appalled as we were at the death of the inoffensive Carnot? Apparently Casimir-Périer[31] has already received threatening letters. They say that Mademoiselle Chiris, daughter of the senator who is a big perfume manufacturer in Grasse, got an anonymous letter saying that if she does not obtain Cesario's pardon, her white gown will be stained with blood on the day of her marriage. Now she is engaged to Monsieur Carnot's son; their marriage banns were published on the Sunday morning, and the father was struck down that evening! Because of the Chiris family, the population demands that besides the Mass that was said at the church for Monsieur Carnot, they also solemnize a funeral service at the Place du Cours, so that the whole city may attend. They say the bishop has consented: "Do whatever they ask of you," he replied to the curate. The ladies [nuns] will not miss it, and Madame Clément will be at their head. As for me, I'll keep to the house. The pilgrimage was hard for me; I need rest.

Good-bye, dear Charles; reply to me before you leave Sangy and send me an outline of your itinerary.

Your affectionate sister,

Émilie

ÉMILIE DE MONTBOURG
TO CHARLES DE CERILLEY
Grasse, August 4, 1894

Dear Charles,

Our poor Marthe has of late been seized so often with attacks of hys[teria] that I've come to be afraid for her reason. The priests and the doctors say that marriage is the only radical cure for this state. So I'm looking all over.

From Bordeaux I'm offered a baron, age twenty-nine, related to some very good titled families. The grandmother, very rich, is still alive, as are his father and mother, so he will have no fortune for a long time; he is general agent of the *cornimphile*[32] of Bordeaux (do you know what that is? I don't), which brings him in 200 francs a month. He makes 200 francs more, somehow or other. I have asked for fuller information. Here in Grasse there is a young man of thirty who came three months before us, as I think I've told you. He has a pharmacy, not in his name, which he runs with another young man, also very serious. It is called Pharmacy of the Future, and has as its motto "Health through Economy" (hence no name). Monsieur Martin—that's his name—never goes to the café and does not associate with a living soul. He is good to the poor and to animals, which gives hope for the kindheartedness that M. so badly needs.

I had information gathered at the town hall in Carpentras, where the family comes from, and I send it to you, asking that you return it to me with your opinion.

M. declares that she doesn't want to be separated from me. If she could find happiness in Bordeaux, I'd follow her there! But . . . in a milieu of counts and marquis, M. would be made to feel her moral downfall, and she would be willing neither to endure the humiliation nor to adopt restrictive habits. Then she would leave everything there flat, and what would my situation be? Monsieur Martin might, in a few years, sell his pharmacy and, in some great center, find a career as a premier drug mixer in the big firms in Marseille or another big city. You see, neither of them has a *sign;* still, a man must keep busy! Tell me your opinion very quickly, for I shall have to have the question asked by a missionary in Marseille, who will write without naming us, and I am eager to have your opinion above all. In the family, you could present him as a *chemist;* at the present time, that's a very admissible career, and even in honor. Pharmacy is not what it used to be, for it uses nothing but products of chemistry and physics.

Monsieur Martin has rented a little country place where he goes every evening after closing the pharmacy, and he doesn't come back until eight or nine o'clock in the morning. The young man he leaves in charge is attached to him like a brother and trustworthy. A wife doesn't get involved in a pharmacy; they would rent an apartment near me. Ponder all this, I beg you, and tell me your opinion.

Good-bye, dear Charles.

Fond good wishes,

Émilie

ÉMILIE DE MONTBOURG
TO CHARLES DE CERILLEY
Grasse, August 9, 1894

Dear Charles,

Your letter of August 7, which M. was waiting for with such impatience, has found her quite cooled, because it seems that another individual has her preference. He's a new stationmaster of the southern line in Grasse. I must pick up this new trail. I haven't yet written to the missionary in Marseille. However, the poor child must need badly to settle down, for she really suffers, and she has terrible headaches as a result. You ask me why I am depriving myself of the stay in Sangy. It's because there are even fewer diversions there than here, because the frequency of M.'s attacks makes Éléonore deathly afraid that people will see the reason for them, and lastly, because it's easier for me to take care of Éléonore here. We have found a shoe dealer of seventy-five, son of General T., also a botanist; he owns properties, one of which is quite near, and he allows us to take walks on it. There M. can shoot at the birds; it is an enclosed area with a little cabin and trees, which allows one to go shooting without chasing about the countryside. And the kind old man is delighted to have someone to talk to when he's tending the mountain flowers he has brought there from his many climbs. You see, Providence does help us sometimes.

To make cider, you begin by crushing apples, steeping them in water in such a way that the water does not run out of the mush unless you squeeze it. Now you put it on the cider press, laying down a bed of crushed apples 2½ feet square by 15 centimeters high; then you put on a layer of well-sifted wheat straw, extending 10 centimeters beyond the apples. On this layer of straw you put crushed apples again, same thickness as the first bed, then straw, and so on, and you squeeze. The next day, you undo the press, you take out the straw, you crush the apples again, adding more water, and you set the whole lot to ferment in a tub of water, in such a way that the apples, well stirred with a strong wooden stick, are thoroughly covered with water. After twenty-four or thirty-six hours, you put this pomace back on the press in the same way as the first time, with a layer of straw between the beds of apples. When you want to have pure juice, you don't mix this second batch with the first. That's what they call *cidre mitoyen* [intermediate cider], the kind the farmers use as an ordinary drink; but when you can't or don't want to make pure juice, especially when you don't have real cider apples, you mix the two batches of juice, and the whole thing ferments in the vat.

You have to put a rather fine basket at the overflow chute of the press, if you want the juice to come out really clear.

Finally, you crush it a third time; it is this liquid, which they call *eau rompue* [broken water]—when the recrushed apples have been squeezed again and allowed to stand once more—that is used to wet the new apples you would have to crush. It never ends! But it seems that the more the seeds are crushed, the more alcoholic the cider is. If you want to add strength, you have only to put sugar into the vat.

M. works on improving her character as much as she can. She did not make the planned trip because of the great heat, and also because of the expense, for if she marries we'll have to go to Paris and reconnoiter to avoid possible embarrassments.

Good-bye, dear Charles, and fondest wishes.

Émilie

Your begonias make us very happy. They are in full flower. Burn this letter when you've noted the way to make cider.

ÉMILIE DE MONTBOURG
TO CHARLES DE CERILLEY
Grasse, August 28, 1894

Dear Charles,

The day I got your last letter, the mail informed me that it was impossible for the missionary from Marseille to involve himself with matrimonial affairs; the same mail brought me an overture from a gentleman of very good appearance with a marriage portion of 100,000 francs. But all of a sudden, M. was brought back in her mind to all she had suffered and for so long! She was seized with such a great fear of marriage that it made her ill. When I questioned M. very intimately, she admitted to me that it was indeed like oil on the fire that she had gone through before, and that did not leave her until the end of the nine months; thus the remedy that the priests think they can point out would only augment the trouble.

For ten days the poor child has had bad pains in her wisdom teeth. She has earaches and headaches that respond only to antipyrine, and which were diagnosed as neuralgia because they were starting to come every four hours.

She's better now, thank God, but I've caught a frightful cold from getting up drenched in perspiration to soothe her. Cocaine mixed with oil does her more good than laudanum in her ear.

The pharmacist has now decorated the store with a superb sign *with his name* on it, to prove to the gossips of Grasse that he has paid for his stock in full. That means nothing to us, since he does not suspect the idea that M. had.

For the moment, the wind is not blowing in favor of marriage at all. We are praying to several saints to obtain the cure of this terrible malady, and M. has had the idea of getting herself received by the third Franciscan Order, in which one may be a *nun in society*. There's a year of novitiate. This third order does not rule out marriage, but it does require chastity, *according to one's state*. Married people belong to it if they wish. No need to go into all the details, which you can figure out on your own. This third order was founded by Saint Francis of Assisi at the request of married people who had a great desire to earn their salvation; he established it in the thought of protecting the honor of young people even while making the propagation of the family more honorable.

If M.'s imagination and nerves could be calmed by it, it would be a great good for her and for us.

It's been 34.5 [about 94 degrees Fahrenheit] since yesterday, the first time it has been so hot, and you catch cold from the heat. I've had a canopy set up in front of the dining room, where we stay so as not to roast completely. We sigh for rain!

Good-bye, dear Charles.

Your affectionate sister,

Émilie

Be very careful about sunstroke! Use your parasol like a real southerner.

1895

MAÎTRE MAURIT, NOTARY AT GRASSE
TO ÉMILIE DE MONTBOURG
March 16, 1895

Dear Madame,
Here is the answer I received from the registrar. The total of debts verified and attested is 11,445 francs. However, I must tell you that the registrar considers it probable that there are other creditors who have not come forward, knowing that the bankrupt has nothing.
This supposition comes from the fact that Monsieur Caron d'Aillot had filed a petition in bankruptcy for 32,594 francs.
You will see what that means.
Sincerely yours,

Maître Maurit

[Note by Émilie de Montbourg:]
Petition in bankruptcy: 32,594, a figure not declared at the time of the marriage contract!

ÉMILIE DE MONTBOURG
TO MADAME D'AILLOT
Grasse, May 19, 1895

Dear Madame,
I have just received a visit from Abbé Bosset, who urgently advises us to return to our original idea of having the wedding at Labastide. It seems that our intentions arouse great envy, as does the possibility of improving

Monsieur Robert's situation. People are so happy to trample on those among the nobility who have been ill-served by circumstances and commercial ventures, to make disagreeable remarks along the route of the procession, and even in the church. Now, I did not think it appropriate to notify my daughter's witnesses of the unfortunate result of that start in business. We are all upset by these revelations! The abbé assures us that a marriage at Grasse, even at midnight, would leave us vulnerable to manifestations of the mean republican spirit and the coarse habits of the populace.

So we thought we must get around the difficulty, without giving you the trouble of having the marriage in Paris. I will remit to you the sum I allotted for the meal we were to give at the hotel, and in that way you'll be able to avoid all the unpleasantness they keep warning us about.

Mademoiselle Yvette, who has just written most pleasantly to M., tells her that you plan to return from Labastide next Wednesday. If you rest your horses at Grasse, do me the favor of coming with Monsieur d'Aillot and Monsieur Robert to lunch with us at noon; we'll come to a better understanding in person on all the details of this sudden change in plans and on the time of the marriage. I hope to hear that this stop is possible for you.

With my very best wishes,

Baronne de Montbourg

P.S. If you have adopted the idea of having the marriage celebrated at Labastide, Monsieur Robert must, right away, before leaving Les Clues, obtain from the mayor authorization to have himself entered on the registers of the commune, as *resident* at an early enough time to allow six months' residence before the marriage, which could take place from the 15th to the 20th of June; he might elect residence on *October 1, 1894*. In that way legality would be observed without any trouble. But this formality is indispensable, and the mayor, knowing the reason for it, will not refuse it.

I hope this letter will still reach you in time; I'm not delaying a bit.

MADAME D'AILLOT
TO ÉMILIE DE MONTBOURG
Château des Clues
Labastide, May 21, 1895

Dear Madame,

I will not tell you that your letter has astonished me; since we know the habits of the region and the ideas of Grasse, that was impossible for us. However, we have, I think, always been esteemed and honored by the persons we have associated with, and we do not understand it; I like to believe that Abbé Bosset, in his eagerness and devotion, may perhaps have exaggerated the matter a bit to himself. However that may be, let us adopt the plan of having the marriage performed at Labastide. The affair, I think, will be only the merrier for it. So we accept your invitation to luncheon tomorrow, Wednesday, although we are dressed like real mountain people: heavy shoes and costumes to match. You will excuse us, given the circumstances. Also, we may have to delay your luncheon, for although we will do everything possible to arrive at noon, we might possibly be a little late.

Robert urges me particularly to remember him to Mademoiselle Marthe and sends you his respects. Monsieur d'Aillot and I send you ours, and we take pleasure in looking forward to tomorrow.

Devotedly yours,

Madame d'Aillot

Information on Monsieur Robert d'Aillot and his family, as well as on his properties, gathered by Abbé Bosset, chaplain of the hospital in Grasse, who got his information from the curate of Mougins.

Age of Monsieur Robert d'Aillot: Thirty-three. External appearance pleasant and attractive.

Health: Since he left Grasse to settle in Mougins, this young man has never been sick. The fainting spell he had on the road to Vallauris was a unique case.

Character: It is good. Without having known Monsieur Robert d'Aillot intimately, the curate of Mougins finds nothing reprehensible in his general relations as known. Monsieur Robert d'Aillot does not have the violent character of his brother, who lives in Marseille.

Cast of mind: He is fairly intelligent, to judge by his appearance. Monsieur Robert d'Aillot is jolly, and is said to be neither sad nor spiritless, but energetic.

Religion: Monsieur Robert d'Aillot is not a practicing believer, but he is far from being hostile to religion, and he does have faith (which is a lot in itself).

Politics: Monsieur Robert d'Aillot is deeply conservative.

Habits: He does not drink, he never goes to the café or the club, he is not thought to be a gambler. There was a little gossip in Mougins about Monsieur Robert d'Aillot and a maidservant assigned to his country place; this is a slight detail, and there will be no young people around him except his wife. The young man does not run up expenses; he is settled and does his business well and quietly. Family fortune: no capital; a rather nice-looking property of 5 to 6 hectares [12 to 15 acres] at Mougins with an oil press. A big house in the village of Mougins in which the whole family lives, sometimes renting parts of it. Another property situated at Antibes. This house is thought to belong to Madame d'Aillot. There are a few current debts: they owed 1,500 francs to a mason, and there still remain 500 francs to pay. As for mortgages, inquire at Grasse. The d'Aillot family lives on the income and the retirement pension of d'Aillot the father, which is about 1,200 francs. The Mougins property also belongs to the mother of Monsieur Robert d'Aillot. This young man has nothing of his very own; he works for the joint estate. There was a bankruptcy and sale of the business by a syndicate. Monsieur Robert d'Aillot runs things in part for his family, taking the milk and vegetables to several markets. Monsieur Robert d'Aillot has two cows and three mares at his property in Mougins.

Monsieur Robert d'Aillot is discreet, serious, and capable of being the head of a family.

Make up of the d'Aillot family: Monsieur d'Aillot, the father, former customs officer in retirement; Madame d'Aillot, née d'Evelands.

Children: (1) the oldest of the sons, Vincent, lives in Marseille with his wife, whose family is from Aix-en-Provence. Vincent d'Aillot in Marseille is a liquor distributor. (2) Marie-Thérèse d'Aillot, a widow with a little daughter, lives with her father-in-law near Grasse. (3) Robert d'Aillot and two daughters, also unmarried. (4) Louis d'Aillot, a medical student who has completed two years of study. (5) François d'Aillot is doing his military service. The sister of Monsieur d'Aillot the father, Mademoiselle Mélanie, who has a harsh tongue, made over her personal fortune to her brother on condition of being lodged and fed and receiving a pension of 300 to 400 francs. She lives with the d'Aillot family.

ROBERT D'AILLOT
TO ÉMILIE DE MONTBOURG
Labastide, June 1, 1895

Dear Madame,
Your letter makes me very sad, and since I want in no way to make Marthe ill, I do not hesitate to do what you ask. I have too much delicacy ever to have wanted to impose anyone on Marthe, and the perseverance you speak of is only the result of earnest observations based on the good

qualities I have been able to appreciate for the last eight years in Césarine; nevertheless, since that casts even the slightest shadow on our picture, I do not hesitate to do what you ask, though I protest energetically and am deeply hurt by the scant confidence of my future wife.

I have too much respect for my family and myself ever to have dared to use, to take advantage of, a woman whom I was paying to work for me, and my conduct for eight years has given no occasion for scandal in the region, which makes me doubt the unfavorable terms these ladies must have thought they heard pronounced about me; moreover, I am such an insignificant person that people are not always concerned about me, an unknown to three-quarters of the population of Grasse.

There, madame, are the painful objections provoked in me by your letter of yesterday; I am sad and upset to think that, although I may have inspired a certain love in Marthe, I have not been able to inspire her *confidence,* the real pledge of mutual happiness; it is this that makes her doubt my feelings for her, and especially the degree of honor and seriousness that I attach to marriage.

As for my handling of my property in Mougins, that's my personal business; I know better than anyone the needs of my land and of my work, which is to tell you that your proposition is not acceptable, and that on that score I must be left to be guided by my own practical experience, which I have acquired at my own expense.

Before I leave you, madame, I ask that you remember me to Marthe and that you yourself accept this assurance of my perfect consideration.

Robert Caron d'Aillot

CHARLES DE CERILLEY
TO ÉMILIE DE MONTBOURG
Sangy, June 16, 1895

Dear Émilie,
The travelers arrived at Sangy yesterday at 2:09, in very good shape. I went to get them with the brand new break[33] and the two horses. Monsieur d'Aillot is very nice; at any rate, we like him very much. He will be a good mentor for Marthe, whose joy is a pleasure to see. Happiness is transforming her.

I am asking Éléonore to keep me posted on your health, with details; get a nurse, for Éléonore will give way in turn, I fear. If you get 250,000 francs for Saint-Savin, let it go quickly. The château will be less and less attractive; it's losing ground each year. If less is offered, keep waiting. I had the guests visit the four farms that have been laid out. Monsieur d'Aillot is impressed; he sees with the eye of the practitioner. I'll show him some pieces of land. We're going to the Minster today to open it up; I'll be there, and no one will pry into anything, you may count on that. How we hope for your prompt recovery! But don't have any illusions: it will be long. Your constitution will win out, but I think that for any lasting residence our climate is forever barred to you. Oh, how sorry I am to be tied down by this cursed matter of the farmer who ended up leaving me; it's serious, very serious.

I'm giving Marthe our 100 francs as a cash gift. Madeleine turned over to her your handsome wedding scrapbook.

Good-bye, my very dear sister; we send you and Éléonore our fondest wishes. I am also speaking for Marthe, her fiancé, and Madame Clément, whom we take pleasure in seeing again.

Your affectionate brother,

Charles de Cerilley

ROBERT CARON D'AILLOT
TO MARTHE DE MONTBOURG
Mougins, July 13, 1895

My very dearly beloved Marthe,

I've received your good letter of yesterday. I'll do anything that will please you; as soon as we're back from Labastide, we'll get busy with building the rabbit hutch to lodge all your little family. I'll bring all the necessary parts so that nothing will be lacking this time; for your part, will you be good enough to take down the public notice and the published banns Tuesday at the town hall. I am too busy to leave here before Monday evening at eight o'clock, so it will be impossible for me to stop at your house, in view of the advanced hour of the night at which I'll pass through Grasse. Besides, I'll already be loaded down, and I fear I could not take on other packages; however, to please you, if you find a way to pass me anything without giving yourself too much trouble, do so and let me know. I will pass through Grasse between eleven o'clock and half past midnight. I am at your disposal for whatever you wish, but it's impossible before that time because of my work. We'll spend a few days at Labastide, then come down here and go back up later; I hope, dear, that you won't be bored. Moreover, I'll do everything I can to make your life as sweet as possible, convinced that for your part you will contribute to making me happy, for in marrying that is the only goal I seek to attain—peace, happiness, and union in the house. I'm pretty well, and warm, and my hay is managing pretty well with this weather; today I'm putting away a good deal, though I would to heaven it were all of it.

Good-bye, dear little wife; I allow myself to send you a kiss while I ask you to believe in my real and sincere love, hoping, however, that it will be shared.

Robert Caron d'Aillot

CHARLES DE CERILLEY
TO HENRI DE CERILLEY
Sangy, July 13, 1895

Dear Henri,
Marthe's marriage contract was signed on the 6th. The marriage, which almost broke up because of Marthe's violence of character, has been delayed more than a week because they did not observe the rules for posting public notices. It's unheard of! I augur no good for the future. The d'Aillots are making a marriage for a fortune in all the crudity of the term. It's a thousand to one that he will console himself elsewhere, and who would dare to reproach him for it? It's a matter of an honest conscience.

Your uncle Paul and aunt Edwige have gone to Grasse and did not learn until they arrived of the postponement of the marriage, which they cannot wait for, seeing that hail played havoc with their vines on July 1 and they have to be present for the insurance company's appraisal. The result is that Marthe will have only her mother and her sister at her marriage. That's tough luck, but it's certainly their own fault.

Many fond wishes from your affectionate father,
Charles de Cerilley

CHARLES DE CERILLEY
TO HENRI DE CERILLEY
Sangy, July 19, 1895

Dear Henri,
Marthe has been married since Thursday, the day before yesterday. Good riddance! Éléonore did not attend the wedding (which was per-

formed at the d'Aillots'), on the pretext that she could not leave her sick mother. Her mother is so weak she told me that Éléonore, with her reserve, would have been uncomfortable in the midst of such gaiety! That's senseless fancy.

Your Aunt Émilie received your present and thanks you very much for it; illness keeps her from writing as she would like to.

Oh, what luck for M.! Her husband is too superior to her in every respect for there not to be consequences.

Your affectionate father,

Charles de Cerilley

Excuse this awful ink stain that has just appeared. If I were an artist, I'd draw swallows flying toward you.

ÉLÉONORE DE MONTBOURG
TO CHARLES DE CERILLEY
Grasse, August 16, 1895

Dear Uncle,

Mama finally has a vacation from plasters, which are being replaced by ointments of iodine mixed with Rousseau laudanum, to prevent any corrosive effect. So we would be fairly calm if it weren't for this marriage.

After Monsieur Robert's second visit, Mama was so ill that I can no longer be responsible if such emotions are renewed. However, that interview lasted no more than half an hour, I think. I had said frankly, in response to a direct question, that the first visit had harmed our patient, but it's useless to talk. I am quite determined not to let him see Mama when he brings his wife, but M. will consider this procedure unspeakable, and we shall have scenes of anger which will bring Mama to a mortal relapse. You can't imagine the harm these visits have done her. Ever since, she has had, most of the time, nights of fever and insomnia that have left her very weak. She is still worried about M. and frightened at the situation that has been made for her. The poor child is completely ensnared, fascinated, and turned away from us, and so she writes us furious letters. And then we have no one to act as a third party. Madame Clément does not count, any more than the nun who was with me in the house. In ordinary circumstances I bless our isolation—you yourself, at present, can only applaud us for having managed to keep it so well—but today, in the face of so much cowardice and brutality, I don't know what to do any longer. If you could make an appearance, the effect would be magical, Mama would pay for an excursion round trip for you, and I could stop being afraid for her. Poor Mama! She would rouse your pity; I beseech you, dear uncle, not to abandon her in this hard trial.

If you could have seen what a rage Monsieur Robert was in just as I came back in! At that moment he was talking about a former comrade who called him "inept." Monsieur Robert must slap him—not in the street, he says, for he'd promptly be hauled into criminal court, but man to man, alone, if he gets the chance. With such a character, you will judge whether I'm right to fear for our dear patient, so delicate and so weak now for over two months. . . .

I'm writing you in haste—I must rest a bit before I return to my post.

Your very worried niece,

Éléonore

CHARLES DE CERILLEY
TO ÉMILIE DE MONTBOURG
Sangy, August 18, 1895

Dear Émilie,

So what *is* going on at Grasse? This silence since August 3, date of the last letter written by Éléonore, with nothing more from you, surprises me, distresses me, and worries me more than I can say.

I wrote you, a few days ago: I was proposing to you that I make some observations to Monsieur Robert d'Aillot on his lack of gratitude for the consideration you showed him (if you think that appropriate). I await your reply, for, as you wrote me, we judge badly from a distance, and it's better to abstain; your silence confirms me in that disposition, and we'll say no more about it.

I hope you're no longer obliged to use the plasters, a painful and debilitating thing; are you gaining some strength? Is your digestion good? I used Bonjean Elixir with success, though it may perhaps be a bit strong for you.

Has Marthe come back from Labastide and the honeymoon? Have you seen her again?

Is Madame Clément enjoying it at Labastide, and is she liked by all? I hope so, for everyone's sake. Since the wedding I've received only Marthe's letter and her husband's in reply to mine, which was prompted by the photograph they sent of the bridal procession.

Good-bye, dear Émilie. I can hardly wait for a good letter to reassure me.

Your affectionate brother,

Charles de Cerilley

Let's be completely agreed that no news means good news.

ÉMILIE DE MONTBOURG
TO CHARLES DE CERILLEY
Grasse, August 27, 1895

Dear Charles,

Monsieur Robert d'Aillot has refused the doctor's examination for M. at the last moment. I was expecting them. Instead, here is the copy of the letter that M. addressed to me; you will know what to think:

"Dear Mama,

"I won't go to Grasse; my husband has his reasons for that. So you can tell Dr. Barand not to bother. We'll see later what we have to do."

Well, what do you say about such a retreat, after making such a racket?

That's not all: the same mail brought me eight pages from Madame d'Aillot, the mother, adding to her son's offenses by implying that all these anxieties about M. come from a brain touched by illness. Then a shameless piece of extortion. She closed by telling me:

"For a month now I've had your daughter at my table, as well as Madame Clément. I treat her as well as I can, and I'm sorry that my means do not allow me to do better; but I am too proud to ask anyone for anything."

Now, when her son came to get the quarterly dowry income of his wife, he told me, in front of Éléonore, that he was going to relieve his mother of the burden his family adds to the expenses, by giving money —that, in short, his household might cost him more than at Mougins. I could only approve of this good idea, having paid my father for board as soon as I was married.

Since he doesn't like to have anyone meddle in his affairs, I didn't ask what he would pay his mother, but I'm quite convinced that he has done so. And the lady, thinking I was not aware of it, passes the collection plate!

Monsieur Barand relished this letter, and strongly recommended to me not to answer it or let myself be led on if I wished ever again to have a moment's repose. However, I would like her to know that I'm aware of it. Monsieur Barand thinks they have all concocted a plan together and that I should let them unmask themselves.

You can understand that all these torments work against my convalescence. I am having a bilious attack, or some worse stomach disorder and I've had to go back to veal bouillon alone. My poor Éléonore also suffers from all these emotions.

Poor M. has let this whole family walk all over her; they will become just so many leeches if this continues.

My very fond greetings, Charles. Pity me. I'm going to have the notary called to revise my will.

Your affectionate sister,

Émilie

CHARLES DE CERILLEY
TO ÉMILIE DE MONTBOURG
Sangy, August 30, 1895

Dear Émilie,

I'm replying to your letter, received yesterday. I was greatly pleased by the proof of the d'Aillots' retreat, which only demonstrates their intentions. Dr. Barand gave you very good advice! No, you must not reply for the moment, and let them hoist themselves with their own petard by making new demands that will demonstrate more and more their self-interested aims; thus you will be better armed. Learn to *see things coming.*

Since any letter demands an answer, you might *merely* reply to Madame d'Aillot that you have it from her son's mouth that he is to contribute in his own right to the household's expenses. I see no drawbacks to that. That will cut short any inclination to make a calculated complaint.

When I advised you to let yourself be exploited a little, that was on the supposition that the medical visit would have created a moral obligation for you. But in the opposite case, *no, a hundred times no.* Play it cautiously, with all possible tact, so as to have all the trumps in your hand.

Still no letter to me from either M. or her husband.

M.'s letter to you shows that they are getting her to talk, and that she is lending herself to it in a regrettable and scarcely filial way. That is especially painful for you, her mother. Be very careful about that bilious tendency, and have Éléonore take care of herself, too.

Be sure to keep M.'s letter; it is very precious.

Tomorrow we have luncheon here with fourteen guests. It's our vacation reception.

Good-bye, dear sister; include Éléonore in our fond wishes.

Your affectionate brother,

Charles de Cerilley

MARTHE CARON D'AILLOT
TO ÉMILIE DE MONTBOURG
Château des Clues, September 5, 1895

Dear Mama,

I'm happy to know that you are fully convalescing; I hope the improvement will hold up and that in a few days you'll be able to come down to the dining room without getting too tired. I don't understand: how have I lied?

Yes, my husband went to Grasse, but he did not want to go receive fresh insults! You ought to be ashamed to have written all the unspeakable things you wrote, not only about him, but also about my whole new family. Do you realize that it's fortunate for you and for me to have found a man who was willing to marry me? Yet to thank him for the honor he was willing to do your daughter by giving her his name, you insult him in the most unworthy fashion! And, running out of derogatory expressions, you don't shrink from writing me that he is plotting with his brother Louis to dispatch me to the next world. For you did write me that; I hadn't said a word to you about it yet, but since I see you continuing your mean behavior toward him and the hatred that drives you, I can't resist writing it to you: I hope that God, in restoring your health, may change your feelings and make you exercise more restraint in your words.

I do not hide from you that I'm very distressed at the way you answered the good letter that Mama d'Aillot wrote you; she showed real kindness in writing you such a conciliatory letter, for everything you could say about my new family you have said: you say you will keep Mama d'Aillot's letters in the Montbourg family archives, but if I'd kept all the letters you've written me and showed them to my husband, don't you think he'd have something to cause you trouble with?

You should thank me for not communicating them all to him. You are wrong to fall out with Mama d'Aillot and to want to cease all relations with my new family: they haven't done anything to you to deserve that!

I hope that when I stop at Grasse on the way to Mougins at the end of October, I'll find you better disposed toward Robert and my parents-in-law, whom I revere.

A thousand thanks to Éléonore for her kindness in hunting for and sending all the things I asked for.

Your respectful daughter,

Marthe Caron d'Aillot

MARTHE CARON D'AILLOT
TO ÉMILIE DE MONTBOURG
Château des Clues, September 10, 1895

Dear Mama,

Your letter pained me deeply. It is impossible for me to go to Grasse to see you without my husband, and I consider that I have been as good as put out of your house. You're very mean to my dearly beloved husband, Mama; he is so good, so perfect for his wife, and he certainly doesn't deserve to be treated this way; the most ignoble thing you could have done was to show us both the door of your home, for a wife must follow her husband in adversity as well as happiness. You want a quarrel, all right, but don't blame anybody but yourself. I won't come to see you except to get my things when we pass through Grasse on our way down to Mougins. If Robert comes with me, I hope you won't shut the door in our face. That would give you a bad reputation among the people of Grasse. So be good enough to send me my light-gray cloth suit, then my coat; also, please, the six rabbits that are still at the villa. We'll get the mothers and the male when we stop by Grasse, which will be toward the end of next month.

I hope your stomach illness will not last long and that you will soon be well again.

I repeat once more to you, Mama, that you cause me much distress by thus treating my husband and my whole family, who have never shown you any but good manners. I would be sorry if you turned Uncle Charles against Robert—that would not be fair. I'm sorry about this falling out, but I can't share your opinion of Robert, who loves me with all his heart, and for whom I have deep affection.

I hope that later you will return to feeling better toward him and my whole family.

My best to Éléonore, for whom I'm continuing to make a collection of stamps of all countries.

Your respectful and distressed daughter,

Marthe Caron d'Aillot

CHARLES DE CERILLEY
TO MADAME D'AILLOT
September 17, 1895

Dear Madame,

I have received the letter that you were kind enough to address to me, and I hasten to reply:

The letter you wrote to my sister and that she communicated to me is indeed the original. I have not kept a copy of it, since my position as an affectionate and devoted uncle makes it my duty not to intervene in these painful discussions, which I wish with all my heart I may not see renewed. I can explain them to myself a little only by keeping in mind, on the one hand, as you say, the very quick-tempered southern character of your son Robert, and, on the other, the illness of my sister, whose spirits must have been overexcited by the serious state of her health.

As for the passage in your letter that misled us, as you now assure me, here it is, as my reading of it and my memory recall it to my mind: *I am too proud to ask anyone for anything.* This after writing that you were sorry your very limited resources prevented you from doing all you would like to do for Marthe and Madame Clément as regards household matters. That you wished, perhaps indirectly, for a supplementary subsidy was bound to occur to us, from your letter, if only in appearance; anyone would agree, if it were proper to consult anyone. Nevertheless, I am glad that we were wrong, and I ask you please to accept my personal apologies.

From a distance, I cannot soundly judge the motives that determined my nephew to oppose Marthe's visit to her sick mother. These motives must be serious to be legitimate. It is not for me, as an uncle, to discuss the natural rights of a husband, who, knowing himself to be short-tempered, has the wisdom not to expose himself to a display of his character that he could only regret. I consider him fully capable of being a good head of a family. What I saw and heard of him at Sangy I liked very much, and I certainly hope his efforts will have complete success with Marthe, who lends herself to them very readily and happily, or so she writes me.

I was very sorry, madame, not to be able to attend the wedding, but surely some circumstance will arise that will provide me with an occasion to make your acquaintance and your family's. Meanwhile, dear madame, please give my best to my niece and nephew, and accept my respects for yourself and Monsieur d'Aillot. Madame de Cerilley joins me in this.

Devotedly yours,

Charles de Cerilley

ÉMILIE DE MONTBOURG
TO CHARLES DE CERILLEY
Grasse, September 22, 1895

Dear Charles,

I have a lot of news to tell you; will I have the strength? I must. Monsieur Louis d'Aillot went to spend his vacation at Labastide. He must have been struck by the healthy appearance of M., so different from the exaggerations of his brother, who was asking him for remedies for a malady that is visibly apparent when it really exists. Madame Clément writes me that simple injections of walnut-leaf water completely stopped the leucorrhea. It was certainly worthwhile to make such a fuss, wasn't it? And has the blackmail been adequately proved?

The picture that I sketched in for you has sufficiently demonstrated, it seems, that I had not overstepped a mother's duty in defending my daughter's health. For Madame d'Aillot the mother was impelled to inquire into the truth about her son's conduct toward me. So she asked Abbé Bosset for an explanation of what happened, urging him to remain neutral and in the conciliator's role that the priest must play in families. The abbé brought me the letter. He replied to her that his conciliator's role could not keep him from telling the truth: that he knew beyond a doubt that I had displayed toward her son and his family all possible good conduct, that Monsieur Robert made two violent scenes with me that gravely compromised my health, that I had fulfilled my duty as a mother by asking for the medical examination for his wife, as he wished, and that by refusing it at the last minute he had pronounced his own condemnation; that the abbé himself had been distressed to see her son fail to take an action that I had a right to ask, as did Éléonore, that on that score he thought he should give some good advice to Monsieur Robert, who had not even answered him.

But what I am forgetting to tell you is that, furious at the blame his brothers laid on him, my son-in-law took revenge by lying to his wife, saying I had turned him against her by telling him many bad things, both about her and about his mother.

Fired up by this, M. wrote to the abbé not to believe a word of what I told him: *that everything coming from me was a lie.* I saw the letter, so I cannot doubt it. Now, last winter, this same girl was reproaching me for making a cult of the truth! . . . The abbé replied that he had enough experience to assess the veracity of the speakers, that he knew that all the good behavior was on my side, and that, even when I could have left her husband in trouble, as many others would have done, over an installment payment due the contractor of their house (the notary with whom the funds were deposited was absent), I had made him an advance of 1,000 francs.

But the day the abbé brought me the letters of these ladies and his replies, I had received in the morning a frenzied letter from M. under the influence of her husband's lies: he had pushed her to write to the abbé. I was so hurt that I could not answer right away. So I waited for the result of the abbé's letters.

Twenty-four hours later, a change of scene! M. thanks me for my good feelings for her, even though she still tells me I am unfair toward her husband. If she wanted to see me alone, I would receive her affectionately albeit with no pleasure, for all she has said about me and written me weighs on my heart, and I'll always be afraid that she'll talk to me about her husband. Éléonore is recovering slowly from her prolonged period of sleepless nights and the successive emotions she has endured. Alas, she clings to the slightest hope, but if I get over it, it will not be for some time. Having the maid sleep in my room at night is enough for me. In the daytime, Éléonore gets help from two persons, and I have to be supported to walk. That's where I stand, not far advanced, as you see. I have her go out with the maid when she is willing. She eats some grapes and takes broth. The two of us support each other as best we can, but we need to have calm and to get away from the coarse d'Aillots.

I have had sent to M. a large part of her winter wardrobe, for at over 4,000 feet altitude it must be cold, and they plan to stay until the end of the month. All my efforts go at this moment to making the whole family promise to stop off at Grasse, which they pass through, right in front of our house. There used to be a convenient inn nearby where one could find a good dinner, good fire, and good welcome, but it's too late for that, these liars, vulgarians and swindlers will not stop there. M. can come back from Mougins with Madame Clément to get what remains of their clothes. I'll send the furniture through an upholsterer. I enclose the list of the objects I intend her to have, and you'll see that in spite of her faults I am generous to M. Éléonore is the first one to urge me to be, although M. has also done bad things to her. I sent her this list and have not received a word of thanks. What do you think about that? Not even an acknowledgment of receiving this list, and she *did* receive the letter, for when I told her that I was sending the three heraldic rings for her brothers-in-law, M. complained that her husband was not getting one. I answered that his was made, too, but that we had agreed he would get it only after his commercial rehabilitation. I know that the three brothers blame Monsieur Robert for the attitude he has adopted toward us from the beginning, but the rings are not being given for that.

Your affectionate sister,

Émilie

Burn my will.

MARTHE CARON D'AILLOT
TO CHARLES DE CERILLEY
Château des Clues, September 30, 1895

Dear good Uncle,

Your good letter gave me great pleasure, and I am happy to note that you at least do not share the hostile feelings that Mama de Montbourg has against my husband and all my family.

I'm very distressed to see that in spite of everything Robert has done to make me happy, Mama still hates him, and I swear to you, my good uncle, that Robert, whose good character you have been able to assess, does not deserve such treatment at all.

You will make us all very happy if you can succeed in changing Mama's feelings and get her to be more friendly to my husband, who is goodness itself *par excellence.* You tell me, dear uncle, to go pay a visit to Mama alone? But if I do, it will only be in company with either my sisters or Mama d'Aillot; that is to say, Mama d'Aillot will accompany me up to the door of the villa, for Mama de Montbourg has asked her not to come see her, and I swear to you, my good uncle, that I will never forget such treatment. Mama de Montbourg is behaving unspeakably. It's a matchless piece of infamy. What do you think?

My husband is away, so as soon as he is back I'll show him your good letter; he will be very happy about your benevolent intervention, for this falling out distresses him greatly. After all he has done for me, he is very ill-rewarded. I beseech you, my good uncle, restore Mama to better feelings toward my dearly beloved husband. I'll be eternally grateful to you.

The meadows are still very dry and have changed into real straw mats; yesterday, however, we had a bit of a storm and it's continuing today. I hope we will at last have some water, which will allow us to get up the potatoes, of which there is a field here.

Mama d'Aillot and also my father thank you and are happy to see that, in spite of the malicious insinuations of Mama de Montbourg, you are keeping your positive feeling and consideration toward them. Please, dear good uncle, and good aunt as well, accept this assurance of the grateful and affectionate feelings of your niece,

Marthe

[Note by Charles:]
Under the yoke.

ÉMILIE DE MONTBOURG
TO CHARLES DE CERILLEY
October 10, 1895

Dear Charles,

Alas! I have had many days of suffering and of disheartening weak spells! My strength is not returning, and the reason has become apparent in recent days. This demon's scenes have definitely curdled my blood once more, the blood I'm trying to build up by forcing myself to eat these gruels that disgust me but are all I can get down; it is so mixed with water that my feet are swollen, as well as my legs, even my thighs a bit. The doctor claims that weakness is the cause of it, that I don't eat enough; but you have to be able to digest, and that's the difficulty! He prescribed pills for me that hurt my stomach so badly that I leave them to go back onto Dr. Clertan's turpentine capsules. On my own, I take a little rhubarb. But this weakness is disheartening, and the slightest emotion, the mere thought of the d'Aillots, brings back pains in the heart and liver, and contractions of the pylorus. Under these circumstances, you judge whether I can, whether I even should, concern myself further with all these disagreeable things that make me so ill. I decided to reply to M.'s entreaties to receive her husband as follows: Stop insisting, you won't get anywhere, and I will not budge.

I'm so resolved to maintain our independence, which cannot be defended here either by a husband, or by a son and a brother, that the maids have been ordered to deny entry to the house to all the d'Aillots except M.; if their insolent arrogance should lead them to force their way in, the order is given to find the police superintendent and have him charge them with trespassing. That alone calms Éléonore, who is always afraid she will see one or another of them arrive. They have no idea of this, but if they have the audacity to defy us, they'll be caught at it.

Meanwhile, although I did not tell M. in so many words that her husband was up to something with his brother, I did think it, since the supposition of illness, the advising and sending of the remedies, came from them; you would have done as much in my place. I even think that the thing has been premeditated ever since Paris, for Monsieur Robert told me that poor M., so sick and so ill-tended, had patches of an odd color on her face. They tried to make a case against her out of everything, and since she wrote me from Paris that he told her, "I haven't blackmailed your mother, but I may," I was warned by my daughter herself. At that time, when she was not domineered as she is now, she said to me, "I think I ought to warn you." Now, if I had not made a fuss and brought Dr. Barand into it, I don't really know what would have happened; what I do know is that Monsieur Louis must be mighty scared that I may jeopardize his medical career by letting his professors know he is allowing himself to recommend and to send to the provinces dangerous medicaments without having the qualifications and authority for that, for he is only a student. You may well believe that I'm leaving him in this blessed fear and that my exposé of the situation, in which I was merely telling M. that she had not understood my maternal solicitude, had that purpose. You can see the result: Monsieur Louis has had his mother write to the abbé, who replied prudently but demonstrated to them that he had seen right through them, and now they are keeping quiet, having requests for reconciliation made now by M. I want no part of them; please understand that and refuse the role of peacemaker that they are asking of you. I remain in my tent, on the heights of my position, and armed at all points. Let them leave me alone. Am I not *right* to show the door to buccaneers who would come and strip me of my living? I told her that she was not to count on my parlor furniture, that I would give her a few pieces we can do without, but that I was not planning to empty my own house, I would not allow anyone to come and move me out of my house, and I would send her via an upholsterer what I could spare for her—at my own expense, of course. But she was not to have any illusions, for I never wanted to see her husband again, and she would have to accept that if she were to turn penitent but not come to see me alone, she would get nowhere by it!

Now Monsieur Robert is trying to make people believe that all he did was ask simple questions about M.'s health because of the illness *her father* left her, which I had not spoken of. To that I replied that, since Dr. Barand declared that the malady was not transmittable, I did not have to talk about it; besides, mere questions would not have put my existence in peril.

One of my doctors, a relative of the d'Aillots through his wife who has no reason to be pleased with their behavior, took pity on me at first and then became a friend. He said to me recently: To my mind, your son-in-law tried to give you a stroke or a heart attack so as to get your inheritance sooner, if the blackmail did not work.

M. finds herself happy in a situation that would not have made my happiness. I'm very glad that she's attaching herself to her new family, and I'm doing nothing to dissuade her from it. You're letting yourself be influenced by the lies of which her letters are full. I know my duties and I'm fulfilling them. But this great love for the d'Aillots is no reason to forget what she owes to a sister and a mother who have been so devoted to her. All their insults will not keep me from setting up her household as well as I can, since the d'Aillots cannot do it in accordance with the custom of the region.

I've put in time at it, but at last I'm coming to the end of what I had to let you know about, dear Charles. The heat is still fierce during the day, and I have much trouble digesting. However, the little I can digest seems to give back a bit of strength to this poor machine, which nearly broke down completely. Good Lord, what a lot of time it takes to restore the functions of bile in the organism! That's because of all these violent emotions.

My very fond greetings. Your affectionate sister,

Émilie

Since you're going to stay a while in Sangy, please look after the cemetery. I've sent you an order from the prefecture. I can hardly wait for the vault to be made.

MARTHE CARON D'AILLOT
TO ÉMILIE DE MONTBOURG
Château des Clues, October 17, 1895

Dear Mama,

I was very happy to give you a hug and a kiss when I passed through Grasse. I hope my visit did not tire you too much and that the swelling you had has completely disappeared. I entreat you not to despair as you do. We arrived safely at Labastide. My health, as you could see, is excellent, my character is more supple and with time will become just fine; little by little I understand more and try to engrave in my head all that a wife should know.

I'm grateful to you for offering to make some flannelette breeches, but, having nothing left to do, I prefer to make them up myself; my excellent sisters will cut them for me and I'll sew them. So if you'll send me the piece of blue flannelette that you bought at Le Printemps, I also think there's another piece of flannelette with gray and pink stripes that you had ordered from the same store to make some jackets for me, I have a pattern here, and I'll make it all myself.

Since you've been good enough to have a border put on Papa's traveling rug, you can add that to the above articles and send me the whole lot, as you did the last time.

Madame Clément thanks you warmly for sending her things to her, but unfortunately these are not the things she needs: the others are locked up in that basket trunk.

The rabbits you sent me are fine; I'm pleased to see that you have a maid who keeps the house very clean; she takes especially good care of my rabbits, from what I can tell from the two that have arrived here.

Why don't you rub yourself with oil after burning a candle in front of the statue of Saint Anne? Or Éléonore could ask Adrienne to send her a flask of oil from the lamp they have burning in front of the miraculous statue of Our Lord in Brussels. I no longer remember where she got the oil she had sent to Saint-Savin for poor Émile.

Anyway, take courage, dear Mama, and keep on believing that your daughter loves you very much and does not forget you.

I send a hug and a kiss with all my fondness as your daughter, and hello to Éléonore, although she wasn't at all nice to my sisters, who nevertheless are charming! I think Éléonore is very stupid to have behaved that way; I am sad to see that she is becoming more unbearable than ever, and that her heart and her tongue have nothing but cutting things to think or say.

With much devotion, your affectionate daughter,

Marthe

ROBERT CARON D'AILLOT
TO CHARLES DE CERILLEY
Mougins, November 25, 1895

Dear Uncle,

I'm taking advantage of a moment's respite from my work to give you my news and talk to you about some very painful things that, even as they break my heart, make me bitterly regret agreeing to become the son-in-law of such a mean woman as my M-in-L.

I will list the things this woman holds against me. First, pulling her daughter up out of dishonor and ignominy, showing consideration and kindness for her; in spite of the horrors and abominations that she never stops spewing on me and my family in all her letters, a good husband who took on his painful task with patience and perseverance to make this girl, a poor lost girl—without education, without manners, without qualities, full of vices and defects—into a nice wife able to take her place in a salon; of having from the beginning refused to be a puppet by not allowing my M-in-L to fulfill obligations that the contract imposed on *me*. Next, my learning about the past, the illness and death of Monsieur de Montbourg, the syphilitic infection left to his wife, and the tainted birth of Marthe, who was covered with syphilitic pocks; Marthe told me that at the age of nine she broke out in a rash, that at the time of her delivery she had others, which they treated with boracic vaseline, and that hardly six or eight months before she had had more outbreaks. I also learned of Marthe's lascivious past, which had been hidden from me with painstaking care; her pregnancy, which was no longer either a simple youthful offense or the consequence of a moment's rapture, as your sister has always so carefully told me, but was, rather, the result of a dissolute and licentious life that began at age fourteen, led in broad daylight in Normandy, to everyone's knowledge up to and including her mother, who deliberately shut her eyes to it, since she did not stop these excesses in spite of the anonymous letters that several charitable people wrote her. And I found that on the day of my marriage I was given a girl in a deplorable state of health, with leucorrhea and such a flow that she soiled her linen every day. Thus it was quite natural that knowing all this, and as a husband concerned about the future, I made a perfectly friendly inquiry of your sister, to help me cure my wife, whom I love in spite of all the wrongs done by her or by her mother, who is trying to disturb the good feeling that prevails in my home. At the time I made this inquiry, your sister was in fact very kind, but, unfortunately, her self-esteem and pride were wounded, and after I left for Mougins, she wrote Marthe letters full of horrors and abominations about me—letters so atrocious that my mother wanted Marthe to burn them before I came back from Mougins, a thing I never cease to regret because they were documents that could justify me in the eyes of the family. Marthe then wrote to warn me against her mother, who never ran out of invectives for me, and to tell me that her mother's aim was to separate us by turning Marthe against me.

When I went back to Grasse I was determined, in spite of myself, to do the right thing; and to be all the nicer the meaner she was to me. That proved impossible in the face of the atrocities she hurled at me, telling me, to begin with, that if Marthe had the pox it was I who had given it to her. At this I sprang up and burst into bitter reproaches in terms that were sharp, it is true, but I told her some home truths about all the lies and deceptions of which I had been the victim in this wretched affair; I said that she had been dishonest, and that she behaved that way to me in order to avoid recognizing the wrong she had done by letting her daughter grow up like a streetwalker, that she was trying to befoul me, and all my family as well, to hide her own filth; she knew very well that she was tricking me and that her daughter was ill, for she never stopped repeating to her: *"If Robert knew everything he wouldn't take you, and you know that you have tainted blood in your veins, so watch yourself."*

Was I right to ask for an explanation? They sent you to see the doctor before the marriage, yes, that's true, but the doctor never examined Marthe. Now, what could he say about it? Nothing except that she had fine color and she could be married. They never told him about any hereditary taint of the blood, and that was what I was terrified of. Then I refused Dr. Barand's visit because I gathered that that gentleman, even if there had been trouble, would not have said so: he has to look out for his own interests in the person of your sister, a good customer for him, better than I, who, thank God, avoid such gentlemen; I no longer had any confidence.

Things have remained at that point. She wouldn't see me any longer, and from that day she launched a series of insults and slanders against me and my family, in all her letters; we have peace for a week, then comes another letter full of insults; I'm keeping them like treasures because, I must tell you, if this state of affairs does not stop, I'm going to bring a suit for defamation against her, which will mean a real scandal for your whole family—she cannot toy with such impunity with a man who leaves her alone, saying neither good nor ill about her, without one day going too far—but then watch out!

Nevertheless, dear uncle, I am heartbroken about this situation, and very often, as I think of the act I have performed and of the gratitude this woman should have for me, I shed abundant tears at the idea that I am denigrated and reviled. If only I were at least left alone, without her always coming and turning the knife in the wound. She is wicked and has a viper's venom, but let her beware of my vengeance. I am kind, very kind, but she must not take advantage of that kindness, for it would turn out badly. I love Marthe; she's nice and certainly does everything to make people forget her past, for which she is beginning to feel horror; her feelings for me are growing, which makes me love her all the more, but I beg you, dear uncle, to use whatever power you have over that woman to make her be quiet, for nothing good will come of it in the end. Even my brother is getting angry at hearing himself vilified by this woman, and you know that unity means strength. You have told me that you like me. I haven't changed, I'm still the same—even though your sister says you wrote that you were not astonished by everything that had happened, for you had judged me the same way and had a low opinion of me. However, at the Sangy station, when you left for Dauphiné, didn't you tell me as you embraced me, "My heart is in it and I am your friend"? Well, it seems that you did not mean that, and you wrote as much in your letter my dear uncle, didn't you? In spite of everything, I believe what you told me, and in my heart I keep the good impression I brought back from my stay with you. I continue to be your friend and to be fond of you as well as of my dear aunt, who is also so harshly regarded.

I was reproached in a recent letter for having equivocated for a moment at your house and in Paris over keeping my pledges. I appeal to you and to my aunt to speak up. They say they should have broken off. Would God that had happened. I wouldn't be unhappy, as I am, and I would have continued to live in peace, honored and respected by everyone, while the person who ought to be supporting me is the first to throw stones at me. Pity me, uncle, for I need your pity.

She claims that I have not kept my pledge; if anyone didn't, it is she, since she promised, at the time of the negotiations, to continue support of the child, and her primary concern during the first three months has been to withhold 150 francs from the sum for the wet nurse. Is that right? Is it honest? Before she could possibly have judged me as her son-in-law, she has usurped certain powers that, unless I were a cretin, I could not put up with. On July 15 she had Marthe make out a receipt for 200 francs, dated July 18 (the marriage took place on July 18), signed with my name, for Marthe's trousseau, and she asks me, in sending me 900, for a receipt for 1,250, plus 200 from my wife, which makes 1,450. When I sent the whole amount she was vexed—that's when I was called a witless Danubian peasant.[34]

Today she claims that she wants to assume responsibility for everything, but why does she need papers in that case? Let her send the total to the wet nurse and whatever else is necessary, and that's that. But no, it is the papers she wants, to play some trick on me that she must have cooked up again in her mean and possessed imagination. Well, I'm keeping these papers; she shall not have them. If she wants to do something, let her do it, or else, if she presses me, I'll do it myself: I'm used to work, neither the task nor the fatigue frightens me, and, thank God, I have good health, which allows me to overcome many obstacles. May God confound this wicked and ignoble woman, who wrote yesterday to tell her daughter that she is enslaved to her parents-in-law, who do not leave her the right to have her own household and who deprive her of food. Such things are frightful! She thinks that she will never stop insulting us because she has me in her pocket; maybe she thinks that I love her two cents' worth enough to let myself go on being insulted. Not having been born rich, I am used to anything; comfort I gladly accept, but if I have to drudge, I have a strong back and stout arms and I drudge night and day.

So this does not give her much hold over me, and I must tell you that I prefer poverty and happiness to money and perpetual war. Now, dear uncle, you are up to date on what has happened since my marriage. You can see how sad it is and that, though I often shed tears over my lost happiness, I still love Marthe and am especially happy to see her developing into a woman.

I count on your influence, dear uncle, to settle these matters, or at least to put a halt to this state of affairs, which will avert a sure scandal.

I leave you now, for I have bored you long enough with my verbiage, and I ask you to forgive me. Please give my friendly greetings to my dear aunt, and I once more declare myself your sincere and devoted friend,

Caron d'Aillot

CHARLES DE CERILLEY
TO ÉMILIE DE MONTBOURG
Sangy, November 29, 1895

Dear Émilie,

I hesitated at first to send you the letter that Robert d'Aillot has written me because of its harshness. But the details it presents are so grave that I think you must read it. Send it back to me, though, because I want to pass it on to Honoré: if some day he has to be involved with me in a guardianship over your daughters, it is absolutely necessary for him, too, to be familiar with all the items in the dossier.

Robert d'Aillot says much more than I knew myself! Who could have told him all that? Even if only half of it were true, that would be more than he needs to arm himself for war. I entreat you to maintain complete silence in speech and in letters; from what your son-in-law says, you never stop recriminating.

I am enclosing a copy of my reply to your son-in-law. I made it very diplomatic, because I don't want to pour oil on the fire. If you accuse me of being soft, you might ask Léon and my son whether I can be tough when necessary.

It's one of two things: either Marthe herself told her husband the whole story, for what it is worth, in which case it's odious to see a daughter give away her mother; or else her husband made inquiries before the marriage, and if someone told him all he says, that's the strongest proof that this was *marriage for money* at any price.

It is clear that someone tried to get a grip on your purse. That shocked you, and you flared up. It might have been wiser to let it go without complaining too much, as long as things had not assumed undue proportions. Today I tell you: be happy to see your daughter married, because with her instincts she needed a husband; she would have fallen into the lowest category of streetwalkers, for she had to have it at any price. I don't think I'm telling you anything new. But get it into your head that you must avoid scandal at any price. Your memory would be ruined, and surely you are worth a hundred times that. Conclusion: silence at first, and then little by little the resumption of relations, all the while sparing personal sensibilities. The time has come for me to speak out straight and clear for the greatest good of all. Take my word for it, don't protest: you may not have told me everything, but I know enough to have a very firm and justified opinion about it. It is mild and humid by day, cool in the morning. I am well.

Your affectionate brother,

Charles de Cerilley

CHARLES DE CERILLEY
TO ÉMILIE DE MONTBOURG
Sangy, December 2, 1895

Dear Émilie,

I am returning to you, enclosed, the letters from Marthe and Madame Clément. Keep the silence you are asked to, but really and truly; in any case, the one who breaks it will be the guilty one. Your son-in-law writes that that's all he asks. If a breach of the silence comes from them, let me know and give me proof, and I swear I'll tell him so clearly. I strongly approve of your good work in taking responsibility for G.'s [Georges, Marthe's son] upbringing and education, but as for being unofficial head of our family, that's *pure illusion* and you must not cling to it. Have yourself authorized to pay for and direct G.'s upbringing and education —that's all you can ask.

M. must be losing her mind if she regrets the acknowledgment granted by her husband, who took the fault on himself so she could go about *legally* with her head high. The moment the acknowledgment is established, isn't it in their interest not to have a ragamuffin for a child? I don't believe there will be a refusal on their part. That would be odious.

In the matter of the guardianship, let's understand one another: I approved of the acknowledgment that you required as a condition for the marriage. That approbation puts me under no moral obligation toward this child, whom I have no desire to know. I shall give Éléonore my moral support after you, if I succeed you in the continuation of this good work. I repeat, you may do it only with the authorization of your son-in-law. Don't try to get around that. As for the role played by Abbé Bosset, I don't like to see clerics poke their noses into ugly matters.

As soon as possible I'll take up your business of a perpetual grant for three tombs in the same row, side by side.

Remember how awful you considered the interference of your M-in-L, who never ceased after your marriage to warn you about your husband's defects out of jealousy of your influence over him. I beseech you not to commit the same mistake. Recovering your peace of mind through silence is easy.

May your equanimity be restored, dear Émilie; it will be a guarantee of long life. I quite understand that a mother cannot draw up an act of accusation against her unhappy daughter. And you must also be aware that those who know a good part of the dismal truth have felt it was their duty not to rend your heart needlessly. Today, faced with danger, I'm forced to warn you against the folly of reckless recriminations. Good-bye, dear sister; fondest wishes to you both.

Your affectionate brother and uncle,

Charles de Cerilley

Send back my copy of the reply to your son-in-law as well. It is part of my dossier.

I'm quite sure that the marquise will not have her son-in-law, if son-in-law there ever is, acknowledge the child her daughter had by a young carpenter. You must not think that what your son-in-law has done is typical. But in his case, the lure of a fortune gave him special courage on that point. Yes, he hesitated to do it. M., too, but your social status and my advice in favor of marriage got the thing accomplished—which you regret now that the marriage has taken place.

ÉMILIE DE MONTBOURG
TO CHARLES DE CERILLEY
Grasse, December 12, 1895

Dear Charles,

Since Madame C. arrived, there has been a new upheaval in my blood and my bile. It's inconceivable: I have never seen anything like it. A bilious sediment covers the skin of my stomach and arms and makes me suffer the same kind of pains in my chest as when I had nursing abscesses. Some glands were probably damaged by those abscesses, and the circulation in that area is more difficult; from time to time I get a fever from it.

The fact is, Madame C. has given me cause for great worry! We must not believe in the happiness that M. harps on in her letters, for when she was at Labastide she once nearly set out on foot to come back here. Another time she told her husband that since he was so unhappy about having married her, they must separate. Several times he threatened to slap her face, which is not at all the act of a kind, tender husband, and yet she does all she can to cater to his despotism.

What frightens me is her weakness of character. I'm very much afraid she won't be able to keep Madame C., who is her safeguard. Madame d'Aillot exercises, it seems, much influence over them all. Well, she's the one who had M. write the letter I sent you expressing unnatural feelings toward her child. Everything is dreamed up between her, her son, and her daughters; M. writes only what she's allowed to. That's the truth of it.

During the week she spent at Mougins alone with her husband and her sisters-in-law, they managed to turn her against her child to the point evident in the letter that I sent you, and they got her to promise to dismiss Madame C. Only, since I'm the one who pays, and they're afraid of the consequences of the family's wrath, they forbade M., and also Madame C., to write me anything about it. Yet they allowed Madame C. to come to Grasse, fully hoping that she would speak to me about it, and they would have put her out the door for being indiscreet if I had betrayed it in any way.

Madame Clément thinks that the complete isolation they want to put M. in is designed to get a will out of her. I think so, too, for the last time she came she said to me without provocation, "The little money I have I'll leave to Robert; I'll destroy the wretched will I made in G.'s favor before my marriage." — "What about your son?" I asked her. "Well . . ." and she made a gesture as if to say, "A lot I care about him!"

When Monsieur R. has attained his goals, the poor wife, who is already not attended to when she's in pain, will be abandoned or worse, if she doesn't have Madame C.

Would you believe that, to worry M., the husband often stoops to speaking in front of her about the women who have charmed him— among others, the daughter of the man he buys milk from, whom he would have been happy to marry! And, stupidly, M. says to Madame C., "Well, if I died, he could remarry whomever he liked—I'd leave him enough for that!" Oh, I'm far from easy about the happiness and safety of my poor child, dear Charles, and what has made my illness worse is not so much the bad faith of this liar, this man so unfaithful to his pledges, in short so despicable, as it is the worry caused by all Madame C. has told me. Just think: your niece is such a slave that if she needs to take an enema she has to hide in Madame C.'s room. They go to the point of counting how many times she urinates! You judge the rest. . . . And that's what vexed them so much about the rumor in town: that it's true!

Monsieur Robert claims that I don't leave him alone. On the contrary, he's the one who takes pleasure in tormenting *us!* Listen: this past summer, while I was so sick, someone rang our bell violently, twice, during the night. The first time the maid got up and wanted to go downstairs to answer it, and I opposed it. Poor Éléonore trembled until dawn. The second time, no one heard it but me, thank God!

Later, when M. returned from Mougins with her sisters-in-law, she told us that in coming from Labastide, as they ordinarily did, as they passed by the villa at three o'clock, the husband wanted to ring the bell. The ladies opposed it, so as not to wake us up. Oh, he passed our door several times, she added with a certain air of malice, and looking right at me. But I remained imperturbable: I would not give them the satisfaction of having annoyed us. Why did her husband ring, knowing quite well that he would not be received? Why would he want to ring when he had no intention of leaving his wife here? That's not the act of a serious man; it's mean.

Now that I'm obeying you by not responding to the irritating remarks that M. writes to me, and now that I'm playing dumb, Monsieur R. has twice thanked me for paying for *the months at nurse,* because, meanly, he proposes to make a ragamuffin and a pariah of the child. If I picked up this burden while saying that I intended to be responsible for all the child's expenses in order to make of him, with the help of God, a man of the social condition he was given, you would be told that I'm insulting the entire family. I think that if you could get them to give me the papers concerning G., there would be fewer dangers for the child to run—for why do they claim rights when they refuse to fulfill the duties that those rights impose?

I'm suffering a lot, both morally and physically, dear Charles. God must lend His powerful hand for me to get through such a trial.

Unfortunately, I'm not the only one affected: poor Éléonore has gastralgia from all these unhappy things.

My very fond wishes to you and to Madeleine and her mother. How is she?

Your affectionate sister,

Émilie

I don't think it would be useful to send that awful statement to Honoré, but if you do, it is only fair for you to send my response as well.

MARTHE CARON D'AILLOT
TO ÉMILIE DE MONTBOURG
Mougins, December 16, 1895

Dear Mama,

I thank you with all my heart for everything you've sent me, including the lamb that you had cooked for me, even though I had told you I didn't know what time I might arrive.

My parents-in-law are kind and tender toward me. Mama d'Aillot, not knowing my constitution well enough, had Dr. Caylat come from Antibes. He's very gentle with his patients. He was nice to me, and will come back Friday with his instruments to examine me in detail and prescribe a treatment for me that will put me back on my feet.

As for my going to Grasse, you mustn't think about it; I wouldn't consent for anything in the world to be parted even for a day from my dearly beloved husband, and I absolutely refuse to go to Grasse. Especially since the situation is pretty tense: you've written too many letters that were worse than offensive and horribly insulting, and, besides, I haven't forgotten that you threw my husband out of the villa. Such actions are hard to forget!

I hope, Mama, that this situation will not continue and that you will understand how immensely you have wronged my husband and my family.

Send me my curling iron, which Madame Clément put in the chest, and also my religious album, which I need to put devotional pictures in.

Dr. Caylat thinks you were very wrong not to have me treated before my marriage.

When I'm on my feet, I'll come get the rabbits, by which time my new rabbit hutch will be ready to receive them.

Affectionate wishes to you and to Éléonore.

Marthe

[Written directly on the above letter:]

Dear Madame,

Be reassured, Madame Robert is better. She has had one little attack since Sunday, when she was in some pain. Her mother-in-law wanted to have her checked as a precaution; it's not serious, however, and Friday they'll find out from the internal examination precisely what is paining her. We'll keep you posted, for she has to stay in bed.

Respectfully yours,

Madame Clément

1896

MADAME CLÉMENT
TO ÉMILIE DE MONTBOURG
Mougins, January 22, 1896

Dear Madame,
I arrived safe and sound, and Césarine met me at the mail coach. I found Monsieur Robert very angry about your letter—he doesn't want to let Marthe go to Grasse any more. She's unhappy about that, and I think she's going to write you. Lately she's felt very fond of you, and on seeing me come back she said, "You bring me back a little bit of *them*" (of you two); then she repeated to me several times that she had pined for me, so accustomed is she to finding whatever she needs at hand. When I showed her your letter today, she said to me, "I just hope Mama doesn't talk about what she writes me." She needn't fear: you won't say anything about it. I beseech you, don't write any medical advice; that makes them too angry, and it's M. who suffers for it. What you were afraid of with regard to François is quite true. Monsieur R. is jealous and has a funny look in his eye. He scolded his wife yesterday evening because yesterday they noticed at Bellevue that she was joking too much with him [François], and her mother-in-law and her sisters gave her a good lecture about it; last night, when I passed on to her your recommendations, the whole thing fell on her like an avalanche, and she is determined to watch her step. The husband, for his part, is on the alert. It's not because he wasn't warned. The honeymoon is drawing to a close, beware; she tells me that since Saturday she loves her husband less. Her visit with you has bound her to you again. Good Lord, how is this whole thing going to work out? She's going to take care of herself during her periods—don't worry, I'm

there—but she's always too trusting, and you have to watch out the minute she's with her h[usband]: she tells everything, she can't keep anything back, it's terrible. So we need to be terribly prudent. I haven't spoken to the mother-in-law about Césarine; let's wait on that. If Monsieur Robert becomes less pleasant with his wife, she'll quickly tire of it, answer him abruptly, and then, you know, it won't be long before she sends everything to the devil. Enough of that. She was wrong to sing her happiness over the rooftops—that's never any good. For now, let her take good care of herself, as I keep telling her, because, given your health, you cannot confront the storm.

M. has been much nicer since she learned that her husband is going to keep me. Poor dear child, she's always getting in the way of her own happiness. She was saying to me just this evening, "If I ever become a widow, I'd never be so stupid as to remarry, it's too late." Let's do the best we can and wait; let's hope they can love each other peacefully *without the honeymoon,* which would be better. I'll keep you posted.

Devotedly yours,

Madame Clément

M. has also had torments of mind, as she puts it. She remembers some pieces of advice you've given her and fusses about it, and I have a great deal of trouble calming her. See for yourself, if she didn't have me there, with whom would she share all these things?

MADAME CLÉMENT
TO ÉMILIE DE MONTBOURG
Mougins, February 10, 1896

Very dear Madame,

I'm quite alone and free to chat a bit with you. Your letter met with everyone's approval. Marthe answered you without showing the letter to her husband; when he remarked on it to her, she answered, "I read it to Yvette." Then he said, "What does that matter? I've told you not to send any without letting me see them," and she promised not to do so.

She is well, so yesterday, Sunday, she went to Nice with her husband; he left her at her sister-in-law's, then picked her up at noon. Today, it turns out that she's not to come back until tomorrow, Tuesday. In the evening, there's a flower show.

This morning there was quite a sendoff. Madame d'Aillot dismissed Césarine. There's something serious behind it, I don't know what yet, and they have hired a housekeeper. Your daughter doesn't know anything yet, since she's at Nice. Her husband will inform her about it, no doubt.

What a lot of things I'll have to tell you next week when I see you. If she spends the three days of Carnival at Nice, I'll leave Monday and return Tuesday. They won't need me here, and I can spend a little more time with you. Dear madame, continue those tactics in your letters. We'll be more peaceful, Marthe will be able to come see you from time to time, and her visits to you at home will do you a lot of good—though you know you mustn't fluster her.

He's behaving better with me and asks me for what he needs. I will have the money from a draft that is to come today. In short, if I can have a little peace, I'll be thankful for it. Marthe doesn't want to hear about religion (for the moment). That's one more passing phase; it used to happen at Grasse. May the good Lord help us—I ask Him with all my heart.

All my fond wishes, dear madame, and rest assured of my utter devotion.

Madame Clément

ÉMILIE DE MONTBOURG
TO CHARLES DE CERILLEY
Grasse, February 21, 1896

Dear Charles,

What you tell me about Marthe's letter to her aunt proves to me that what I feared is happening: pouring, as you say, oil on the fire may be causing the hyst[eria] to progress. On the occasion of Mardi Gras [Shrove Tuesday], I had Madame Clément here for twenty-four hours; I'm still sick in bed from it, with very painful digestive problems, though the vomiting has finally stopped today. Marthe spent five days in Nice with her brother-in-law and sister-in-law during the Carnival, her husband joining them to spend half of every day.

Dissension is coming into the family: just recently Monsieur Robert, in front of everyone at the table, had a business discussion with his mother that led to anger and foul language. The father and mother are trying to find ways to play a dirty trick on their son by harking back to the 13,000 francs they had to give up for the settlement of his bankruptcy. Although this sum was given to him, in the marriage contract, they would like to have the interest on that sum paid to themselves, to establish a precedent they could take advantage of later on. Naturally, Monsieur Robert is not happy and complains that they are pressing him to get more money out of him. The mother declared in her anger that she wanted no part of the young couple in her house as of March 15. Then she reflected that she was cutting off her own supplies, since little by little she has succeeded in having Monsieur Robert furnish her with wine, oil, laundry service, beans (of which they eat a lot), pastry, figs, and 50 francs in cash a month for the meat and bread. Madame Clément works for everyone and irons all the linen. Then she [Madame d'Aillot] came back and said she'd wait until their house was built.

This mother, who is capable of doing anything for money, rented space *in her house* to the family of a maidservant who had been R.'s mistress, and whose dismissal she had got us to demand. This wench has gone back to serving everybody, and it's Monsieur R. who is paying. Marthe was stupid enough to let the girl be forced on her, and even to become very fond of her. This girl flatters her to her face and makes fun of her behind her back, to the point of calling her an idiot. She has become the mistress of Monsieur François, the son who is now back from his military service and is waiting for a position as a customs officer.

The other day Madame d'Aillot, who had blamed this son for going after the serving girls while the eldest *"had had the good sense to spend two years pursuing a noble lady whose husband was at sea,"* saw fit to keep watch over Monsieur Fr. and found him in the serving girl's bed! A great racket ensued, and the girl was put out the door. But, wouldn't you know, that ninny Marthe, whose husband was away, took the side of the bad girl and her brother-in-law with such violence she brought on another scene that almost led to blows between her and the sisters-in-law. The ninny has quite a thing for that brute François, whom the husband leaves alone with her much too often. All the loving exaggerations you've quoted to me don't calm me, for I've been fooled by it. She pretended to have a great attachment for one person but showed it all to others. Monsieur Robert noticed these more-than-fraternal attachments and has watched them, but since he himself creates the perilous circumstances, I think it's a contemptible scheme on his part, and a snare into which that ninny may fall.

That's the milieu she is in, a poor child in whom two strong moral levers have been destroyed: mother love and filial love. Nor is there any respect for paternal authority around her. They talk about the old men who don't croak fast enough. The men's religion is confined to criticizing the priests, and the women's is only a sham.

You understand fully that she's not allowed to write me about any of this, and that she's been forbidden to say anything to me during the three appearances she's made here. I can't comment on it in my letters to her, for that would mean the immediate dismissal of Madame Clément, whom I must rely upon for Marthe's moral and physical well-being; so I'm devoured by worry and can do nothing but pray for her!

After Marthe's great scene, the mother complained to Monsieur Robert, who demanded that his wife beg pardon on her *knees!* You see what a position she's putting herself in among these arrogant people who have already trampled her so badly! The mother, in a frenzy, wanted to write me, then thought better of it and indicated to Madame Clément her great fear that I might learn about all these ignominies.

Yet in the midst of all this violence she doesn't stop thinking, and— as a trial balloon, I think—she said to Madame Clément, "But they'll have to do something about little G., we can't leave him with peasants. I'll be his tutor. I'll take him in and bring him up here *as my son's child."*

When Madame Clément presented this idea of Madame d'Aillot's, I told her, "If she speaks to you about him again, tell her that in taking responsibility for G. we meant to educate him, at our expense, for a man's career, but that if he's taken away from us, we won't give anything more." I suppose the lady was counting on a living out of the 600 francs I'm paying the wet nurse. She'll leave it at that, I hope, but if the opposite happened—good Lord!—you might expect anything. And how is one to reconcile this woman's pretension with the letter from Marthe that you've read? Really, one can get lost in this labyrinth of double dealings.

Monsieur Robert is going through the 6,500 francs he took last month so fast that he will soon find it impossible to pay for the construction of his house in full, or for much of the furniture they will need; I must make sure I'm in a position to come to the aid of my daughter, take her back if necessary, so it's impossible for me to absorb added expenses. This illness is also costing me a lot, and my life is so necessary that I must look after it and neglect nothing to preserve it. There's a long piece of writing.

Good-bye, dear Charles; my very fond wishes.

Your affectionate sister,

Émilie

MADAME CLÉMENT
TO ÉMILIE DE MONTBOURG
Mougins, February 22, 1896

Very dear Madame,

I will not write you at length this evening—I'm very tired and it's late —but above all I want you to have news, or you'd be worried. The father is still very ill; they think he's past hope. Dr. Caylat couldn't come yesterday and didn't come until six o'clock today, after a telegram. I find him very negligent, and they say in Mougins that he gets *tipsy*. When I went to fetch him in his villa on Wednesday, he spoke to me about you but would not discuss anything else. He was very polite to me, since I was recommended by you, dear madame. That does not surprise me, but I found that he already smelled slightly of rum, and seemed a bit *emotional.*

Aunt Sophie has sent her picture and her husband's with a nice letter of congratulations to her dear niece, so happily transformed, *she* says, into a serious and elegant young woman, to which Monsieur Robert replied today by praising to the skies those responsible for the transformation.

I don't know what keeps her from writing you; each day she puts it off, but it'll be tomorrow, I think.

I leave you, dear madame, and wish with all my heart that things may go better, but the poor child is not changed at all. She is still the same, with perhaps a little more self-assurance because she feels she is a *lady* —that's all. Her husband dominates her, though if he went at it too hard, she'd bite him.

Most devotedly yours,

Madame Clément

ROBERT CARON D'AILLOT
TO CHARLES DE CERILLEY
Mougins, February 26, 1896

Dear Uncle,

We have just been struck by a great misfortune: my poor father, who was eighty-five but enjoyed flourishing health, was stricken last Monday with pneumonia, which took him from us after a week's illness; he retained all his faculties until the last moment, and he departed from us yesterday evening at five-thirty. We are all in the disarray that such an event causes, especially one so unexpected.

Please inform my aunt about our misfortune, I send her my best wishes.

Marthe is well, still happy, and joins me in offering you our warm regards.

The situation at Grasse is a little better, for which I am happy and thank you very much.

Dear uncle, please accept the fond regards of your devoted nephew,

Robert Caron d'Aillot

[Note by Charles:]
Continuous comedy to make us think M. is very happy with him.

CHARLES DE CERILLEY
TO ÉMILIE DE MONTBOURG
Sangy, March 1, 1896

Dear Émilie,

Robert d'Aillot has written me of the death of his father, and also sends word of Marthe's continuing happiness and their better relations with Grasse: he thanks me for my good offices in restoring harmony— which means they've realized that the blackmail will not work, and wish, I think sincerely, to get back in our good graces. I replied with the tone the circumstances required, moderate and prudent.

I'm returning Madame C.'s letter. You have one very simple way to check on whether M. has really changed to some degree: to see it with your own eyes when she comes to visit you. It is so natural that it is bound to happen and shall happen one of these days. I think there's some truth in it, and you can only be happy about it. It's the same story as with most girls after they marry: an equilibrium is produced because Mother Nature is satisfied.

Yes, I think there are going to be rough financial disputes among the d'Aillots, whose situation is worsened by the loss of a great part of the deceased father's pension. It's fortunate that Marthe's marriage contract clearly specifies that the father and mother give up what they were owed from their son's bankruptcy; on that score, they would have been tempted to plead poverty to you if they hadn't found out the uselessness of *blackmail*, which is the hobby of many who have gone broke—you have to defend yourself against it energetically.

Good-bye, dear sister; share our tender wishes with Éléonore.

Your affectionate brother,

Charles de Cerilley

MADAME CLÉMENT
TO ÉMILIE DE MONTBOURG
Mougins, March 6, 1896

Dear Madame,

I'm always afraid my letters may worry you too much, and then I want to write you again to reassure you. Marthe has remained sad since the last scene she had with her husband. He maintained to her that she would never be a good mistress of a household, that she thought only of trifles, that she was not like other women. They spoke to her about it at table, and her mother-in-law also rebuked her; the poor child promised to do better, but she champs on her bit in silence and does nothing but say to me, "What a shame I married, how I miss my mother's villa. My poor mama, how I pine for *the two of them*"; then she says to me, "Good Lord, what if you had left, for I wanted to let you go. . . . At least you're a bit of them, I can talk to you about them, I can think out loud." She's very gentle at that point, and begs my pardon for having made me cry so much —she knows very well that she's been harsh. I tell her to take courage, she assures me that she won't give me any more trouble—or you, either—but I know from experience that when she is on good terms with him she changes toward us. Can it also be the coming of the famous Louis that again got the husband worked up? I don't know a thing about it, but the honeymoon seems to be quite over. She's frightened of the future. She doesn't dare tell you anything—she's so afraid he'll find out, for she has a terrible fear of him. Her periods have lasted only three days, with little flow. All that business of Césarine hurt her, but she mustn't look into that too closely, it's just too bad.

Well now, dear madame, we must take heart. I'd like to see her happy. She had a hard time writing the letter she sent you because she wanted to put in something completely different, which wasn't possible; she kept squirming in her efforts to find expressions and saying to me, "If Mama only knew how to read between the lines, she would see perfectly well that I'm not saying everything." She kept asking me if you would be pleased with her letter; anyway, what do I know? Let's pray hard for her, she must cheer up but still be firm. She promises to listen to me (until further notice).

My very fond wishes,

Madame Clément

She kept saying to me this evening, "I don't love Robert very much any more."

MADAME CLÉMENT
TO ÉMILIE DE MONTBOURG
Mougins, March 10, 1896

Dear Madame,

I have no doubt that the letter your daughter sent you Sunday hurt you very badly, but be assured that she wrote it only because she couldn't do otherwise. Her husband certainly noticed it: he said to her, "You wrote that to please me, but you don't mean a word of it." Your letter put them all in a fury, and the poor child no longer knew what to say. She's been very unhappy the last three days and has done nothing but say to me, "*If only I could escape.*" For five or six days he had been rougher with her, noticing that she didn't keep up with anything, so much so that on Sunday morning, before writing her letter to you, she said to him, "I see perfectly well that I can't keep up with a household like another woman. I'd rather go back to the villa." You may well believe that he doesn't want her to go. Then he said, "You don't love me, and that's not right." Anyway, it was sad to see them so. He finally got her by being sweet. This evening he stopped to think; so they're back together for now and she's starting to defend him and thinks he's fine. Yesterday he was ugly and mean, etc.; would she say that this evening? You see, dear madame, how she tosses back and forth, it's sad for us all. We both feel deprived not to be able to see you. She has been sorry lately for having married, and misses all the comfort you surrounded her with. She's repeated it to me often enough, but this evening she kept saying, "No, I won't leave him." He can have his way with her. . . .

Above all, he must not suspect anything. I'm having my letter passed along by Madame Martin. I strongly urge you not to get upset. I say that, yet I torment myself badly over this state of affairs, which we can't do anything about.

Dear madame, accept my sincere affection and my devoted wishes for yourself and Mademoiselle Éléonore.

Madame Clément

ÉMILIE DE MONTBOURG
TO DR. CAYLAT
Grasse, March 11, 1896

Doctor,

I see from my daughter's letter that they're trying to convince her to use a pessary, a subject about which I have already indicated to you my repugnance. Moreover, I have learned from competent men that not only is this method painful, which can bring on nervous reactions in certain temperaments, it can also have such serious consequences as inflammation, infection of the uterus, etc.

I write to you now to declare that I *formally oppose* it, as well as any operation, and that not only would I not pay you for that, but if anything happened to my daughter from having taken your advice and your medication, I would spare nothing to make you atone for it.

You would do better, in everyone's interest, to insist that my daughter come to be treated in my home, for you know very well that in her present circumstances she can have neither the rest nor the comfort she needs.

I'm keeping a copy of this letter, which will go by registered mail, so, should the occasion arise, you cannot claim ignorance of my resolutions as an excuse.

I send you, doctor, precisely the consideration you deserve from me.

Émilie de Montbourg

ROBERT CARON D'AILLOT
TO CHARLES DE CERILLEY
Mougins, March 12, 1896

Dear Uncle,

The better relations we noticed with your sister have not lasted long. I am weary beyond measure of this existence, which will make me ill unless in some way or another I put a stop to it. In what follows I give *in full* the text of two letters addressed to Marthe, filled with slanders and insults about me. Here they are:

Grasse, March 6, 1896. Dear Marthe, I think I should point out to you that your dress with the blue diamond pattern trimmed with astrakhan cannot be dyed black, because it's mostly cotton. The gray dress is all wool, so it will take well, but make sure about the beige. I can hardly wait for you to be settled in the chalet, my dear child, for as long as you don't run your household yourself, you'll never get any experience and you'll be thought incompetent. On another count, I have to warn you that I'm being tracked down by several members of the family, who would like to have me seriously involved in a long-range task that would take away from me the resources at my disposal for you. When I mention getting you settled in your new house, they claim that it's a way of robbing me of it because your husband puts too much ill will into seeing this house finished ever to have intended honestly to make you a home of your own. And yet it's promised, and a piece of your estate has been turned over to your husband for it. Did he ever hurry the notary to transfer the funds to him *to pay the workmen!* So at this moment you all are keeping everyone busy, and I swear I will press whomever it may concern because if you're not settled in by April 15, I won't pay any more, and then you'll have to make out on your own as best you can for the furnishings. But why put me to this trouble?

And so forth. There is nothing special about the end of the letter, and I shall pass on to the other without any comment except this: I intend and I want to be master in my own home. Whatever I may do, I am not in any way allowing this woman to meddle in my affairs, which do not concern her at all.

That said, here is yesterday's letter, which is even worse.

Grasse, March 10, 1896. Dear Marthe, do you know what a pessary is? No, you don't, do you? Well, it's a large ring of bone, an instrument of torture that is inserted into the body and that you won't be able to endure. You would have nervous attacks, maybe tetanus! Listen, in Normandy, where the women carry enormous milk jugs on their shoulders by holding them with their arms in the air, there are frequent cases of a fallen uterus. How many have come to tell me of their sufferings! I would advise them to go to the doctor. He would advise the pessary; the husband didn't want to pay the cost, so I would donate it; two days later the wife would come and tell me, "Madame, I couldn't bear it." Yet these women had stronger and less nervous constitutions than yours. . . . After a few such disappointments, the doctor advised a rubber ring, less hard than the bone one, but it had the drawback of taking on a bad smell and had to be taken out often to be washed and freshened, and replacing it was a difficult matter—in short, the women gave up on it and switched to a girdle of coarse linen, very primitive and hardly attractive, but it didn't cost them much. The one made by the truss manufacturer Capron has been adopted by the ladies of the Faubourg Saint-Germain. That's the one I've proposed, and you're wrong not to accept it: even if it does you no good, it will at least not do you any harm, and since I'll be paying for it, it won't cost you anything. This said, I turn to the other subject of the letter. First of all, let's establish some principles that seem to be forgotten. You have no right to ask me for an account of my actions or to make observations to me on the way I may use my money. On the contrary, both divine and human laws subject children to the comments, and if need be the criticisms, of their parents. I think your mother-in-law has not abdicated that right over you, and I have the same right over your husband, although he affects not to recognize it and to *treat as pinpricks* what you must regard as, and what in fact are, *observations* and matters of reflection for you. Since I keep my pledges with rigorous exactitude, I may call to task those who don't. Your husband had promised that you would have your own home as soon as possible; what did he do about that? He had time, *good weather,* and money, but he didn't have the experience necessary to guide the workers. He did have access to the experience of his brother Vincent, who drew up the plan. So it's *entirely his fault* if the house isn't finished. The public and the family judge it the same way, but he won't always be able to trifle with me, and if *for your sake* I have had the generosity to look ahead, try to take advantage of it and recover a little practical energy. As long as Monsieur Robert persists in the bad course he has adopted, it is clear that there can be no understanding between us. If he had shown himself to be the kind of son and brother we had naturally expected, it would have been different; but let him take a good look at himself and he'll recognize that he's gone off on the wrong track. The liquidation of his father's estate will bring him expenses. Is this the moment to sour the good will that could be useful to him? Is this the moment to impel me to give him a lesson in punctuality by delaying the quarterly payment, just as he has delayed the completion of the house—for which, as the local business people know, he has demanded work? I promised you a table to dine on and twelve chairs, but not *the complete furniture for a dining room.* A number of things will be lacking when you move in, and I would have looked after it gladly, but if the house is not done by April 15, don't count on me! You know that I don't talk through my hat; try to read between the lines, for the position you're letting yourself be put in does not allow me to write any more about it. I enclose a ticket of admission for your father-in-law to the pious league of prayers for the souls in purgatory. This will assure him of several Masses a day. Give it to Madame d'Aillot for me. Since you tell me you two cost the household money, I must assume that she will insist that her son keep his promise to finish up the work on the chalet swiftly so that you can be in it by April 15. I send my fondest wishes to you, dear Marthe, while urging you more than ever not to let yourself be made the instrument of observations that are not your own, observations that no one around you has the right to make to me.

(Signature)

There, dear uncle, are the letters your sister writes—without any provocation from my side, I assure you, for if anyone is indifferent toward this woman, it is I. So she has resumed hostilities. This time I'm determined to take radical steps to make her stop. I leave it to you, except that whatever is to happen to me, and however much it may cost me, I'm determined to bring suit for slander against her before the courts, so as to obtain the silence that I, for my part, am keeping and that, following your wise advice, I have been very careful not to break, having always had complete confidence in you. The matter is more serious than it seems to appear to you, and here's why: my mother-in-law, instead of keeping quiet and telling herself that with her daughter married she had no more voice in the matter, has permitted herself to judge harshly the decision I made in having our family doctor take care of Marthe during her indisposition. She wrote him a letter, whose contents I do not know and about which Dr. Caylat didn't say a word to me when he came to see my poor father during his illness, but yesterday she sent him another, registered, of which I can give you the following résumé:

Sir, I must warn you that I oppose the application of a pessary, as well as any kind of operation, and I'll hold you responsible if anything should happen to my daughter and make you atone for it by any means whatever.

I urge you strongly to insist to my daughter that she come to be treated in my home, because in the circumstances in which she is living, she can have neither the comfort nor the care she needs. No use your continuing to visit my daughter, for I will not pay you.

I send you, sir, precisely the consideration that you will deserve, I hope.

(Signature)

That's the summary of her letter, which I can send you in full if you are interested. You must understand, uncle, that, above all, I'm a man, and that, on pain of passing for the worst of imbeciles, I can no longer put up with such a life; it is making me ill and might put me in bed or drive me to some regrettable extreme. So I beseech you to exert all your influence to end this state of affairs, for, I repeat to you, I'll be taking counsel and collecting a dossier (and it is voluminous) while awaiting your reply. I'll put it in the hands of my attorney in Grasse with instructions to prosecute, no matter what scandal such a suit may cause, because I'm sure to come out of it, and my family as well, with head high, while the slime and the mud of the de Montbourg family will have been stirred up and will besmirch the name more than it is already—and that is saying a lot. Such conduct is shameful.

I'm heartsick, dear uncle, to have always to be talking to you about such painful matters, but you must understand how much such a situation hurts me. I love my wife and she loves me; I have made of that little monstrosity that you knew a woman like other women, I am a man of extraordinary justice and I am careful, in view of the bad reports, not to meddle in any matters having to do with my wife's relations with her family. Everything she says, I'll swear to before God, and if we go to the law court, I'll have my wife put on her oath to say it, I won't even set eyes on it, and it will be of her own volition that she will make her observations. Oh, no, I'm the one, I'm always the one who's the *bête noire,* and who is treated like a bandit. Well, then, do everything you can to put a stop to it, and forcefully, for otherwise I'll proceed, and then beware.

Please forgive me, dear uncle; I've bored you long enough now, but I know your kind heart, and that's why I beseech you to take an interest in me in these circumstances. I ask you to convey my very best wishes to my aunt, and I send you the fondest of greetings, from Marthe and me.

Robert Caron d'Aillot

MADAME CLÉMENT
TO ÉMILIE DE MONTBOURG

Dear Madame,

What more can I tell you? He wrote Monsieur de Cerilley a long letter, which he read me. You will learn its contents from your brother. Aunt Sophie has written Marthe to tell her to hurry up and get settled in her house because you're being pressed to come to the aid of a family that's hard up, and if it is delayed further, you'll have to give in. They cannot believe it's true, and say you're contriving all that to speed up the move.

Good-bye, very dear madame; I send you all my affection. I'm distressed to see you so little appreciated in this family, and I foresee so many troubles awaiting us all. *Still silence;* they seem nice enough to me, but can I trust it?

All my friendly wishes and thanks.

Madame Clément

MADAME CLÉMENT
TO ÉMILIE DE MONTBOURG
Friday evening, 10:00 P.M.

Dear Madame,
   Good Lord, how your letters get us into trouble! You'll learn from
Monsieur de Cerilley how angry he is and what he wants to do.
   I entreat you, in your own interest as well as in ours, do stop! Your
daughter is not in danger, and I'll do everything I can to spare her trouble,
but don't write such letters any longer—we're expressly forbidden to write
you. Don't be astonished if Marthe doesn't answer; as for me, I've had it
repeated to me *several times,* so I had to give in, there was no choice. I'll
pass news to you through my sister; that is, I'll put a sealed letter inside
my letter to her, and she will send it to you. I won't use any other ways
any more, but you must either not speak of my letters, or else have me
come back with you, for he would put me out unhesitatingly if he knew
I've been writing you for a long time. It's more serious than you can
believe. Marthe doesn't say much; she loves her husband at the moment,
and you know she doesn't get to the bottom of things.
   If you only knew how distressed I am to see you so upset and how
I beseech you to end all hostilities in your own interest and Mademoiselle
Éléonore's. You're a little better, but now you're going to make yourself
ill again with all this turmoil.
   Please do believe, dear madame, that I sympathize greatly with your
concerns, but she *is* married, and since she's standing up for him and
telling everyone that she's happy, there's nothing to be done. The law is
on his side and he's not mistreating her and he's her master. You would
get nothing but grief and serious trouble if you tried to be useful to her
in spite of herself. Believe me, I'm weighing things coolly; in heaven's
name, don't initiate struggles with them, for you'd be cut to pieces. That
is certain.
   I send you my most affectionate greetings. I don't want to worry you,
but one must give warning when one can.
   Devotedly yours,

Madame Clément

CHARLES DE CERILLEY
TO ÉMILIE DE MONTBOURG
Sangy, March 15, 1896

Dear Émilie,

My sciatica is better, though I've had a lot of pain. Two days ago I
wrote to your son-in-law along the lines you indicated, the gist of which
I approve of. He promised, he got the money to finish his chalet, so he
must keep his word. If he doesn't give you satisfaction, unless there are
valid reasons, he won't be looking out for his own interests. I discussed
this subject with *precision* and *tact.* But now, this morning, I get a long
letter enclosing copies of two of your letters in which I find nothing to
criticize in terms of the content, although the form leaves something to
be desired. There's also a summary copy of the letter you addressed to
Dr. Caylat, which I'm copying: "Sir, I must warn you that I oppose the
application of a pessary as well as any kind of operation, and I would hold
you responsible if anything should happen to my daughter and make you
atone for it in every possible way."

This, says your son-in-law, is only a summary of your letter. Is it
verbatim? If so, *you have gone beyond your rights, you're going out on
a limb.* I've often told you that you tend to work yourself up in many
situations. You take violence for firmness, and you spoil the best of cases
in this way. You've given your son-in-law an advantage over you, and he
takes advantage of that to tell me that if I don't succeed in getting you
to quiet down, he'll bring suit against you for slander, and his dossier is
ready.

That may all be bluster, for where would it get him? The financial
result would be disastrous for him, as I see it, but he's counting on your
fear of scandal and on your maternal solicitude, not a pretty thing to do.

Final conclusion: you must be silent, and declare without rhetoric that
as they do, you will do. That's all. If you approve of that formula, I'm ready
to pass it on to Mougins. Your son-in-law is mighty careful not to speak
of either the chalet, or the money received to complete it, or his promise
of separate households. He wants to be his own master, *that's all.*

Parents certainly have the right to advise, to remonstrate if need be,
but there are limits to be respected, as regards form and even as regards
content. Think back over your whole life and tell me if you have never had
occasion to jump the tracks. It has happened to me, I confess, but more
rarely than to you. I owe you the truth in this delicate situation. For
goodness' sake, don't dance on the tightrope; don't blind yourself to the
consequences of Marthe's marriage, which might perhaps be different

with another husband; it is certain that you would have found serious drawbacks elsewhere, and, *such as he is,* I think you're still fortunate that things are what they are. Sophie is entirely of my opinion, for she, too, knows the situation.

Look, here's a passage in the letter sent by Marthe to Edwige recently. Just roll this over your tongue: "You see, dear aunt, he's so fantastically my good lord and master, my beloved pussycat, that I'd like to lay the whole universe at his feet. If I had twenty lives to give him, I'd give him all of them. I mean to tell you by this that I devote myself body and soul to this sweet pussycat; he's so kind, there's nobody like him, and I adore him, this sweet bunny rabbit of mine, my idol, my everything! . . ."

Well, what do you say to that? In any case, in the face of this amorous exaltation, I recommend that you be very reserved in your observations. Marthe writes to her aunts to contradict you and prove her perfect conjugal happiness; that's part of the d'Aillots' policy. As for you, don't put yourself in the wrong, even formally.

I shall not leave your son-in-law unaware that I do not take at all seriously the threat of a defamation suit, which smacks too much of blackmail (harmful to its author).

Just look at what happens in other families and see how parents intervene with less violence in their children's households, even while holding their own ideas, which at bottom are very just. You yourself have always been reproached for this. Allow me to repeat to you: it's the duty of a devoted brother I am fulfilling, and with all my heart I want you to understand me.

I'll leave you, for right now I'm in pain. My very fondest regards.

Your affectionate brother,

Charles de Cerilley

ÉMILIE DE MONTBOURG
TO CHARLES DE CERILLEY
Grasse, March 17, 1896

Dear Charles,

Yesterday evening I felt so rushed that I forgot to send you the copy of my second letter to Marthe, in reply to the one she sent me after my letter about completing the chalet, of which, unfortunately, I did not keep a copy. But I remember it well enough to recognize whether Monsieur Robert made an exact copy. Send me his brief—I'll send it back to you —for it is important for me to know as fully as possible what to think about this person without writing again. I've said what had to be said, and I won't return to it. Futile reiteration is not among my habits.

As for the doctor, I'm very glad to have got there in time. One of two things must have happened: either Monsieur Robert summoned him to Mougins—for which there was no need, since Madame Clément says that Marthe is well—and to excuse himself wrote the account you quoted to me yesterday, or else Monsieur Robert went to Antibes to reach an understanding with him once more. The scoundrels must have thought it ingenious and entertaining to make me pay the expenses for causing my daughter to suffer. But the doctor must have been concerned to keep her on his list of patients; to show his helplessness in this shoddy affair, he must have turned over my letter. I had no choice of means, my brother, I had to do what I did. Remember that if I had acted as some others did at that time, our sister Clémence would have died in desperation in the madhouse, as her husband had decreed. Having had one sister who died insane (or so they said), you would all have settled your children as best you could, and it would have gone on for generations; so there are times in life when one must go off the ordinary track.

You must remember that after receiving disturbing reports on this Antibes doctor, I had him come here to judge him for myself. To try to win him over to his patient, I told him I would be responsible for paying his fees. Then, having learned that his medicine had led to a setback and that my daughter was very weakened, I wrote him to ask him to change the temperature [of the enemas], requesting that he send me his bill after each series of five visits. He answered me that he not only stood by his forty-seven degrees [Celsius; 116.6 degrees Fahrenheit], but advised adding enemas at forty-five degrees [113 Fahrenheit]. . . . At that point I called in Dr. Barand, who blamed the temperature. Then Providence sent me Madame Clément, who understood and lowered the temperature; and so the setback was not repeated. You see, you have to outwit wicked people! My poor Marthe has made a will in favor of her husband. I'm going to have a great deal of trouble saving her!

Help me, please. Why don't you tell Monsieur Robert that a husband who loves his wife and cares about winning her family's esteem remembers to consult that family when she's ill and needs special care? How, if it were your daughter, would you take the mystery surrounding mine? When one has nothing to hide, one doesn't hide! And when someone does hide, it means that person is guilty.

Good-bye, dear Charles.

Your affectionate sister,

Émilie

CHARLES DE CERILLEY
TO ROBERT CARON D'AILLOT
Sangy, March 18, 1896

Dear Nephew,
My last letter crossed in the mail with your indictment of your mother-in-law. My health is better, the weather is fine, the sun is shining—everything impels me to gaiety. So we'll tell each other some home truths with a good laugh.

I have read yours carefully, and here is my impression: you're getting up on too high a horse and using language too strong over matters that do not warrant it, apropos of my sister. You offer me a performance of Tarasconais fantasy[35] transported into Provence, a benefit performance. In point of fact, the text of my sister's letters that you copied is not at all blameworthy for its content. Only the form might be toned down, but be good enough to remember that you're attacking her character; use your mirror, I beseech you, and look at yourself in broad daylight. Then, my good friend, you speak too much of your rights, and not enough of your duty, which consists in observing your given word—to wit, finishing your chalet with the money your mother-in-law gave you for that purpose. You don't say a word about that in your letter, but instead get indignant because someone has reminded you of it. Now, is that reasonable?

You speak of a suit for defamation, and a scandal, with such assurance that one would think it doesn't affect you. Well, no, I don't believe it one bit; unless you're going crazy, you cannot blithely ruin your present and your future—no offense to the disinterestedness that you profess, but which cannot be. You're the one who would be guilty of defamation by revealing to the public what it has no need to know. When my sister complains or criticizes, she does not address her letters to the public!

You haven't given me your reason for not finishing the chalet, although you copied out all my sister's grievances on that score. That is strange.

My sister's maternal solicitude is on the alert, the more so because you keep your wife from communicating freely with her. Your aunt and I would not be happy if our son-in-law kept our daughter in such secrecy.

Be good enough to recognize the situation you have been creating, which is not acceptable considering all the kind things my sister has done for your household. I am speaking as freely as you did, and you cannot be shocked at this since you've set the example. This is the precious guarantee for me that you will recognize here only my well-intentioned and cordial friendship for you.

Whereupon, dear nephew, I offer you my handshake with all my affection. Your aunt sends her best wishes to you, and also to Marthe. Your affectionate uncle,

C. de Cerilley

CHARLES DE CERILLEY
TO ÉMILIE DE MONTBOURG
Sangy, March 18, 1896

Dear Émilie,

I am much better, beginning to walk and not sleeping badly. Enclosed is the draft copy of my letter to your son-in-law. I tell him some home truths in an almost jovial way, so they might get through. Do you think perhaps I'm too pointed? Read me carefully, forgetting yourself so you can judge it better. If you find nothing to change, send it back to me and it will be copied *as is.* Offer me any constructive criticism and I'll ponder it. On the matter of speaking frankly, you see that I know how to do it when I see fit; in any event, quite a few people know that about me full well.

I think your son-in-law will have no reason to welcome my letter. It was time I told him how I feel, clean and clear. My term "benefit performance" means blackmail on his part, which is clear as day, but the crude word isn't in it, and shouldn't be for the moment.

In speaking of your maternal solicitude, I had to consider that your letter to the doctor overstepped the bounds, risked seeming partial, and thus rendered you unable to defend yourself usefully; keep that in mind. Along these lines, much must be forgiven the lapses of a mother's alarmed heart.

For some days now my pen has not been lying idle. Fortunately, my status as a recluse gives me plenty of time for this.

And here is the fine weather; it's almost warm, and quite a few plants are budding. A little fresh air does me a lot of good.

My expression "Tarasconais fantasy transported into Provence" is meant to tell your son-in-law that he's playing the role of Daudet's Tartarin de Tarascon. I didn't want to use the raw term, but that certainly is the gist of my thought, and he'll understand it perfectly well. Good-bye, dear Émilie; my fond wishes as a very devoted brother.

Charles de Cerilley

Talk less than ever and don't stray from that formula: *As you do, I shall do.* You'll be strong that way.

ROBERT CARON D'AILLOT
TO CHARLES DE CERILLEY
Mougins, March 19, 1896

Dear Uncle,

I am replying to your letter and giving you the few items of information that you ask me for. Let me start by telling you that in getting married I had no intentions of accepting anyone's tutelage, having my actions and gestures commented on, discussed, and directed. I wanted to do as all young people do on starting out in life: to try to fashion for myself a family and a home. This is by way of telling you that I do not concede to my mother-in-law, whether motivated by solicitude or any other purpose, the right to discuss my actions or to meddle in my private affairs, especially in so far as they in no way contribute to making my wife unhappy; on the contrary, her happiness is pure and perfect among us. That said, let me explain why I'm still not in a home of my own, even though I very much wish to be, and unfortunately cannot firmly set the moment when I will be. The contractor—a man from the region who is comfortably off and has been the family mason for the last thirty or forty years—promised orally to complete my job by the end of October; at that point another job came along and he took on both at the same time without hiring more staff. (I went to a local man in large part because later one cannot go to a contractor from a neighboring town to have a roof repaired or a tile laid, for he would not take the trouble.) If he had refused me, I would have looked elsewhere; but he accepted, and I had to put up with my contractor, who wouldn't pledge his word in writing, telling me he didn't want to have any trouble. Besides, he knew very well that even if he had been bound in writing and had been late, I'd never have dared take him to court, for fear of ending up with the whole countryside on my back. So I had to put up with it and try to respond to his delays by jolting him often; these delays have brought me to the present and threaten to last another month or two, in spite of all my urgings. So it's not because I'm not paying that the house is not progressing; it's not because I don't want to move into a home of my own that the house isn't finished; it's not because I'm dishonest that I don't want to give my wife a home of her own, since I'm the first to suffer from not having a house—it keeps me far from my work and forces me to get out of bed at two-thirty every morning to leave for Nice. So these are gratuitous insults hurled at me by your sister, and I want you to bring them to a stop; otherwise—whatever happens and whatever is to be the result—I'll drag her before the law courts, because this situation is intolerable. We are above all people with a heart, and love of money does not impel us to insult our neighbor without a cause. My whole family is outraged by this behavior, and I warn you that we will all join forces to make her keep quiet if you don't feel you have enough influence to do that. I want and intend to be master in my house, I forbid her to meddle in anything that concerns me, and since she pays no attention to that, I hereby break off my relationship with her, so she will have no excuse to intrude in my affairs. You think the fear of being disinherited will make me crawl; no, a hundred times no, and even if I end up having to beg for my bread, I mean to make myself respected above all. If she gives someone else her pittance, she will prove once again that the promises made at the start of the marriage were nothing but an act she put on, the better to deceive me. That's the gratitude she promised me in her salon (holding my hands in hers) when I consented to marry her daughter, to whose bastard I was giving my name—it is so true that today dishonesty dwells everywhere, even among the most Christian people, or those who so style themselves. I'm outraged, dear uncle, at having to drink the cup of gall to the lees, at being steeped in ignominies. There are no horrors or abominations that have not been heaped on me and my family—I've been called an assassin and a despoiler. I have these letters, and I'll produce them at law; then there will be light, and people will see which of us two deserves the esteem of the public (since she talks so much about the public); we'll bring it into the light, into broad daylight, the life of shame that in full knowledge she let her daughter lead, from the age of fourteen. We'll establish with certainty whether I'm the one who could have infected my wife, as she has accused me, both orally and in writing, of doing, or whether it comes to Marthe from her father and mother. I hope that afterward, when all the smallest details of her life are known to the public and our life has also been brought into the light, we'll see who stays clean. Such subjects are so painful to me that I must stop, so as not to weary you any further. I have a heavy heart and am in a state of jangled nerves. I'm counting on your influence to restore peace and spare me the pain of this scandal, which would have repercussions throughout France. So do apply all your knowledge to this and keep me posted, for I remain determined to take action. My dossier is ready. I think your indisposition will not last, and I say prayers for your very prompt recovery. Marthe is heartbroken over all this. She tells me to send you her hugs and kisses to share with my aunt. My mother, too, appreciated your good wishes, and thanks you for them sincerely; and I, dear uncle, even as I repeat to you the grief this situation causes me, ask you and my aunt to accept my fondest greetings.

Robert Caron d'Aillot

Grasse, March 20, 1896

Dear Charles,

When you composed your draft of a reply to my son-in-law, had you received the four letters I sent to you—one from Marthe, my reply, the one I sent to the doctor, and one from Madame Clément? If so, I think you're wrong to criticize my letter to the doctor, and circumstances prove me right, since it produced a good effect: Madame Clément writes me today that Marthe is getting better and better. The scoundrels saw themselves outwitted and got scared! So there's no more question of painful methods or of an operation. Good Lord, give me support instead of blaming me. You did well to send to me your draft, which otherwise is very good. I don't know whether Monsieur Robert will understand by "benefit performance" that you mean "blackmail," but he will still certainly feel that you are joshing him pleasantly.

Apropos of defamation, do be sure to tell him that he is switching the roles: he's the one who would be committing defamation by revealing to the public what it has no need to know. When I complain or make criticisms, it is by sealed letters addressed to my daughter, not to the public.

I hope that your *corrected* letter will have a good effect. He's a sharp one, and you have to hold him in all the more since his father is no longer around—and since his mother, seeing things only through his eyes, is no help. But he's fundamentally a coward, like everyone who is wicked through stupidity. If Marthe, who was such a willful terror at home, could only persist in managing her husband firmly and vigorously, instead of letting herself be tyrannized, it would be she who would lay down the law, all the more so because she has the sinews of war—the money. But she lets her morale be ground down, and permits the good she still had left in her heart to be snatched away. If later on the husband complains, the answer will be that it's his handiwork.

Don't fail to return to me the letters I've sent to you, also, if you will, my son-in-law's indictment, which I'll return to you after making a copy.

Your affectionate sister,

Émilie

Thank you for your brotherly help.

Sangy, March 20, 1896

Dear Émilie,

I'm returning your letters and your son-in-law's brief that was addressed to me. Send it back to me, please. The copies of your letters from your son-in-law are verbatim. I do find a good deal of fault with your letter to the doctor: it would get you hanged and you don't even know it! No doubt if I as a father disapproved of a given medicine, I'd oppose it energetically, but I would not go threatening to make him "atone by any means whatever." You were making an accusation in advance, which is a big mistake. That's the way thoughtless violence has often spoiled the finest pages of your life; if you attempt to deny it, it simply means you're still compelled to go off the track. Anyone who knows you well must judge you thus.

Yes, I can add to my tentative reply to your son-in-law an observation on the charitable work to which the family is inviting you, and me, too —that is, a work to which I would also contribute my support. I think that giving him that bone to gnaw on will produce a happy effect. As for telling your son-in-law that I don't take his Tartarinades seriously, I think that's useful; for too long he's been battering my ear with them; he's getting too big for his britches. So just keep in mind that he has no interest in knocking over or breaking the cookie jar. If he was acting on impulse, he'd better not muff it, for then his regret would be bitterly sincere, but *too late*. However, if you're afraid of it, I agree to suppress that passage in my letter, though with regret, I assure you. Oh, if only I were constantly at your side, I would avoid many mistakes for you. From this distance, I get there too late. Good-bye, dear Émilie.

Your affectionate brother,

Charles

Madame Clément is right to tell you, "Be prudent." It's important that she remain at Mougins. You keep seeing crime everywhere. It's your ailment, repeated far too often: given a principle that is fundamentally true, you often push it too far and are put gravely in the wrong by the form you employ, which is often a serious mistake that can spoil the content. Do you acknowledge this?

ÉMILIE DE MONTBOURG
TO CHARLES DE CERILLEY
Grasse, March 23, 1896

Dear Charles,
Now the cat is out of the bag! This is a new bit of blackmail by Monsieur Robert. You'll see from Madame Clément's letter that they said in front of her that the chalet costs would mount to 14,000 francs. The budget was for a third of that, and it seems impossible to me that his brother Monsieur Vincent, who drew up the plan for him with an estimate of 6,000 francs, could have made such a bad mistake! Would the engineering firm that employs him keep him on as an architect if he was that far wrong? What do you think? It's likely that Monsieur Robert spent the money designated for the chalet on something else, and would like to use blackmail to get more to pay for his house. If I hadn't pushed him to finish it, poor Marthe would have been condemned to several more years of living in her mother-in-law's house. To win over Sophie, Monsieur Robert wrote her a long letter, which I hope she'll send me.

You'll also see that Madame d'Aillot is reverting to her idea of taking little Georges in. These people definitely have no shame. What a situation for Marthe, and what worries for us! Considering that Monsieur Robert could not bear her little dog, who wasn't doing him any harm, and Marthe had to give him away so he wouldn't be kicked to death, what would happen to the poor child *"who interferes with his career,"* as he said to me in reproaching me for insisting on the acknowledgment. Besides these worries, think of the position this would put the young household in, before the family and society as well. A while back you were very much opposed to the child's presence in the region.

And how inconsistent they are, wanting to take *into the mother's house* this child who barely three months ago was a piece of dirt, etc. That's because the father of the family was alive three months ago and still inspired respect; now they must think that anything goes. To be sure, if they take back the child, whose expenses they had certainly pressed me hard enough to take on as my responsibility, I won't contribute any more for him. Nor will Éléonore provide clothes for him; they'll have to make out as best they can. But at this point we can't tell what they are up to —we've just got to wait and see.

Meanwhile, the unworthiness of Marthe's character is becoming so evident to us that if she herself won't help salvage it, I'll really have to make up my mind to abandon her to the lot she's making for herself.

Good Lord, what a difficult daughter, and how badly she responds to all the kind deeds, all the devotion we've offered her!

My fondest wishes. Send me Monsieur Robert's letter.

Your affectionate sister,

Émilie

There's no further question of pessary or operation; my goal is reached, and the anger of these unmasked scoundrels doesn't astonish me. Poor Éléonore is bowled over by Madame d'Aillot's idea, after the disputes of three months back!

CHARLES DE CERILLEY
TO ÉMILIE DE MONTBOURG
Sangy, March 23, 1896

Dear Émilie,

I'm sending you the enclosed letter from your son-in-law, which I hope you'll profit by.

I'm awaiting your reply before writing to your son-in-law. Do weigh carefully everything he says. If, in spite of all my efforts, the war keeps breaking out again, I can't do anything more about it. You think you must use violence, when ordinary diplomatic firmness would be wiser. If Marthe were unfortunately restored to you, or if she wanted to run away some fine day, what would you do with her—never mind the scandal? And if you happened to die, what could you do for her? Where the goat is tied it must browse, the folk proverb says. If I were you, I wouldn't talk any more about either the chalet or the separate household. It's up to Marthe to insist that her husband keep his promise; for *if* she should prefer living in the parental home, so as not to have the nuisance of running a house, which she doesn't know how to do, would you insist on a separate household on the strength of a promise that was made to you? Marthe will always lack a rational will, and you won't always be there to make up for it. So act as though you didn't exist. Confine yourself to *diplomatic* advice. If that's impossible for you, groan in silence for the sake of peace and for fear of worse.

I'm not satisfied with the condition of Madeleine's colon: there's a chronic irritation, sometimes there are touches of mucus, from time to time a little blood, and almost all the time a feeling of fatigue. The treatment is long.

You must resign yourself to seeing the d'Aillots speculate on your daughter's income. I repeat, it will be worse after you are gone. It's inevitable—you can do nothing about it, or very little. You can't punish your daughter for lacking character, and since she appears to be something of an exception, people won't fail to tell you it's your fault, for indulging her too much. You can see what your son-in-law is already saying in the letter I'm enclosing.

March 25

I got your letters yesterday. I'm polishing up my letter to your son-in-law, taking into account your corrections and insisting on every husband's duty to come to an understanding with his wife's immediate family regarding the medication to have her take when seriously ill—and also on the private and rightful nature of your remonstrances, which have not been destined for the public; that would make *him* the one doing the defaming.

Don't lose sight of the moral state of your son-in-law since the frightful admission Marthe made to him about her private life from the age of fourteen. This is extremely serious, and it redounds against you for your alleged lack of supervision, whatever you may say. Forgive me for reminding you, but I must if you are not to lose your head. No, I don't like the way you closed your letter to the doctor, with the consideration he "will deserve" (sic). In the first place, that's insulting. Oh, women! And the tone of the letter! Bad, bad—I've got to be frank with you; put up with it, or I'll keep quiet entirely, and with everyone.

I'm feeling better and better, but it's a slow climb, very slow.

Good-bye, dear Émilie; this fine sun should do you good.

Your affectionate brother,

Charles de Cerilley

The explanations for the delay on the building are excellent, *if they are true.* Barring proof to the contrary, you must accept them as good, but your son-in-law makes them known too late, and, as it were, as needed.

CHARLES DE CERILLEY
TO ÉMILIE DE MONTBOURG
Sangy, March 25, 1896

Dear Émilie,

I'm returning to you the letter from Madame Clément, who is very useful to you at Mougins. Yes, it is likely that two new pieces of blackmail are being prepared for you *if you're willing to let it happen.*

1. Very exaggerated cost of the chalet, which they whisper is to come to 14,000 francs after an estimate of 6,000—a chalet whose completion you have demanded; they'll make a lot of noise about that.

2. Their bringing Georges into their home; they'll cry poverty until you pay the same expenses as for the wet nurse.

You have no moral or legal right to oppose your son-in-law if, worshipping today what burned him yesterday, he receives into his home the child he acknowledged as *his own.* From the moment of acknowledgment, the child cannot be taken away from his immediate family. Oh, by the way, I repeat that, for my part, *I don't ever want to see him.* Please tell this to anyone whom it may concern. Moreover, *while I'm alive,* my cesspool would be filled to the brim if anyone brought her to the Minster. You must understand that I will not have anything to do with actions that would make us a public spectacle.

Marthe will always give you trouble through her fickleness and her absolute lack of character. So behave, as much as you can, as if you were no longer in this world—I insist on this good advice—and be very sure of what you want. If they see you get up on your high horse, there will be no end to their demands. If I were you, I'd avoid undertaking commitments for which no one is grateful to you once first thank-yous are over. It would be preferable to send a little from time to time as a subsidy, fully voluntary and well motivated. Need is more imperious than any theories. But since they need you, see to it that they earn your help. If not, let them sweat it out; that will even be just and moral. Help out, but don't take on their responsibility lightly. Good-bye, dear sister. My letter to your son-in-law is in the mail.

Your affectionate brother,

Charles de Cerilley

ÉMILIE DE MONTBOURG
TO CHARLES DE CERILLEY
Grasse, March 27, 1896

Dear Charles,

I can't write you at length, for I am in considerable pain, but I want to protest against my son-in-law's lies. No, I never spoke to him of gratitude for marrying my daughter, and I never made him any promises for the future, nor held his hands in mine except in giving him the common handshake now in fashion. I've never concerned myself with his personal affairs except in insisting on that promise of a separate household, because Marthe told me she was suffering from her status as a daughter-in-law. As for her health, I couldn't help worrying about it, since they were keeping her medication a mystery to me. I thank you for making the necessary corrections in your reply.

Can one count on a sense of honor in a man who lies to the point of taking an oath that he doesn't look over his wife's letters—while he's keeping her under such moral pressure that she can't write one line without his say-so—a man who prides himself on having his wife swear a false oath to the law?

I'm sending you a letter from Madame Clément that reached me yesterday evening. You will see that Marthe is inclined to tell her aunt Edwige about Georges's birth. Do you think she can have come to that decision of her own free will? Meanwhile, we can't say a thing without compromising Madame Clément. What can Monsieur Robert have in mind? He knows that that branch of the family has not been informed about the matter.

Madeleine's being indisposed worries me as it does you. It seems probable that material remaining there too long must have produced irritation. Find out from her doctor whether, after the colon has been cleared, an enema of calf's-head bouillon—or calf's-foot bouillon, for that matter—often repeated, wouldn't be good for this condition.

As for Marthe, I've said everything I should say. If I have been neither understood nor accepted, that's too bad; I go back under my tent, fully determined to do as they will do. For the moment, all missives and correspondence have ceased, and that will last as long as their bad attitude does.

I can't copy Monsieur Robert's letter today, but I'll return it to you later. It's quite certain that not all his excuses for the building delay are true. The exaggeration of the cost is the proof. Monsieur Robert is indeed the son of his mother, who while passing the tin cup says, *"I'm too proud to ask,"* but who does her blackmail just the same.

Good-bye, dear Charles.

Your affectionate sister,

Émilie

CHARLES DE CERILLEY
TO ÉMILIE DE MONTBOURG
Sangy, March 29, 1896

Dear Émilie,

If your son-in-law has the gall to write to Edwige about Marthe's misfortune, I'll write and tell him just what I think of him. That means he's capable of anything, and I'll break off any relationship with him—but I think it's a new type of blackmail. From the threat to the act is a long way, except in a case of madness. I'm very glad that thanks to the letters from Madame Clément who is on the spot, you at last understand the need for silence, and that you are detached *in fact* from everything that is happening and may happen at Mougins. You would have done better to practice this from the start. Marthe has neither head nor character; she is fickle to the utmost degree and will sacrifice you, her mother. So pray for her and do *nothing more* by way of show of force. As for Georges, let them do as they like, *without saying a word;* and as for subsidies, at least practice the adage, *As they do, you will do.*

But *no commitment for the future,* for then it's farewell to the acknowledgment. That's what happens when rights are conferred outright. Be sure to dot all the "i"s so they can't make false inferences from isolated facts. Keep a copy of everything.

Your son-in-law has not acknowledged receiving my letter. I suppose he wasn't expecting my new tone, inspired and motivated by his own.

Good-bye, dear Émilie.

Your affectionate brother,

Charles de Cerilley

The doctor has already advised the calf's-foot enema for Madeleine, and your opinion has decided her to do it. Thanks to you on her behalf.

MADAME CLÉMENT
TO ÉMILIE DE MONTBOURG
Mougins, March 31, 1896

Very dear Madame,

I did indeed receive my sister's letter at five o' clock this evening. Your writing looks a little different; I'm afraid you may be ill. I'm very worried about it. I have great hopes of visiting you next Monday, provided he doesn't say no. Marthe gently insinuated to him that I could fetch the rabbits now that the rabbit hutch is dry; he didn't answer, but he seemed to be more accepting than refusing. I'm very happy about it, and so is Marthe.

Yes, I did urge Marthe not to write to her aunt Edwige, and she won't do it. Moreover, he is calm, and there's no more question about Georges —he absolutely doesn't want him about, and he's right. Marthe is no longer all for Césarine: she's on the ladies' side. He got a letter from Aunt Sophie that put him back in a good humor. He had me read it, and I'll tell you all about it. He's also calmed down on the score of Dr. Caylat, who isn't saying anything any more. Dear madame, after such an assault a person needs rest. I'm shattered by it—if you only knew how painful it is to be silent when one would like to speak. The house is coming along a bit. Two rooms are tiled, and I think the month of April will move it ahead a good deal. Now Marthe is saying that she will be sorry to leave her in-laws. What is one to do? The poor child is really temperamental; I think she'll always be that way. She misses you, just the same, and will be very pleased to get news of you.

I hope you're well and not fretting too much. She speaks of you pretty often. You know how inconstant she is in everything; she's still steamed up against religion; she often has headaches, though less than before; morally the Easter holidays were very trying for her; she's as she used to be at Grasse, only she uses more trivial expressions, copying those around her. This evening at table their cousin was saying, in speaking of the two brothers, "You use expressions that should never be found in the mouth of an aristocrat—peasants speak better." The mother is certainly the cause of it. She should have corrected all that as she went along.

Marthe felt pains around the heart last Tuesday and Wednesday, and again a little this morning. She thought something might be starting, although nothing indicated it; it's a combination of weak digestion and her usual state, for you know that in Grasse she felt the same thing at the time of her fits of hysteria. I'll give her some water-lily powder, which I think will do her a lot of good.

Dear madame, do give my best to Mademoiselle Éléonore, and for yourself, please believe in my sincere devotion.

Madame Clément

MARTHE CARON D'AILLOT
TO CHARLES DE CERILLEY
Chalet Marthe, April 3, 1896

Dear kind Uncle,

I don't want to let my husband's letter go off without adding a few lines to assure you that I haven't forgotten you or my dear aunt, either. I'm very pleased that Robert likes me. I have no other will but his, which makes me find everything pleasant and easy to do.

We have a charming cousin whom I'm going to take as a model so that, as best I can, I can complete on my own what my husband has made of me, and never leave the straight and narrow path. What sort of weather are you having at Sangy? Here it's nice one moment, but then the mistral takes over with a great racket, though fortunately it doesn't last long. Still, its visits are not very pleasant.

I've gone back to painting. Robert is showing me how to draw, so I can make my own models when I don't have any others at hand.

I leave you, dear kind uncle, not wanting to tire you by too long a letter.

Fondly, your very devoted niece,

Marthe

CHARLES DE CERILLEY
TO ÉMILIE DE MONTBOURG
Sangy, April 9, 1896

Dear Émilie,

Received your letter and Madame Clément's, then saw the doctor, who came on a house call. I spoke to him about pessaries, bone, ivory, and rubber. He maintains that all are very useful and never cause accidents, that if they are sometimes wearing, that's because people need another *shape* or another *size*. So you see you shouldn't rule them out *en masse* and on principle on that score. The doctor urges you to consult a specialist, perhaps in Nice. I'm very glad I spoke to the doctor about that.

Your handwriting seems shaky, and I'm afraid you may be quite weak. I beg you: live in calm, see things from above the battle and as if you were no longer there—not an easy thing, I know, but you get much too upset, and it's always been that way with you. I share in this failing a little, though to a much lesser degree. Let Marthe and your son-in-law arrange their life as they please; be dead to them from that point of view; I beg you, do that.

My fondest greetings as an affectionate brother,

Charles de Cerilley

We're becoming immobilized, Madeleine and I: the slightest trips break the equilibrium of our health. Everything has an end, alas!

Marthe had written me to ask for news of us and to sing to me her conjugal happiness. I replied to her that real happiness doesn't need much broadcasting to be taken seriously.

MARTHE CARON D'AILLOT
TO ÉMILIE DE MONTBOURG
Mougins, May 11, 1896

Dear Mama,

I hope you're in good health, and Éléonore, too. For my part, I'm very well, perfectly well.

I'm still *very happy* and I'm taking advantage of Madame Clément's going to Grasse to write you a few lines. We are hoping to move in next week, and Madame Clément is taking the measurements of the windows.

It would be nice of you to get everything ready that's left for me to pick up at the villa. Madame Clément will go to Grasse again to help with that. I have a pretty covey of chicks, which is a good exercise for my patience. The rabbits are well.

I think you might quit dressing Georges in blue and white, now that he's three. When you write his wet nurse, give him a good hug and a kiss for me.

Keep taking good care of yourself. Fondest wishes to both of you.

Your affectionate daughter,

Marthe

MARTHE CARON D'AILLOT
TO ÉMILIE DE MONTBOURG
Mougins, June 6, 1896

Dear Mama,

We arrived safe and sound. I slept well last night and didn't cough too much. My pussycat was kind enough to get up twice last night to pull up the covers over his little wife, who had kicked them off in her sleep.

My dearest asks me to thank you warmly for his ring, which gives him great pleasure.

I was very happy to see you, believe me. We both send fondest wishes from the heart to you and to Éléonore.

Your affectionate daughter,

Marthe

P.S. If you find the mesh from one of the landing nets, send it to me; also my gray slippers, which I left in the night table. Then please send me a half-box of charcoal drops to take away bad breath; you'll do me a big favor, for that makes me very uncomfortable.

ÉMILIE DE MONTBOURG
TO CHARLES DE CERILLEY
Grasse, June 9, 1896

Dear Charles,

The twenty-four-hour visit from Marthe and Madame Clément gave me great pleasure, but also great pain, for the poor child admitted to me that she has suffered cruelly from the behavior of her husband's family and of her husband himself, who gets worked up too easily.

Oh, how inspired I was to insist on their completing the chalet, and how I reproach myself for not having done it sooner. D'Aillot's mother gets everything she can out of her son, and they're constantly out of money. Monsieur Robert, always inclined to blackmail, was not ashamed to send my daughter to me without a sou to get herself some shoes and gloves. I gave her 50 francs a quarter for her clothes. Out of those 50 francs she also bought some clothes for her husband.

I think he'll let his wife come again other times. Marthe is coughing a lot. It's a cold, they say, but it needs to be taken care of. I called in the doctor, who, though he found nothing serious, would nevertheless have liked to study this condition for a few days. But the poor child is so afraid of her husband that she doesn't dare tell him she saw a doctor here. She will take cough syrup in Madame Clément's room. I found her sad, paler and thinner. Robert is definitely stupid and wicked, and Marthe admits that, crushed by all those people, she hasn't been able to make a place for herself. Now that's going to change: she must manage little by little to establish her influence and her independence. Monsieur Robert told her to be *proud of herself*, which gave her a bit of a lift in her own eyes. The mother-in-law, sisters-in-law, and aunt are going away to spend four months at Labastide; during that time Marthe must establish herself at home and not let them flock around her when they come back.

The furniture will go tomorrow. I'm also sending them supplies for setting up house. That's the present of bread and salt that the Russian empire gave the czar as a welcome.

Vanity would have had me send over all the furnishings right away, so as to have a luxurious housewarming, but that's beyond my means for the moment. Besides, I myself did not get completely set up right away. They'll proceed like others, step by step.

If among the items of livery I gave you there are things that don't suit your servants, please send them back to me, for Marthe will be very pleased to have them. They have a young man of eighteen in their service.

At last Monsieur Robert's brother is in Marseille, in the customs. That's a bit of good riddance anyway!

The confirmation of the enslavement I suspected for my poor Marthe distressed and upset me very much. Her husband's stubbornness will make her independence more difficult to achieve. She felt happy in our devoted and sincere affection, and promised us to try to come more often, but I'll have to pay for her visits, I suspect. She begged my pardon many times for her ungrateful actions, provoked by her surroundings. Would you believe that when she tried to stand up for me her sisters-in-law kept saying to Monsieur Robert, "Come on, now, give her a good whipping to shut her up!" Her mother-in-law makes her believe we're detested here, which is not true at all; on the other hand, the villagers of Mougins don't say hello to Madame d'Aillot and her daughters, whom they loathe for their insolence. Fortunately, their hats are off to Marthe, who, for her part, is the *nice* Madame d'Aillot.

The poor child was greeted here with affectionate respect by our tradesmen, who showed they were delighted about her getting established soon in the chalet.

My very fondest wishes, dear Charles.

Your affectionate sister,

Émilie

ÉMILIE DE MONTBOURG
TO CHARLES DE CERILLEY
Grasse, June 16, 1896

Dear Charles,

I thank you for the 500 francs you sent me, which arrived just in time, for I had almost nothing left. Thanks, too, for the livery items you returned to me for Marthe, though, as a matter of fact, the stuff won't go well with their carriage, a sort of uncovered wagon, very inconvenient.

Being owed money by an upholsterer to whom I did a favor once to help him avoid going bankrupt, I proposed to Marthe to have this man make her some curtains for her bedroom, as I had consented to the draperies requested by Monsieur Robert. But the solid fabric, blue-and-yellow canvas, doesn't suit him; he wants a very lightweight kind of thing that the tradesman doesn't have, and I can't oblige him, after all, to go to great expense to supply what he doesn't have. I'm not going to let myself be pushed to the wall by Monsieur Robert; since what I'm offering doesn't suit him, I withdraw, and let him do as he pleases. He's going to be furious again, but what can I do about it?

Recently old Aunt Mélanie, having had reason to complain of their behavior, said to Madame Clément, "I had had the idea of putting into the chalet what china I had left, as a surprise, but I won't do it." Madame Clément told that to Marthe, who repeated it to her husband, who succeeded in persuading the poor aunt that she had promised that china and got her to give it to him. Marthe, when she came, told me that story and tried to play the same trick on me apropos of my mirrored wardrobe. But I'm not Aunt Mélanie, and I intend to prove to them that they won't get me to act like her. You have no idea of the squalidness of such characters! And yet Marthe suffers from it to such a point that *she declared to us that she had sought several ways to destroy herself.* Now that the harpies are at Labastide, she'll have only her husband to cope with, and she will, I hope, be less unhappy. But she missed the boat from the outset by letting everyone trample on her. May God be willing to help her little by little to resume her place.

My very fond greetings, dear Charles.

Your affectionate sister,

Émilie

Poor Éléonore suffered cruelly from a chill in her ear caught on the day of loading up for Mougins. Now she's better, but as for me, worrying has again given me digestion problems.

ÉMILIE DE MONTBOURG
TO CHARLES DE CERILLEY
Grasse, July 19, 1896

Dear Charles,

I'm uneasy about not getting any news of you. Here the heat is so intense that everybody suffers to some extent. Marthe and her husband are staying at her sister-in-law's. I'm not without worry on that score, for that lady—a dry, greedy hypocrite—has a good deal of influence on her brother. She doesn't like Marthe, and I know she is quite capable of self-seeking schemes that the husband would be happy to adopt. I can hardly wait until my daughter gets back to Mougins, then comes to see me here again. I pay for her trips here and give her money for her errands, among which she always includes the finest clothes for her husband.

That's how I get a few visits nowadays! It does her good, for she gets a few things off her heart, which is turning back toward me. They've left Madame Clément at Mougins. That's one more worry for me. Oh, my brother, how unhappy we are when we can't trust anyone!

Sea bathing, too exciting for Marthe, is completely forbidden. Nevertheless, Monsieur Robert had a bathing suit packed for his wife. To let you judge the man, I will tell you that, just so that he could strut about on the beach in fine clothes, he *pawned* the ring he had given his fiancée—or, rather, it was Aunt Mélanie who gave it. How do you like that? I won't let him drag me down into poverty, I swear to you! When one is hard up, one stays home! Keep this a secret—burn this letter—for poor Marthe would be ruined if he found out that I know what is going on.

My fondest greetings, dear Charles. Please let me have news of you.

Your affectionate sister,

Émilie

ÉMILIE DE MONTBOURG
TO CHARLES DE CERILLEY
Grasse, July 24, 1896

Dear Charles,

It's from Marthe herself that I got what I wrote you concerning the ring. Do you think I would be capable of inventing such an infamy? Madame Clément knew the whole thing and hadn't dared tell me about it for fear of grieving me. How did Marthe ever consent, you ask me? My dear, she has to think well of everything her husband does, on pain of being threatened; what makes her dismal role even worse, she was trying to win my pity for that specimen, who was pretending to weep as he took the ring to cart it off to the pawnshop. I'd rather not talk about this added ignominy, but I fear that the jewelry and silverware I've given my daughter will go the same way!

Anyway, now they're back in Mougins.

Try to cut down on your trips, since they tire you so, dear Charles, and at least enjoy the quiet your sciatica imposes on you. At this time of year, all rheumatics are in more or less serious pain. My very fond greetings.

Your affectionate sister,

Émilie

Chalet Marthe, August 3, 1896

Dear kind Mother,

I'm taking advantage of my husband's having gone on an errand to write you a bit. The letter you passed along to me touched me deeply. How kind you are, dear Mama! I could never match all your kind deeds in return.

Since yesterday's letter had nothing in it that could offend my dearest ratkin,[36] I showed it to him. When there's nothing in your letters that could anger him, it's better not to make any mystery of them. Only I didn't let him see the letter you wrote to Madame Clément, for my poor pussycat would have been jealous to see that we each had one. Eventually, I think, he'll become closer to you, you who always say at the end of your letters how much you love me. He would like to get such a greeting, too, I see perfectly well. But if you write me again, don't talk to me about this letter I'm writing you right now. As always, you must be very careful in your letters to me.

Everything you sent us has given us the greatest pleasure, and the napkin ring went right to his heart; he's using it. I'm so happy about it, he's full of kind deeds, poor little rat.

I hope to go see you some time this month, but at the moment it's much too hot. Don't mention my letter when you write me.

A big hug and kiss from the heart to you, also to Éléonore.

Yours,

Marthe

Chalet Marthe, August 11, 1896

My very own Mama,

I'm taking advantage of the fact that my dearest isn't back yet to write you right away that I had a good trip.

This first letter I'm writing you now will be followed by a second one when the ratkin is back, for, obviously with my dear tyrant watching, I'll have to write you to tell you I had a good trip. I really have to be tricky with him. I'm keeping the can of tea for Madame Clément and me and not telling the ratkin about it. I'm very happy to have been able to stay a few more hours with the two of you. Forgive me my interjections; I'm sorry about them, but I'm so upset that I can't hold back, and what can I do? I talk about everything.

Your ducks are very beautiful. Thanks again, dear kind Mother. I wish I could stay with you, but I have to reckon with my temperament, and, besides, I'm head over heels in love in spite of the dagger I'm chained to for all eternity.

Madame Clément does as I do: she takes her courage in both hands, and then we are patient. Time and especially God are great masters.

I send you a big hug, such a big hug, dearest Mother mine. Prudence and silence everywhere. Rest easy. You have once again lighted, as did Abbé Bosset, the torch of honor in me. A thousand thanks. I want to be worthy of our ancestors, not scorned by them. I also want to do honor to the motto I've chosen for myself: happiness lies in devotion and duty.

Your affectionate daughter. Oh, my beloved mother, how dearly I'm paying for all my stupidities!

Marthe

A thousand kisses to Georges.

ÉMILIE DE MONTBOURG
TO CHARLES DE CERILLEY
Grasse, August 13, 1896

Dear Charles,

Marthe's visit shook my nerves so badly that I couldn't give you an account of it right away, and it's still hard for me to use my pen today. The poor child is so unhappy! This time she admitted it to me in tears, and, since I was reproaching her for writing to everyone about a happiness that is anything but real, she told me that she was forced to by her tyrant. Her stay at Sainte-Maxime was a torture, with the mother-in-law working up her husband against Marthe all the time. They never stopped saying cutting things to her, reproaching her for her past, accusing her of wearing out her husband, who is even more passionate than she is; and in public he says that having received his wife in bad shape he *never* sees her.

Now, it was two ladies whom that family knows—one is a cousin—who told that to a friend of ours, right out in the street, but Madame Clément assures me that, on the contrary, he's after his wife night and day! Since they got back to the chalet, not only have the insults and threats continued, but the poor little thing was actually *beaten* . . . a slap that left a mark, a kick and two slaps that left black-and-blue spots. I saw the imprint of the last one, though she's been threatened with death if she informs her family about anything whatever that concerns them! When she cries, he laughs at her and threatens her with blows. Yet she works for him constantly, she does all the mending, her own and the household linen. Madame Clément bears witness that Marthe does everything in the world to satisfy her husband, that she goes much too far to anticipate his fancies, and that she gets nothing but reproaches for it. The poor lady is extremely distressed about it—and Monsieur Robert is also trying to bring *her* to the end of her rope, by overwhelming her with work so that she won't be able to stand it any more and Marthe will be alone, completely at his mercy.

I recommended to Marthe that she do what she can to keep Madame Clément, for I won't pay for anyone else! Meanwhile, Monsieur Robert has had thirty liters of alcohol distilled from loquats for his personal use, and he's starting to drink brandy. That's all we needed! . . .

The moral situation is very sad, but think of the pecuniary one. When he got married he apparently was in debt for the four cows he had been keeping. Instead of paying for them with the profit from the milk, he stubbornly insisted, despite his parents' advice, on buying five more, very big ones, without making sure of a buyer for the milk, most of which had to be thrown away, since he would never use it to fatten pigs. In spite of the 1,250 francs a quarter, he borrowed 600 francs from a man to whom he already owed money. Wanting to have another 600 francs, he took to the pawnshop the 3,000-franc set of diamonds I had given Marthe. To make matters worse, his tastes for comfort and luxury continue to grow. Forty to 50 francs' worth of perfume doesn't seem to him too much for his person! He has just spent 50 or 60 francs on a set of special beer glasses. He has himself served like a sultan and does absolutely nothing himself. It won't be long before he allows himself the luxury of a mistress! Would you believe that he was shameless enough to boast to his wife and Madame Clément of having spent in Paris the 200 francs that Éléonore had given her sister as a wedding present—and that Marthe was silly enough to entrust him with buying something there for the house—with the Parisiennes, "whose a——s smell so good"! He contracted there a malady that his brother the medical student treated. That's what gave Marthe that irritation he kept carping about; you can see that in the long run everything comes to light, or at least many things are discovered, and I hadn't been wrong! Do you see now why he backed away before Dr. Barand's visit?

Thank God, Marthe's health is now good, though this doesn't keep grief from making her thin and pale.

He also boasted of making the scenes in front of me that you know about, with the intention of bringing on my death, and of sending his brother to ring the bell at our door during the night to worry us all, especially me, though he knew I was so ill.

Marthe urged me never to let him in the house, for he has nothing but homicidal intentions toward us. She herself feels so insecure about her life that she wanted to make her will, and implored me to ask you to hold a copy. I'll send it to you open; after you've read it, seal it. I gave her 100 francs so she could buy herself what her husband refuses her and Madame Clément, for he is in charge of all the household details and sometimes he's very miserly for others. I also insist that she must always have enough to pay for her trip home if she can't stand it there. I offered to take her back so that she would be safe, but she answered that she needs a husband too badly and that she loves him despite everything. She urged me not to give *him* money, because he would become insatiable. I again loaded her with household supplies and will send her two kilos of cooked ham because Monsieur Robert's elder brother is coming to spend Saturday and Sunday with them—father, mother, two children, and the maid make five persons. So you see that in spite of their wretched behavior, I'm not abandoning Marthe, whom adversity is bringing back to us.

Fondest greetings to your dear family from Éléonore and me, and all my warmest wishes to you. I'm glad to know you're in good company.

Your affectionate sister,

Émilie

Add this long letter to the dossier. I haven't the strength to copy it over.

ÉMILIE DE MONTBOURG
TO CHARLES DE CERILLEY
Grasse, August 20, 1896

Dear Charles,

I hasten to send you the will that Marthe asked me to pass along to you, for she has complete confidence in you and your son. Since her misfortune is known, there's no longer any reason not to tell Henri about it, and we hope he will sympathize by supporting Éléonore when she needs it. That scum Robert d'Aillot shouts the worst insults and bitterest reproaches at his wife even while their poor little maid is serving at the table or eating in the kitchen, right next to the dining room. He has no more decorum in front of the workmen he employs. Well, never mind, Marthe is so worthy, so kind to everyone, that people are sorry for her and have more esteem for her than for the rest of the family put together. Everybody tips his hat to greet her when she shows up in the village, so Madame d'Aillot has urged Monsieur Robert to let her go there as little as possible; but he doesn't keep her from going to Mass on Sunday, and the people of Mougins make a point of greeting no one in the family but Marthe.

Apropos of the tuberculosis he claims Éléonore has contracted: if she wanted to get married, that could do her a disservice, but since she doesn't want to, it seems to me it's better to say nothing about it right now. It's a weapon you must be sure to keep in your hands, but will he dare to get back into correspondence with you?

His conviction that I won't live long makes him dig himself deeper into the abyss of his debts without blinking an eye, surely thinking that after I'm gone he'll be able to force his wife to part with her fortune to pay them. Would you believe it? He complained to Madame Clément that Marthe *has no vices!* "If she was at least like other women," says he, "BUT SHE HAS NO VICES!!!" So what's his tactic? He's trying to demoralize her with his conversations and the reading he has her doing. With his threats, his reproaches, his accusations of all sorts, he's trying to destroy her reason, and by all these methods combined he'll destroy her health.

I told you he'd allow himself the luxury of a mistress. He has said to his wife, "I don't want to give you any children, but I'll give some to my mistress, and I'll bring them up with your money." And when the poor child, worn out by her moral suffering, said to him, "Then kill me right away, that would be better!," he replied, "No, *there are crueller methods.*" . . . And he forces his wife to write to everyone that she's happy! Is he atrocious, or isn't he?

Did I tell you that he has declared he will refuse to endorse the sale of Saint-Savin unless I promise in writing not to disinherit Marthe? Since I will not make that commitment, I'll stop trying so hard to sell it.

He also said he would oppose our keeping little Georges at our house, though he doesn't want to keep the boy at his. However, there is still time to reach a decision, and circumstances may change in the meantime.

Since the vegetable garden is ready to be planted and has been much appreciated, I'll send some cuttings to Mougins, and some more hens for the barnyard. Such things keep Marthe busy and divert her—and will also be useful for the household.

My fondest greetings, dear Charles.

Your very affectionate sister,

Émilie

MARTHE CARON D'AILLOT
TO ÉMILIE DE MONTBOURG
Chalet Marthe, October 15, 1896

Dear Mama mine,

I received this very moment the hamper, which gives me great pleasure, for I was almost out of Bayard wine and laxative, as I told you yesterday. By the way, don't send any kind of letter via your messenger: we must be cautious, for we two are risking nothing less than our heads. When Robert writes him, have Uncle Charles say he doesn't approve of Robert's taking the child into his house. We have to take so many precautions, I have to dissimulate a lot. I'll pretend to be keen about his idea of taking in the child. Since we must anticipate everything, suppose Robert, thinking I agree with him, writes Uncle Charles that I am in favor of taking Georges into our house. But you will know the contrary, so you'll be able to clear it up for Uncle Charles and explain my trick. I don't want to have Georges with us, because he's better off where he is, but I really do have to play tricks with Robert. Robert wants to place the child at his mother's so as to double her income. I don't want my son to be with that woman. However, I'm scared to death of Robert, and I don't have the courage to stand up to him, knowing very well that he wouldn't shrink from killing me if he knew I'd told you. So be careful: don't answer this letter, for your reply wouldn't reach me before he gets back, which, as I've already told you, is Saturday evening. Do answer my preceding letter, which you should receive today, with Georges's photograph. I'm sending you this letter anyway, but don't answer it, and be prudent, prudent, my dear mother, about anything and everything. You're the pearl of mothers. I'll tell Robert I've received a hamper and have thanked you for it, so there's no need for you to write me and mention I'm again asking for laxatine syrup since he knows you sent me some. I'll write and thank you for sending me the food for the dogs when Robert is back; that way everything will come out for the best.

I'm all yours, dear Mama, my fondest wishes to you and to Éléonore. Madame Clément thanks you with all her heart for all you do for her.

Marthe

My head's bursting from all this writing. I've had enough. Be careful —I'm terribly afraid of my husband.

ÉMILIE DE MONTBOURG
TO CHARLES DE CERILLEY
Grasse, October 16, 1896

Dear Charles,

I'm sending you the two letters that I received from Marthe yesterday evening, so you can judge the situation more accurately. What is clear to me is that Monsieur Robert has two aims: (1) to contribute to his mother's well-being by means of Georges's allowance, which he thinks he can continue to get me to pay by making me think he's at the chalet when he's at his mother's house; (2) to exasperate his wife, whom he will continue to revile by using the most dishonorable terms in front of the child, as he does in front of the servants and the workmen—even by maltreating the child as he did the little dog, his scapegoat, who had to be given away so as not to be killed. Maternal feelings won't be able to put up with that: Marthe will do something violent and they'll take advantage of it to make people think she is crazy. On the advice of his brother Louis, the perpetual medical student, he's already subjecting her to emotions that could cause serious problems, from what I've been told by competent people. The situation is getting tense, as you see, and it's important for us all to be agreed to defend the mother and child against these fierce wolves who have neither heart nor honor. God grant that Monsieur Robert writes you! It will no doubt be to ask you to get me to continue to pay Georges's allowance, on the pretext that he needs it to take Georges in. Neither in that case, nor in any other, would I consent to it.

I shuddered, my kind brother, to learn that a little rashness made you so sick, and I thank God for having saved you once more. But, for heaven's sake, look after your health—at our age life itself is endangered. You ought never to be left *alone,* since you can't resist giving in to your need for activity. Bear in mind that you're indispensable to those who love you, and particularly to us, for you are our only good defender in the circumstances we're in.

To go study mushrooms as a science would be a fine occupation for a naturalist in the country; but for you to study them by experimenting with them as food is a supreme rashness that I beg Madeleine to watch out for, and that I implore you not to commit. Saint François de Sales says not even the best mushroom is worth a thing, though in this region there are some that have a good reputation. But, then, aren't there enough decent vegetables that can be eaten without concern?

If you want a change, cultivate Vilmorin's novelties: some of them are really good, and your tired stomach will be happier with them than with the ever-suspect mushrooms.

Éléonore is better since she's been taking Bellac charcoal and inhaling ozone with the vaporizer.

But for the constant turmoil caused by the d'Aillots, we'd be returning to health, but there's always something new with them, and I think it's according to some atrocious design. My fondest wishes, dear Charles, to you and to Madeleine. Let me have your news in detail.

Your affectionate sister,

Émilie

Put Marthe's letters in the dossier.

ÉMILIE DE MONTBOURG
TO CHARLES DE CERILLEY
Grasse, October 30, 1896

Dear Charles,

I was unable to acknowledge earlier my receipt of the 800 francs you sent me with your letter of the 24th. A bout of intestinal illness caused me so bad an upset that, given my natural weakness as well, I've been left deaf, tottering, head spinning—or at any rate everything spinning around me —breaking out into a cold sweat after the slightest exertion. Some light bouillon gave me back a little strength, and I managed to get up yesterday.

Madame Clément, in acknowledging receipt of her month's pay, told me that Monsieur Robert's scheme is not for right away. Perhaps it was only a trial balloon, and Marthe's attitude has made him afraid to insist at this point, for he's a coward as well as mean. Perhaps he hopes that winter and illness will get the better of me? In short, right now there's a lull. But he never emphasizes the rights given him by law, for he will exercise them only for Marthe's and the child's unhappiness. You must understand that he never speaks about the boy without spitting in scorn, and always in the most disdainful terms. The sight of Georges would excite him still further; he would revile the mother even more, teach the child to insult her, and the village children to insult the child.

I'm expecting Marthe tomorrow evening. Her letter, which, without saying anything, shows traces of tears, is still worrying me. Alas! You can't understand the wickedness of her husband; you believe it only on solid proof. He's atrocious. I don't see how she can stick with a creature so unworthy of her respect. I suffered morally a great deal in the past to keep a home for my children, for that's what gave me courage; she doesn't have such a motive, since by a despicable plan he drives her to hyst[eria] without giving her feminine temperament the satisfaction of a pregnancy. How can she let herself be insulted, flouted, threatened, and even beaten without leaving, since her suffering is all for nothing?

This time Marthe is coming on the pretext of seeing the dressmaker who used to make her clothes before she was married. Her husband, who shamelessly takes her allowance away from her, thinks I'll be paying the bills, since the dressmaker is mine as well. But he's wrong: I'll send her to the notary through whom the quarterly payments are made. These payments are quite enough to feed the household, the barnyard, the dogs, pay the doctor and the pharmacies—expensive for these ladies—Georges's allowance, Madame Clément, all the trips to Grasse, and the pocket money. I shall not let myself be imposed on for Marthe's upkeep, which is included in the contract. Just think: to avoid taking anything away from their 5,900 francs, I'm putting on my account the taxes and all the expenses for Saint-Savin. You can see how they're taking advantage, and I'll stand fast on the dressmaker.

My very fondest wishes.

Your affectionate sister,

Émilie

You understand how painful these sad anniversary days are for me. Did you get the hamper?

MARTHE CARON D'AILLOT
TO CHARLES DE CERILLEY
Grasse, November 4, 1896

Dear good Uncle,

I'm taking advantage of being at Mama's, and not having my husband's will weighing on my own, to inform you that, in case my husband forces me to write you that I insist on having Georges at home with me, I wish to *declare to you that I do not want to have the child in my house* because of all the drawbacks and troubles that would result for him and for me. Keep this letter a secret, for I am risking my neck. If Robert knew of this letter and the others you have in your possession, it would not be beneath him to maltreat us, Madame Clément and me.

I'd rather, dear uncle, that you burn my last two letters: they are full of incorrect expressions, but I was so angry I couldn't restrain myself. Whatever trials the future holds in store for me, rest assured that I'll always remain worthy of your respect and the family's.

Don't answer my letter. I'm heading back for Mougins, so, dear uncle, you must not correspond with me, for my husband turns upside down and inside out the letters Mama writes me, and scrutinizes every word to find something he can use to his advantage, either against me or against Mama.

Entirely yours, your very devoted niece,

Marthe

P.S. If you wish to write me, I'd be glad to have news of you and also of my aunt, but don't ever speak to me in your letters about the child or anything pertaining to him: you'd get me beaten to a pulp, dear uncle. Keep it in mind. I make the same recommendations to my aunt.

[Note by Charles]:
Proof of the husband's terrorism over his wife.

HENRI DE CERILLEY
TO ÉMILIE DE MONTBOURG
Lyon, December 27, 1896

My very dear Aunt and Godmother,
Adèle joins me in sending you, and also Éléonore and Marthe, our most fervent wishes that 1897 may bring you, first, good health, and a period of consolation after all the griefs you have been through and with which we sympathize with all our hearts. Papa has told you how we came to be informed of your maternal trials. I would have wished to talk to you about them at greater length had it not been for my feeling of discretion, and also for distance and, lastly, a sense of prudence regarding correspondence, which lends itself to confidences only up to a certain limit. Be that as it may, we are linked by the tenderest bonds of affection, and you three,

as my cousins, can count on my devotion in the fullest sense of the term. I have too much of the professional habit of reliving the past for my heart to forget your beautiful familial devotion—if, indeed, I needed to be reminded of how kind you have been to me and of how tradition has piously preserved your role as replacement for Grandmother de Cerilley.

As for us, we have our bitterness, too. My mother-in-law's will disinherits Adèle with the full rigor of the law, and the ineluctable conclusion will be that my wife will be obliged to return a considerable part of the dowry of which she has received only four-fifths, although seven years ago I got married on the assurance of a letter from the deceased promising that 300,000 francs would eventually come. The entire fortune remained with my mother-in-law.

Our two babies couldn't be in better health, but Adèle has for some time had a bronchial susceptibility that gives rise to concern and meticulous precautions—without, however, being distressing, according to the doctor, who checks her breathing frequently.

As for me, I'm in very satisfactory health.

Your superb carton of mandarines is the delight of great and small, who thank you with all their hearts and send their fondest greetings to you and the cousins.

Your affectionate godson,

Henri

1897

MARTHE CARON D'AILLOT
TO MADELEINE DE CERILLEY
Chalet Marthe, January 6, 1897

Dear Aunt and Godmother,
I'm quite late in sending you my New Year's wishes. Believe me, though, for all that, that they are nonetheless sincere and affectionate. Robert adds his for you and our good uncle, to whom I also send mine.

I hope, dear aunt, that you're all well again. I wish our Uncle Charles would completely give up the tough jobs that tire him so: they'll do him in unless he drops them.

We are now settled in our chalet, and I'm doing my best to run my home, which I'm very fond of, taking immense pleasure in the duties of mistress of the house. Since Robert's affection succeeded in taming your willful Marthe, I've started to do as others do and look after my house. For the rest, dear aunt, I don't at all want to sing my praises, for I'm terribly far from deserving the compliment of being called a good homemaker, not having your talents and your experience in everything.

Please give everyone around you, dear aunt, our most affectionate wishes for happiness, and keep for yourself the fondest of all.

Your very devoted niece and goddaughter,

Marthe

[Note by Charles:]
Keep. Letter written under her husband's influence.

Dear Charles,

I did indeed receive the 600 and 1,200 francs you sent me. The farmers, without knowing it, did me a special favor, for I recently had to send Marthe 2,000 francs to spare her and her husband the unpleasantness of having their possessions seized. They had already received second notices on some bills, and the creditors wouldn't wait any longer.

Monsieur Robert has sent the list of sums paid on the construction of the chalet, and those of the suppliers and workmen, which have to be paid right away. I called in the notary, who drew a new agreement in the amount of 10,000 francs. In this document, Monsieur Robert acknowledges that he has already used 8,000 francs (of the 16,000 he has received) for this construction and that, should the marriage be dissolved, he would owe his wife 10,000 francs, which has been used for the construction. He had expressed all his gratitude for my help, and wishes the past did not exist, but I'm in no hurry to see him again, for he is in cahoots with his family to try something new with Georges, which would just lead to a new rupture, for I shall not yield.

He, for his part, acts sweet to his wife and speaks of the child in touching terms, wanting to have him with them, etc. His mother threw herself at Marthe's knees, begging her pardon for treating her severely. They even had Simone, her sister-in-law's child, clasp her hands before Marthe as if before the Holy Virgin! . . . It's nauseatingly squalid! And all this to cajole Marthe, and consequently us, so that we would hand over the unhappy little fellow, whom they cursed and loathed so! But they hope first of all that I'll continue the allowance, and then that the sale of Saint-Savin will bring in a capital worth coveting.

I'm beside myself with indignation, and I'm ill from it, my brother, for I think they're capable of every kind of low trick, and Marthe of every possible weakness.

As for being taken in by their marionette shows, nay! And as for the capital provided by the sale of Saint-Savin, Marthe's share will come in the form of French-government annuities—this is determined by the contract—and I'll have the rest in my hands, reflecting the share I possess. For the moment the d'Aillots won't be able to cash in any of it, but the idea of money affects them as fresh meat affects wolves!

Marthe is proud and happy over the drawing-room furniture. Right now I'm also having a coffeepot in britannia metal sent her for when she entertains her husband's family, and I'm embroidering her a workbag with the family coat of arms. You see I'm doing everything possible to set her up properly in her household and in society. Unfortunately, her husband and his family have done her much damage. Oh, my dear, how many usurped reputations there are in the world!

I send fond wishes, with anguish in my heart, but also tenderness.

Émilie

CHARLES DE CERILLEY
TO ÉLÉONORE DE MONTBOURG
Sangy, January 20, 1897

Dear Éléonore,

I received this morning the letter from your mother enclosing Marthe's, useful for the dossier, and yours, which I fully approve. Yes, it's very important for little Georges not to go to Mougins for a long time. This is something to impress on your brother-in-law by emphasizing *moral* considerations, as well as social. Bear in mind that he has his rights, against which we cannot move without putting ourselves in the wrong. This is a trump card we must not put in his hand. Henri agrees on this; several times he and I have discussed with wisdom, prudence, and firmness the policy to be pursued. The extra sum of 20,000 francs for your sister to be taken out of the available amount would not be known to your brother-in-law until the opening of your mother's will. If he refuses the condition, they're deprived of it and you are armed for all the rest. It would be insane of him to refuse. Until your mother dies, they'll be dominated by the *As you do, so I shall do, and so you will receive.* I marvel at his demand to know what is coming up from now on. If he dealt with me on this subject, I would have plenty of reasons with which to oppose him.

I cherish the hope of visiting you toward the end of January, after I spend a few days in Lyon. I'll stay at least a week, at whatever hotel you say, for I don't know the city and I want to be as near you as possible. Barring health problems, you may count on me. It will also be very useful for conferring—I certainly don't expect Monsieur Robert to give in at the first shot. *As you do, so you will receive* is a powerful formula—a formula to conjure with. It's just as strong as the force of inertia when handled well. Being strong is not allowing a hold on oneself.

You understand the usefulness of a codicil in your mother's will for this 20,000-franc favor, *on condition* that the *entire* direction of little

Georges will be left to you until *he is of age*—you can't go beyond that, for it would be against the law.

You don't seem to welcome this idea of an added bequest, with conditions, yet it is wise policy, which I have discussed thoroughly with your cousin Henri, an intelligent and careful man.

Yes, your mother is right in saying we must not stress the idea I first suggested to Monsieur Robert, that little Georges was a product of a youthful folly on his part, which would take away from you any reason to concern yourself with him. This idea is just, but since we must base ourselves on logical reasoning if we do not wish to appear to be acting out of tyrannical caprice, I think we should stick with *financial* and *social* considerations. This term is vague, I know, but I have masses of reasons that I can formulate—each one stiffer than the last—but only *in extremis.* One example: Monsieur Robert cannot love this child—he has expressed this to his aunt, not to me; consequently no devotion at all, the more so because they are *very needy.* Marthe's avowals reinforce this argument frighteningly.

I'll be responsible for reducing him to *reasonable* silence. As for southern follies, if they come up, I'll say to him: If we are to reason, we need calm; otherwise I'll remove restraints on my tongue.

Good-bye, dear Éléonore; my fondest wishes to you and to your mother.

Your affectionate uncle,

Charles de Cerilley

ÉMILIE DE MONTBOURG
TO CHARLES DE CERILLEY
Grasse, February 13, 1897

Dear Charles,

Léon's death caused me sharp grief. Our brother caused himself much pain with his imagination, but his children caused him terribly much more—tearing his house away from him in his lifetime, at the very moment when, having at last managed to acquire a line of work that was right for him, he could have rediscovered a little peace of mind thanks to the success of his vines. The grip of miserable poverty on a permanent basis, what a painful feeling, especially when one isn't used to it!

Madame Clément's albumen problem is better, but her stomach still cannot digest anything except milk. Now Marthe is starting to be very hard on her: after refusing to let her come, she's going to send her to me. Oh, dear Charles, you tell me to mistrust a lull and fear a new bit of blackmail! There's all too much to tell you on that score, but I was waiting till you returned to Sangy.

So let me tell you that no matter how much I've given, Marthe has recently been asking continually for more. Instead of paying all their debts, they've started acquiring more, chasing around all over; they even rented a room in Nice to go see a show in the evening, stabling their horses for the night at the hotel—and paying, of course! Marthe told me that they were paying cash for everything, *which is not true!* Nor did they get the diamonds out of the pawnshop, though she assured me they had. So it's no use my skimping to help them, for they both lack the sense to stay within the limits of their wealth. Why feed two horses, if they've been obliged this year to buy 300 francs' worth of fodder? Why wear out your clothes by being incessantly on the road in an open carriage? Why constantly employ men when you're thirty-five years old and before your marriage you knew how to handle tools? Now, from his easy chair, smoking, Milord watches the gardener work for hours on end. Marthe does not allow me to comment on this, and she's constantly begging. Well, I got angry, and after threatening her many times, I told her that I would send no more supplies and that they'd better base their budget on that. You can imagine the furor, for Madame d'Aillot knew very well how to profit by contributions, too! But I'm determined to maintain this resolve: they're taking advantage of my kindness and straining their ingenuity to tell me a lot of nonsense.

Here's something that will amuse you: one evening when there was a high wind, I get a letter from Marthe saying that she was very worried about the nasty cold her husband had caught and begging me to send her some medicine *right away.* Now, since the maid had a bad cold herself, and there was no mail pickup later in the evening, I waited until the next morning. The pharmacy student took the remedies to the post office on his way to go eat at the hotel right across the street. He was more than a little astonished to find Monsieur Robert at table there—he had come on his bicycle! . . .

That evening, the notary came and told me that my son-in-law had come to his office to familiarize himself with the document of apportionment and settlement among my children. I asked him if Monsieur Robert had a bad cold. "Why, no," said he, "he didn't cough once." — "But is he hoarse? Is his head congested?"—"Not at all, madame; he's in perfect health."

So what was Marthe's intention? If I had refused the errand, neither she nor they would have failed to scream that I am hateful and pitiless; I had the remedies sent, but the pharmacist put them on their account, which seems fair to me. Also, the minute I saw her, I told Marthe she had only half fooled me: she would pay for her lie. I cited to her the two men who had *seen* her husband without a cold.

They also tried to make me believe Madame Clément had an incurable illness, so as to make me pay for a replacement. But I answered that after Madame Clément they'd better not count on my paying for a servant for them.

Finally, Marthe came the other day to talk clothes with me apropos of a wedding she is to go to, that of a first cousin of Monsieur Robert's. The occasion would also involve a meal after the wedding. They had just received their quarterly payment and were better off than I, so I turned a deaf ear. Then she treated me to a scene of high sentiment with regard to Georges, saying she can't go on without him, that she absolutely must have him, that her husband wants him, etc. I answered that my resolutions on that subject would not change, and that if they take him back it's forever and at their own expense. She cried, stormed a bit, and calmed herself very quickly when Éléonore, who returned from some errands and was informed of the attempt, replied with great calm, "Well, that will mean a lot of savings, but for us! You won't get anything more out of it."

Good-bye, dear Charles; my very fondest wishes to you and to Madeleine, who must be very happy to have you back.

Your sister,

Émilie

ÉMILIE DE MONTBOURG
TO CHARLES DE CERILLEY
Grasse, February 24, 1897

Dear Charles,

Madame Clément arrived with a woman from Mougins, but without a word from Marthe. The doctor in Grasse found no trace of albumen in her urine, which he brought to a boil in our presence, in an iron spoon over a lighted lamp. He was sorry that the doctor from Antibes hadn't done the same at Mougins. That's saying a lot in a few words! Not finding any of the maladies dreamed up by his colleague, he advised getting back little by little to a normal regime. He also advised a hygienic girdle to hold up her stomach, which is very stout (like her mother's and her sister's).

He says that the mere weight of this part of the body disturbs the digestion by pulling on the organs and can bring on ailments of the digestive tract.

Everything I'm learning proves to me that it's past time for me to stop being bountiful, and that I'd be wrong to go on depriving myself of so many things for the sake of people who take advantage.

The chalet is becoming a banquet house, what with all the supplies I'm sending. When they don't eat there, they go eat elsewhere—also drink, Marthe as much as the gentlemen. To complete the picture, she smokes. Both things are strictly forbidden for her. Madame Clément and I can neither criticize nor advise, for the husband approves whatever harms his wife.

They rented a room in Nice to go to the casino and the shows. Monsieur Robert even had Marthe play roulette; since she won 8 francs, she'd like to begin again, and she'll get taste for it! In short, all they think about is good foods, clothes, pleasure, and deceptive ways to drag money out of me to amuse themselves and also to supply the family. So I'm determined to withdraw my help; they've got to arrive at what's reasonable for their position and make their property yield something to live on. My resolve to leave Grasse is quite firm; since I don't want them to learn about it until we're settled in somewhere else, please don't say anything about this. This way I'll have a little peace around us, for she won't come treat me to scenes of emotion and sessions of lies any more. Éléonore, too, needs calm for her health.

I'll keep Madame Clément here until they ask to have her back, and I will not let her go without making conditions, because of her health.

I've just had a lot of pain because of a piece of bread no bigger than a little walnut. You see where I still am.

Your affectionate sister,

Émilie

ÉMILIE DE MONTBOURG
TO CHARLES DE CERILLEY
Grasse, March 23, 1897

Dear Charles,

Here we are very busy over the health of Madame Clément, whose distended stomach worries us very much. Since he arrived, the doctor has been trying to find out what could bring about such a state. Either the Mougins doctor has been badly mistaken three times, or he has tried to claim great merit for saving her from illnesses she did not have. The cause of this dropsy remained unknown until a few days ago, when sharp pains in the liver and vomiting of green bile revealed the trouble to be in the liver. A powerful purge with calomel relieved her yesterday, she is better able to digest milk, her abdomen has shrunk a good deal, but the left leg and thigh are painfully swollen. I'm waiting for the doctor to figure out what to do. I'm suffering from fatigue, which has made the sciatica I had been suffering from lately go to my chest. So now I'm down with bronchitis again and incapable of taking care of Madame Clément. I've taken on a nurse to tend her. That dear lady accepts as her due all the cares and expenses she imposes on me, and would scream "robbery" if I didn't pay her the salary that in point of fact she's not earning.

From Mougins they're writing her letters that are more or less warm, depending on whether her health is better or worse, for they would have wanted her, before she left, to give all her furniture to the chalet—they were even displeased that she took along her keys, because they won't be able to snoop around, as they had no hesitation about doing in her absence, with Monsieur Robert the first to do so. While she was sick there, they were trying to extract her money from her on the pretext of small loans! . . . All that is ignoble, and unfortunately poor Marthe lets herself be dominated by the harpies that surround her! . . . Since Marthe wrote impertinent things to me, and her husband has allowed himself some new vituperations directed at me, I haven't been writing to Marthe any more, and will do so only when she has apologized. But I've twice sent her a laxative syrup that she is using to advantage for her health, plus some plants from our garden for hers at the chalet. You see that I'm not utterly unbending, and that she might at least write me her thanks! . . . But in that world of theirs people appreciate nothing but money and things to eat, so the rest doesn't count. I will do my best to patch up Madame Clément sufficiently for her to resume active service, but I will not replace her.

My very fondest greetings, dear Charles.

Your affectionate sister,

Émilie

ROBERT CARON D'AILLOT
TO CHARLES DE CERILLEY
Chalet Marthe, April 3, 1897

Dear Uncle,

You will receive under separate cover photographs of us and also of the chalet. I'm happy to be able to send them to you, for it gives me an occasion to write you. I'm really lazy when it comes to letters, I admit it, although corresponding with relatives is very pleasant. I think of you nonetheless, dear uncle, from time to time, especially of the kind welcome I received from you when I stopped at your house; the memory of it has remained engraved on my heart and will never be effaced. So I beg your pardon for not writing more often; the reason for my silence must be ascribed to the factors already mentioned and not to indifference. Our life is calm and monotonous as ever; diversions and amusements are not abundant far from the hubbub of the cities, so one day's life is much like the whole year's. As for news, I can announce to you with happiness the fortunate change in Marthe. Molded and reshaped by my care, she keeps very busy and does her best to think of everything, especially since Madame Clément has been away (you must know of her illness and departure for Grasse). The feelings that seemed extinguished in my wife have been rekindled, and that contributes to make her sensible and serious. Today, my dear uncle, the former Marthe—the one who led such a stormy and disorderly life—no longer exists, and in her place I have a pretty little wife, sweet, amiable, charming, who has added to her moral beauty a pretty physique. I'm proud of her, and it's with love that I regard and contemplate my handiwork and rejoice in announcing it to all her family. My happiness, dear uncle, would be complete if things could go well with Grasse. On that subject, alas, I cannot speak with enthusiasm, for they will not recognize that I love my wife, and they never speak of me to anyone without hatred and scorn, calling me a tyrant and a play-actor when necessary. All that is very sad, I admit; it's the ugly other side of the coin for me, especially since I don't think I've deserved such treatment. I'll be so happy when I can live in good understanding without being subjected to the perpetual crises which always occur, whether about boots or something else. I very much look forward to seeing you and having a chat with you: some things are too long and hard for one to put down on paper, and, unfortunately for us, the distance is too great, for I'm convinced that you'd succeed in bringing peace into this house and would finally make it understood that I don't deserve the severity I'm treated with and the harsh words about me they let fly to Marthe from time to time. I keep hoping that time, the great master, will remedy all this, and that, I assure you, is my sole and only desire, just as making my wife what I've made of her was my sole aim and my only hope.

I leave you, dear uncle, with fond regards,

Robert Caron d'Aillot

ÉMILIE DE MONTBOURG
TO CHARLES DE CERILLEY
Grasse, April 12, 1897

Dear Charles,

Thank you for having sent to me the d'Aillot letters. I've made Madame Clément the judge of them, for she has lived with those people enough to judge the veracity of the husband. The fact is that Marthe dresses and does her hair to her husband's taste, that she's acquired, in company and everywhere, an aplomb that goes beyond the measure of good taste, and that for those around her *(when she does not fear them)* she has become quite difficult.

She no longer has the heart of a mother, a daughter, or a sister; everything goes to coquetry and animal passion. If she has gained on the physical side, she owes that to her age and to the Creator of all things; the husband has no reason to glory in it. For my part, I'll never be grateful to him for making her lose the good she still had in her, to replace it with affectations that have no substance and rest on nothing solid; let an accident or an illness keep the husband from satisfying the overstimulated needs of the wife, and there will again be reason to fear everything for her!

I fear that the poor child is preparing great moral and physical troubles for herself, and other griefs for us. So I'm pleased with myself for having resolved to leave Grasse. As soon as the season and my health allow it, we'll look for a place to live.

Madame Clément's condition is still disturbing. The doctor was telling me yesterday that we should take advantage of the progress she has made to send her to her family, because later that will no longer be possible.

He doesn't think the cirrhosis is absolutely established, but he has noted a serious stomach and liver condition and an acid dropsy that comes and goes but seems quite intractable. By lancing it they can prolong life when the swelling threatens to stifle it, but the two doctors don't believe a cure is possible. It's hardly encouraging, and the cousin has not yet replied. The doctor from here, who knows about our health, would like to see her with her family. Tomorrow will make a week since Madame Clément's letter went off!

I'm glad to know you're with your children, my good brother. Do share our warmest wishes with them.

Your very affectionate sister,

Émilie

Dear Madame,

I would have answered you Sunday, but, having learned that everybody was going to Antibes today, I preferred to wait until today when I can chat freely. Marthe is in a good mood; she knows I'm writing you but did not give me a letter for you because she has a bad headache and needs calm—she is certainly attached to you and loves you both. Your leaving grieves her very much. In her mind you were near, and if one day she were to need you, that seemed easier to her. Let's hope we won't come to that, but she loves him less and is seeing things more clearly. Will that last? I don't know. He doesn't do anything extraordinary; it's still the same thing. When the family has gone, we'll be more peaceful, for he submits to the influence of his mother, who is not at all amiable.

Marthe is keeping nicely busy in her household. She has much to do —three lovely broods of hens to look after, then her cooking, which she does well. She's so happy to have me back, she calls me her Mama Clément and she must have regretted my leaving, for she often used to say, "If ever she comes back, I'll spare her; if I'd helped her a little, she'd have been less tired." Her husband, for his part, said to me, "Since she's known you were coming back, she's been happy. We missed you." Then why didn't they write that? It would have pleased us. I'm following my diet well. I haven't thrown up since I arrived, and every other day I put down a pot-au-feu, with a half-kilo of beef.

It's a very good thing I came back. Marthe is so happy. We both work, and Monsieur Robert is quiet, he comes and goes. She's not so sad any more; apparently she was very bored. Dear madame, don't worry: she won't do anything stupid, for she's very calm and is turning back to her own people. I think this will last, especially since she no longer has that fervor that kept her from seeing clearly.

My most affectionate greetings, dear madame, and all my best to Mademoiselle Éléonore.

Your wholly devoted,

Madame Clément

ÉMILIE DE MONTBOURG
TO CHARLES DE CERILLEY
Grasse, May 22, 1897

Dear Charles,

To answer your letter of the 16th, I was waiting for more detailed news of Madame Clément's return to Mougins. These days Monsieur Robert inspires such great fear by checking on letters that she waited until the whole family went to dinner at their cousins', and even then she addressed her letter to our pharmacist in Grasse, who had it passed on to me. Do you see how the gentleman sees to it that people are uncivil toward me? He concerns himself with making me suffer worries and impolite behavior, being unable to do anything else for the moment.

Marthe has no thought of trying to get money out of us, and her ideas of suicide, which often haunt her because her husband's absolute tyranny exasperates her, are unfortunately very serious. She hasn't the courage to make herself independent, and Madame Clément is so afraid of not keeping her position that she overdoes her services for the tyrant. So she is only a comrade in captivity, when she might do better. I've certainly tried to make her understand, but she's very much her own person! All the same, her presence is a help for Marthe, who was bemoaning her absence without daring to say so, for she is forbidden to be grateful to me for anything at all. She's happy to have that meager help, and will make use of her more sparingly so as not to wear her out.

It's Montpellier we're thinking of going to, choosing a pleasantly situated quarter. In a large town there are more resources of all sorts, and Éléonore will have more diversions; then there are good doctors, and we'll be far enough off so that Monsieur Robert's bicycle won't give us any frights. Marthe will even be able to escape him more easily via the main line of the railroad, if he makes her too unhappy. I'll give Madame Clément 100 francs in reserve against that eventuality.

My very fondest wishes, my kind brother.

Your affectionate sister,

Émilie

ÉMILIE DE MONTBOURG
TO CHARLES DE CERILLEY
Montpellier, June 21, 1897

Dear Charles,

We've been here a week, but the trip was so hard on my bowels that after spending a morning searching for an apartment, I had to get to bed. Diarrhea with bloody mucus and gastritis required that we send for the doctor, who was not able to come until the attack was over. He found me very weak and prescribed packs of glycerophosphate with bicarbonate of soda, milk to drink, and rice, for the gastritis comes back. You see how delicate I've become. Éléonore, while walking in town, slipped on something sticky and, in moving suddenly to keep from falling, must have sprained some muscle in her back, for it's been hurting ever since; she contents herself with putting oil on the painful spot and won't let anyone touch it.

Here we are in the ladies' pension run by Franciscan nuns. They have given us four rooms and a toilet, with food and service, for 15 francs apiece, which is to say 30 francs for the two of us; heat, light, and laundry are extra. I'll be allowed to have Georges here until he is old enough to put in boarding school to prepare for his first communion. In the house there's a lady with two little boys who go to school every day. But I want another room available for Marthe, in case she should come to see me or be too unhappy in her new family. I need this room, in any case, to store excess furniture.

The mother superior is very nice, and the girls who serve us are polite, gentle, and obliging. Here we'll be at peace. Being served in our rooms, we remain independent of all gossip and scandal, and we won't have to fear Monsieur Robert's breaking in or carrying on to win over our servants. Éléonore was in a constant state of suspicion and fear of everything in Grasse. Here she will relax from her worry and care, and this tranquillity will make her accept the cloistered calm of the house. She will do the errands, and that will give her exercise. The botanical garden is close by; it's lovely, they say, and people take their needlework there as they do at the Jardins du Luxembourg in Paris. It will become our walk.

We're going to catch our breath, here, from this first trip before starting to pack in Grasse. The apartment won't be free until August, and our lease in Grasse doesn't end until September 29, which gives us time.

If you don't answer immediately, wait until we're back in Grasse.

Your affectionate sister,

Émilie

Please put the enclosed letter in the mail, since I don't want people to know our new address yet. Don't tell Marthe anything: her husband wants only to annoy us to make us ill.

ÉMILIE DE MONTBOURG
TO CHARLES DE CERILLEY
Grasse, July 6, 1897

Dear Charles,

Marthe came and surprised us yesterday morning, crying poverty as always, and *not having had enough to pay for the bus trip from the station, so they gave her credit until evening!* . . . That's the way my son-in-law behaves! And *he* had come on his bicycle and had a good dinner at the hotel! I gave Marthe 40 francs so she could wait until her quarterly payment; but I'm quite sure he won't have left her anything. My daughter provides for everything, for all he does is morally isolate her more and more. I found her paler and thinner. She's quite changed since her photograph was taken. Now, you know how he glorified himself, how he sent that photograph to the entire family? Why such a rapid change? I'm worried. Marthe has no energy left: her fear of her husband's anger and blows paralyzes her.

She warned me that if we take little Georges in with us, we'll bring on ourselves scenes of violence from her husband. I told her that this question had to be resolved soon, because if her husband continues his systematic opposition, I'll stop sending anything to the wet nurse. She's hoping that this woman will keep Georges for free until they gain from my death—which they hope will be soon (I'm speaking of Monsieur Robert)—the means to pay her. Or else they'll have the child brought back by the nurse and will keep him (if Madame d'Aillot is willing). Until they can send him to secondary school as a boarder, he'll go to school in the village of Mougins. Now, this milieu of peasants, then that of the chalet, where husband and wife compete in swearing and lie to match, the example of all these mockers of old age and of priests—all that does not constitute a desirable moral atmosphere for a child. Madame Clément has suffered greatly from their manners and conversations, worse than trivial, which shocked her ears and eyes, and yet she wasn't born yesterday! Her mother tended cows and her husband was a building contractor who had started with plastering and housepainting. You see that circumstances reinforce my motive for not contributing toward a *bad* education.

My very fond wishes, dear Charles.

Your affectionate sister,

Émilie

ÉMILIE DE MONTBOURG
TO HENRI DE CERILLEY
Grasse, July 7, 1897

Dear Henri,

Since Madame d'Aillot, by her breaches of confidence, has let you know about our misfortunes and you have assured me of your sympathetic support, I'm going to appeal to that in all confidence, for I take you to be a trustworthy gentleman.

You must be aware that the person who helped arrange for the marriage introduced the situation with the express stipulation of acknowledgment of the child and inviolable secrecy about all this, even toward the family. Monsieur Robert gave his word—I have the declaration of it in writing. You know how he kept that word? I've paid his debts so he could redeem his good name, and given money for building their chalet. Well! He refuses to do anything about redeeming his good name; I've had a very hard time getting him to finish the chalet and so obtain the independence of the household. You see what concessions have been made to him. A few days after the marriage, and while I was very ill, he came and treated me to murderous scenes in the course of which he reproached me violently for having demanded that he acknowledge the child, saying that I had thus shattered his career. He displayed his hatred for this poor little creature, who after all is not responsible. (There's a whole dossier on this squalid undertaking in your father's hands.)

Now, in a few months we absolutely must take this child, who is four and a half years old, from his nurse. To end up with a career you have to start in time. Monsieur d'Aillot has changed his tactics. He doesn't want to let me take the child, who will still need a mother's care during the few years before he becomes a boarder in secondary school. We'd like to send him to a nursery school where there are well-brought-up children. Madame d'Aillot will have no other resource than the village school, where the child will learn bad things rather than good; and since, thanks to the bounties Monsieur d'Aillot confers on his family, he is always in poverty, where will he get the means to clothe this child and get him an education, this child whom he is counting on making a victim of blackmail against us? You may well believe that we won't let him put this over on us, I assure you. On the other hand, poor Marthe, already so humiliated, so morally isolated by her husband and his family, understands very well that she'll be made to suffer even more in front of the child, and for him and even through him, so she doesn't want his presence, all the more because, already tempted several times to do away with herself, she's afraid she won't be able to endure an added load of grief. Her husband has told her that if we took back the child, he would come renew the scenes of violence, which would be terrible this time. She has entreated me not to bring them down on us; she herself is so afraid of being beaten or roughed up that she has no will or energy left and couldn't defend a soul any more. I would like a solution within three months, for after I am gone—and my frail existence is hanging by a thread—Éléonore will bear the burden as the survivor, and that assurance will give her a purpose for her life. It would mean for the two of us a certain peace of mind regarding my two daughters. Éléonore will strive to temporize further by having him given lessons in reading and writing at the nurse's. What do you think?

If you are agreed, I'll ask you, my dear nephew, to stiffen your father's resolve for a vigorous declaration; for in all this, I have not always been fully satisfied with his attitude. He has often blamed me because I, being at closer range, saw faster and truer than he. Monsieur d'Aillot flatters him, and he lets himself be taken in too much by the acts put on for him. The situation is serious! Don't tell your father I'm appealing to you: he's jealous of the supremacy due him by virtue of his age and his status as head of the family. We must spare his susceptibilities, but you yourself might turn the conversation to this subject and give your opinion squarely as having sprung from common sense: "Since my aunt is going to leave Grasse, why shouldn't she take this child with her to start his education?" Don't get me in trouble with your father, who would not forgive me if he knew I was appealing to your youthful energy. I confess to you that I would not have done so, fearing to compromise us all with him, but Éléonore has so much confidence in your tact and your prudence that I think I'm doing well to yield to her urging.

My fond wishes to you, dear Henri, and also to your wife and children.

Your affectionate aunt,

Émilie

MADAME CLÉMENT
TO ÉMILIE DE MONTBOURG
Antibes, July 7, 1897

Dear kind Madame,

I'm very grateful to you for your letter, the candies, which came in very handy, and your thoughtfulness in sending me my month's pay in advance. If I had known, I would not have appealed to Monsieur Robert.

I still had 70 francs, though I needed 80; but if Marthe had been willing to enlighten you, she could have told you that her husband, the day I left Mougins, had asked me to advance him 50 francs, since he had some debts to pay and had no money in his pocket! He's always that way! Since he sold some hay, I figured he'd pay it back to me in the course of the month. He had some nerve!

But I'm going to pinch him, I promise you, if he doesn't pay me back by July 18. That's too much. *About this whole letter not a word to Marthe, please.* She forbids me to tell you that he left for a week in Marseille yesterday; but I told Madame Martin, not knowing that she'd keep it from you; we'd have taken advantage of this occasion to write each other and enjoy a bit of freedom. Marthe comes to see me every other day, and a while ago I had to get angry; she wanted to leave at night, on foot, for Grasse, and come back the next morning, as if her health permitted anything like that! And she'd get in trouble with him if he found out. As for the little one, Monsieur d'Aillot is going to write the family to get their opinion. They all ought to advise him to leave the child to you; get ready for that. Otherwise he's stubborn. Yesterday he was all keyed up: he doesn't want to have an enemy later on; he wants to bring him up in his own way of thinking. Yes, teach him to despise his mother! It's inevitable, poor little fellow—he'll hear it said and he'll believe it! It's sad! What a calamity that Marthe, so intelligent and keen, has let herself be dominated to the point of not having 10 centimes in her pocket to check a package. That did grieve me. I could never have let myself be abused to that point, and he has no business leaving her without any money that way. It's terrible! Marthe is not happy and never will be. She won't leave him and she tells him everything. Unfortunately, *he* takes advantage of her weakness and leads her around like a dog! Don't you see, it's dreadful that she's so afraid! One can say it, but there's nothing to be done. Please, not a word of all this—you wouldn't want to make trouble for me. He certainly takes advantage of being alone with her to make her more afraid. How I'd like to be well again, to be back with her. The poor little thing, I scolded her good and proper for her weakness. Alas! Where is the energy she had as a girl? And must a person stoop so low for a man!

I needed to unburden myself a bit with you, but I'm paining you, though you like to know. Don't let her suspect what I'm telling you, I urge you once again. Be very careful when you see her not to make a mistake.

Dear madame, good-bye. My health is not too bad. I'm very tired of everything that's going on. My poor head can't take any more. My fondest wishes, with all my heart.

Devotedly yours,

Madame Clément

ÉMILIE DE MONTBOURG
TO CHARLES DE CERILLEY
Grasse, July 9, 1897

Dear Charles,

Since you often accuse me of exaggerating in my assessments, I'm sending you Madame Clément's letter.

You see that the presence of the child at Mougins would present a frightful increase in troubles for Marthe! It's infamous to make a daughter disdain her mother! You see from Madame Clément's letter that Monsieur Robert steeps his wife in insulting words, since she says, "The poor little thing would hear and believe." Marthe's getting pale and thin, she has no more energy; I'm seriously worried about her. She'll die of consumption if she doesn't destroy herself, for she feels her dismal situation, and has only one feeling left: *fear!* Yes, the fear of being beaten, even killed, by that wicked man, who treats her like a *dog,* Madame Clément says! Who keeps her from complaining to her family by threatening her, and who writes sweet words to you aunts and uncles! He forces his wife to write that she's happy, when it's just the opposite! Therefore you must come to an understanding with Sophie, so both of you may make her understand that the child's place is *with us* who are willing to take charge of him, that for them it's all a matter of advantage, and that if he wants Georges to be kind to him later on, he must give us reason to judge him favorably, whereas ever since his marriage he has done the opposite of what he should have done, even in his own interest. But don't allude to the poverty to which he subjects Marthe so as not to refuse anything to himself; she would pay dear for that! What is unfortunate is that she is *giving* him everything, or that she lets him take it to have peace!

I leave you, dear Charles, weary and unhappy to see that Marthe is weakening to the point of abdicating all dignity.

Your affectionate sister,

Émilie

ÉMILIE DE MONTBOURG
TO CHARLES DE CERILLEY
Grasse, July 11, 1897

Dear Charles,

Did you get my letter enclosing Madame Clément's? Yours distresses me, for I see that Monsieur Robert is succeeding only too well with you in his game by obliging his wife to write you about her spurious happiness. You will not believe that finally, after all her moral sufferings, she will dare at last to tell the truth on this point!

Listen: Madame Clément was on very poor terms with Éléonore and viewed her position in the household as ill-assured. So she clung passionately to the idea of marriage for Marthe, who promised to keep her in her house. To make this marriage happen, seeing me fall ill, she hid from me many things she heard in town that would have made me decide in the negative. She also hid from me what Marthe had to endure from that whole family at Labastide and at Madame d'Aillot's in Mougins, to maintain her situation; she herself had to swallow countless affronts. She let me be torn to bits and calumniated by all. Now that she is very ill, she feels remorse for having compromised my daughter's happiness out of personal self-interest, and failed in the duties that my trust and her salary demanded. She has made up her mind to tell more of the truth, but she's still under the impress of terror that Monsieur Robert inspires in her. You see, this is the first confidential letter she's written me, and that was only when she was quite sure he had left for Marseille. So you must regard as *true*, in large part, what you find too odious to be *credible*.

As for being unable to pay for the seat on the bus, that's *absolutely true!* Marthe told the conductor she'd pay in the evening and he should pick her up as he passed in front of the villa. The man forgot to stop, and she was obliged to go back on foot by the short cut. I had an errand boy carry a big basket, and our trusty woman took Marthe's bag, went to the station with her, and kept her company until the train arrived (it was late). This woman *saw* the bus conductor demand that Marthe pay for her seat in the morning. Both women scolded him for forgetting to stop on his way back down for the evening train. Even at Antibes, Marthe hadn't been able to check her empty basket and pay for it until that evening! You see to what sufferings Monsieur Robert's self-love condemns my daughter! And *he* doesn't deny himself anything! This trip to Marseille is a pleasure jaunt, the occasion a meeting of the "Touring Club," which these gentlemen have signed up for with the loafers from Provence, who are many. I learned that from the newspaper, and also from the Martin family, for Marthe would have been very careful not to talk to me about that useless expense. He enjoins her, under most terrible threats, to hide from me all that concerns them; and, as I've told you, fear, a sickly fear now, paralyzes all energy in her! Madame Clément is still a support for her that her husband puts up with. If she comes to lose her and we are far away in Montpellier, won't Marthe be seized with despair? I don't dare hope that energy will return to her: she's too enervated, and too morally isolated by all the bloodsuckers that surround her. So I'm perplexed, and were it not for the necessity of taking Georges back from the nurse and getting Éléonore away from the unending emotional crisis we have here, I wouldn't have the courage to go so far away from the poor child. But this must be *really effective,* Éléonore must be able to attach herself to the child for the present and future and not constantly have the fear of seeing him exposed to everything in that family. You haven't given me any answer on that matter! Your goddaughter is not satisfied with your silence. So tell us clearly what you intend to say to Monsieur Robert. If you fear the responsibility of making a decision, consult with Henri, who is destined to succeed you as head of the family. Since he knows all about Georges's existence, one may, and even should, bring him up to date on everything that concerns him.

You find evil hard to believe in, dear Charles. Our sister Clémence would have been a victim some time ago, if Providence had not had me stand in the way. Fortunately, our father was alive then! The wicked need to feel a man's hand—women's devotion cannot suffice.

Your affectionate sister,

Émilie

MARTHE CARON D'AILLOT
TO ÉMILIE DE MONTBOURG
Mougins, July 12, 1897

Dear Mama,

I entreat you on my knees not to write me any more as you have done. Fortunately, your letter and the money order didn't fall into the clutches of Robert, who is away again. I didn't dare tell you, I was afraid you'd scold me for not opposing still another trip, considering we are strapped, but I can't stand up to my husband, as I keep telling you. He's coming back tomorrow evening. I myself went to the post office to cash the money order for 10 francs. Thank you, dear Mama. I'm keeping that sum for when I might need it. When I go to get the quarterly payment, we'll have a good chat together, but until then, no more letters that I can't show. I'll answer your letter of July 8 tomorrow, when he's back, for that one he can see.

I've burned your letter with care. Burn mine, but don't be so imprudent as to write me like that. Damn it, be careful about your letters: you're risking getting me a beating. I've carefully hidden my 10 francs; he didn't take off without leaving me some money, but I'm keeping what you've sent me just in case I need it.

My very fond wishes, dear Mama, to Éléonore, too; I'm taking the letter to the post office myself.

Devotedly yours,

Marthe

ÉMILIE DE MONTBOURG
TO CHARLES DE CERILLEY
Grasse, July 16, 1897

Oh, you bad brother, you want to make me die of worry on your account! So that cruel eczema on your arm was not enough to teach you a lesson! I hope you've been thoroughly cleaned out, to bring down as fast as possible that swelling in your head? You crazy kid, can't you play dead when faced with a hoe or a pick? That's easier than my playing dead when faced with Monsieur Robert's indignities to my *daughter,* and yet you never stop laying down the law about them to me!

But you, you can try to lessen your troubles by giving up that little glassful that always goes with your coffee. Who knows whether you don't take others during the day? Well, I formally accuse those glassfuls of maintaining, of provoking in you a certain agitation, a factitious strength, which you try to expend to the detriment of your health. So I entreat you to give up these stimulants, the best of which are worthless. It mustn't be any harder than giving up smoking, and some people manage that. Set me that example of energy and I'll hope to succeed in playing dead by sheer will power! Is it a bargain? Let's not go back over the past, dear Charles. We've tried to fulfill our duty from our individual points of view. For my part, I haven't had the satisfaction of seeing human justice passed on the rascally actions of Monsieur Robert. He's been able to strut about at his ease on his earthly scene. But the time for mercy will pass, and then, before divine justice, I'll be able to cry out all I want and can hope to see the wicked punished. I live in that hope. I've told you our plans; try to get things decided for the best between now and then! Éléonore is quite of my opinion; it's time. But what we cannot accept is Marthe's stoicism in the face of misfortune. If it were your daughter, you'd speak of it differently.

My fondest regards.

Your affectionate sister,

Émilie

ÉMILIE DE MONTBOURG
TO CHARLES DE CERILLEY
Grasse, July 21, 1897

Dear Charles,

I'm very happy to have better news of your health, and I ask God to strengthen your good resolutions for the future, for, you see, every imprudence becomes serious at our age, and we must avoid them out of affection for those around us.

I'm also glad you realize that it will soon be time to take Georges from the nurse, and I thank you for being willing to take in hand the opening of these negotiations with my son-in-law. But since he has just received his quarterly allotment, we must wait a bit. In a month, money will already be scarce in his house, for he always has a lot of bills to pay, and the tradespeople let him go along like that. The butcher, the baker, the trader in hay and bran, charcoal, and the others are lying in wait for the quarter to come! So we must wait at least a month to broach the question. This question must be settled in my lifetime and in yours, since you have some influence on this obstinate man. We must give Éléonore some guarantees to continue our mission, but what guarantees are possible? You see, that's something we have to establish. I am not at all satisfied with Marthe's health: she's getting thinner and paler, there is less and less moral depth to her. She no longer looks anything like the photograph! She is obviously overdoing, and that has repercussions on the brain and may bring on, I fear, after the erotic excesses, physical atrophy and a short life! Start with that if you want to follow the self-interested game of that individual! He's taking advantage of this progressive weakening to terrorize her. She has at present, I tell you, an unwholesome fear. Didn't you notice in Madame Clément's letter that Marthe has told several people that she fears being beaten for getting a spot on her dress! Yesterday, Madame Clément let me know that she had had visits from Mougins, and that there is talk there of domestic scenes in the chalet.

Here we have intense heat, and I really wish I could cure the chest pains that have been gripping me since Monday's visit—without applying a plaster! Oh, Lord!

We'll have to handle her child's situation without involving her in it, for she's no more than a tool in her husband's hands.

Your affectionate sister,

Émilie

ÉMILIE DE MONTBOURG
TO CHARLES DE CERILLEY
Grasse, August 7, 1897

Dear Charles,

I want to tell you about Marthe's visit. She arrived last Tuesday unannounced and didn't leave until Friday evening. The whole time, she never stopped complaining about her husband, and she insisted on doing so in front of the maid who has been serving us for four years, a spinster respected by the entire town, thinking that her testimony might be useful. She repeated to us several times that her husband insults her in every way *in front of the servants,* that he threatens to beat her constantly, even to kill her, that he hit her on the head with a shoe because she refused to look at a photograph or lock of hair of one of his mistresses, that she got a kick for being found asleep in the daytime on the chaise longue I gave her, that he frightened her so by waking her at night with sudden noises, hooting on the stairs and at the door of her room, that her nerves are shaken to the point where, while he was off traveling for pleasure, she almost had brain fever because the balky mare he told her to drive ran away. And yet, before all these upheavals and frights, she remained more courageous than fearful. Her sister-in-law found her so ill that she called in a doctor from Cannes during the night.

In spite of all her entreaties, she couldn't put a stop to the cries and noises her husband was making to annoy her, except by threatening him. Now, when something white is seen at night, he tries to make her believe it's the soul of a dead woman. I urged her not to believe her husband if he tells her about ghosts and makes her hear strange noises, and to say right away, as we did for the bell-ringings at our door during the night, "That's him." Let's not be weak enough to let ourselves be impressed to satisfy his meanness!

You understand that these murderous tricks, recalled from the cobbler Simon, who used them on the unhappy Louis XVII, can be practiced on poor little Georges as well.

Marthe has urged us to keep a good watch, and was worried about what kind of setting we'd be in, for she thought that in order to have a garden we'd have to be almost in the country. I told her to rest easy, we'd be in a big town and in a house with many other people. But nothing more. She told me her husband kept saying that since we are not making known the place we are moving to, we're quite capable of not giving our real address. That made us think of using general delivery until further notice, when we're at Montpellier. M. has warned us that her husband used to say that if he knew a way to kill us (without incriminating himself), he'd do it right away; that if he weren't afraid of the police, he'd come and strangle us. A little while ago he was doing research on how he might have me locked up *as insane!* He told her I have the worst reputation here. "Oh," answered the old maidservant, "it's just the exact opposite: Madame and Mademoiselle, who pay cash for everything, who are good to the poor and the sick, are missed already, and they say: 'It's really a shame, the good ones go away and the bad ones stay!' "

Marthe is afraid that, after we leave, her husband will blacken our reputations in every way, and asked this maid, whose judgment is respected, to defend us against calumnies. Monsieur Robert claims that I run him down in public? But my dear, that wouldn't be honorable for us; it's the common people who, knowing he's poor and still under the weight of his bankruptcy, since he won't redeem himself, say when they see him pass, "See, there's a great do-nothing and a glutton who doesn't lift a finger now that his wife brings him enough to eat." Two persons have repeated to us these words of the local people. In Provençal they're more vehement than in French. When Marthe said in front of the maid, but without speaking to her, that they had only 24 francs left in their house, she couldn't help speaking up, for she was indignant: "How can that be, madame? It was two weeks ago that I took 1,250 francs to the notary for the quarter! So what does Monsieur Robert do with that money? He managed to live before he married, but he worked then, and now he's a do-nothing and a glutton and has to be supported by his family."

You see, the public's opinion doesn't need mine; but he prefers to blame me for the way his conduct is judged. Liar that he is, that's not hard for him! Would you believe that he wanted to make Marthe think that if we learned that he beats her, we'd rub our hands with satisfaction and say, "Ah! All the better, we're winning!" Isn't that abominable?

Recently he wanted to force his wife to write me a letter of insults, absolutely gratuitous. He reproaches her for not making violent scenes when she comes to see us, and crushes her with mean remarks when she returns. He told her, if you can believe it, that all I send them is things I don't want for myself, because I consider their house a dump! Now, it was with the idea of being useful to them that I was doing it. I went right away to a secondhand store that will buy from me whatever I don't give to those who are happy to receive it, and in exchange for three pieces of furniture I'd promised them, I declared, on the advice of the notary, that I needed a receipt for *everything* I've sent since the marriage and that I've given *to my daughter.* This was with the double purpose of preventing any seizure of the furniture, which will be acknowledged as *part of the dowry,* and also to keep them from putting the furniture among the acquisitions held jointly; for her sister-in-law has already said to Marthe that this furniture belonged to her husband's family.

A man of any sense would recognize that he has used the wrong tactics, but, arrogant and stubborn as he is, will he want to change his? It's doubtful.

The diamonds I gave Marthe are still in the pawnshop! He says he'll redeem them at the end of the year, probably by getting a new loan.

I've instructed my notary to write to the pawnbroker that if they're not redeemed before the time of the sale, he (the notary) must ask the pawnbroker to sell them to him. This is naturally on my account, but not in my name. He tells me that the loan amounts to no more than 600 or 800 francs on the value of 3,000 francs.

Marthe has instructed me expressly to tell you and Sophie that if her husband makes her write you that she's in agreement with him to take Georges back from the nurse and take him in with them, or if he writes you this himself, *you mustn't believe him;* but that you should act upon your own counsels without mentioning her, so as not to expose her to bad treatment or blows. She promised me not to run away from Mougins except as a last resort, for she knows his temper, and even though he makes her life an agony with his mean remarks and terrors, her husband knows very well how to handle her. I've told nothing but the bare truth, without commentary, as I always do, and I don't understand why you think I'm too emotional, in my place you would be as worried as I am.

This is a really long letter, which has left me very tired. My fondest greetings.

Your affectionate sister,

Émilie

MARTHE CARON D'AILLOT
TO ÉMILIE DE MONTBOURG
Mougins, August 9, 1897

Dear Mama,

We went to see Madame Clément two days in a row, for she's very tired. She's still vomiting up everything she eats; chicken doesn't go down any more, nor bouillon with *jus anglais,* [37] she can keep down nothing but iced drinks. She's so weak she can't get up any more. We're afraid of a crisis from one moment to the next, which has us extremely worried. She can't turn over in bed by herself any more; she's really pitiful. She's nothing but a skeleton now. We'll go see her still more often, and I'll keep you posted. I'm sending you the receipt you asked for, signed and made out by my husband on official paper. I got the leeks and the lettuce planted. Thanks for all that. One of these days I'll send you the case that contained the *grignons,*[38] plus the apron, a napkin, and a bag holding a hamper, both of which I'd completely forgotten in the workroom. The heat is still very intense, and we've also been having a terrible wind that is drying out the poor fruit trees.

Pray often for our poor patient.

My fondest greetings to you and to Éléonore.

Devotedly yours,

Marthe

MARTHE CARON D'AILLOT
TO ÉMILIE DE MONTBOURG
Mougins, August 10, 1897

Dear Mama,

I'm writing you even as things are happening. Robert isn't going to Labastide now; I don't know when he'll go. Madame Clément is so bad I'm afraid she won't get through the week. I've sent you today the receipt you asked me for. I don't know if it will suit you as it is, but don't ask me for another one, for I've had a lot of trouble getting this one. I still urge you to be very discreet: with a man like the one I have, you must. I don't know when Robert will write Uncle Charles and Aunt Sophie. He doesn't talk about it any more, but, please, be very careful about what you write and say, for when I think of what might happen if he came to know everything I've told you, I shiver with fright. I've kept some money out of what you've given me and put it in a safe place. I put in my writing desk only a little something for the household. My temperament keeps me from living with you, but some day, when time and the years have appeased my ardors, I'll come and join you. But I'll be easier in my mind about you when you're no longer in Grasse. Don't ever write me a letter on the sly from Robert, for you'd get me killed—keep that well in mind. I no longer remember what you've told me regarding Saint-Savin, and I haven't spoken to him about it at all. He asked me if we'd talked about Georges. I replied that I'd asked for news of the boy, and that's all I told him.

Now, dearest Mama, though I love you dearly, believe me, I'm doing you a favor by not going with you. I'll manage not to get beaten, and I'll never give my signature, I promise you, so rest easy. Be careful, I entreat you. Always prudence.

Marthe

MARTHE CARON D'AILLOT
TO ÉMILIE DE MONTBOURG
Mougins, August 24, 1897

Dear Mama,

Our poor friend's sufferings are over forever: she died yesterday evening at eight o'clock. Her burial takes place tomorrow, at eight in the morning. We'll both be there, of course—she had no one left but us, poor woman. So it's over, quite over. Of her nothing is left, I'll never see her again, never, never. It's when people aren't there any more that you feel just how dear they are to you. I wish you'd give me the photograph of this poor lady; it's in the big album. You're not doing anything with that portrait, and I would be so glad to have it that you can give it up for my sake.

I'll go spend the day after tomorrow with you. Pray for our poor Madame Clément, dear Mama; it grieves me so not to have her any more. I would certainly have liked to see her again one last time, but Robert was afraid it would have a bad effect on me to see Madame Clément dead, and he asked me so urgently not to go see her that I'll do so only to accompany her, with Robert, to her last abode.

I'll see you soon, then, dear Mama. My fondest greetings. Poor Madame Clément.

Devotedly yours in tears,

Marthe

MARTHE CARON D'AILLOT
TO CHARLES DE CERILLEY
Mougins, August 25, 1897

Dear good Uncle,

Our poor Madame Clément has ended her sufferings in this world. Her burial took place this morning at Antibes. We were both there. I feel much grief over this death. Madame Clément loved me very much, and I was devoted to her. I feel how dear she was to me in the pain I suffer from this separation, unfortunately eternal. The poor woman died fully conscious. She spoke of her death with admirable calm and courage.

Everyone in Mougins mourns her loss: she had succeeded in winning every heart.

I hope, dear uncle, that you're in good health and are not tiring yourself out too much, for I know you sometimes overdo it a bit. I'm keeping very busy in the house. Robert is satisfied with me. That's a precious encouragement for me.

Let us have news of you, dear good uncle, and do believe in the affectionate wishes of your niece and nephew.

Marthe

[Note by Charles:]
Keep.

MARTHE CARON D'AILLOT
TO CHARLES DE CERILLEY
Grasse, September 4, 1897

My very dear Uncle,

Taking advantage of being at Mama's, I'm anxious to make my situation clear to you: believe absolutely everything my mother tells you about my husband, who's a nasty man. Speaking of you and the whole family, de Cerilleys as well as de Montbourgs, he says, not only to me in private but to all the people we know, that you can shove it, and shit on you!

He told me, shouting at the top of his lungs, that if he found some bastard capable of killing my mother and my sister, he'd give 50 francs for it. He has told me that not only in anger, but also quite coldly, and the statement was heard by my servants and the people coming back from their jobs. I'm not exaggerating a thing. He's even told me he'd shoot Georges to death.

Dear uncle, I'm a woman, a wife and a mother, and I don't want anyone to kill my son. My temperament forces me to stay where I am, but, I implore you, keep my son under your authority, without taking him in with you. Read between the lines—I'm in a rush because of the train.

Devotedly yours,

Marthe

[Note by Charles:]
Keep.

ÉMILIE DE MONTBOURG
TO CHARLES DE CERILLEY
Marseille, September 13, 1897

Dear Charles,

This evening we'll be in Montpellier. You can send your answer to my last letter there, the one in which I enclosed a very important and disturbing letter from Marthe. But don't give out our address to anyone. My son-in-law will try to get it by all possible means. Forbid the post office in Sangy to give out our address under any circumstances. *This is very important to our safety.* I'm sick at heart to leave my poor Marthe defenseless in such a situation, but I must save Éléonore, who has done nothing to deserve the wicked schemes of that evil Robert.

Answer me soon. We'll soon be sending our furniture van to Montpellier. To throw off pursuit, we directed it to the Marseille station at the time of our first trip, with the permission of the stationmaster; you'll approve of that. All these precautions are a great nuisance.

Your affectionate sister,

Émilie

Since it is not prudent for my address to be divulged, I beg you not to give it to *anyone*—to Marthe even less than to others.

CHARLES DE CERILLEY
TO ÉMILIE DE MONTBOURG
Sangy, September 16, 1897

Dear Émilie,

I was waiting till you got to Montpellier to answer you: Henri, who is here, and I find much to blame in the extreme precautions you're taking to conceal your address. In the long run, it will astonish many people and give rise to a thousand assumptions that can only harm you. You are taking at his word the calculated terrorism of your son-in-law, who is exploiting Marthe's fear. It's an infamous scheme, and you are only reinforcing it in her mind. What have you to fear behind the bars of a convent? Absolutely nothing: ponder well what I'm telling you, and meanwhile I promise you absolute silence.

Madeleine has been feeling consistently low lately: she had such pain in her stomach she thought she was not long for this world, but fortunately she's had a letter from the doctor declaring that her fears are baseless and that she can go on to age eighty with her intestinal infirmity. That has visibly reassured her, and I bless heaven for it: her state of mind was breaking my heart. Her condition is chronic and derives from rheumatism that has settled in her intestines. The proof is that she has had no more pains in her arms and hands. Her sister had rheumatism in her neck and is well now, so it's the same principle in another form.

What arrangements did you make with Marthe so she can give you her news? She must know where to write you. Oh, I wish I could give her morale a boost, but it's impossible to do so directly. They take advantage of her weakness, and they exploit her credulity odiously. God grant that she may profit from the lessons of wise energy you've been able to give her so that people will reckon with her more than in the past. The key for the future is to arm Éléonore in such a way as to keep her brother-in-law in check through self-interest. Such means, well employed, will be all-powerful. Henri understands this perfectly, for he is a man of energy and good counsel. After I am gone, you can have confidence in him.

Pick out in Montpellier a good magistrate recommended by the mother superior of the convent. Let him know *everything,* like a confessor. That's a must. I'm convinced that he'll approve of everything that Henri and I are advising. You'll have to tell Sophie yourself how you want her to correspond with you, because of the address, which I am not giving her. All that is too much! I warn you that in the future I will refuse to associate myself with a measure that I consider frightfully compromising for you, for Éléonore, and also for Marthe. You're making yourselves look like criminals in hiding. In heaven's name, get hold of yourself; you've never strayed this far. If your son-in-law, encouraged by your fright, has the audacity to pursue his schemes, I will take responsibility for shutting him up by writing him just one letter. So don't be afraid.

Good-bye, dear sister.

Your devoted brother,

Charles

ÉMILIE DE MONTBOURG
TO CHARLES DE CERILLEY
Montpellier, September 19, 1897

Dear Charles,

The mother superior has given me your letter. Your card pleased her very much, and with the furniture van arriving the same day, she did her utmost to spare me the pleurisy with which fatigue and the change of climate were threatening me. Evidently the rheumatism was traveling. A heavy perspiration and a fire in my room saved me one more time, plus the potion that has often done the job for me. I certainly should have expected this trial, which is going to keep me indoors for some time. Patience! First I have to stay alive.

I'm sorry we don't agree about the precautions we have to take for our correspondence. But you wouldn't find them so ridiculous if you knew how we've been spied on lately. Someone was right there inside the station to listen at the ticket window, and when we asked for Marseille, the ticket taker said to me in a strange way, "Ah, it's for Marseille?"—"Yes, sir."

Since our van was also registered for Marseille, they were thrown off the track, as were the big-ears, of whom there were not many, for we chose a holiday, when many curious people are elsewhere. To learn what day we were leaving, Monsieur Robert had his wife ask me questions every day; I kept sending things up to the last minute, and announced by letter that a message would not be coming until two days later. That way we kept our departure secret. Let me tell you that a little while ago a son-in-law whose wife was leaving with her mother lay in ambush in a neighboring compartment of the train and fired on the unfortunate women through the partition. Judging from Monsieur Robert's remarks that are flying around the countryside, there might have been as much done to us.

Some friends whom I asked to write me care of general delivery urged us to adopt a pseudonym, so that Éléonore would not be spied on and followed. You see, these people are even more cautious than we are! Here, inside the house, we can't change our names. I know all too well that we can't always hide, but let me be the judge of when to take off the mask. You're making a snap judgment when you take for childish errors precautions deemed necessary by people who know that wicked man better than you and we do.

My fond greetings, dear Charles.

Your affectionate sister,

Émilie

MARTHE CARON D'AILLOT
TO ÉMILIE DE MONTBOURG
Château des Clues, September 24, 1897

Dearly beloved Mama,

I'm taking advantage of my husband's being out hunting to chat freely with you. Oh, Mama, how unhappy I am! He's become so mean, so mean, since we've been here! His mother works him up against me and, right in front of me, she runs his wife into the ground, and yet I don't stop being good and devoted (more than he deserves, Mama, as you well know). Oh, I entreat you, don't ever let my poor child come to Mougins —he'd kill him, I'm sure of it! You were right, Mama, to tell me that he never would love my poor Georges! I still had illusions, but they've disappeared. What a wretch! To think that all my life I'll be bound to such a creature! I've heard some *nice* things about his family here. If my tyrant eventually lets me go see you, I'll give you the name of the worthy person who has wept with me and consoled me, and who's going to mail this letter for me. On my way out hunting this morning, I'll stop by her house; she, too, has suffered at the hands of the d'Aillots.

I had a terrible quarrel with my mother-in-law and my husband yesterday about the 13,000 francs they want to steal from me. *I declared to them that I will never sign anything,* and that since I got married under the dowry system, which means my husband can't dispose of my fortune without my signature, they can just stop counting on having one from me.

I've recovered my energy, Mama, and even if my husband were to ask me for my signature at gunpoint, I would never consent.

Have no fear, darling Mother, I will not weaken, even if that despicable man threatens never to come near me again. I have water-lily powder, and I'll take some to keep my wretched temperament from going against my will, which is iron. If some day Robert runs away from his household, that doesn't mean I should do as much; I want to leave him completely in the wrong. I don't respect Robert, but by dint of tenderness I want to bring him back to God, to do as you do, my blessed mother, so that one day we may all go to heaven together if possible. I'm leading a martyr's life, but what does that matter if the result is good? You've restored my faith, I believe in an afterlife—thank you, my darling mother! Don't answer me—be very careful not to—we'll be leaving this accursed place on Monday. I'm taking care of myself, my tonsillitis is over, I assure you. If I had needed the potion, I'd have taken it, but the sausage and gargling with boric acid have put me completely back on my feet.

One more tender caress, dear Mother, and for you, too, poor sister. Forgive me once again for having torn your heart so; I'm paying for it fourfold, and that's just. God wills it, no doubt. May His will be done and not mine! Above all, don't answer me. I'll write you another letter for my husband to see, probably tomorrow. Silence, prudence.

Your daughter, who embraces you in tears,

Marthe

MARTHE CARON D'AILLOT
TO ÉMILIE DE MONTBOURG
Château du Fermet, October 4, 1897

Beloved Mama,
Robert has gone for a walk in Grasse, so I'm taking this chance to write you a few words.

I'm writing from the home of my uncle Alexis Tavelle du Fermet and his wife, my dear good aunt, where I came for lunch. They're sorry for me with all their hearts for having to live with such a creature. They said to me, "We don't understand such people. Your husband is a scum!"

In your next letter, dear Mother, don't mention family or anything that may get me struck. As for the idea of some consolation from my mother-in-law and sister-in-law, you mustn't count on it, for they laugh at my tears.

From Monsieur Martin I ordered four bottles of glycerophosphates and two bottles of syrup; I had my period twice during the month of September, and very abundantly, which left me worn out, and I need to live for my son. If you have received my letter of September 24, you should put these words in your next letter: "Pats for your dog Dick." I've got to have dauntless courage, and my poor Madame Clément is surely watching over me from the heights of heaven. When Robert goes off somewhere, I'll make myself some broth and I'll take good care of myself with the money contained in your letter. Since we have only 20-odd sous left, I don't want him to rob me of what you've sent me, so I've hidden it with care.

Don't worry about me. My resolve is unshakable though my heart is shattered. Thank you, thank you, dear, ever-so-kind Mother and sister. Who knows when I'll see you again? I don't want to leave him—you know why—but how hard atonement is! Mama, once again I'm weeping as I write. I love you, believe me. Keep my Georges near you. How I regret giving him such a father as Robert! Above all, don't talk about this in your next letter.

Your grieving daughter,

Marthe

Big kiss to my dear kind sister. Thank you, thank you.

MARTHE CARON D'AILLOT
TO ÉMILIE DE MONTBOURG
Chalet Marthe, October 18, 1897

Beloved Mama,

Thank you, dear kind Mother, for your 100-franc bill. I've hidden it carefully, and no one has a prayer of finding the hiding place. Since Robert has gone to Grasse to get the quarterly payment, I'm taking this chance to write you freely, for you know that I have to write and rewrite in front of him my letters to you. Such slavery is very annoying for me, but I can't do a thing about it. I'll take every opportunity to write you when he isn't here, for it's so painful to me not to see you any more, Mama darling, and kiss your beloved face. Mama, Mama, I'm crying, oh, yes, I'm crying as I write you. How much courage, how much resignation I need to endure such a life. Last week my husband did nothing but insult me, shouting such infamous things at me that if I had not fled to the far end of the property (which is not very big), I would have ended up doing him in, so outraged was I to hear myself called such things. The *bitch*es, *whore*s, *two-timing slut*s and all the rest kept pouring out of his mouth as from a fountain. My, he's created a fine reputation for himself in the region. Everyone is sorry for me and thinks I'm unfortunate, for I always behave nicely to him; it's such a crying injustice that one person in Mougins reproached him for it, telling him vehemently, "Frankly, Monsieur Robert, your wife is too good to deserve the kind of life you give her. You're lucky to have found her. Before you married her, you lived like a poor peasant, just like me." My husband apparently left shamefaced—I mean shame-faced as anything. They never refer to me without saying "that nice Madame Robert." I tell you all this, dear Mother, not to boast of all the respect I may have won by my way of acting, but to give you a clear picture of public opinion concerning me.

You can't write me under the cover of Madame du Fermet any more, for she went back to Nice; this good aunt was seized again by a painful nervous ailment that threatens her heart at the same time. Last year she almost died of it, and if I lost her, my good aunt, I would be very unhappy, for she thinks of me as a second daughter. How many times she has told me, "Ah, Marthe, how I wish you'd married my Eugène; I wouldn't be so alone, or my husband, either." So you must now stop engaging in any hidden correspondence. As for me, I can continue writing you when Robert is away somewhere. Don't worry.

Although Robert shows many signs of repentance, I keep on my guard, for he's so changeable that I can't count on him. Anyway, while I have peace, I take it; but I beg you, darling Mother, not to write anything that might put him in a fury, for I'm so weak I don't need scenes. I am flat on my back in bed with diarrhea. In the seven days I've been sick, I've gone at least eighty-odd times. I was expecting the doctor yesterday, but he couldn't come. No doubt he'll come tomorrow. So rest easy, however much pain and anger you may have had in reading this letter, which is very long for my feeble condition.

Accordingly, I must rest from time to time. Don't write me, either general delivery or otherwise, on the sly from Robert, I implore you. It's too serious, and I need an infinity of peace and tranquillity; keep that in mind.

I send kisses, beloved Mother, more tenderly and caressingly than ever. I am like a little girl toward you, darling Mother and tender sister, and I love you both very much. Again, a thousand tender caresses. Warm greetings to my uncle and aunt.

Marthe

[Note by Charles:]
Truth emerges at last from Marthe's mouth. What martyrdom!

CHARLES DE CERILLEY
TO ÉMILIE DE MONTBOURG
Sangy, October 25, 1897

Dear Émilie,
Yesterday I received a very proper letter from your son-in-law, with a word added by Marthe. Believing that we might be going to Antibes, your son-in-law puts himself at my disposal for any information and is glad to be seeing us again. He gives me news of Marthe, saying she's almost cured of her diarrhea. Not a word about you. It would be well for me to see her so as to hear with her ears and see with her eyes, in order to broach the question of Georges at long last. His very proper letter makes that visit possible; otherwise, could you imagine me going to Mougins to hear things rejected vigorously, and under his roof! It's not very practical. If it weren't a question of money, it would be best for the nephew to move out. That's a way of proceeding that we can study. Tell me what I should do and your way of going about it, so I can judge it from my side, after which I'll offer you my observations.

Just tell me where you got the idea *that I deny what is odious:* that's a reflection that came rather lightly to your pen. My entire life is a protest against that, and it would be only too easy to prove to you the opposite. Be aware that I am at the same time firm and reflective, that I make up my mind in my own time. I guard against any excitement as long as the hour for action has not struck.

That much said, I repeat to you that I'm frightened by the facility with which you talk about separation and divorce for Marthe if necessary (and what would make it necessary?). You know very well that the material consequence for her will be *the street*—you understand me clearly—*the street,* as long as age hasn't *utterly* cooled off her morbid ardor. She herself has even had the honesty to tell you so, or just about.

So take good care not to pour oil on the fire; that would be a matter of conscience and enormous responsibility for you. Consider also that if Marthe ran away to your house, there would probably be a lawsuit, and that your son-in-law is unfortunately only too well armed to make you play a most disagreeable role before the law, as regards lack of maternal supervision, or lack of elementary perspicacity, even disregarding the possibility of outright chicanery on his part. In truth, are you thoroughly considering all that?

Let's agree clearly from the start that Marthe lacks the necessary equilibrium, especially in the circumstances, and that on account of it absolute credence cannot be paid her, any more than her husband, all of whose wrongs, and odious speculation, I recognize. You have no grip on him except his self-interest, and I can't believe that unless he is absolutely mad, he wants to provoke disaster now, much less in the future.

Good-bye, my dear sister.

Your affectionate brother,

Charles de Cerilley

MARTHE CARON D'AILLOT
TO ÉMILIE DE MONTBOURG
Chalet Marthe, October 28, 1897

Dear Mama,

I did indeed get the bismuth, and if you didn't get news of me, it's because I was expecting an answer to my letter of the 20th of this month, a letter in which I asked you for a few bottles of Eau de Vals No. 3, from the Vivarais spring. It's very good for my stomach, which mustn't be offended or else it balks, and then gastritis and all the rest come on. I'm better now; the stools are much less frequent and so the nights are better; the days, too, but the weakness is still there. My poor tom cat is so attentive to me, he prepares soups for me himself, makes sure I don't get too tired —in short, he's very nice, and his tomcatteries do me a lot of good and make me accept my trots with patience.

I'm very grateful to you, dear Mama, for offering to have me spend my convalescence with you. That would be a real happiness for me, but it's not a possibility right now. The maid I had left me abruptly, on a passing whim, and the one who has replaced her is so clumsy that sometimes she puts my patience to the test in a way that would make the Father Eternal scream aloud. What I am saying is that my presence is useful in the house—I can't leave my poor darling alone. What would become of that poor tom cat without his tabby cat? Good Lord! Later on, when my pot has become an elegant flatland (that is to say deflated), I'll come to you; I've no lack of desire to be with you, but we must take events into account.

I won't be able to send you the rug, for my illness has obliged me to leave it unfinished, but I'll paint something for the two of you. The bag has also suffered an enforced delay; it's only little by little that I'm getting myself back to work, and I don't do much of it at one time. A great big hug and kiss to you, dear, dear Mama, and also to Eléonore.

Devotedly yours,

Marthe

ÉMILIE DE MONTBOURG
TO CHARLES DE CERILLEY
Montpellier, October 30, 1897

Dear Charles,

I've just got a letter from Marthe, who's better, although the diarrhea still hangs on. That is completely contrary to her constitution. Her husband is still making soup for her, which doesn't reassure me at all. This ailment came on following the affront that the Mougins peasant presented to Monsieur Robert apropos of the scenes of demented frenzy that he presents to his wife. No, is it not possible that his immense arrogance, which is incapable of acknowledging a wrong, has tried to take revenge on a victim gagged by terror? An intelligent maid, devoted to my daughter, is replaced by an incapable idiot who drives her mistress mad. They say that maid left on an impulse. I don't believe a word of it! She was a witness that had to be removed. You ask what makes me think that you deny facts you find odious—why, dear brother, in your own correspondence! Last July, after a visit Marthe made to Grasse during which her heart had finally overflowed and let me know how enslaved she is in the matter of her letters, the poverty in which her husband keeps her, the scenes and insults she endures, I wrote you about it, and you made the following reply (I'm copying): "The (moral) isolation, the slavery and fear in which you think Marthe lives, *I don't believe in it*, because either it's true or it isn't true; if it's true, it's so revolting that your son-in-law would compromise himself gravely thereby for the present and for the future. So it must be untrue, which would fit in admirably with blackmail."

So you think that Marthe is committing blackmail in collusion with her husband? Well, *that is not so!* Besides, her mother-in-law and he reproach her for not doing so.

To your most categorical denial I responded with circumstantial details which shouldn't have left you any doubt about the veracity of the facts cited. But you didn't utter a peep. I've kept a copy of my reply, appended to your letter.

My poor child is expressing such a desire to see you and also her aunt, and *soon,* that she might well have something to talk to you about in private, but *will she be able to?* I beg you urgently, dear Charles, when Madeleine is recovered from her trip to Hyères, go to Mougins and see Marthe, but beware of Monsieur Robert. He will spy on you and will make his wife pay dearly for her confidences.

My fondest greetings, dear Charles.

Your affectionate sister,

Émilie

MARTHE CARON D'AILLOT
TO ÉMILIE DE MONTBOURG
Chalet Marthe, October 31, 1897

Dear Mama dearest,

Since Robert has left for Labastide to join the family crowd, I'm seizing my chance to chat freely with you, whom I love so much! First of all, I want to thank you with all my heart for everything you do for me. I don't know what words to use to express my gratitude to you. Alas! The thought that I can't go and see you breaks my heart, but that is absolutely impossible as long as my maid is untrained. I can't leave Robert alone with this girl, who, though thoroughly upright and decent, is possessed of a rare ignorance when it comes to cooking, even the simplest kind. And, then, Robert is so afraid of his mother, who has forbidden him to let me go see you. It would make you hold your sides laughing to see this big fellow, who plays the bravo with other people but hides in a mousehole when this woman has spoken. Yes, I repeat, it would be a laugh if it weren't so cruelly sad and painful for me. Yet he's almost promised to let me go see you later on. I could do nothing but bow to it. What else can you expect me to do, run away from him? Oh, no, good Lord, with a temperament like mine it would be terrible; to get along without Robert, not have his caresses any more, that would be frightful. I would embarrass you horribly. I have a man, I'm keeping him, and trying to fret as little as possible. I already have enough to worry about as it is, for his meannesses gave me the dysentery I've had for four weeks.

He has asked my pardon, and you know I've granted it. But I was in pain yesterday, and I feel very tired. First of all, when I go off the diet, the slightest bit, I get the runs terribly; also, any hot liquid makes me go like a fountain, so I take milk and all liquids lukewarm (I got the unfortunate idea of having cocoa with milk in the morning, it started up the dysentery again, which had stopped for three days so that I thought I was cured). Oh, yes, indeed! It came back stronger than ever. I'm going to resume taking pomegranate-peel tea—that's what's done me the most good.

May the devil take my mother-in-law! There is one I'd trample on happily. What a filthy slut! I hate her so! The day she croaks, I'll have a *Te Deum* sung at Sainte-Réparate in Nice for a mercy granted! May God's lightning strike her, the old bitch, really! I get a little relief from saying all that, dear Mother, but I think a whole lot of other things about her as well. If I go see you some day, we'll have a long talk, for I have so much to tell you.

I'll stop now, because I want to write to dear Éléonore, too. I send you a hug with all my strength, Mother darling. In spite of your anger at seeing your daughter treated so, don't write me anything that will make him hit me, for, my God, I'd blow out his brains if he struck me. And I repeat, I need calm, for my strength is not great. Once again, a thousand fond wishes, Mama, Mama mine.

Marthe

[Note by Charles:]
The truth comes pouring out; tyranny cannot hold it back.

Dear Charles,

I'm sending you a letter from Marthe, who is seriously in the grip of an enteritis that I think is being badly treated by Dr. Caylat; he has given her injections of naphthol and now he's treating this illness the same way. Try to find out from Madeleine's doctor if, on the contrary, enteritis shouldn't be treated with emollients of all sorts. I'm worried to death and in despair at being so far away! If Marthe decided to let us care for her, I'd write her that we'll be in a ladies' pension and near some very good doctors when we want them.

You have every right to go see your sick niece, without being invited; it will be enough to give notice of your arrival. You will judge on sight what's to be done. Your relations with Monsieur Robert aren't the same as ours. He hasn't insulted you as he has me, he hasn't blackmailed you as he has me, he hasn't calumniated you as he has me, he's not the ingrate to you that he is to me. So his pride can allow him to look you in the face.

If he asks for our address, you're to answer: "But you know where Marthe addresses her letters to her mother?"

I grant that Marthe does not have the maturity of character that she could use to take advantage of the circumstances in her favor. Now she bends, now she gets too carried away. If after every one of her husband's scenes she had set conditions on the pardon she granted him, she'd now be mistress of the situation. But she lacks experience, she lets herself be terrorized—as did, alas, poor Madame Clément, who also let herself be morally isolated. But just because she is forced to write what she doesn't mean, which she contradicts when she finds the chance (you know that very well, since she has written you from my house), that's no reason to deny her unhappy situation and abandon her to her unhappy lot without trying to relieve her as much as possible.

How can you do that wicked man the honor of believing he is susceptible to logic? Or believe in the actions of Providence? He mocks both, one as much as the other, and if, even as he destroys his wife by making her miserable, he would nevertheless like her to survive us to collect our bequests, he desires even more that we should die quickly so he can more easily get the better of the mother and child. We don't have any illusions, because we know from a certain source that he wants the death of all who get in his way—even those he owes money to, for he forgets that the heirs will see they are paid just the same.

So you see clearly that it is not *mad terrors* that make me so worried for Marthe and for Georges. You will understand, I hope, that Éléonore, so weary of all that, is afraid for herself when she has to go out alone because my strength is failing and I am unable to breathe outdoors most of the time.

When you've had a rest, don't forget my poor Marthe. Once you are satisfied about her health, if she thinks she can entertain her husband's family, I fully authorize you to order in Antibes or Nice a three- or four-kilo pâté, a nice 4-franc cake, some sausage and two nice capons to roast. Marthe likes to entertain well. You'll give her 200 francs from my strong-box in Sangy, and I'll reimburse you from here for all the expenses of the trip and meals. But above all, look to her health so she doesn't get worn out; look to the family's welcome. Try to bring home to them the salutary thought that our family is not losing interest in any of its members.

Will they let you have any private talk with Marthe? If they do, make sure of the security of the surroundings, for the walls have ears! Besides matters of health and behavior, try to find out whether Monsieur Robert has borrowed anything, as he said he wanted to, whether he has had anything signed, where they stand at this year's end. I know that neither the chalet nor the furniture can be seized, thanks to the recognizance I had Monsieur Robert make out to my daughter, since it's part of the dowry. I know that the diamonds I gave my daughter (3,000 francs) are at the pawnbroker's, and that if they're not redeemed by the end of the year, they'll be sold by the shop at a miserable price. What kind of an act will he put on for me this year to get the 500 francs he needs to redeem them?

Never has Monsieur Robert spoken to me about his business affairs; I've prompted Marthe to tell him that if he showed more trust in me, I'd see what ought to be done. But that man is so false, so deceiving toward those who have dealings with him, that he is neither able nor willing to set forth his situation honestly. First of all, he would not accept any suggestion for reform, and he doesn't know how to get away from the behests of his mother, who demands what is not due her. When she feels there is money in the chalet, she absolutely needs some—she's a wild beast smelling fresh meat.

I'll leave you, dear Charles, for this is a very long letter, although written in several sittings. My fondest greetings, and I ask for news.

Your affectionate sister,

Émilie

CHARLES DE CERILLEY
TO ÉMILIE DE MONTBOURG
Hyères, November 13, 1897

Dear Émilie,

The trip went off well, in three stages, but by the time she arrived at Hyères, Madeleine was at the end of her rope—her poor abdomen very sore, her features drawn, and her stomach obstructed.

Let's come back one last time to that delicate question of my trip to Mougins.

I set on it one absolute and well-considered condition, that you authorize me to give your son-in-law your real address if he asks me for it, and not your text, which you haven't pondered: "But you know where Marthe addresses her letters to her mother." That doesn't make any sense, for he knows very well that that's not where you are. I cannot play a ridiculous role in his eyes, unworthy of a man. You're both mesmerizing yourselves with fears that have no serious basis. Your son-in-law, who is dealing only with women, enjoys terrorizing them, and not for anything in the world do I want him to imagine that I'm wearing skirts; conse-quently, if you persist in your idea, I must tell you with regret that the only way I can respect your will is *not to go to Mougins.* Yes, that's final.

Furthermore, to go to *his house* without being invited either by him or by my niece with his consent, is out of the question for me. Can you see me arriving at his house, even with an invitation, and being lodged and fed at his house! Or else—and this is beneath consideration—staying at the hotel and paying them only one or two visits!

When Madeleine is in a condition to do without me from a Saturday to a Monday evening, I'll go to Mougins *if we are agreed on all points.* If not, no. Also, you don't make it clear whether I'm to pass the 200 francs to Marthe *openly or secretly.* I assume it's *secretly,* but you must tell me clearly nevertheless. As for how to do it, that would be easy to figure out on the spot.

I'm returning Marthe's letter to you, enclosed. No doubt enteritis is treated by emollients. The Lyon doctor treated Madeleine solely through diet, with no medication. Little to eat, little to drink, absolute rest, corset to support the abdomen. No raw vegetables or milk products ever, white meat but not at night, cooked fruits and vegetables, but never any acids. That's it, and that's why we don't see any doctor here.

In my capacity as an uncle who has criticized your son-in-law sharply in writing to him, I must avoid the tactlessness of indiscretion. How to go about the invitation business? He's not at all eager to see me, that's certain: it wouldn't cost him anything to come here, but he still wouldn't come, I'm sure of it. As for proposing to him that he bring his wife to our house, a house he doesn't know, that's sheer fancy. In any case, tell me, given your system of forwarding mail, does Marthe know you're in Montpellier? That's a dangerous mystery that has all the worst possible features.

With a mind at rest, I want to start weeding out and organizing Marthe's dossier. I have a delicate job to do there, cutting down a good many of your letters. I've kept everything. Oh, how flamboyant it is, and painted in compromising colors! It's not even good to show your lawyer, for there's too much imagination in it. None of this invalidates the main point, but it does it much harm—the best cases are often lost for that very reason. Your son-in-law must fear me a great deal, because I've said little and he knows I'll wait for him till the cows come home. I repeat to you that too often you have seen crime everywhere. There's quite enough real evil without our having to double and triple it in our imaginations. That's the tendency of your nature, and those cases where you've been right have given you an excessive confidence in your judgments. The lamentable flightiness of certain persons often causes them to be called criminals. I have strong proofs, and until I see proof to the contrary, your son-in-law will be in my view an ill-bred, foul-mouthed boor when he's not checked. From that to making him out a man capable of anything whatever, one must have more to go on than you do. Oh, if Marthe had a balanced character, she could make herself respected and feared by everyone around her who is taking advantage of her! In spite of themselves, they're forced to follow the morality of self-interest—after all, with a stroke of the pen can their crafty policy be punished in this world. But we have to bring that home to them forcefully.

Good-bye, my dear Émilie.

Your affectionate brother,

Charles de Cerilley

CHARLES DE CERILLEY
TO ÉMILIE DE MONTBOURG
Hyères, November 17, 1897

Dear Émilie,

I'm sacrificing a good deal of personal dignity to your maternal devotion by going to Mougins this coming November 24. I'll make the first move and declare to your son-in-law that my opinion as a man has always been that you have not been concealing your address since you left Grasse. Your ill health is an excuse and will give him great pleasure. That's what I foresee, even as I prepare him a reproach fit to make him blush.

I am announcing my arrival at Mougins for the 24th by today's mail, so that Marthe may have all the benefit of advance notice. If your son-in-law has the unhappy idea of protesting against the concealment of your present residence, I won't hold back from telling him your reasons.

So don't talk about divorce or separation any more, for apart from the religious aspect, what sort of remarriage could poor Marthe contract??? That's just a matter of common sense, and your lawyer can conclude only as I do—*if he is well informed about the situation,* which doesn't seem likely to me.

It's very good that Marthe's dysentery has subsided, and it's only natural for the stomach to go on ailing for a while. So don't worry too much. I'll find out whether there is an analogy with Madeleine's condition, and I'll give you a detailed report.

I'm tossing my letter in the mail quickly. Good-bye, my dear sister.

Charles de Cerilley

CHARLES DE CERILLEY
TO ÉMILIE DE MONTBOURG
Hyères, November 20, 1897

Dear Émilie,

If I weren't already expected at Mougins for the 24th, your text of the answer I am to give your son-in-law about your address if he asks me, which is likely, would make me decide not to go. This false nose you're sticking on me doesn't suit me, and I warn you that if your son-in-law asks, I'll answer that since your health required calm, I advised you to leave Grasse, and that, as to your residence, I must observe a silence that I as a man would not observe for myself. That's the least I can say without passing for what I'm not. Don't try to convert me to your ideas on this point; I'm absolutely inflexible on it. Under the fallacious pretext of not creating difficulties by revealing that there are divergences between you and me, you would have me play a part that I flatly reject, and, rather than play it, I would simply go back under my tent. Pay close attention, for you can and must take me at my word. Women are allowed weaknesses that men are not; that's why I don't want to seem to have seconded yours.

I'll take care of your errands in Mougins, and bring what you ask me to.

I'm expecting an answer from your son-in-law, whom I asked if it is indeed at Antibes that one should get off the train to take the bus for Mougins.

Good-bye, my dear sister; fondest wishes to you both.

Your affectionate brother,

Charles de Cerilley

Rest assured, at the same time, of my prudence and personal dignity vis-à-vis myself and my nearest. It is a matter of tact and dignity, both of them things that command respect.

CHARLES DE CERILLEY
TO ÉMILIE DE MONTBOURG
Hyères, November 21, 1897

Dear Émilie,

Your son-in-law hasn't answered me yet to tell me the railroad station where I am to get off to get the bus to Mougins. I think it's either Antibes or Cannes, but I want to be definite. Why hasn't he answered? He may be away, but then doesn't his wife open his letters from the family? Answer me by return mail, and if I should postpone my trip by twenty-four hours, I'll do it. If I were sure there was ill-will behind this, I wouldn't make the trip at all. The two-kilo pâté made of poultry and veal chopped very fine and jellied, is ordered for Tuesday evening and will cost.................................... 10F.
Nice Bresse chicken......................... 5F.
850-gram can of wafers .... 4F.
Total .... 19F.

I know very well that your son-in-law's answer may come this evening or tomorrow, but his lack of haste clearly proves that my visit does not give them the slightest pleasure.

I'm taking this note promptly to the mail.

Your affectionate brother,

Charles de Cerilley

CHARLES DE CERILLEY
TO ÉMILIE DE MONTBOURG
Hyères, November 23, 1897, 11:30 A.M.

Dear Émilie,

A riot of letters, but I feel that you need to be kept promptly up to date on the details of the present moment.

I've just received your package of effects. I'm carefully removing every trace of Montpellier.

At the same time I've received a wire from your son-in-law, who tells me precisely this: "Mougins, November 23, 10 A.M. Reply sent Saturday the 20th, don't know why not received. We expect you Wednesday, 4:16. Will be Cannes station with carriage. Best. Robert." I'd written Marthe Sunday to notify her of my arrival on the 24th, asking her why her husband hadn't answered: absence, or loss of my letter.

I told her about the 200 francs to be passed along to her husband for the care of her health. I also told her that I was bringing from you pâté, chicken, and wafers. All that is worth a lot more than the wire. I'd be quite surprised if my letter was lost, although it's not absolutely impossible. I have to pretend to believe it. If you hadn't already spoken to Marthe about the 200 francs to go to her husband for her health, I'd give him only 100, and 100 secretly to Marthe. But you speak to Marthe about it in the letter you've asked me to give her. In my opinion, that's too much *at one time* for your son-in-law. No way to reduce it now, because he knows about it. I expect to be fussed over, as a matter of policy. Rest easy, I'll be on my guard, and yet I'll leave nothing undone to sound out the situation now and for the future. My status as uncle gives me the right to inquire *out of solicitude.*

It was high time that wire from your son-in-law arrived. His silence had a bad odor. I would have gone anyway, having announced myself, but the horizon was darkening.

I'll write you either from Mougins or on my return and with all the details you desire, which I will collect.

Your affectionate brother,

Charles de Cerilley

MARTHE CARON D'AILLOT
TO ÉMILIE DE MONTBOURG
Mougins, November 27, 1897

Dear Mama,

First of all, I want to thank you with all my heart for offering me the dynamo-vital machine, which does me a lot of good. I've also received the five plaques you sent me, and I'm using them with the same success. Thanks to this treatment, the diarrhea is stopping as if by magic. The fluid that was constantly running through me will finally disappear completely with this treatment. You spoil me much too much, dear Mama, with all the nice pretty things you sent me via our dear uncle, whom I was very happy to have for a few days, unfortunately all too short. Anyway, I'm nonetheless pleased to have entertained dear uncle, and I did the best I could. My tom cat certainly joined me in surrounding him with affection. The Bresse chicken, dear Mama, was tender, and the jellied pâté well chopped and good—I mean good good—I really relished it. I was able to eat a little of the white meat,[39] though I couldn't cook it in the pot-au-feu, but in the oven instead with a well-prepared stuffing, not spiced, but just as it should be. The bouillon, though prescribed for me, is not tolerated by my stomach. It makes me trot to the toilet like a cat with the runs, so I rule it out absolutely from my diet. I take my peptone in a thin bouillon that doesn't make me go.

The 200 francs, dear Mama, also gave me great pleasure. They'll be useful to me for all the other things I might need, and I can't thank you enough. Éléonore needn't worry, I'm not going off my diet at all, and all alcoholic spirits are carefully removed from it as well as wine. So be reassured both of you. I want to repeat that I'm very well cared for by my husband, who, in all truth, incessantly surrounds me with affection, with care, and with all sorts of attentions, which touch me very deeply. If he weren't there to give me a hand in the duties of the household and cooking, I don't know how I'd make out, for my maid, although beginning to do her cooking better, will always be a real dolt, I very much fear.

I can't yet write a word to my dear Éléonore to thank her for her note, so heartfelt, but I'm only putting that off. I say yes, yes, to the *foie gras* spread; it will go down admirably—yes, yes. Thanks, thanks, with all my strength, which is starting to come back. I have two hot-water bottles, the copper one on my feet and a glass bottle on my belly, my big eiderdown quilt and two blankets on the bed, so you see I'm good and warm and there's no reason to fear for me. I'm not taking any showers as long as I'm sick.

As for my coming to your house for you to take care of me, I certainly love you very deeply, but, as I keep repeating to you, I don't want to stay away from my husband long. I need him, so I'm staying here; don't be offended, but that's the way it is. I can't get along without him.

Again, a thousand of the fondest greetings.

Your very affectionate daughter,

Marthe

CHARLES DE CERILLEY
TO ÉMILIE DE MONTBOURG
Hyères, November 28, 1897

Dear Émilie,
   Got back to Hyères yesterday at two o'clock. I come now to report to you on my mission. When I arrived in Cannes, your son-in-law was waiting for me with his carriage. At Mougins, Marthe, happy to see me, was with her two sisters-in-law. At first they seemed to me rather stiff, but gradually everyone relaxed, for they stayed there a fairly long time. My casualness put them at ease.
   The next morning I chatted alone with Marthe, who was in bed, and I gave her your 100 francs in secret. Then Robert came into Marthe's room, and I gave him the 200 francs from you, which he thanked me for as if it were from me. I repeated: It's from your mother-in-law for the care of your wife. Another *anonymous* thank-you.
   He and I went out for a walk, talking of this and that. Then, at one point, as I was speaking of you in general, he tossed me the anticipated question: "Where is she, anyway?"—"Oh," I replied, "I can't tell you; that is to say, I don't have permission to tell it, and since you yourself are opening the subject, I'm going to be frank with you, while still respecting the secret, *which is not mine.* Well, I advised your mother-in-law and my niece to leave Grasse, from the moment their life, from their point of view, became troubled there. They accuse you of ringing their doorbell several times at improper hours to frighten them, which could produce harmful effects on fragile women." He defended himself on that score rather poorly, but, pretending to take him at his word, I added, "That would have been a deplorable trick, at the very least," and he agreed.
   I then brought up Georges and asked him his intentions, since he's already well up on yours: to wit, that you want to take over from him care of the child and reduce him to zero. He balks and refuses to withdraw entirely.
   I pointed out to him that his financial means did not allow him to pay for a complete education, and that as long as you and Éléonore were disposed to do it, he had much to gain by giving you satisfaction within the limits necessary to safeguard *the personal dignity of each party.* He accepted this in principle, with the details to be discussed later. Thus he asked to see the child often enough for the child to consider him as his legal father. That's fair; moreover, he reserves the right to discuss it with his mother, who is in Paris for a month in connection with the marriage plans of her doctor son.

It seems that before Marthe's marriage, you divulged some very imprudent confidences to your future son-in-law on the subject of your husband's health, even before the birth of your daughter. From this he concluded, after the wedding, when confronted with certain phenomena, that her blood was tainted. That being the case in his view, he had no wish to have defective children by her. Now that he has consulted with doctors, had it checked, and seen there's nothing in it, he'd like to have children, he tells me, but she can't, as a result of a slightly displaced womb.

The prospect of never having a child by Marthe binds him to little Georges. He told me that very seriously, in a tone I find prettier than nature, but which I applauded eagerly, to encourage him in it.

Marthe is pleased with herself on account of the attentions her husband pays her. She really loves him, in spite of the domestic scenes that have taken place. Moreover, she declares that she needs him, and acknowledges that she has lacked balance in her behavior with him. The fact is that she's reasoning much better now, answering more to the point and with a clarity that gives her more respect. She really needed to be tamed, but she could have used a northern bridle, more diplomatic than the southern variety, which often hurts by its violence.

The moral effect of my visit was considerable, and for the good. They had strong prejudices, and these have vanished, or at least they seem to have. In short, I'm in a position to be heard with open ears, which is a lot.

The pity was that Marthe at the start of the marriage admitted to her husband everything about her acts and deeds and about your statements on the subject. In all good faith, didn't you exaggerate? Put yourself in your son-in-law's place!

In your letters to Marthe, you spoke of the d'Aillots in a way that compromised you, for your son-in-law has read most of them. The war was inevitable, and would have broken out in the same way on any other ground. You see, I've learned quite a lot about it.

My firm and moderate tone made your son-in-law take me very seriously, and proved to him that urbanity in observing the forms did not exclude the greatest energy.

On my return here I found your son-in-law's reply, dated the 20th, *but* the stamp is postmarked the 24th–25th, proof that it was mailed at the same time as his wire. It's obvious that at first he didn't want to see me. Today he's delighted about it, for he didn't know how I would behave. He was very nice, as was I, even while telling him home truths as sugarcoated as possible to make them go down.

They found your culinary presents excellent, and your 200 francs to your son-in-law definitely had a marvelous effect. On that score, Marthe told me her husband would certainly give them to her, since they were intended for her health. I had her repeat that twice, it surprised me so.

Here is the cost of my trip:

Train trip one way there	10.55F.
To Robert	200 F.
To Marthe	100 F.
To the maid	5 F.
Presents to the servants	3.50F.
Return train trip	10.55F.
2-kilo pâté	10 F.
Chicken	4 F.
Wafers (1.075 kg.)	6 F.
Total:	349.60F.
You sent me	100 F.
Your cash on hand with me	249.05F.
Surplus expenses (a mere trifle)	0.55F.

As for my two lunches at the railroad stations, they are on me, since I would have eaten at home at Hyères anyway.

It's still pretty hard that your daughter doesn't know your address, but I kept silent out of respect for the secret you want me to keep. She is fully determined never to sign anything. Lastly, she finds that her husband has been much gentler for some time. I hope that my visit and all our conversations will have happy consequences, that the sharp edges will be smoothed down bit by bit, and that if it remains impossible for you to resume relations from a distance, there will at least be a direct and practical epistolary *modus vivendi*. I'd like that very much. I've done my best; the role of impartial and fair intermediary is sometimes quite difficult. Your son-in-law listened carefully to my judgments on his verbal lapses. Let me speak to you with the same brotherly frankness, and tell me likewise whether I've carried out your ideas well.

Your affectionate brother,

Charles de Cerilley

ÉMILIE DE MONTBOURG
TO CHARLES DE CERILLEY
Montpellier, November 29, 1897

Dear Charles,

I was waiting with much anxiety for the account of your trip to Mougins, and I thank you a thousand times for not keeping me waiting.

I hope your visit will have produced a good effect for my poor Marthe. But you have now seen for yourself that my generosities of all sorts leave my son-in-law indifferent, since he affected to thank only you. And yet, what haven't I done for them? If their chalet is furnished, whom do they owe it to? Nevertheless, in the eyes of this family, I'm petty and stingy, because I don't intend to furnish for anyone but the young couple.

I'm very happy to know that Marthe's enteritis is not so serious as might be feared. You don't tell me whether she was able to eat some of the jellied pâté and suck on a bit of chicken.

Monsieur Robert lied to you once more in telling you that I divulged confidences about Marthe's health. *That's not true at all.* He's saying that now to give himself a reason for having tried to ruin his wife's health with harmful injections to keep her from having children, which would have threatened her life if I hadn't raised a hue and cry. He carried his infamy in lying to the point of assuring his wife that I had said to him, in the famous conversation he is imagining, "I've done everything I could to help Marthe have an abortion, and I really don't understand how that failed to happen." I got that from Marthe, who was quoting it to me as one of her husband's lies. How horrible! On the contrary, didn't I do everything necessary to bring that wretched pregnancy to a successful conclusion? But that's the man for you!

He lied to you, and in the postmark you have the proof of his lie about why his answer was delayed. What's more, the wire he sent you, in which he tells you he answered on Saturday the letter you didn't write him until the next day, Sunday, is a rather nice proof of a lie. It's the expected money and his wife's urging that made him decide to send the wire, and he sent you the letter at the same time, stupidly—sometimes liars fool themselves.

But I declare to you that if Monsieur Robert had shown the slightest regret for his wrongs, I would have reopened my house to him because of Marthe. The chaplain of the hospital at Grasse tried several times to get him to express this regret, but each time he answered that he did not acknowledge *any wrong* on his part.

Good-bye, my dear Charles; my very fond greetings.

Your affectionate sister,

Émilie

MARTHE CARON D'AILLOT
TO ÉMILIE DE MONTBOURG
Mougins, December 10, 1897

Dear Mama,

This morning I received a little case full of new things to spoil me, for which I thank you with all my heart. But a letter would have given me even more pleasure, for, frankly, I don't know how to explain your silence as well as Éléonore's; if one of you is ill, the other might at least, it seems to me, give some sign of life. I'm very upset not to receive anything from your quarter. I've cried about it. Yes, yes, you're both monsters. I've enough problems with my illness without your alarming me like this—I don't need any more, you always say in your letters, but you're giving me some.

I'm much better. I have no more blood in my stools, or viscous clots. My diarrhea is still there, a little, but it's getting less frequent, only four or five times in twenty-four hours.

You must be very cold. Here the weather is fine. Don't worry about me: I have a fire in my room, and the sun comes in the whole blessed day.

I'm doing appliqué work on sackcloth—that is, I cut out and pin up the pieces of cloth you've sent me from Grasse. That doesn't tire me, but other kinds of sewing and such, I still can't get back to. I completely forgot to tell you how much Marie thanks you for the scarves you sent for her children. That dear Marie, I use her from time to time (she doesn't take full days), she gets a lot of work done, and above all she has a rare honesty, which is unusual nowadays among domestics. She's one more of those old pieces of family furniture of bygone days, but, alas, a species that is disappearing like everything else in this world!

Since I'm going to write a note to Éléonore, I'll leave you now, so as not to get too tired, for in the process of regaining my strength I still must take it terribly easy.

My fondest wishes to you, dear Mama.

Marthe

ÉMILIE DE MONTBOURG
TO CHARLES DE CERILLEY
Montpellier, December 13, 1897

Dear Charles,

So that you will understand the delay in correspondence that worried Marthe, I must explain the quite involuntary cause of it. *As soon as* your first letter arrived with details about Mougins, I answered my daughter's letter containing your little note, written as you were leaving her. As always, I addressed it, put it inside another envelope, and sent it to Edwige. Since the postman came by while she was away, however, the maid, through an excess of caution, put it in a drawer that is rarely opened and forgot to tell her mistress about it. It was quite by chance that Edwige found it, and I for my part was tormenting myself for not receiving news even while I was being taken to task for not writing!

That was being treated as obstinate silence. How people judge falsely when they want to find fault with someone!

Yesterday you sent me Monsieur Robert's letter complaining about the bad effect produced on his wife's health by this worry; I'm sorry. I didn't wait for the second letter that he said Marthe was to write, and that I haven't yet received, in order to reply right away that the person who had undertaken to put my letter in the mail had totally forgotten it and made her excuses for it to me, after at last doing her errand. Will they believe it?

But I marvel that my son-in-law concerns himself so much about the small cares I may involuntarily cause my daughter through a delay in the mail, whereas he worries so little about those, the far more serious ones, that can be caused by the discussion concerning Georges. Since we are to leave him with the nurse one more year, and you were advised of this, I was hoping that would give Marthe the time to recover morally and physically.

His letter is very proper: it would fool those who don't know him. He wants to take advantage of the effect he has tried to produce in you by his display of feelings that you found "prettier than nature," and he is so sure of it that he throws himself in your arms and assures you of his need for calm in family relations—when his wife is seriously ill from the scenes of all sorts he has treated her to for three and a half years!

To come to that point, he must in your presence have eaten a good piece of his mother-in-law[40] and must think he has an unshakable hold on your esteem. That would be amusing for the gallery if we could forget about the prospective gunshots for the child, the regret expressed at not finding a bandit for hire to destroy us. . . .

You tell me that I'll be blamed for using his powerlessness to pay the expenses for the child. I don't care a rap, for you get a grip where you can on dangerous creatures of this type.

For the rest, let's await good advice.

My very fond greetings.

Your affectionate sister,

Émilie

CHARLES DE CERILLEY
TO ÉMILIE DE MONTBOURG
Hyères, December 17, 1897

Dear Émilie,
   Your last letter includes various mistaken notions which I will try to correct.

   Contrary to what you think, your son-in-law maintained a very great reserve concerning you, and did not, as you say, in my presence "eat a good piece of his mother-in-law," which I would not have tolerated. To the single grievance you articulated about his health—broken down, you say, because he lacks a beard, for you a certain sign of acquaintance with Saint Veronica[41]—I could only tell you that that sign was no proof at all and that your language was blameworthy. When I explained the motive and the causes of your leaving Grasse, based on his being rightly or wrongly accused of ringing bells or having bells rung at your door at improper hours with the intention of troubling your rest and consequently your health, I told him I myself had given the advice to get out of there. He defended himself, but mildly, and I strongly censured the action, whoever had taken it. Now, who had a guilty interest in doing it? You see, I tightened the vise very hard, but in a way that would allow my ears to stay open to hear everything. So you're wrong to think he made me his dupe with his fine pretenses of feelings. I'm fully persuaded that I did a lot of good for your young family through my reflections, forcing them to think for the present and for the future. Both have often let themselves be carried away about things and needed a counterweight of calm. God grant that my intervention may bear lasting fruits. Marthe told me *in private* that she had made good resolutions in that regard, and I strongly encouraged her to. You see, it's prudent for you not to take at face value all her reactions and expressions.

   I didn't set before your son-in-law any of your probable conditions concerning Georges, so the field is open. Now, since you don't seem to value my ideas on this subject very highly, I ask you to seek advice from your lawyer about it, and get him to formulate it in writing, which will have more weight in your son-in-law's eyes. I'm willing to serve as intermediary in this way, but I can take personal charge *only of what I can fully approve.* It's for this reason that I demand a complete picture, with all its details, and by another hand than mine.

   Well, the verbal violences of your son-in-law in moments of *very understandable* irritation aren't worth a thing. Good Lord! How I wish I could convert you two to that just idea! But you're both hypnotized, and in your eyes I am wrong. I'm very sorry about it, since that disturbs your health and the tranquillity of your everyday life. It's a great pity.

Good-bye, my dear Émilie.

Your affectionate brother,

Charles de Cerilley

CHARLES DE CERILLEY
TO ROBERT CARON D'AILLOT
Hyères, December 26, 1897

Dear Nephew,

I thank you for your affectionate letter, received yesterday, and for the good news you give me of Marthe's health.

Your aunt has been back to life for a month: color, pulse, strength, moving about easily, gaily; everything is going much better. She hums often, which is a very good sign. In short, I'm delighted at this significant return of health, which I dared not hope would be so prompt or so marked. We haven't arrived at a complete cure—oh, no—but everything makes me think we're on the way. To get there safe and sound, she'll have to stick rigorously to her severe regimen and come back south to the Midi each winter. What I say about your aunt may apply to your wife.

For myself, here is what I suggest you say to your mother-in-law concerning the things she wants to do for Georges:

1. Your mother-in-law to choose the educational institution, which you will be called on to approve before he's placed there. Absolute liberty for you to see him there, and all your rights and duties as legal father to be respected (up to you to formulate them, naturally).

2. All expenses concerning Georges personally charged to your mother-in-law, and, in default of her, to your sister-in-law Éléonore until he can be self-sufficient.

You are requested to approve these arrangements or to make such suggestions about them as you deem appropriate.

Please, my dear nephew, share with Marthe my most affectionate wishes.

Your uncle,

Charles de Cerilley

MARTHE CARON D'AILLOT
TO ÉMILIE DE MONTBOURG
Chalet Marthe, December 28, 1897

Dear Mama,

I could hardly wait to get your news, and I was beginning to despair when your letter came and restored a little balm to my heart.

I'm rather better, even much better, but still have the runs to some extent. I've put myself on a diet—that is, Robert implored me to go on one, for it's probable that I would never have done it by myself. So, dear Mama, here's my menu until further notice: semolina soup with butter, lentil soup with butter, green-pea soup with toast. The last is a kind of soup I have my cook make; she is getting quite knowledgeable.

My menu is as varied as possible without departing from the doctor's prescriptions, and since mussels and oysters are allowed, I regale myself from time to time with them. I get ocean mussels at Nice. My tom cat goes and gets me some himself; to do him justice, he doesn't neglect any occasion to please me. The oysters come from the Gironde. They're fresh, very good, and not too dear, which is a big point.

I'll probably send you, some time next week, a parcel-post package containing Éléonore's bag of postage stamps, which will contain a cockle that you don't have and a little night-table runner. I made it—that is, I painted it on sackcloth—last year (it's not so well done as if it was by an artist, but anyway I made it, with all the patience I now have).

I'll also put in with those little things the cross you gave to poor Madame Clément. She is someone who never leaves my head. I think of her always, and she will always remain in my memory and my heart.

I send you, dear Mama, and also to dear kind Éléonore, our very fond and affectionate wishes for the New Year. Let's hope that 1898 will be less rich in sad events than 1897. Both of you, be as happy as possible. I'd like to tell you that *viva voce* as I kiss and hug you very hard, but since destiny has arranged otherwise, I can only bow beneath its hand. I love you dearly, Mama, I do, and you may be sure that I never doubt your heart, darling Mother. I can't wait to resume my customary way of life, but with this accursed stomach ailment I have to take so many precautions I'm driven wild. If it weren't for my tom cat, who makes sure that I take my soup as directed and don't eat too fast, I'd have long since told the diet, the remedies, and everything else to fly away.

Yes, now I can have a little bread—very little, but still bread—with the *foie gras,* which goes down perfectly. Thanks again and always, dear Mama, for all you do for me.

I'll leave you, Mama. A thousand more tender wishes from your daughter.

Marthe

I *would* like to have a little box for knickknacks, if that's not too much trouble. I'd enjoy it a lot. I can't find any here.

CHARLES DE CERILLEY
TO ÉMILIE DE MONTBOURG
Hyères, December 29, 1897

Dear Émilie,

Thanks, first of all, for your thoughtfulness, both of you. The beautiful glacéed melon that reached us this morning will make quite an effect on January 5 at the private lunch we're giving, and we'll tell where it came from.

I'm sorry I passed you Robert d'Aillot's last letter, for you read too much between the lines. You were mistaken about his phrase ". . . thanks to the severe diet I've put her on, to some extent by force, with help from Mama, immediately the illness that wouldn't stop torturing her has almost disappeared, and the stools are becoming insignificant." In fact, our doctor had Madeleine follow a diet so severe that anemia was becoming very pronounced. Now, I who can judge on sight, both about Marthe and about Madeleine, can only approve her husband on the severity of his diet, because I've seen with my own eyes that Marthe would be likely to go off it, for she doesn't stick with anything.

Once you reach the point where you want no part of any text or treaty with your son-in-law, there's nothing else left but to live from day to day. Choose the institution you want, act as you please without consulting him. *He won't say anything,* but if the occasion should arise, you're arming him by violating and rejecting his rights as a father. Marthe asked me if she would not do well to have me destroy her will, since her husband was manifesting good feelings. I dissuaded her from this, pointing out to her that it might be useful for her to keep it, as long as she did not think it appropriate to make another one. She acknowledged that I was right. As for leaving Mougins, for a longer or a shorter time, *she doesn't want to.* She needs to stay there, she told me in a conversation alone with me. So don't be too alarmed.

Your son-in-law is not formulating any request except not to be left

223

out. If you give him satisfaction on the point of personal dignity, every-thing will go like clockwork, and you'll get all the authorizations. But if you appear to be putting him in a bad light before the public by making offensive restrictions, you're much better off living from day to day, and keeping Georges in fact under your personal, absolute tutelage. No one will make any objection, but think of the strange situation you'll be creat-ing for this child, who may perhaps not come to Mougins until he's of age!!! What will relations be between him and his parents? It's a long time now that I've been harping on this subject, for you're always finding obstacles to it; you only have to live from day to day, since *time,* as you say, is a great master. I've already written something in this general sense to Mougins. It seems to me the case has been settled.

Good-bye, dear Émilie.

Your affectionate brother,

Charles de Cerilley

Marthe complained to me *in private* that you pitched too hard into her husband, who saw your letters. She begs you to keep absolutely silent. All alone with me, she didn't seem to me as much of a martyr as you suppose. Marthe herself admits that she has often exaggerated *on her side:* bear in mind that very freely expressed admission.

MARTHE CARON D'AILLOT
TO ÉMILIE DE MONTBOURG
Mougins, December 29, 1897

Dear Mama,

I'm reopening my letter to smother you with thanks for all the count-less things to spoil me which you never stop showering on me, as does Éléonore, who is clearly the best of sisters to be always thinking how to divert a poor patient like me. That's a real act of charity on her part, for I'm terribly bored with taking all the precautions necessary for my condi-tion, and now or never is the time to say I'm up here with them. You're very kind, too kind, dear Mama, to add a 100-franc bill to all your other lovely favors. Thank you, thank you; that way I'll get oysters and mussels a bit more often. I don't know what words to use to express to you all the affection and love that my heart holds for you, darling Mother. If only I could hang on your neck, embrace you with all my strength, as I gladly would; but, alas, I won't be able to budge for a long time; my bowels have been so scoured out that I can't even allow myself to go often to see my dear d'Artagnans[42] and my beloved little pullets, for as soon as I take trips of any length on my little legs, the stomach and the lower-back pains grip me right away. What an old crock I am. I don't look so well as when I saw you in Grasse. You know, it'll soon be three months that I've had the trots, and that ailment is far from charming.

I renew all my wishes for the New Year to you and also to my dear sister, Éléonore. I thank her for the pretty books she's sending me. As soon as they're received, I'll hurry and give her my assessment of them, but I'm sure in advance that they can only be interesting, for Éléonore is surely a good judge in such matters.

I leave you with regret, but I'm a bit tired. I've picked up my needlework again a little, but I get tired quickly, so I can't do much at one time.

Again, a thousand trillions of tender wishes from your daughter,

Marthe

1898

CHARLES DE CERILLEY
TO ÉLÉONORE DE MONTBOURG
Hyères, January 3, 1898

Dear Éléonore,

Your letter gives us great pleasure because of the good wishes it contains; but I see that your mother is more and more susceptible to bronchitis. She's wrong to be alarmed about the condition of Marthe's health. Your aunt had a much worse time of it, and the doctor put her on a much more severe diet than Marthe's. *You have to do that during the acute stage.* Robert d'Aillot was quite right to make her follow the severe diet *to the letter.*

I'm sending you the letter your sister has just written to your aunt for New Year's Day so you can judge her condition. Now, what I've seen with my own eyes, heard with my own ears, all alone with her, proves to me that her letter is sincere.

My trip to Montpellier has been decided on in principle, but the date is uncertain.

I'm trying with all my power to dissuade your mother from going to Nice to take care of Marthe there; *Marthe has no need of it.* Moreover, she wouldn't want it: she doesn't want to leave her husband or her home; nor should she, for leaving this way on account of her health, when there were plenty of women around her, would be viewed askance by the public. A woman who is concerned about her good name should not open herself up to criticism. These observations are mine only, and for you two alone.

Good-bye, dear Éléonore. Your aunt joins me in sending you and your mother her timely best wishes, very special, and surely without the usual banality of New Year's Day. We both send our very fondest greetings.

Your most devoted uncle,

Charles de Cerilley

MARTHE CARON D'AILLOT
TO ÉMILIE DE MONTBOURG
Mougins, January 4, 1898

Dear Mama,

I thank you for your offer to take care of me at your house, but in spite of all your kind attentions and your affection for me, you'll never be able to replace my husband; I tell you this once and for all, so you'll get it through your head. Also, I don't want to go into a ladies' pension. Oh, no, good heavens, I don't want that at all.

I did indeed receive the packing case with the kilo of chocolate, the box of tapioca, the wafers, and the cheese; all that was welcomed with great pleasure, as I've already told you in my letter of December 31, which no doubt you haven't got yet.

I recommend to you an herb tea of wild geranium; that's what's going to complete my cure definitively.

I'm going to send you on Thursday a parcel-post package containing Éléonore's bag, your runner, a box holding a sample of a new product that very nicely takes the place of shortening, oil, and butter, very pleasant-tasting: vegetaline (vegetable butter), derived from coconut, sells for the modest price of 14 sous a kilo. We've been using it for some time and I find it very economical.

I frankly admit, dear Mama, that your letter put me in a bad humor, and that even though I love you with all my heart, I won't leave my husband, who's indispensable to me, or my house. But poor you, what would you do with me after I'd been with you a week without my tom cat? No, no, dear Mama, I have a man, I don't leave him. Thank you just the same. I thank you for your offer, but it's impossible.

A loving hug for you, and one for the dear *invalid.*
Devotedly yours,

Marthe

ÉMILIE DE MONTBOURG
TO HENRI DE CERILLEY
Montpellier, January 5, 1898

Dear Henri,

Marthe has had a relapse, which coincided with the return of her mother-in-law, who is very hard on her. There's some improvement at the moment. God grant that it may last! When he saw her so sick as a result of the perpetual scenes he puts her through, her husband must have been frightened. I didn't hide the fact that the doctors I've consulted in her behalf attributed this illness to distressing emotions and preoccupations, which must stop before any medical treatment can bring on a cure. I wrote that the husband had a real self-interest in preserving his wife's life, because on her life, her health, and her happiness the future really depended. He must have given it some thought even as he complained of what he calls my "thrusts," for he knows he would lose a great deal if he lost his wife!

It was at that moment that your father went to Mougins, and Monsieur Robert was well aware how to soft-soap him to win his sympathies. He inaugurated for his wife the loving attentions not customary until then, and Marthe, in her happiness, didn't tell your father all she had to complain of. My brother, enchanted, made himself my son-in-law's intermediary to obtain from us, apropos of little G., concessions that we must not make, for the engagements he would get in return would be only illusions, since legally he could at any time resume his rights. As for promises from him, even in writing, since he treats them as *fictitious* and doesn't keep them, we never believe them, because he has neither heart nor honor! But your father was so well taken in that I've had to battle for two months and get advice from a lawyer, a former jurist. This struggle has been distressing for me, I assure you, for I should have been able to count on my brother, whom I keep informed of everything! I've put into this all the calm and patience I can muster, so that our fraternal affection may not suffer from it.

Ah! You're right, my dear Henri, to abominate that aristocratic class *when it lacks honor,* because then it lacks its fundamental virtue. Its members are all the less commendable in that the honorable past of their ancestors crushes them! Those who have only pride in the virtue of others are taking a wrong road that leads them astray. But, thank God, there are still gentlemen like you, and the race of them is not lost. My fondest regards to you, dear Henri, and also to your wife and the children. I like to rest my heart upon you, and Éléonore does the same.

Your affectionate aunt,

Baroness de Montbourg

ROBERT CARON D'AILLOT
TO CHARLES DE CERILLEY
Mougins, January 8, 1898

Dear Uncle,

I did indeed receive your letter, and the propositions it contains are completely to my taste in principle, and, except for a few remarks that I'll submit to you in a few days in an official way, you'll have nothing left to do but transmit them. In principle, however, I accept what you propose without modifications, and I'll be happy if the matter can be arranged to everyone's satisfaction.

Marthe is better. Her diarrhea has stopped and the stools have become regular, once a day. However, since yesterday, she had a few windy episodes, which were fortunately not followed by storms. I attribute this relapse to a chill, for at the same time she had a sore throat and some pains in the lower back. In two or three days there will be nothing left of it. She hasn't gone off her diet, which she will keep to for a long time with a rigor that I'm supervising. It's such an annoying malady that it would really make a saint lose patience. Anyway, more than ever we must keep a stout heart against bad fortune, and that's what we're doing. I leave you, dear uncle, repeating that in a few days you'll receive a letter accepting your propositions, which you may submit to the interested parties.

Please accept, dear uncle, with my fondest greetings and Marthe's for the two of you, a cordial and affectionate handshake.

Robert Caron d'Aillot

CHARLES DE CERILLEY
TO ÉMILIE DE MONTBOURG
Hyères, January 22, 1898

Dear Émilie,

It's too bad that there isn't any hotel near your house; but a quarter-hour's walk doesn't frighten me just as long as it's not two or three times that. I'd rather have the hotel room than that of the man who rents carriages, but for lack of the former I have no prejudice against the latter, if it is just as clean. I don't care at all about luxury, especially for three or four nights. What you tell me about the Montpellier road system will make me wait for a drier season. I accept with pleasure the hospitality of your table, but I warn you that I'm of an ever greater frugality. Lunch: a dish of meat and vegetables, a dessert or two, a cup of coffee, and that's it. In the evening, ditto, minus the coffee. I don't eat meat on Friday, when my health is good. A bowl of milk when I get up in the morning. I'll find that at the hotel, no doubt.

Madame Milan has told me that during the acute stage of her enteritis, she used to take two enemas in a row: the first made with camomile flowers to empty the intestine, the second with starch. For Madeleine it was with boric acid; then the doctor gave up the boric acid to rely only on the diet, with which we are making out well. Above all, you need much calm, physical and moral.

I'll do everything I can to go back to Mougins, fully convinced of the usefulness of the trip by the moral influence which resulted from the first one. You amuse me with your fear that my mind was seduced. I thought I was protected by my age. Bless Providence for seeing I was heeded. That results at the same time from my impartial character and from the way I took their attempt at blackmail by answering your son-in-law and his mother. You were afraid of the effect of my tone. You see very well today that it is good, and so good you think I've been cajoled too much.

I assume that your son-in-law will come here next week; between now and then, prepare your answer to the letter of his that I've sent you. Write me as soon as possible, so the postman will not deliver a letter from Montpellier that he can see. The postman puts the letters into a basket that we hoist with a string after hearing his ring. Your son-in-law might very well come out of his room and see the letters *on their arrival.*

Good-bye, dear sister; share our tender wishes with Éléonore.

Your affectionate brother,

Charles de Cerilley

ÉMILIE DE MONTBOURG
TO CHARLES DE CERILLEY
Montpellier, January 25, 1898

Dear Charles,

Either you didn't transmit our propositions in their full tenor, or my son-in-law takes no account of our conditions, for he persists in maintaining his legal rights. If he holds to his claim, we, for our part, refuse all commitments for the present and for the future. But we will be able, *of our own free will,* to continue the work we've begun for Georges, under the supervision of men who know the channels leading to the *grandes écoles,* [43] and from there to a liberal and honorable career. We two alone are to be the judges of the moment when the child can be entered in an educational institution, the choice and place of which we reserve to ourselves. Nor do we accept the term "personal expenses," which is too flexible; we'll be the judges of what is necessary.

Let's also talk about the circumstances of what my son-in-law calls "the business"! Until now, in his receipt for the quarterly payment, he used to put simply, "Received from my mother-in-law, Madame de Montbourg, for quarterly payment on the dowry annuity of my wife, the sum of . . ." This time he thought he should add, "Received from Madame de Montbourg, having no known residence . . ." Why not say "with neither hearth nor home"? That would be even better! Isn't that just one more impertinence as thanks to me for sending the money so promptly?

I certainly hope that Marthe's health will allow her to stay at your house in Hyères while her husband goes to Marseille and to Aix. Try to inspire in her the courage to withdraw her son from a milieu that is dangerous for him and distressing for her, as she knows well. That's her *duty* and her *right.*

My fondest greetings.

Your affectionate sister,

Émilie

[Added at bottom of preceding letter:]

Dear Uncle,

Mama wants me to tell you that she does not at all believe it was the pleasant emotions caused by the idea of the trip that made Marthe ill again, but the rather very painful idea of discussing Georges. God grant that her husband may bring her to you and everything will turn out for the best.

Éléonore

MONSIEUR MARTIN
TO ÉMILIE DE MONTBOURG
Grasse, February 11, 1898

Dear Baroness,

Yesterday Madame Martin had the pleasure of seeing Madame d'Aillot, a pleasure that was markedly shared. Your son-in-law was at Cannes that day. The two ladies were able to talk for a quarter of an hour without a witness. At first your daughter wouldn't say anything, but, finally convinced that it was for her own good, she offered a glimpse of the life she is allowed to live. She cannot write *one* line *to anyone* without her husband's permission and review; she never has a sou at her disposal, which meant that the 50 francs that you sent to her were welcome. Nevertheless, that sum was not accepted at the outset, for it is awkward for Madame d'Aillot to receive money unbeknownst to her husband. On Madame Martin's urging, she consented to take it, which seems to have brought her real happiness. But she urged us to be sure to remind you not to mention the 50 francs in your letters to her, for her husband, who reads everything she receives or sends, would not fail to ask for an explanation that could not help being stormy.

Our duty, madame, is to tell you that your daughter has become quite thin, which is nothing extraordinary with the diarrhea she has. From what she says, she goes no fewer than twenty or twenty-five times a day, and according to the doctor there's nothing that can cure her except constant attention. Madame d'Aillot likes fish, and that's almost the only food she digests well. Unfortunately, at Mougins she can't get it for herself as often as she'd like. Could we arrange a scheme to have her get some from Grasse from time to time, by way of the cheese merchants? We'll do as you see fit.

Madame d'Aillot will never leave her husband, she declared to my wife. She doesn't think it is possible for you to take care of her in a villa at Nice or in its environs, for, she claims, her husband will never put up with seeing you.

Nevertheless, *Madame Martin's opinion* is that if we persist on this count, Madame d'Aillot, seeing her health weaken from day to day, would finally go to your house on condition that she would see her husband, every day, though he must never meet you face to face.

Your daughter has a rather serious case of enteritis, and to the material cares that can be given her should be added the moral tranquillity that is refused her. Recently, Madame d'Aillot spoke ill of you, and Madame Robert replied as she should and tried to put her out the door of the chalet. Then the son arrived and ordered his wife, Madame Robert, to entertain her mother-in-law—if not affectionately, at least politely—when she visited.

There are so many things to tell you that in spite of myself my style betrays my haste. I'll ask you, madame, please to forgive the incoherence that you will note in my letter.

It seems that next March 26 Monsieur d'Aillot's brother who is a doctor in Paris is to be married. It's more than likely that Monsieur Robert will go to his brother's wedding. Your daughter has promised to let us know of this departure, and then Madame Martin would hurry to Mougins. Between now and then, madame, you'll have the time to make such preparations as seem best to establish lasting and secret understandings among your daughter, yourself, and us. On leaving the chalet, Madame Martin gave a little present to the boy who serves your daughter. It might perhaps not be impossible to make use of him if we pay him. There is also a servant girl, but she doesn't seem very intelligent, and we would have to fear she might betray her mistress to the advantage of her master.

It is quite understood, madame, that in your letters to Madame d'Aillot there must be no talk of Madame Martin's visit unless she has spoken of it herself.

I was forgetting to tell you that in front of her sisters-in-law Madame d'Aillot had given my wife a pompous eulogy of her husband.

Madame Martin and I beg you both, madame and mademoiselle, to take good care of yourselves in your struggle against the flu, and to believe we are your very devoted,

Martin

P.S. Madame Robert, in fear that some day her husband may find himself in your presence, urges you to burn all the confidential letters she may have written you.

MARTHE CARON D'AILLOT
TO ÉMILIE DE MONTBOURG
Mougins, February 14, 1898

Dear Mama,

I forgot in my letter of the day before yesterday to ask you for a little money, to make a present for my brother-in-law Louis, who is to be married some time in March. I've never planned to attend the wedding, especially since I'm sick, and my husband won't go, either, because of the expense the trip would involve.

I've had to give up the horrible stag-horn tea mentioned in good Monsieur Devaux's recipe, which made me want to vomit. I'm obliged to go back once more on wild-geranium tea, which causes me no nausea. I also drink rice water that has lemon slices cooked with the rice, which makes an herb tea that greatly calms the thirst I feel. I alternate cups of the geranium and the refreshing herb tea. Since I write you in the evening and I have the good habit of sleeping on my chaise longue after supper, I'm half asleep as I'm writing. I also wanted to write a word to Éléonore, but I want to sleep more than I want to write, so I'll put off that occupation until later.

My very fondest wishes, dear Mama.

Devotedly yours,

Marthe

ÉMILIE DE MONTBOURG
TO CHARLES DE CERILLEY
Montpellier, February 19, 1898

Dear Charles,

I'm sending you a new letter from Marthe, who, you'll see, delayed a request for money as long as she could, and is making it only on orders, for she thoroughly detests all the d'Aillots. You will admit that Monsieur Robert has no lack of nerve—after all, he got the quarterly payment a month ago!

If the notary hasn't yet sent the 300 francs, he won't take long to do it, and in that case I would ask you to advance 100 francs, for I mean to prove to my son-in-law that whatever he may do, I'll do what I think right. I think you'll go along with me on this: if I refused, my poor daughter would suffer from the horrors they'd say about her mother! But in sending the 100 francs, you might say that a young woman always likes a ring and that you can find a lot of very pretty ones for much less than 100 francs. From you, Monsieur Robert will take it well; I can't give any advice, as you well know.

You left here, my dear, an excellent reputation as a paragon of husbands, respecter of nuns, and best of brothers! You may well believe that I join the chorus with enthusiasm and that we've gained in the esteem of these ladies by having such a paragon in our family. When they learn that you're on friendly terms with the brother of their bishop, that will be even better! By the way, be sure to keep his address, for we might need him.

I'm very happy about the long talks we've been able to have, which are useful in the situation because of the impressions they've left us, on both your side and mine. I've got more confidence in your support, and you've seen that, even while keeping myself on the defensive with dignity, I bear no hatred. As for the mistrust, it's necessary for our safety. My fondest wishes, dear Charles.

Your affectionate sister,

Émilie

ROBERT CARON D'AILLOT
TO CHARLES DE CERILLEY
Mougins, March 11, 1898

Dear Uncle,

Your letter gave us pleasure, as did the announcement of your visit for April 13. Marthe is very well, and this time I hope that the enteritis has finally been fully cured. However, we take precautions to avoid a dismal return and its consequences. I'm happy about it; she's regaining her strength and visibly putting weight on, her appetite has come back, and I'm often obliged to check her ardor for fear of a relapse. In the last few days, she's had some very painful facial neuralgia. I attribute it to weakness, and I treated it with cerebrine, which had a marvelous effect. I hope it'll be conjured away by certain precautions we are taking against the cold; the foul weather we're having at the moment is in large part the cause of these ugly surprises.

The automobile race had to face frightful weather, so the poor drivers were hardly brilliant when they passed along the Antibes plain; those riding motor tricycles[44] were so covered with mud that only their eyes were clear. They were sad to behold. With good weather it would have been of great interest; it's really too bad.

I'm happy to have made one more adept at cycling. You see it's not so hard to learn, and I'm sure you'll soon be ready to undertake a cycling excursion. That will be very pleasant, and next year we'll take some bicycle trips around Hyères. I encourage you to stick with it and not take your few falls seriously—that's the right way to get the hang of it!

My situation is making good progress. This morning I saw the registrar of the Commercial Court of Antibes, who told me he had received the order to post it; once this is done, he'll send a laudatory letter about me to the public prosecutor's office, signed by the president of the court, saying there was no opposition to the rehabilitation, that I deserve in every respect, and so on—those are his words, which I repeat to you in the belief that you'll be pleased to be kept up to date on this affair.

I leave you, dear uncle, begging you to give all our fond wishes to my aunt, while keeping a large share for yourself.

Robert Caron d'Aillot

MARTHE CARON D'AILLOT
TO ÉMILIE DE MONTBOURG
Mougins, March 26, 1898

Dear Mama,

I thank you with all my heart for offering to send me dishes all prepared so I don't get tired, but our sister-in-law and her husband will not be here till August or September. How good you are, dear Mama, to be always thinking of your daughter. Thank you, thank you; you thought of my birthday, dear Mama; thanks to you, and to kind Éléonore, who also thinks of her sister Marthe. Your flannels give me great pleasure. I know, I no longer have my poor Madame Clément, and I miss her a lot. I see it every day: although I work, she did so many things in the house, and of course it was she, while now . . .

My tom cat is very nice to me, poor little devil—honest, he's nice to his little wife. My coveys, dear Mama, are coming along well. I have three hens brooding ducks and one brooding pullets whose hatching I'm expecting Tuesday. You see, if all these coveys succeed, we'll have quite a bit of poultry for the market, and this year we'll sell some of our pullets and ducklings.

I thank you very much indeed for taking an interest in these hatchings. All these mama hens give me plenty to do, honestly. Every morning I get them up to have them eat and drink. The first ones who started brooding get back on the eggs themselves, but the others make a frightful racket in the kitchen. That's where I feed them, for, to spare me the trouble of coming and going to the chicken coop, my tom cat has had me install the brooders in the dining room, and I feed the hens in the kitchen.

I'm very glad to know you're better, dear Mama beloved; take good care of yourself, please. It's true you have Éléonore to keep an eye on you, as you say.

Still more fond wishes from your devoted daughter, dear Mama.

Marthe

MARTHE CARON D'AILLOT
TO ÉMILIE DE MONTBOURG
Mougins, April 13, 1898

Dear Mama,

Our dear uncle arrived in good health and not too tired. He's staying with us until Sunday evening; although it's not much, we're very glad to have him longer than the last time.

I'm very glad to know you're well enough to take a few rides in a carriage, from what my uncle told me. Apparently Éléonore is well, too. Good, all the better. I'm happy about this good news, believe me, dear Mama, for it gives me much distress when I learn you're ill.

What a lot of goodies, dear Mama! Why, this roast of veal is beautiful, and how good it will be; and this pâté in its golden crust makes my mouth water; this cake, which will be devoured with eager gourmandise—everything has been received with open arms. I renew all my affectionate thanks, also for the pretty Scotch stockings, the excellent quince candy, the chocolate drops, letter paper, flannels, and the books that Éléonore added to all the nice things you sent me via Uncle Charles. The bottles of champagne you spoke to me about in your next-to-last letter would have been welcomed with the greatest pleasure in other, less sorrowful, circumstances, but my uncle and aunt thought this was not an occasion to go popping champagne, and we fully agree with them, for, with that poor tomb barely closed, we can hardly be full of joy. I thank you just the same, dear Mama, for thinking of it. That will be for another time—thank you, thank you.

I'm very well. My enteritis is leaving me alone, so both of you should be reassured about me. Besides, my uncle may write about it. I'm not going to seal my letter this evening, so he can tell you a little about me.

I'm going to hug him, it'll seem as though it's you, dear Mama, whom I love dearly, believe me, please.

I thank Éléonore very much indeed for these two volumes, which give me pleasure. Jules Verne writes with such spirit, and there's always something to learn even while enjoying a pleasant diversion. Yes, I enjoy it, so thank you again.

Marthe

Robert tells me to thank you personally for all the nice things you sent us via our uncle.

[Added at bottom of preceding letter:]

Dear Émilie,
On my arrival at Cannes, I found Monsieur Robert's carriage and the young family at the station, happy to see me back.

Marthe is very well and looks well; moreover, she is very happy and is on the best of terms with all the members of her new family. I'm very happy to see that and I hope it will remain unchanged.

Tomorrow I'm driving Robert and Marthe to Nice and having them to lunch.

As you see from Marthe's letter, all your errands have been done and received with personal gratitude well expressed.

Good-bye, dear Émilie.

Your affectionate brother,

Charles de Cerilley

CHARLES DE CERILLEY
TO ÉMILIE DE MONTBOURG
Hyères, April 19, 1898

Dear Émilie,
I'm not using my mourning stationery today, for my travel journal is bound to be long and I need a lot of room. I came back last night in frightful weather, and found Madeleine not badly off and happy to see me back.

Before I relate each day to you, let me tell you quickly that Marthe is very well and very happy. This is positive and visible, and she repeated it to me several times in private. It is so true that she would like me to destroy the will that, as you know, she entrusted to me last year. I got her to agree that she would let it remain in my hands, since her happiness is still too recent in date. For example, she ardently wishes you to destroy or put in a safe place the few letters she wrote you while fed up with her

238

husband, in the acute period of their quarrels, for, she says, if suddenly you were not there and if, there, they find these letters under seal, and her husband learned of them, that would mean the definitive loss of her happiness. This is very serious, so we must reckon with it. My opinion is that you should not put these letters in a position to be placed under seals, an operation that your son-in-law would have the right to demand, even from a distance. That said, I resume the narrative of my journal.

First day, the 13th: Marthe came to Cannes with her husband to get me at the station. In the evening, Madame d'Aillot and her daughters came to supper, and your provisions (pâté and smoked ham) were served that very evening; the roast of veal was cooked the next day. I clearly stressed what you'd sent when I spoke to Marthe, who said how good you were. On that score, a little murmur of approval.

That same evening I gave your son-in-law the 100-franc note. Again anonymous thanks, but see what I did next: the next morning, Marthe comes into my bedroom alone to talk, and tells me that her life is very happy and that she thanks her stars for the behavior of every member of the family without exception. "Then," I said to her, "why does your husband, apropos of your mother's presents, which I simply brought, affect to say 'Thank you, uncle,' and not 'Thanks to my mother-in-law'?" At that moment, enter Robert, and I continued my observation by saying, "A tip of the hat, even from your enemy, demands reciprocity, doesn't it? Consequently, a present given requires a token of gratitude."—"No doubt, uncle, no doubt, and I commission you to say it to my mother-in-law."— "But," I answered him, "it's better that it should be you who commission your wife to say it *on your behalf.*" He and Marthe agreed to that perfectly. He's even inclined to write you his gratitude if he were sure of pleasing you. I dissuaded him, because one mustn't go too fast on one side or the other.

On the 14th, after lunch, we all went up to Le Fermet to Uncle Tavelle's. We were received in the garden; M. was very nice with me. I exclaimed over the view and, after talking about several subjects, asked Monsieur Tavelle du Fermet to let me admire the promenade around the château, from which you get three views, the main one being of the sea, in the direction of Nice. He and I were alone. Quickly I take the opportunity to broach the d'Aillot question and that of the young couple. He's up on everything, blames his nephew and those around him for having several times humiliated Marthe for a past that was the result of a morbid state. We agreed on all points.

On the 15th I took Robert and Marthe out for the day: a walk before lunch at 11:15, then cafés, then a visit with his brother the architect, then for a big carriage ride outside Nice, around the residences of the queen of England and Monsieur Félix Faure.[45] Then refreshments: beer and Bavarian cream for Marthe. Finally, a visit to the nursery incubator, where we saw a baby who had come into the world at six months weighing 1 kilo 60 [about 3.5 pounds]. I paid *all* the expenses of this little excursion, which do not exceed 23 francs 50, and I had a very nice time myself.

Marthe was delighted with this little trip to Nice, as she told me over ten times.

On the 16th, we dined at Madame d'Aillot's, and she put herself out for me, though I could not do much justice to it, for away from home my stomach gets rebellious.

Finally, parting at the Cannes station in beastly weather, Robert repeated to me, "Good-bye, uncle, try to keep up the good work." "Yes," I replied, "but help me." And that's understood.

Conclusion: this second trip completed the good work that the first one started, for it's dating from the end of September that not only has calm returned, but also the attentions, the little favors, have been regular. Never the slightest allusion to the past—in short, not the least little cloud, Marthe affirmed to me several times. She tells me to thank you with all her heart for the 100 francs in gold that I gave her *secretly*. I asked her what she did with this secret resource: she uses a bit of it for herself, a bit for the household when there is need. "But, then, your husband notices something abnormal?" She simply answers him, "That's my little reserve fund," and he doesn't insist, and doesn't nose about, but guesses perfectly well without saying so that these funds don't fall from the moon.

Marthe wants very much to have the new and latest photograph of Georges, which you spoke to her about. The first picture is still on their bedroom mantelpiece.

Marthe asked me where you were, but I maintained an inviolable silence. The poor child longs to see you and also her sister. That's fine, but what's too bad is that she doesn't want to have children at all, and says so.

Now Robert explains his fear of not having children in future by some problem with the position of the uterus, and not by the atrophy of the ovaries. Yes, the injection of the sublimate is indeed medicinal in *such and such a dose,* but it will sterilize at *another dose.* A speculum examination, I've told him, would get him clear about any defect in position of the uterus. In any case, that will never be a cause for regret in Marthe, and that distresses me for her. I've kept to myself my inner feelings, for maternal feeling is either *there* or *is not.*

I don't think I have forgotten anything in this journal.

I'm glad to have carried out my mission at Mougins—to your satisfaction, I hope—and to have given your children the pleasure of the day in Nice when they didn't have a centime to spend. That's my personal present, and also that of our household.

Good-bye, my dear sister.

Your devoted brother,

Charles de Cerilley

ÉMILIE DE MONTBOURG
TO HENRI DE CERILLEY
Montpellier, April 25, 1898

Dear Henri,

Your father has written me that Marthe is to come to Lyon next May 5 to undergo a rather serious operation, and at the same time he forbids my talking to him about it by letter so as not to worry my sister-in-law, from whom they hide things that can upset her. But since you'll have my brother at your house before the operation, please bring to his attention, *in private,* the dangers that may result. Here, next door to our apartment, a young girl succumbed just lately to an operation on the uterus which the surgeons claimed *always* succeeded. It was to make her periods less painful. Just think of the parents' regrets! Now for Marie, the problem seems to be an abnormality that doesn't keep her from living, and which nature by itself might perhaps modify with time.

At the death of my first child, emotion had caused a displacement of the uterus in me, but in those days they didn't go in for operations lightly, and with the use of a pomade of belladonna the organ returned to its place in time! I would have consented to spend my life stretched out on a chaise longue; as for an operation, *never!* Nowadays the doctors too readily risk the lives of women, and make many victims. I thought I must write you about it, dear Henri, because you have influence with your father and it is urgent to counteract the medical profession's current tendency to use and take advantage of the patients they know can pay for the talents of the surgeons.

And while you're at it, you really ought to try to dissuade your father from his infatuation with the bicycle. At his age, the shaking up caused by falls is not without danger, and you know he's just had one rather brutal one. I haven't been able to make him give up this exercise.

My brother's two visits to Mougins have contributed to Marthe's happiness, because these cowards are afraid of the beard, and he has set himself up as an energetic righter of wrongs, *for others.* You see it's not hard *for a man* to make them pull in their claws, while they play the villains in front of women! Oh, for the good old days when Queen Berthe span and knights were bold!

With that I leave you, dear Henri. With fond wishes from the heart, your very affectionate aunt,

Baroness de Montbourg

ROBERT CARON D'AILLOT
TO CHARLES DE CERILLEY
Mougins, May 30, 1898

Dear Uncle,

It's a long time already that I've been wanting to write you, but I've always been kept from it by diverse circumstances, the main one being my hay harvest, which was a source of enormous concern because of the weather: the first half went very well, but I've had unheard-of trouble with the second half, to keep it from rotting.

Marthe is still quite well. We thought for a moment we could announce to you a great piece of news, obvious proof of perfect health; unfortunately, after a clearly marked delay of fourteen days and various symptoms the presence of which I haven't yet got over, we had to give up hope for the moment, though we may begin again next month. That certainly proves that Marthe's health has made great progress and that her enteritis has made her turn over a new leaf, about which I couldn't be more delighted.

Before I can respond to my mother-in-law's requests, please give me the result of your negotiations.

I leave you, dear uncle, with very fond wishes to you and my aunt. Marthe joins me in sending the same.

Robert Caron d'Aillot

ÉMILIE DE MONTBOURG
TO CHARLES DE CERILLEY
Montpellier, June 29, 1898

Dear Charles,

Here is the layout of our villa here. On the ground floor: salon, small parlor, dining room, kitchen, and outside storeroom, bathrooms; on the second floor: my bedroom, staircase, Éléonore's room, a spare room, and English-style bathrooms; on the third floor: maid's room, two big closets, which I use for linen and hanging things; one storeroom, and finally a gazebo for lovers of scenery, fireworks, or the geography of the sky; under the stairway is a cellar that serves as a butler's pantry. Farther out and facing the door of the villa, a wood box with a supply of firewood. You see it's pretty complete; we're perfectly independent here. Four mail pickups and four deliveries a day. The mailbox is opposite the landlord's house, fifty paces from ours.

Our maid seems to suit us; we pay her 30 francs a month, which makes 360 francs a year. But since she has two children and an old mother and she has had to leave her husband, who is settled in with another woman, and she had nevertheless to bear the entire cost of the household, we'll be obliged by our charitable heart to give her something extra from time to time.

I'm very glad you find my letter to my son-in-law suitable. It cost me much effort. Éléonore thinks I looked as if I am recovering from an illness. The fact is that I have become quite constipated again. I'll continue our incognito as long as possible, for it's our security. The well-proved indiscretions of Monsieur Robert made staying at Grasse impossible for us. He'll do as much here to be unpleasant to us and do us harm. Now that my physical strength is diminishing, I can't live a nomad's life without striking a blow, and if we were obliged to leave Montpellier, this time it would be for America. Come what may, that's no joke, I assure you, but we'll manage to find peace at all costs.

My very fond greetings, dear Charles. Don't expose yourself to sunstroke. Your very affectionate sister,

Émilie

CHARLES DE CERILLEY
TO HENRI DE CERILLEY
Sangy, August 24, 1898

Dear Henri,

Important and serious business! Marthe has run away from Mougins to take refuge at her mother's. Monday morning I received a wire from R. d'Aillot phrased thus: "Very serious, urgent matter here Mougins. Inform mother-in-law, Marthe missing—Signed Robert." Two hours later, wire from your aunt: "Marthe here, your presence urgent, situation serious —Signed Émilie." During those two hours between the two wires, I thought it might be suicide. I answered your aunt and Mougins that my health, sorely tried by the heat, prevented me from risking, at my age, a serious danger. Your poor aunt didn't think about that in her panic. I'm waiting for details, for I still have only the wires. I assume that R. d'Aillot was brutal and Marthe fled. The matter will be investigated in the family first, and I'm going to hear everything with calm and impartiality.

I'm inviting your aunt to follow the advice of her attorney, for she has mistrusted me for a long time. She thinks I'm biased.

Fondest greetings from your affectionate father,

Charles de Cerilley

ALEXIS TAVELLE DU FERMET
TO CHARLES DE CERILLEY
Nice, August 28, 1898

Dear Sir,

I've received your letter of August 26, and I had already received two letters from Madame de Montbourg, informing me of the distressing affair. I hope there's nothing too serious in all this; Marthe seems to me to have followed the prompting of an overheated imagination, or at least I like to think so.

I cannot imagine the consequences of a lawsuit without fearing for both parties, so I'll do everything I can to spare them that. Thus I'm fully disposed to help you in finding a way toward a friendly agreement, and I put myself entirely at your disposal in that aim. Please tell me, sir, what you think can be done, and what I am to try to do in conjunction with you.

Very sincerely yours,

A. Tavelle du Fermet

I'm going back down to Le Fermet next week, and I'll see Robert.

CHARLES DE CERILLEY
TO ÉMILIE DE MONTBOURG
Lyon, August 28, 1898

Dear Émilie,

Arriving last evening after a deadly-hot day, I received this morning, forwarded here, your letter and your son-in-law's, the latter enclosing a note, which he asks me to get to his wife.

Henri thinks, as I do, that the letter is very exaggerated, but that Marthe, too, may well be exaggerating, that the thing to do is to temporize, to be calm and firm and not do anything abruptly. If the facts are well established and it's evident that a permanent separation should be maintained, it would be much better to reach a friendly agreement sanctioned by a document under a judge's authority, though in his private chambers rather than in open court. For in the latter case your son-in-law would defend himself, and if he burned his ships, he would bring to light his wife's entire past, which would be lamentable for all, and for you in particular. Then again, hysteria is cured only by the frosts of age, and for quite a few years you'll be living on top of a volcano. You haven't thought enough about these dangers. Lastly, can Marthe prove the death threats uttered against her by her husband? If so—well, then, no remedies, they must separate completely.

I'm afraid I see exaggeration everywhere. Marthe's past has proved it to you many a time, and furthermore she speaks about her husband violently in her letters. You did well to write to Monsieur du Fermet; for my part, I did so, too. His opinion will weigh a great deal with me, for he must know his nephew well.

Good-bye, dear Émilie. Give the enclosed letter to Marthe for her to judge. My fondest wishes. As for me, my health stands in the way of my braving the heat, and it's bad of you to act as if you don't believe it, even insulting to me, which I tell you for your good.

Your affectionate brother,

Charles de Cerilley

When the time for a solution has come, then my presence will be useful; but for studying the case, what would be the use of my making the trip, which could only be for a short time? And we are far from having ideas in common all along the line. I'd rather see you listen to strangers who may think as I do in the majority of cases, if they are well and fully informed.

CHARLES DE CERILLEY
TO ÉMILIE DE MONTBOURG
Lyon, August 30, 1898

Dear Sister,

Your maternal sorrow obscures your gift for penetration, in which you have absolute confidence. Then, too, you seem to forget that you've complained to me of the *unconscious duplicity* of your own daughter Marthe. That's one of the characteristics of hysteria, and Dr. Brouardel diagnosed it. You believe at face value and *literally,* today, the most serious of allegations; you declare war, you talk law courts to your son-in-law *without waiting for* the requested advice. You want to believe it's no longer a question of hysteria; thank God, you say, and you go marching forward without reflecting that the hysteria is still there in fact, and that it will be calmed only by the frosts of age, which your daughter is nowhere near. Until then, can you answer for what may happen? I repeat, if the death threats were really uttered, the couple must have a definitive separation, though without a lawsuit. An amicable document can be drawn up, and Marthe's everyday life will then be the object of precise supervision if possible. The past makes one skeptical about the future. Don't be indignant at this reflection, which would be made to you less considerately by your son-in-law's defense attorney.

I'm at your disposal to transmit to Mougins your request for Marthe's effects. But where are you going to have them addressed, and to whom?

Ask if it's true that the day she was expecting her husband back, or one of the preceding days, she threatened to shoot those who were trying to calm her. There's a fact to elucidate, and it's serious, too. I have your son-in-law's letter alleging it. I listen, I take note, I provide myself with documents.

According to your letter, the girl visiting at Mougins probably said to your son-in-law in front of Marthe that he had every right to beat her, and that he should strangle her while she was asleep. If this scene is taken literally, it is not credible; you would have to prove everything. Mightn't that be, rather, a remark heard through a door or misreported?

You're going to get into a real case of child sequestration if before any regular decision is made and unbeknownst to the legal father, you take Georges back from the nurse, especially if you are concealing your residence. I've told you that several times, and there's nothing I can do about it. You can see very well that I can't be any use to you, since you almost never listen to me.

You complain bitterly that I revealed to your son-in-law that Marthe had taken refuge at your house, but without telling him your address. You're letting yourself be blinded by fear, which makes you unfair to me and keeps you from examining the situation thoroughly. You've never considered for a minute that your son-in-law is armed by law with rights over his wife; that because she had vanished from his home, he had the right and the duty to look for her everywhere, and that's what he had begun to do through personal inquiries and by demanding the help of the law. To stop him in this could only be unfortunate. I thought I should tell him that she was with you, but, I repeat, without telling him where. You absolutely insist on hiding, so *I'll respect your secret;* but do you think, if he wanted to, your son-in-law couldn't discover your retreat by virtue of his rights as husband, which only a decision in law, to which I'll return in a moment, can take away from him? How? Good Lord, the route would be very simple: armed with your letter saying that your daughter *is in a respectable home,* and with mine saying she is at your house, Robert d'Aillot would have only to go find the procurator and ask him on the basis of that information to put him in position to recover his wife. Not knowing how to get at you and for greater speed, the magistrate would address me or Edwige, whose address is known, to get yours, then, summoned officially, we must not even appear to make ourselves the accomplices of a *sequestration.* I don't mean to tell you that all this will come about, but I'm trying to prove to you that the thing is legally possible.

Furthermore, no one will think that Marthe, fleeing from her husband, is going to be in *a respectable home other than her mother's.* What's the sense in this equivocating, when you come right down to it? All it can do is hurt everyone. Anyway, the physical terror that your son-in-law inspires in you has no basis in reason, especially now. He has never maltreated his wife physically that I know of, and it is in his interest to be proper with you all.

You can't rely exclusively on your daughter's word, when she's a prey, at least morally, to very great overexcitement. You must not make yourself out to be of her party and at the same time the sole judge of the opportuneness and the efficacy of a lawsuit. You must, as I tell you, check on the accuracy of her statements; the poor child has suffered a great deal, that's certain, but doesn't her distress make her greatly magnify the causes of her sufferings?

Believe me, I implore you, in order not to compromise her we must above all know the truth thoroughly, and act only upon well-proved facts.

The procedure to follow, it seems to me, should be this: for you to ask the procurator, yourself or through your counsel, to make an *official* inquiry into all the facts argued by Marthe. As a magistrate he has ways of getting information unavailable to relatives, who, moreover, would not have the necessary authority to loosen tongues and bring out confidences that would verify Marthe's complaints—grounded complaints—I don't say they're not—but that must be absolutely *proved* as a reality before we proceed with an affair which will have terrible consequences for the present and for the future.

Once this inquiry is made, which cannot be done completely except by a magistrate, we'll deliberate in the family on the real situation and the course to adopt. At that point, fully enlightened, you'll find me ready to help, as you've always found me in all the serious circumstances of your life.

If I didn't sense that you're so unhappy, our too-frequent differences in views, and especially your unfair and painful suspicions, would make me want to abandon my efforts.

Let's join forces as best we can, for our task on earth seems not to have ended, if Providence so decrees.

Good-bye, dear Émilie. Ponder all I'm saying to you, don't hurry to answer, and wait for it to be cleared up by your counsels, enlightened *by you and by the communication of this letter.*

I send you, and also my nieces, fondest wishes with all my heart. My children do the same.

Your affectionate brother,

Charles de Cerilley

CHARLES DE CERILLEY
TO ÉMILIE DE MONTBOURG
Lyon, September 1, 1898

Dear Émilie,

Pass my letter on to Marthe after reading it carefully, and tell me what Monsieur Tavelle du Fermet wrote you and what you replied to him. That will guide me in the reply I have to make him.

Marthe's head was overheated by jealousy over the familiarities she reports her husband taking with the girl who was visiting Mougins with *his sister* for two weeks. That's still ill-advised and dangerous for Marthe, with her morbid temperament. If I am right, everything that has happened was a consequence of that, and we are confronted only with an attack of fever. Well, you don't break up your present and your future over a fever attack.

Answer me quickly, and outline the course I am to take. If we understand each other, all will go well; in the opposite case, I can only remain under my tent and moan.

My fondest wishes.

Your devoted brother,

Charles de Cerilley

Lyon, September 1, 1898

Dear Marthe,

I am pained to see that I'm misunderstood by the three of you. I know very well that you are unhappy, and that you've hidden it from me on your husband's orders. I've done what I could to develop in him the spirit of our family, thus providing some balance with the spirit of self-interest. As my reward, you consider that I was beguiled. I entreat you to examine with care the heart of the matter: what do we find there?

1. No material maltreatment; that is, you haven't been beaten.

2. Motives of jealousy, common to many other women who, though in a much better position than you to take offense at this, nevertheless do not run away from the conjugal home on that account alone.

3. The scorn that has been shown you is the most serious thing. I've talked about it with Monsieur Tavelle du Fermet, and he condemns it. But put your hand on your heart and tell me whether, at certain moments in a conjugal quarrel, it is so astonishing that your husband has reproached you for certain unfortunate facts that he learned about only after your marriage. Hasn't he a right to attenuating circumstances?

4. The threats of death, articulated on one side and the other, seem so unnatural that only an inquiry, and a well-conducted one, can prove the facts or their exaggeration, an inquiry that can only be unofficial, for I disapprove of a lawsuit that you will lose, I very much fear. Oh, I know I'm not believed, but I hope that outside counsels will have the power to make themselves heard.

Independent life is so sown with dangers for you, my poor Marthe, that if I could foresee the result of the inquiry that your uncle Tavelle du Fermet could conduct without making noise, I'd be the first to tell you to go back to your husband, who, if he has committed regrettable mistakes, will take your temporary flight as a lesson and a warning, which his own endangered self-interest will make even more effective.

I entreat you both not to lose sight of the baneful consequences of a scandalous lawsuit. If you need a knight to go back to Mougins, I offer myself to serve you as one the moment I'm free. I suppose the thing will be possible, and I wish for it with all my soul. So, meanwhile, no impulsive follies and no oil on the fire. Come now, tell me: doesn't what I'm telling you here seem sensible and stamped with the good mark of the family spirit? If you say no, let's say no more about it, and leave it to the grace of God.

Is the inquiry useful?

Yes, if the grievances expressed are serious in fact, but not if they rest only on forms of expression unfortunate for you both. Indeed, on the score of morality, you both toss reproaches at each other's head, including some very ugly words.

The inquiry will bring out bushels of mud but will not wash your stains, which need only silence. Up to you, Marthe, to see, in soul and conscience, whether you have much to gain from an inquiry, which I somewhat doubt. For both of you to lose is much more probable. So consider well while there is still time. Carefully reread your husband's letter, which I sent to your mother. Put his plea for his case through the mill of your criticism, and without prejudice.

Good-bye, dear Marthe. I hope you'll reflect sagely on this and will have no further doubt of my devotion. My fondest greetings from the heart to you, also to your mother and your sister.

Your affectionate uncle,

Charles de Cerilley

CHARLES DE CERILLEY
TO MARTHE CARON D'AILLOT
Lyon, September 9, 1898

Dear Marthe,

I'll be laconic in my reply to your long letter whose purpose is to sound me out on the question of divorce. I reply clearly that neither I nor the rest of the family will accept that, and that if the case should arise, you women will proceed alone *with all the consequences.* If you obtain it from the court, it will indubitably be pronounced against you, which means you'll pay the court costs for it in cash to your husband. And, then, how do I know what the court would order? Now that you're at your mother's and that we're far from being agreed on several points, it can't be fitting for me to keep your will, which you entrusted to me. On my return to Sangy I'll send it back to you care of your mother by registered mail.

I'm waiting impatiently for the reply from your uncle du Fermet on the inquiry he has been asked to conduct. It's quite rare to see an uncle of the same family make such an inquiry! It's a token of very great confidence, but will he conduct this inquiry seriously? I doubt it, for I expect him to disqualify himself as being too close a relative of his nephew.

Then again, your husband accuses you flatly of having deceived him in his absence, in his house and in his bed, with a servant, the one I saw last winter at Mougins. He didn't speak of this in his first letters, and he may say that he learned about it only a few days later. Suppose he's inventing it all—everything, including the witnesses he says he has? That would almost be asking to be convicted of odious calumny, which the law would punish rigorously. It's for you to see the strong and the weak sides of this dismal new question. I must seem to you too calm in facing it, but that's only for a while. I'm seeking the light and it's no easy matter: you yourself put on an act for me, you say, at Mougins, yet you were *alone with me,* and I entreated you to tell me the truth about your happiness at home. You seemed very sincere to me then, as when, on your own, you told me, *alone with me,* that you wanted me to destroy the will you had entrusted to me. I dissuaded you from doing it to safeguard an unknown future. You'll certainly admit that I wasn't beguiled at that point? So, then, who was? You. And the proof is that you long resisted the appeals of your mother, who takes upon herself responsibilities that she should foresee better.

All your grievances, large and small, clearly depict a situation where we find on the part of the husband:

1. Loveless speculation as the sole motive for his marriage.

2. Disdainful moral treatment which he wrongfully denies, but which, in the case in point, you can hardly use as a legal weapon.

3. Blackmail in dealing with your mother, and from which you have suffered by the privations he imposed on you.

4. But we don't find material maltreatments, and as for his private conduct, don't make the court laugh by showing yourself to be jealous—especially you.

5. Your husband declares he doesn't want you any more, so the battle will be joined only over the annuity to pay him—for the court will allot him one. What will it be? More than half, probably, because he has no fortune. What will be said about what happens after your mother is gone?

6. Since your flight took place *on the very day of your husband's return, it seems to have been in fear of his return,* and why? He's using that as an argument. Are you sure you have nothing to reproach yourself for? Can you oppose witnesses to witnesses? Oh, I can hardly wait to see clearly in this! I'm suppressing my emotion and imposing calm on my mind in order to judge the facts properly.

Good-bye, my poor niece. I send you all my affectionate but very sad greetings.

Your devoted uncle,

Charles de Cerilley

P.S. Did you go for dinner at the mill with your maid as a two-couple party with Guillaume and his wife? Same thing at your house—soup, onion pie, several bottles of wine, a half-liter of rum, scenes of orgy, drunkenness on your part, protest by your maid that you had forced her to go along with it under threats.

Two sheets of stamps for documents amounting to 1,000 francs were brought to your house. Your husband fears you may have written promissory notes to buy silence. This Guillaume, wife, and children have left the region and crossed the frontier. According to your husband, you apparently went to get Victorin at his place, followed by your maid at your command. What a web of horrors! Oh, who's going to be confounded? I'm keeping the original at home, and I'm inviting your uncle to get his nephew to tell him all he writes me, so that he may verify it on the spot, using his experience as a lawyer who has the habit of it.

Think of me what you will, but at least have the good taste not to treat me as an enemy, so as not to force me to drop you.

If, unfortunately, the case is heard before the court, your husband, who knows *all your past by your own doing*—and he's proved it to me, to my great surprise—will have everything brought into the open by his lawyer. These precedents will give credence to the present accusations, and to the witnesses called. That's the very great danger I point out to you.

Ah, I deplore your flight! The inquiry will tell what its real reasons were.

Today, in the face of your husband's accusations, any return is impossible, and now you're at a fearful impasse. If your mother should fail you, you must *cloister yourself voluntarily* with your son in a house with severe and protective discipline.

You must not ask for the divorce:

1. Because you're a Christian, and in our society divorce is a stain unless one has married a monster of iniquity whose name honor forbids our bearing. Here that is not the case, in spite of all the grievances you have, which don't have the importance you give them.

2. I don't think your husband will ask for it, because he has no interest in emphasizing that he married you only out of interest in a fortune.

3. He will prefer to retain the right to have you watched over as grounds for blackmail, I suppose. As husband, he will have your residence indicated to him by the police: now that the struggle is in the open, he has the right.

Your mother is talking to your Aunt Sophie about his having imposed a mistress on you. If to your knowledge and in your sight he kept a concubine in your house, that is indeed a case of an imposed mistress. That's a serious tort that the law mentions. But mere gallantries—even risqué ones such as ugly but not serious play with the hands—in front of you do not add up to the term "imposed mistress." What may have gone on outside on the part of your husband doesn't amount to it, either. You'd still have to prove that he deceived you outside.

CHARLES DE CERILLEY
TO ÉMILIE DE MONTBOURG
Lyon, September 16, 1898

Dear Émilie,
 If my lumbago compounded with sciatica did not set an invincible obstacle to any travel, I'd leave right now to go to you. You must already be prepared for the unhappy news that has just been confirmed by the letter I've received from Monsieur Tavelle du Fermet, of which here is a verbatim copy:

Le Fermet, September 14, 1898

Dear Sir,
 In accordance with the desire you express in your letter of the 8th, I have questioned the various persons Robert indicated to me to verify the very serious accusations he has formulated against his wife. To tell the truth, I didn't believe a word of them as long as they were in his mouth because of the exaggeration that seemed to me to be attached to his story. I am obliged to admit that everything has been confirmed.
 Anna, a domestic, confirmed to me with details all the things which her mistress is accused of from Friday, the day of Robert's departure, on. Marthe went to dine at the mill with a reaper and his mistress. She presumably drank to excess (I have sometimes noticed her tendency to do that). At one o'clock in the morning, in the company of her maid, she went looking for a young peasant by the name of Victorin, took him away with her, and spent the night with him. The following evening, Saturday, the act was repeated; she was still in bed with Victorin on the Sunday morning. He did not come Tuesday, but on Wednesday Marthe went and picked him up again in the field where he was working, on the land of a landowner who

confirms the fact. They had supper together at Robert's, killing a duck for this supper. They sent the little serving boy to dine at his mother's so as not to have him as a witness. This boy and his mother confirm this part of the deposition. On Thursday, more love feasts at the mill; Victorin's behavior in going to the barber's that evening to get prettied up attracted attention. On Friday Marthe had her bedsheets washed by a woman who received her confidences concerning Victorin. Finally—a significant circumstance—the reaper, his mistress, and Victorin left the area only a few days after Robert came back home. Marthe's leaving on the very day her husband arrived takes on, in the presence of these facts, a significant coloration. Since Robert had been absent for a week, the earlier grievances would not explain her leaving. Jealousy would explain it no better, for that motive, exacerbated by a delay of several days in his return, should have been attenuated by the announcement of that very return. It is easier to understand how fear of the disclosure of what had gone on led Marthe to run away.

However that may be, you see what the inquiry would produce if it were legal and official. The persons I heard have given details it seems difficult to invent, and the testimony of the main witness, Anna, is confirmed by the less important facts she relates. So I persist in believing that it would be useful to hush up this affair with a divorce for which less scandalous reasons could be found; this can be worked out, but we have to come to an agreement. I'm hardly sorry for Robert, who got only what he was asking for; I won't get involved in a lawsuit, because I don't want to be publicly associated with a marriage the conditions of which had been hidden from me.

Along that line of thinking, I am at your disposal and Madame de Montbourg's, who seems to me deserving of sympathy and worthy of our concern.

Very sincerely yours,

A. Tavelle du Fermet

Consider carefully this report from Monsieur du Fermet, whom you have long regarded as an earnest man in whom one might have the greatest confidence. Weigh thoroughly the facts he expresses and the testimony he cites, and ask yourself whether a law court wouldn't be strongly impressed. On the other side, we have Marthe's absolute denials. Charge her solemnly to tell you the whole truth, for the moment is solemn and of the utmost gravity. If according to the appearances it is all unfortunately true, or for the most part true, *we must,* as Monsieur du Fermet says, quietly rule out a public lawsuit, which would be atrociously scandalous, and reach a settlement, toward which, on your advice, we will all work.

You don't tell me just how your address was discovered by your son-in-law at his uncle's; I assume *you* had given it to the uncle.

The visit from two officers of the vice squad, instigated by your son-in-law, is the start of a blackmail attempt which can only harm him, and I'm telling him so.

What you tell me about little Georges's condition is very disturbing. I'm telling your son-in-law that the expert care of two doctors is being lavished on him, and that in spite of that there is uneasiness. I'm telling him what condition the boy has and promising to keep him posted. Be ready to do so.

I'm worried about your health, my poor sister, in the midst of these terrible trials. I embrace you and your daughters with all the power of my devoted affection.

Your affectionate brother,

Charles de Cerilley

CHARLES DE CERILLEY
TO ROBERT CARON D'AILLOT
Lyon, September 16, 1898

Dear Nephew,

I am notifying you on behalf of my sister that little Georges, who is at her house, has been very sick with dysentery for a few days. The doctors' most expert care is being lavished on him. In spite of that, uneasiness exists. I'll keep you posted.

I have received your uncle's dismally detailed report. I'm communicating a copy of it to my sister, and when I have her answer, I'll get in touch with him.

You sent two policemen from the vice squad to my sister's; I disapprove of this very blameworthy, unjustified trick, now that you know your wife is at her mother and sister's. If one goes by your letters and Marthe's statements, and on the other hand your uncle's circumstantial report, what would result is that on each side there are serious grievances whose proportion remains to be established. This will take time and an impartial spirit that I shall not abandon.

Please believe, dear nephew, in my desire to see this dismal affair brought to the most equitable solution for both parties.

Charles de Cerilley

CHARLES DE CERILLEY
TO HENRI DE CERILLEY
Sangy, September 22, 1898

Dear Henri,

Reply received from your aunt, who seems very impressed by the report. She recognizes that appearances are against M., who has written an indignant denial to her uncle du Fermet! She didn't see Victorin, who was in the fields, but only her mother-in-law, to whose house she had gone to get some vegetables; she learned some very serious things about R. the very day of his announced return, and since she would have reproached him sharply for them, trouble was to be feared. That's why she fled, she says. *That's weak.* R. d'Aillot has written his grievances to Sainte-Apolline with threats of scandal in case of any but full and entire satisfaction. Sophie has just passed along to me this letter, which I add to the dossier.

Little G. is a bit better; they hope to save him. The bloody stools have stopped, but he is still very weak. I've notified the legal father, at the same time inviting him not to have recourse to dirty tricks and threats of scandal, for we won't give in an *inch* to those ways.

Your affectionate father,

Charles de Cerilley

CHARLES DE CERILLEY
TO ÉMILIE DE MONTBOURG
Lyon, September 22, 1898

Dear Émilie,

Your answer reached me here yesterday morning. I was eager to get it so as to be able to acknowledge receipt of his report to Monsieur du Fermet with some knowledge of what was what. I can only repeat to him Marthe's absolute denial without adding anything to it.

Now, between you and me: it's not enough to deny, we must go after each accusation and attack the testimony against her with other testimony that will destroy it, or at the very least cast enough doubt on it to create the presumption of an odious calumny, since, you tell me, Marthe is loved and esteemed at Mougins, and not her husband.

So it's absolutely necessary for the attorney, when he returns, to make an inquiry to verify Monsieur du Fermet's findings. If Marthe, despite her protests, is not cleared by this second inquiry, she will be regarded as guilty and will be forced to line her husband's pockets with gold to avoid a public scandal.

Or else there will be a hearing *behind closed doors,* I suppose, but everyone knows that the day of the hearing ends up being known by the public, which then embroiders on what it can learn of the story.

Submit to the divorce asked by your son-in-law, I suppose, but *don't ask for it.* Principles aside, I don't want to be associated with a stain on the family.

I would very much like to know what terrible thing Marthe learned about her husband *the very day of his return* from Mougins. Is that worth the trouble? Why not tell me, when I'm seeking the truth in the interest of all of you?

I'm writing to your son-in-law and copying out for him the whole passage in your letter which deals with Georges, then telling him of the indignant protest of his wife, who wrote about it to his uncle.

I'm saying nothing to your son-in-law about the inquiry, except that his wife will have to exonerate herself on the basis of proofs still to come. I add that I am inviting you all to be patient in this search for the truth, *for we won't yield an inch to threats, which could only be a very bad business for the party that should use them.*

Tell me, did Marthe cite the testimony of the curate of Mougins? Then Victorin's neighbors could say whether he absented himself from home for several days in a row, since your son-in-law affirms that his fling lasted *several days.*

Alas, appearances are terribly against her! She's got to destroy them or cast doubt on them; otherwise she's condemned in advance. Good-bye, dear sister. I hope that if you save the poor child you'll all be in better health. Share among yourselves my fond wishes as an affectionate brother and uncle.

Charles de Cerilley

CHARLES DE CERILLEY
TO HENRI DE CERILLEY
Sangy, September 26, 1898

Dear Henri,

I've learned from Montpellier of little Georges's death. Marthe continues to deny everything resolutely. She thinks Victorin fled so as not to be called as witness against her husband. As for the cook, she wouldn't be surprised if her husband had gone to bed with her! You see how they smear each other. There's no making sense out of it, and too bad for the guilty ones if they go ahead with it. I fear there is shame enough for them all, and I leave it to their individual and reciprocal initiative.

Just imagine, your aunt was planning to have announcements of her grandson's death with the names of the father, mother, grandmothers, and *uncles, aunts, and relatives!* I protested about it, not wanting to be laughed at to my face in our region. So it's decided that announcements will be limited to the Midi.

The death of the child is heavy with consequences, present and future. First of all, it's one less anchor for the mother.

Your aunt seems to be faltering in the defense of her daughter, who continues to deny everything. I foresaw it. But I'm seized with doubts on all sides. What an ocean of muck, what a sea . . . of shame!

M. denies having gone to wake up Victorin accompanied by Anna. She doesn't know where he lives. Then is Anna lying? M. says that her husband had the mania of believing she was sleeping with one, then with another, and she had finally come to put up with it. In any case, it's not when one has such suspicions that one leaves one's wife *alone* for two weeks.

Marthe also says that her husband used to get a big laugh at the way he deceived me, and at my naïveté (in which she herself connived by her own personal behavior); how shameful all that is! If I didn't restrain myself, I'd answer him with vigor, but what's the use? I've plenty of time for it.

Good-bye, dear Henri, a thousand tender wishes.

Your affectionate father,

Charles de Cerilley

ÉMILIE DE MONTBOURG
TO ADÈLE DE CERILLEY
Montpellier, September 30, 1898

Dear Adèle,

Thank you for the sympathy you show us, and also for addressing it to my poor Éléonore, who had taken so to heart and so maternally the difficult task that Providence seemed to entrust to us. The decrees of heaven are unfathomable and our affliction very great, but in the midst of our distress, we have left the certainty of the eternal happiness of our dear little one, with the consciousness of having done everything possible to keep him.

Because of the prolonged heat waves, we would have left him in the country until mid-October, but on arriving here, Marthe, fearing that her husband and her mother-in-law would take him as a hostage and make a child martyr of him, asked urgently to have him come, and since the other young children who came back here during the last few days were and still are in good health, we had reason to hope it would be the same with Georges. God did not will it, and His will was done. Alas! He took my son from me and I had to submit!

My daughters ask me to thank you tenderly for your sympathy. Éléonore will answer as soon as that is possible for her. She's exhausted with grief and with the care she's given; the little one wanted only her, in spite of the nurses, who never failed. Marthe is crushed with grief, emotion, and the calumnies of her husband, who is blackening her reputation in every way.

Fortunately, our attorney is coming back from vacation and will be able to guide us in this dismal affair, in which avoiding the effects of an odious piece of blackmail requires the greatest prudence. My brother had given so many proofs of his interest in the wretched play-actor who is tormenting us that he was absolutely counting on Charles's intervention on his behalf.

My fondest wishes to you, dear Adèle, and also to Henri and your children. My daughters join me in this. Don't leave us without news of you.

Your very affectionate aunt,

Baroness de Montbourg

CHARLES DE CERILLEY
TO HENRI DE CERILLEY
Sangy, September 30, 1898

Dear Henri,

R. d'Aillot has written a letter full of threats against his m.-in-law, whom he makes out to be responsible for little Georges's death—*a death,* says he, *that was bound to happen, since the boy was an obstacle.* What does that mean? Is it a murder? I'm answering him that he's out of his mind, for to save the child we exhausted all the resources of the healing art and of our own devotion; that I take his letter to be a declaration of war; and that, like his uncle du Fermet, who broke off with him, I was going back under my tent and shall observe silence in this regard, signing my name without greeting. Monsieur du Fermet, for his part, writes me that he doubts the veracity of the testimony he collected, and thinks the judges will doubt it, too, so you see the affair is beginning to take on the color of aggravated blackmail. We may perhaps be able to wind up with an infamous plot hatched against Marthe to cast a shadow on the cause of her flight. This new, honorable attitude of Monsieur du Fermet, after this report, is very precious. His nephew is making mistakes that can catch him out. Marthe continues to protest her marital innocence with constant energy. This, set against her husband's blackmail and the disappearance of the two chief male witnesses, is cause for reflection. I now doubt Marthe's guilt and I lean toward seeing a violent fit of jealousy as the sole cause of her departure from Mougins.

> Your affectionate father,
>
> Charles de Cerilley

ÉMILIE DE MONTBOURG
TO CHARLES DE CERILLEY
Montpellier, October 3, 1898

Dear Charles,

My Éléonore is very ill. This dysentery won't stop—she's so weak, her stomach is so delicate, it will be a miracle if we save her. The doctor hasn't concealed from me that the cure is difficult. Oh, my brother, how unhappy I am, and broken by so many sorrows at one time! Really, it's too much!

The attorney is coming one of these days, but how am I to have a head for everything? And the wicked man is pressing and multiplying his horrors to snatch away a part of his wife's fortune! But she'll need it; besides, she's not disposed to reward calumnies of which she can hardly wait to be cleared. She can't remain under such accusations!

At this moment, Monsieur R. reigns at Mougins by terror, threatening all those he knows to be in Marthe's favor. But on October 10 he leaves to do thirteen days of military service on maneuvers at Draguignan and Avignon. We'll try to use that time, if God helps us with Éléonore.

I can send you fond wishes only very sadly now, dear Charles.

> Your affectionate sister,
>
> Émilie

Montpellier, October 4, 1898

Dear Henri,

I was very touched by your letter, so heartfelt, which I was far from expecting. Would you really believe that my husband didn't ask me one single time (and he knew G. was sick) for news of him, nor did he send me anything when he learned of my poor son's death—never mind an affectionate note, I just mean a few decent lines. Nothing, not a word. Oh, I know very well that he couldn't love him, but since he prides himself on having great feelings of lofty propriety, he might have written a letter that was, if not tender, at least decent. Anyway, let's say no more about it; it's finished, now it's quite finished. I'll never go back with him again, and I hope a good divorce will make me completely free of him. At least you, dear Henri, have a home full of tenderness where, I'm sure, you share with each other the common sorrows and joys. That always ought to be the case, but unfortunately not everyone has your good heart and feelings as fine as the two of you do.

This language in my mouth must surprise you, but I've suffered so much in the three years since I've been married that I've put some lead in my head, as they say in our mountains, and, my word, the suffering and the experience I've acquired at my own expense have matured my character, I assure you. Suffering is a tough schoolmistress, I promise you! There are few women, I really believe, who have suffered more cruelly than I, for nothing has been *spared* me, *nothing, nothing.* You ask me if I have proofs that Robert went to bed with that girl. Well, really, I wasn't there, but I noticed it just the same because my husband lacked finesse—and he must have neglected to do something, for I noticed it very clearly. If I see you some day I'll give you more details, but it's not proper to do so in a letter of mourning, so read between the lines while waiting for clearer explanations.

To increase the griefs with which our mother is overwhelmed, Éléonore has, as a result of all these events, caught a violent dysentery just like the one that gave me such a hard time last year. We have to hope she'll pull out of it all the same, but since she is much less strong than I am, she suffers more from it. And you know that to get her to take remedies calls for a crusade, for she has always been stubborn as a mule, but that's a family malady: poor Émile was a good bit like that and I'm very much so, too, and Georges was, in his own way, more that way than all the rest of us.

I am taking the liberty of giving you a hug, dear Henri.

Devotedly yours,

Marthe

Sangy, October 9, 1898

My very dear Aunt,

I was painfully surprised at the announcement of this bad news. I knew that Éléonore was very tired just lately, but I wasn't expecting such a sudden dénouement. My poor dear aunt, what a terrible new trial God is sending you. I am close to you in thought, and my prayers join yours for our dear deceased. One has to be a mother, my dear aunt, to understand your great sorrow to its full extent. And it's a small consolation, isn't it, to feel that one is not alone to weep for and to miss the one who is no more. As soon as I can go to the Midi, my first visit will be to you, my dear aunt. I would so much like for us to be able to offer you all our consolations *viva voce* and tell you again of our affection, which you know already. My dear papa is with you, I know. I'm very glad of it. At such a time he will be very useful to you and will give you a little courage. Give him a big hug and kiss for us. Marthe must be very hard hit: it's so sad to see one's sister go. I'm doubly sorry for her in the sad circumstances that she, too, is in. I very often join my sorrows to yours, for the Holy Virgin never abandons those who turn to her.

Good-bye, my very dear aunt. I send you a tender embrace, as well as to Papa and Marthe.

Your niece, who loves you fondly,

Marie

ÉMILIE DE MONTBOURG
TO CHARLES DE CERILLEY
Montpellier, October 11, 1898

Dear Charles,

Thank my sisters and their children for their sympathy. At the moment it's impossible for me to reply, for I must conserve all my strength to put in order the many letters and prepare the memorandum that will be based on them, and that's not easy because of my weakness and the headaches that this work gives me. This morning, Victorin told me that last winter, when Monsieur Robert was leaving for Paris to attend his brother's wedding, leaving his wife very ill with a return of the enteritis as a result of their numerous scenes, *he heard Monsieur d'Aillot threaten his*

wife, saying he would blow out her brains with the revolver he was holding
in his hand, because she wouldn't sign a note. Marthe stood up to him
valiantly. Victorin will testify to this in court. He told me, "Madame, I've
been witness to so many things distressing to Madame Robert that it's
hard for me to remember them all. But what comes back to my memory
I will certify. I don't believe any other woman could have withstood so
much suffering." I get him talking so I can line him up behind our
grievances. God grant me the strength to help in Marthe's defense; but
I feel that in taking Éléonore from me, God has taken away a part of such
time as I had left to live.

Send me, please, the model for the death notices. The Marseille
Salésiens,[47] whose fellow worker my poor child was, will print them.

Thank you with all my heart for all you're doing for me. It's charity
to one of the living dead who is spared no bitterness. I embrace you all
with all the heart I have left.

Your most unhappy sister,

Émilie

ÉMILIE DE MONTBOURG
TO CHARLES DE CERILLEY
Montpellier, October 12, 1898

Dear Charles,

While you can surround my dear Éléonore with your tears and prayers, I am obliged to remain in the breach and continue classifying the
documents useful to Marthe; for the emotions and memories of all she
has suffered bring back her susceptibility to enteritis.

Yesterday, the lawyer answered Maître Tassin, who had sent me a
letter with a complaint of adultery filed in the court at Grasse by Monsieur
d'Aillot. The complaint was returned by the court, which did not see fit
to prosecute. But the husband was authorized to seek damages in a civil
case.

Marthe has received a good letter from Mougins assuring her of the
sympathies of the inhabitants. Victorin tells me that the husband and wife
will have the energy to sign for Marthe at the inquiry we're going to
propose to the attorney. Victorin will have a look, and he's suggesting a
courageous and discreet man who can do the thing with discretion. This
fellow, who is naturally timid, is furious at Monsieur d'Aillot: he'll move
heaven and earth to punish him for having tried to ruin his reputation,

until now spotless, and since the court has recognized his innocence by returning the complaint to Monsieur d'Aillot, he has regained his courage and will pursue him to the end, he says. In any case, to begin with he will tell in detail all he knows. The inhabitants of Mougins would be happy to see the d'Aillots humiliated, for they detest them. God grant that the return of the complaint by the court may give them the courage to attest to the good and honorable conduct of my daughter since her marriage, and to the knowledge they've had of the outrages and mean actions endured by Marthe. I hope that the woman who wrote today will be willing to acknowledge that she gave my daughter a meal when she was feeling sick from hunger because Marthe's husband had locked everything up! And to think that that scoundrel, stuffing his pockets with the cakes and goodies I sent my daughter when she was convalescing, nibbled them all day right under her nose, and in front of the servants! . . . Those are the little attentions with which this husband, who claimed to be so affection-ate, surrounded his wife! All Mougins felt sorry for her and accused my son-in-law of making her die of hunger. Now *he*, to be sure, is going to invoke the rigor of the diet he imposed, but he exaggerated it on purpose to weaken his wife both physically and morally, hoping that by continuing the scenes, of which there were plenty, he would get the better of her energy, so as to wangle whatever he might want of her fortune. I'm at the end of my rope, but I want to send you a very tender embrace as I thank you for everything you're all doing for me.

Your heartbroken sister,

Émilie

MARTHE CARON D'AILLOT
TO MADELEINE DE CERILLEY
Montpellier, October 15, 1898

Dear Aunt,

I would have answered your good letters sooner, but I'm so dazed in the midst of all these misfortunes that you must please excuse me. I thank you from my heart for the kind words your letters contain, but only time can give me the consolations that do not fail those who, like me, are endowed with an energy that nothing can shatter, for I need a rare firmness of character to stand firm in the breach and defend myself against my scum of a husband, devil take him.

Don't worry about my future: I'll provide myself with an occupation in harmony with my tastes, and the experience I've acquired at my own expense will defend me against the weaknesses of the heart.

Besides, I'll never leave my mother, I'm staunch at my post, and to a valiant heart the rest is easy. Never will I give my mother the slightest grief: the poor good woman has enough in her parcel of sorrows without my coming along blithely to add new miseries.

By spreading a few good deeds around me and keeping actively busy, I'll console myself bit by bit, but for the moment the wound is bleeding, I swear to you, dear aunt; anyway, patience, time will tell.

Devotedly yours with the best of my heart, your heartbroken niece and goddaughter,

Marthe

ÉMILIE DE MONTBOURG
TO CHARLES DE CERILLEY
Montpellier, October 15, 1898

Dear Charles,

Very few inhabitants of Sangy attended my Éléonore's funeral! The attorney only wrote me a letter of condolence. I'm expecting him today. The notary advised me to leave everything in trust for Marthe until her situation is settled, so as to avoid any trouble with Monsieur d'Aillot, who might well play dead if his wife doesn't sue him.

Marthe has been threatened so often that she no longer remembers which note Victorin heard her husband threaten her over!

In answering Clémence, I told her that Marthe had been with me for five weeks now, having been obliged to leave her husband, who was making her too unhappy. I said nothing about the child or his death; it's no use.

Marthe will only go out with Louise, to the market or to the cemetery; that's enough for her for the moment, for the weather is getting bad, and her teeth hurt when it's damp.

The chicken coop is ready to receive the hens; in winter they'll sleep in the little room opposite. I'm buying some rabbits to keep Marthe busy, and Victorin will sow some vegetables that she will cultivate. These little occupations interest her.

Would you do us the favor of making a summary of Marthe's situation, to complement mine? But don't put off sending the dossier you have at Sangy.

My very fondest greetings, dear Charles. I don't know how I can live with such desolation. It seems that I'm made to suffer.

Your unhappy sister,

Émilie

MARTHE CARON D'AILLOT
TO CHARLES DE CERILLEY
Montpellier, October 16, 1898

Dear Uncle,

I've just received a good letter from the mayor of Mougins; he wrote me in place of his mother, who has long been suffering from poor eyesight. I thought you would be pleased to see this letter, and I am sending you a verbatim copy of it. You'll see how much I was esteemed at Mougins and how everything Monsieur Robert says rings false; it's nice for me, in the midst of my grief, to see that at least I can count on the support of the mayor of Mougins: that's a good trump in my hand. I also hope soon to have other letters, just as good, from the rest of the notables of Mougins.

Robert d'Aillot will spit in the air and his calumnies will fall back on his nose—that will serve him right.

Mama seems to be a bit better these days. Lord, she's not very valiant any more, poor dear! But I do my best to spare her any arduous work. You can count on me, as well as on Henri: I'm with my mother and I won't let go of her, rest easy; I repeat once more, I'm staunch at my post and nothing will make me budge from it.

I leave you, my dear uncle, to attend to some household affairs. Devotedly yours with the beat of my heart, and my warm respects to my very dear aunt,

Marthe

ÉMILIE DE MONTBOURG
TO CHARLES DE CERILLEY
Montpellier, October 16, 1898

Dear Charles,

Monsieur d'Aillot didn't consider himself beaten: yesterday a local process server brought Marthe a summons for next November 4, to appear before the court in Grasse and hear herself condemned for adultery. We're expecting Maître Tassin next Tuesday; he'll outline the course to follow. I told you he sent to the lawyer in Grasse an order to stop payment of the quarterly allotment, which will be entrusted to the presiding judge of the court so that he may determine the arrangement for paying court costs and also the support the husband is to provide his wife for the duration of the proceedings. There won't be much left for Monsieur d'Aillot, or for his unpaid bills: creditors beware! Maybe that will make him a bit more pliable.

Marthe goes out every day, but her head still hurts on the side where her husband hit her more than once with his fist; her left ear is completely deaf and the right one is starting to go. Tomorrow she is consulting a specialist, for I fear an abscess in the head. Oh, poor child! Why did she stay so long with that brutal creature? The letter from the mayor of Mougins will show you that she has kept the high esteem of the region. That will give the attorney courage.

My very fond greetings.

Your afflicted sister,

Émilie

CHARLES DE CERILLEY
TO ÉMILIE DE MONTBOURG
Sangy, October 17, 1898

Dear Émilie,

What you tell me about your health worries me. Get your doctor's advice. No doubt you do well to set all your affairs to rights, for with a gentleman like your son-in-law you should have everything in order without waiting for the law, which, in such a case, is slow and systematic.

I do think they know here about the birth of Georges, for when François told his cook about your daughter's death, she said, "That's the one who . . . the one who . . . " She didn't finish. François emphasized her maiden status to cut it short. Me they ask if Marthe has children; I continue to answer no.

I'm going to get busy on the summary of Marthe's situation. Up to now I've been too absorbed. People hear that I'm back, and they make claims on my time.

Here's the copy of the bill that the curate gave me, at my request, for the first-class funeral of poor Éléonore; I did well to advise you to have four assisting priests, not six or eight. Incidentally, that's what was done for Émile.

Bill:

Curate's fee	30 F.
Funeral at Sangy	10 F.
Set fee for the use of the church	10 F.
Mourning	10 F.
Churchwarden and bell ringer	20 F.
4 choir boys	8 F.
Organist	5 F.
4 assistant priests	80 F.
Lunch for the 4 assistant priests	10 F.
Total:	183 F.

The price of an ordinary grave is 6 francs; since that of Mademoiselle de Montbourg is double the proportions of the others, the churchwarden leaves the estimating of that to Monsieur de Cerilley.

I favor 10 francs for the grave, since the dimensions are not quite double. The bill for the tapers, large and small: 48.25 francs. I gave the pallbearers 20 francs. I gave the curate two bottles of your Bordeaux, and from me a bottle of fine brandy.

I'm going to send you what I have of Marthe's dossier. I've held on to the correspondence previous to her marriage, for it's useless to produce it. We think of you and of Marthe at every moment. I'm eager to know what Maître Tassin's plan of campaign will be. At Mougins, they're not stirring. Wouldn't it be better to make a financial offer before attacking? If they accept, we can avoid a lot of scandal. If they're afraid at Mougins, they will accept, and that would be better for all. We'll come to an understanding for the divorce or the separation. Monsieur du Fermet can help in that *unofficially,* but not otherwise.

Good-bye, dear sister. Share our affectionate condolences with Marthe.

Your very devoted brother,

Charles de Cerilley

ABBÉ BOSSET
TO ÉMILIE DE MONTBOURG
Grasse, October 17, 1898

Dear Baroness,

Madame Marthe will allow me to address to you the reply I owe to her letter of yesterday. Poor mother, the good Lord is crushing you. I can find no fit expression for my sympathy. Only God can alleviate so many bitternesses. I ask Him to do that with all the fervor I am capable of. May He be pleased to help you to carry so heavy a cross. Is it possible that He has withdrawn from you that sole succor, that excellent daughter who seemed so indispensable in your painful struggles?

So there you are alone facing a tough duty, and, however deserved repose might be, you must go on desiring to live. You must not lose courage. The daughter you still have left would be too unhappy—what am I saying—she'd be lost without you. You must live to help her overcome the difficulties that await her. So revive your courage, madame, and live. You still have one great duty left. Its accomplishment will be your joy and one day, perhaps, you'll be a little consoled by it for all the disappointments that are overtaking you.

Don't make any extreme decision at this moment concerning Marthe. I don't know whether a rupture would be favorable to her, or whether an understanding might not be better. In the letter she writes me, she's already talking to me about remarrying. I'm very much afraid that with her you'll never be on solid ground. I don't want to advise anything, madame, before having read your own words. Here I want to dwell on the sympathy I feel for you in the misfortunes that have followed one another so rapidly. I seek in vain among everyone I know, without finding anyone so sorely tried. Nor have I ever met a greater energy, either. You mustn't lose it in your present despondency. God is preserving it for you and especially for your only daughter, who so badly needs it.

Write me a word yourself as soon as you can, and believe, madame, that I am your very sympathetic and devoted,

A. Bosset

MAÎTRE TASSIN
TO ÉMILIE DE MONTBOURG
Montpellier, October 17, 1898

Dear Madame,

I did indeed receive your letter of October 15. You tell me that

Madame d'Aillot has been summoned for November 4. If it's to reply to a request for a divorce, her presence in Grasse will be *indispensable;* she will have to present herself in the office of his honor the president.[48]

The law obliges this magistrate to attempt a rapprochement and try to bring about a reconciliation between the spouses.

In case he has no success, the president will authorize your daughter to maintain a residence separate from her husband's for the duration of the proceedings, and he will set the sum you owe to Monsieur d'Aillot, which he can constrain you to pay him by having an order served on you by virtue of the marriage contract.

I advise you to accompany your daughter if nothing stands in the way of it.

Devotedly and respectfully yours,

Maître Tassin

CHARLES DE CERILLEY
TO ÉMILIE DE MONTBOURG
Sangy, October 19, 1898

Dear Émilie,

I'm sending you my résumé of Marthe's situation. I drew it up concisely and methodically, not as a plea but as notes to submit to your attorney.

Since the summons is for November 4 at Grasse, it seems to me that Marthe's *presence* there is not necessary, but her attorney must go there to defend her; the court having sent back the complaint to its author, the latter thought to frighten you by appealing the affair to the justice of the peace to make you capitulate. If Marthe feels she is innocent, she must defend herself at any cost. Oh, those wretched notes are going to have a dismal effect in spite of the explanation of them I give! What does Maître Tassin think about it? The letter from the mayor of Mougins must be put in the dossier.

Have you conferred with Maître Tassin? What is his plan of defense? Does he favor offering an annual payment to avoid the scandal of a lawsuit, even behind closed doors? Anyway, the scandal will explode before the justice of the peace in Grasse on November 4, and then there will be nothing left, I assume, but the decision of the court to which the justice sends the case.

I have ordered the cross (wooden) for poor Éléonore's grave. When do you want the memorial service to be held? Before we leave on November 15, so we can be there? I believe one requests only two outside priests, at 10 francs a head and not 20 as at burials, or else no one but the curate of Sangy? Let me know in advance.

All the people I talk to express a keen sense of sharing in your distress over the extremely sudden death of poor Éléonore.

The day before yesterday I sent you your wills, which have no further *raison d'être* and must be redone, as soon as possible. I'm swamped with details and have only the time to send both of you our fondest wishes from the bottom of our hearts.

Your affectionate brother,

Charles de Cerilley

CHARLES DE CERILLEY
RÉSUMÉ OF THE D'AILLOT AFFAIR
October 1898

1. Monsieur R. d'Aillot contracted a marriage exclusively for money by accepting the concession. He knew of the existence of his future wife's child, and her hysterical ailment, with *all the consequences that would have outside of marriage.* He counted in advance on the coming death of his future mother-in-law and s.-in-law, and told me of the information he had on that point, in view of their state of health.

2. So Monsieur R. d'Aillot knew about the hysterical ailment, since, at Sangy, he said to his future aunt, Madame de Cerilley, "Can you imagine? Marthe asked me practically to anticipate the marriage, which I refused to do." His wife now affirms that the proposition came from him.

3. Seeing that his m.-in-law would not die to suit his desires and might last, he began to disturb her rest in every way at Grasse, and it is for this reason that Madame de Montbourg fled so far away and hid her address from him, so she might get the rest that was necessary for life.

4. Monsieur R. d'Aillot dominated his wife by terror and repeated threat, so that the family should be deluded. As for me, an uncle, I declare I was his dupe because my niece was forced, by reason of her false position, to put on the same act for me in order to have relative peace. Monsieur Tavelle du Fermet admitted to me (April 1898) that his niece had been made to suffer unjustly a great deal, but that the situation was much better. I had gone to Mougins at the end of November 1897.

5. Madame R. d'Aillot's child dies at Montpellier of dysentery. Mon-

sieur R. d'Aillot writes me that he holds these ladies responsible because, he says, they had no right to take the child away from the nurse without his permission. Now, he granted and left material charge of the child to his mother-in-law and his sister-in-law, yet he dares to write me, *"The child has died; that was bound to happen since he was an obstacle."* This smacks of an accusation of manslaughter, and calls for an interrogation by the law. It's very serious.

6. Madame R. d'Aillot's flight can be explained by too keen a sense of jealousy combined with a conjugal life of tyranny. She attests that her husband indulged, before her eyes and those of several witnesses, in excessively free carryings-on with Mademoiselle L.S., which no wife would have been able to bear right *under her eyes.* If she didn't leave the very day after her husband went away, that was because she wanted to mature her plan.

7. On his return, Monsieur R. d'Aillot expresses his surprise, his sorrow, his despair, his tenderness for his wife, in a tone that smacks of calculated exaggeration. See his letters in the dossier.

One week later, seeing the situation lost, he changes tactics and passes over from sentiment to threat, for above all he needs money—much money—to avenge his outraged honor. It's only then that he produces his accusations of adultery with his ex-domestic. We ask his uncle, Monsieur Tavelle du Fermet, to make a friendly inquiry, and the result brings doubt into his mind. See his letter in the dossier. The testimony he collects is vitiated by implausibility, the proof of which is that the court in Grasse sent back to its author the complaint of adultery after a second inquiry made by the honorable justice of the peace.

8. My niece, inexperienced and absolutely ignorant of the value of money, gave notes to acknowledge care and devotion to her person, in the thought that her leaving was for good. They will try to use against her this apparent attempt to buy the silence of witnesses. I repeat, Madame R. d'Aillot in this circumstance was unaware of her inexperience, and what shows it is that she didn't make out a note for the man her husband assigns her as accomplice.

9. Madame R. d'Aillot, when she thought she could have complete confidence in her husband, and was very infatuated with him under the influence of her morbid temperament, made a free avowal of all her lapses in conduct before the marriage. A woman who acts thus proves beyond question her blind, absolute devotion to her life's mate. Also, throughout the time of their union, Madame R. d'Aillot's conduct is irreproachable, and the voice of the public is for her. How are we to suppose her conduct all of a sudden completely changed?

10. Guillaume the reaper was sick, as was his wife, and my niece was their Sister of Charity. There's nothing in the testimony of Anna resembling the orgy related by Monsieur R. d'Aillot, and Anna's testimony *must be carefully weighed.* Guillaume, who blames Monsieur R. d'Aillot, thought it prudent not to be called as a witness against him. Victorin, the alleged accomplice, took only a short absence and has come back to Mougins, where he is at the disposal of the law to defend his innocence and the truth.

11. In matters involving scandal, except for very hardened characters, many people at first prefer to flee or be silent, as if they were accused of stealing *the towers of Notre-Dame.*[49] The law is accustomed to these foibles of the human heart.

MARTHE CARON D'AILLOT
TO HENRI DE CERILLEY
Montpellier, October 19, 1898

I learned, to my distress, that your trip from Montpellier to Sangy was not very good for your health. I like to believe that in a little while there will be no trace of illness left. I'm enclosing the prescription I promised you, which I think will be good for your persistent cough. Little by little, Mama is beginning to get back on her feet, but she doesn't coddle herself, and if I weren't there to repeat, in every possible tone and rhythm, that she must not tire herself out, she'd soon be flat on her back in bed—and damn it all, this is not the time for it, especially because that foul husband of mine has had a process server give me a summons for November 4 before the court of summary jurisdiction in Grasse to hear myself condemned as an adulteress and to pay damages and interest. That's typically d'Aillot. What do you think of that gallant man, who prides himself so on being gallant! I'll leave here on the 31st of this month so I can rest before going before the court. My attorney will come to Grasse, which means that I won't be alone.

I'm in quite a hurry to have this affair ended, for I'm thoroughly bored with it. I leave you, my dear Henri, to give room to Mama.

Devotedly yours, and most affectionately,

Marthe

ÉMILIE DE MONTBOURG
TO HENRI AND ADÈLE DE CERILLEY
Montpellier, October 19, 1898

Dear Henri and Adèle,

Allow me to answer you both at the same time; although Marthe thinks I'm a little better, I'm really not up to the constant emotions that are sapping my poor person.

Our attorney finally came. It was his wife's health that was keeping him. He got Victorin to talk and set an appointment this morning in his office to question him further and give him his instructions on what he will have to do in Mougins with the help of his friends. I did well to retain him, but he'll leave today. God grant that Monsieur d'Aillot may not know he came here.

Marthe tells you, my dear Henri, that her husband sent her a summons to the court of summary jurisdiction for November 4. I doubt that your father can go there. As for me, I don't have the strength: I'd fall by the wayside, and Marthe still needs me. How pitiful we are! I send my fondest wishes to you both and to your children.

Your brokenhearted aunt,

Émilie

ÉMILIE DE MONTBOURG
TO CHARLES DE CERILLEY
Montpellier, October 20, 1898

Dear Charles,

I waited till the conference with Maître Tassin had taken place before replying to your letters of the 17th. Victorin left yesterday at one in the afternoon and should have arrived at his sister's in Nice, where he'll stay a few days before going back to Mougins. In his office, the attorney pressed Victorin hard with his questions *and demonstrated to him that if adultery is proved, he'll get six months in prison for it. The poor boy answered, "Sir, I'll still tell you the same thing: that is that I'm completely innocent* of everything they're charging me with and that it's a calumny from start to finish, an evil trick of Monsieur d'Aillot's because I've seen and heard too much of what he made Madame d'Aillot endure. I'm well known to the inhabitants of Mougins, since I was born there, and I very much hope that the mayor and others will give me a testimonial of irreproachable conduct. My neighbors have already testified that I've never slept away from my mother's, and they will not refuse to attest it in writing or in person." It is agreed that Maître Tassin will subpoena them. He gave Victorin a big sheet of paper with the following heading: "We attest that during her stay in Mougins Madame d'Aillot the younger has always maintained exemplary conduct; that she has won our sympathy, esteem, and respect, and that if she left the region, it was because of her husband's mistreatment."

Victorin is *to charge his trusted friends to have this signed in secret* by as much of the population as he can, for one can do nothing publicly and openly.

I've strongly urged him to have the cook and trusted friends of his frighten Monsieur d'Aillot's other witnesses about the consequences of their false testimony, because I will not let it go at that.

Our attorney told me yesterday that it's indispensable for Marthe to be backed up at the November 4 hearing by the presence of a man of the family. He will ask the prosecuting attorney for a closed-door session, because the nature of the accusations brought by Monsieur d'Aillot, which will necessitate sharp replies, can only harm the two eminent families. You might ask Monsieur du Fermet to act along those lines with the Grasse magistrates. Maître Tassin considers that, at the point where things now are, Monsieur d'Aillot needs a crushing judgment in his favor, because all his correspondence since his wife left can be exploited against him. His mean ruthlessness in pursuit of gain makes him very inconsistent. Maître Tassin firmly believes he will be condemned by *his own doing* and will not be proud by the time he leaves the court.

Tell me whether I may count on you to join Marthe in Grasse. She'll be going on the 31st, with Louise.

Marthe isn't immoderately worried about her husband's lies and is getting ready to reply in an indignant tone and with head held high, strong in her marital innocence. As for the past, the attorney says there should be no mention of it, since Monsieur d'Aillot accepted her hysterical past and knew of it full well, from what he related at Sangy. I'm at the end of my rope! With bad digestion and stomach pains, the present crushes me and the future frightens me.

My very fondest greetings, dear Charles.

Your afflicted sister,

Émilie

CHARLES DE CERILLEY
TO ÉMILIE DE MONTBOURG
Sangy, October 20, 1898

Dear Émilie,

I'm uneasy, as you are, about this ear trouble of Marthe's; no doubt the plasters are clearly indicated to purge and divert the fluid. But, good Lord, why was the poor child silent about her husband's brutality? And on what occasion did he indulge in it? Maître Tassin must make a detailed note of it. That will be very useful to him. Oh, I understand very well now that she got such a turn, she was terrorized, and it's important to bring that out vigorously in the proceedings. I think my résumé will be useful to Maître Tassin, he'll see how to treat intelligently, without going beyond the moderation of prudence, the liberties Monsieur Robert d'Aillot took with Mademoiselle L.S. You'll tell me, no doubt, that Maître Tassin will go to the hearing in Grasse on November 4.

Should Anna play the part of false witness and odious ingrate, it will be quite just to have her punished by the law, if Maître Tassin finds a way and thinks it appropriate. Do call his attention to that.

Before accusing Monsieur Robert d'Aillot of physical brutality upon the person of Marthe, we must have legal proofs—that is, testimony other than Marthe's. Without these, he will cynically deny it, and will use the unproved accusation to scream calumny, which would seriously count against her. Ponder that well. Marthe's presence at the Grasse hearing: (1) would be pernicious to her health, because of the violent emotion that would inevitably result from the proceedings and her husband's presence; (2) Marthe might be intimidated, and that would greatly damage the defense strategy of her attorney, who will be much more comfortable alone; (3) in all lawsuits of this sort, decency requires that the directly interested parties have themselves represented by their respective defenders. Personal appearances in divorce cases are made only in the judge's chambers. Speak about all that to Maître Tassin. Give him my address so he can write me if he has something to ask me.

Maître Tassin acted wisely in sending Victorin to his sister's in Nice, for in Mougins he might perhaps not have been at ease. On the other hand, his being in Nice will surely be interpreted by Monsieur Robert d'Aillot in *his* favor. It's a good thing that he came back to Mougins for a certain number of days during which his ex-master said nothing to him at all. *That's something to note.*

Keep me posted on Marthe's health. I hope this fluid will be easy to clean out, but we must act promptly.

It seems to me that the law cannot condemn Marthe on the basis of appearances, and what makes me think so is the court's return to its author of the complaint he lodged before it. So it's pure scandal they're looking for, to try to intimidate her. Once the rumor is public, one has nothing to lose by defending oneself and defying him to give any proof, if Marthe is sure of her innocence. All the same, what a horrible trial! And how sorry I am for you both! Courage, and may God give victory to the truth. A thousand tender wishes for you both, from us both.

Your very devoted brother,

Charles de Cerilley

ÉMILIE DE MONTBOURG
TO CHARLES DE CERILLEY
Montpellier, October 20, 1898

Dear Charles,

I wrote you this morning, but your letter of the 19th has just come and I hasten to tell you that what's involved for Marthe is not a justice of the peace but a court of summary jurisdiction, a summons for adultery sent by Monsieur d'Aillot. You see he pushes his blackmail right to the limit! Maître Tassin does not approve an offer of money, because that would be acknowledging a shameful guilt. This unworthy husband must be scourged by the law. *The attorney absolutely insists that Marthe be there to reply to her husband's reproaches,* if the occasion arises, but as I was saying to him this morning, *she absolutely must be accompanied by you or your son. That would be an immense favor to do me,* for my strength is not coming back. Impossible to get into a railroad car, and my bowels are so exhausted that the movement of the trip would cause me an outbreak of dysentery or enteritis. Your grapes are very useful. My thanks to you both.

Maître Tassin comes back tomorrow. I'll give him your résumé, and between now and then I'll keep putting in order the useful letters from the beginning of the marriage, so as to clarify the situation from way back. I haven't received the dossier you must have sent me from Sangy. Did you register it? As for the wills, they're arrived and destroyed.

Alas! It's cruel not to have time to weep for my Éléonore in peace! . . . Marthe is continuing her treatments, but her morale is suffering and having an influence on her blood.

Will it be possible to repair the harm caused by this atrocious villain?

These perpetual upheavals have given the poor child a turn. A thousand fond wishes.

Your affectionate sister,

Émilie

ÉMILIE DE MONTBOURG
TO CHARLES DE CERILLEY
Montpellier, October 23, 1898

Dear Charles,

In a little while the doctor will put leeches behind Marthe's left ear, and tomorrow they will put some behind the right one, to try to avoid a very painful operation. I'm seized with a bloody diarrhea. Will it prove to be enteritis or dysentery? God knows. In any case, I'm going to put my will in the mail, registered, tomorrow—today the offices must be closed.

My son-in-law has had sent *from Cannes* a second summons to his wife for November 4, no doubt so more people will find out about it, unless it's one more attempt at blackmail. This summons comes from his attorney.

You see how calm I am. And this torment to know whether you will accompany Marthe—that's a very great service you would do me, my brother. I've received the dossier you sent me.

Marthe's spells of breathlessness are nervous. She's beginning to suffer from celibacy, but walks and sedatives will do her good. The doctor has understood her condition. Poor child, she would still need me a lot! But I'm glad that you're fully aware of all she's suffered, so you may be willing to take her under your protection. God will do the rest.

My fondest wishes, dear Charles, and I put myself in the hands of Providence.

Your very affectionate sister,

Émilie

ÉMILIE DE MONTBOURG
TO CHARLES DE CERILLEY
Montpellier, October 25, 1898

Dear Charles,

Immediately upon his return, Maître Tassin came to bring me a letter from our attorney that he found on arriving home. Monsieur du Fermet went to see him to resume the negotiations over money so as to avoid, if possible, the scandal of a lawsuit; he expresses the desire to come to an understanding with you personally, but in person. Maître Tassin will be able to devote, right now, five or six days to our affairs in Grasse, where he will arrive on the morning of the 2nd. Later that will be impossible for him. Consequently we must not think of getting the affair postponed. Maître Tassin absolutely insists on *your* presence. Henri can't have the same effect on Monsieur du Fermet. As for handing over money, Maître Tassin advises leaving Monsieur d'Aillot the 10,000 francs that belong to Marthe on the chalet and to add to them 10,000 francs given outright in order to hear nothing further of this good-for-nothing. The partial sale of Saint-Savin is going to help Marthe free herself of this tyrant.

During this stay at Grasse, we'll accomplish the necessary formalities for the divorce and the regularization of Marthe's situation at my house. They've put the leeches behind Marthe's left ear; they drew a lot of blood, yet she still suffers. Thursday or Friday they'll begin anew, on the right side.

With me it's enteritis, made very serious by age and weakness. But I still must live—that is, hang on to pull Marthe out of the devil's claws.

I've sent my will, registered; Marthe hasn't made hers yet. Even though I press her, she'll do only what she sees fit.

I'm confined to bed. They're going to find me one more person so that Marthe can get some exercise.

I have time only to send fondest regards.

Your affectionate sister,

Émilie

CHARLES DE CERILLEY
TO ÉMILIE DE MONTBOURG
Sangy, October 25, 1898

Dear Émilie,

Yes, you may count on me to assist Marthe at Grasse, where I'll arrive on the evening of the 3rd at the hotel you designate, the one Maître Tassin is using; he is doing well to see Marthe's witnesses ahead of time.

Monsieur Tavelle du Fermet must want the closed-door session. It's better to let him act himself, for if we seem to seek the privacy, they'll exploit this appearance of fear.

I'm expecting to hear a tale of horrors. Our attitude must be worthy and firm, without letting our indignation upset us, for we must inspire respect in your fine son-in-law. Get it into Marthe's head that she mustn't burst out in anger before the court. That would be ruining herself. Let her be firm, calm, dignified.

What did Maître Tassin say about my résumé?

Good-bye, my dear, sorely tried sister. I pray God to assist you. On my feeble part I'll do what's humanly possible.

Charles de Cerilley

MARTHE CARON D'AILLOT
TO HENRI DE CERILLEY
Montpellier, October 27, 1898

Dear Henri,

Since you have a week free, I'd feel a lot easier if you came to be with Mama during my absence, for she's very weak and I'm uneasy about leaving her alone—with some nurses, it's true, but it's better for you to be near her in case they have to send me a wire. I beg you, dear Henri, to release me from my distress by coming Sunday, for I'm going to leave Monday by the 7:15 A.M. train, and I'll be at Grasse at 7:00 P.M. So I really need you.

Be our very affectionate interpreter to your wife. Excuse me for telling you what to do this way, but I'd be a lot calmer knowing you were with Mama. I have enough problems with my private griefs without having also the anguish of knowing that Mama has no one from the family.

I'm sending you from Mama 50 francs for your trip.

Devotedly yours,

Marthe

HENRI DE CERILLEY
TO CHARLES DE CERILLEY
Lyon, October 29, 1898

Dear Papa,

The enclosed letter will bring you up to date. I'm leaving for Montpellier tomorrow, Sunday. I couldn't refuse from the moment it was known that I had official leave from Sunday the 30th to Sunday November 6th,

and, frankly, my aunt deserves too much sympathy from me not to respond to her appeal.

But I can't stay beyond November 6. From Montpellier, I'll write
every day to you in Grasse.

Fondest greetings to you and Mama.

Your affectionate son,

Henri

CHARLES DE CERILLEY
TO ÉMILIE DE MONTBOURG
Grasse, November 3, 1898

Dear Émilie,

Things are shaping up very well: the gentlemen on the d'Aillot side
were terrified at all the correspondence of your son-in-law, who has sunk
himself. It's at the point where they're going to accept what is due on the
chalet and on other debts, altogether about 18,000 francs. They'll give
back the furniture and the pawn tickets. The divorce will be at Marthe's
expense.

The November 4 hearing will not take place. The remainder of the
divorce proceedings will not take place until later, when I'll be at Hyères,
free to bring Marthe here when the spouses must appear in the chambers
of the presiding judge. During this proceeding, which will take at least a
week, Marthe will stay with us at Hyères.

Monsieur Tavelle du Fermet was just fine.

Today Monsieur Robert d'Aillot is to attend the second conference
at Cannes with these gentlemen; they prefer that I should not be present.

This morning I'm taking Maître Tassin to Marthe's so he can give her
an account of the first interview, and if there is a complete and signed
agreement, Maître Tassin will leave Cannes to go back to Montpellier.

This evening at quarter past five I'll take Marthe to her lawyer's so
that he can give her an account of everything, and get to know her.

If it is all finished, Marthe, Louise, and I will be able to return to
Montpellier Friday morning.

I didn't dare to hope for such a success. Your defenders are able and
intelligent. Both counsel and attorney congratulated me on having collected all the correspondence, which casts a prodigious light on the whole
affair and will give us the victory. They read the important parts to our
adversaries, who were convinced of the blackmail and sensed that the
game was lost for them.

The cornerstone of the plea is Marthe's morbid irresponsibility, and her husband, *in his letters,* applied himself to demonstrating it.

The counsel's strategy is for Marthe to issue an appeal to her husband to take her back (a matter of form to win the high ground); if her husband accepts, she will refuse on the grounds of the grave insult of his accusation of adultery. We must set up our batteries so the divorce may be pronounced against the husband. This evening everything will be over for the moment, and if it's not too late, I'll write. I'm preparing a memorandum, and if necessary I'll sketch for you the final result, for you must be thirsting to know it as soon as possible.

Good-bye, dear sister. I can hardly wait to see you again and to find you better. This letter will do you good. A thousand tender greetings for you and Henri, whom I'll also be glad to see again.

Your affectionate brother,

Charles de Cerilley

MARTHE CARON D'AILLOT
TO HENRI DE CERILLEY
Montpellier, November 17, 1898

Dear Henri,

I would have written you much sooner if I hadn't had so much pain in my ears; yesterday I had a little operation performed on my left ear. The operation was not too painful. I feel better and I hear better, too, though I am not completely well yet.

But that won't keep me from going to Grasse to finish with Monsieur d'Aillot.

Mama is better, fortunately, for she gave us quite a fright two or three days ago. The doctor asked for a consultation with Dr. Grasset, who is one of the stars of the medical school at Montpellier. These gentlemen declared to me that they hoped to save Mama but that recovery would take a long time. I asked them if I could get away, and they said yes, I could go to Grasse, there was no danger for Mama.

Just the same, I've been worried these last few days and one day I was even on the point of sending you and your father a wire. Now Mama is better, but she caught a chill getting in and out of bed to go to her wheelchair. To get our dear patient to take some quinine it took a regular crusade, as they say, for your dear aunt is far from being docile, so when she tells me I'm stubborn, I reply that I get it from her and from my poor father.

I think we're going to have quite a job to get her to recover from this malady, but the loss of poor Éléonore is a big factor—grief is sapping her strength. I cannot, to my very keen regret, be for her what Éléonore was. I do what I can, and when you do what you can you do what you should. But I beg you to believe that it's infinitely distressing to me not to be able to do better. So I implore everyone not to speak to my mother about my sister, for every time she talks about her, she gets such attacks of fever that her life is in danger. I can't write you at very great length, dear Henri, for it tires me because of my ears.

Devotedly yours with all my heart,

Marthe

MARTHE CARON D'AILLOT
TO HENRI DE CERILLEY
Montpellier, November 23, 1898

Dear Henri,

Your good letter gave our dear patient great pleasure. She thanks you very tenderly for it.

Unfortunately, I have no good news of her health to give you. She seemed to be improving, but the day before yesterday she gave us a terrible fright. Mama spat pure blood several times, then her chest got congested, and since the day before yesterday she's been breathing with such difficulty that it rends your soul. The doctor found her completely depressed, and this morning he found her much worse than yesterday. It seems she told the sister that her heart wasn't beating well: the left side is very congested, and a plaster placed yesterday evening didn't work very well. I asked the doctor what he thought of Mama's condition. He said to me, "I think she's in very bad shape."—"But," I said to him, "should I wire my uncle?"—"Not yet," said he, "but maybe later."

If I see Mama worse tomorrow or the day after, I'll send a wire to your father, dear kind Henri. It's frightful: during the three months that I've been here, two human beings have gone off, and yet another grave is yawning for someone dear to me. How unhappy I am in all this. Fortunately I have Louise, who is a big help to me in this illness, for she assists me with all her devotion and has to take care of me into the bargain. Really, she's *just a gem*. We have an old cook who is very sweet and who does all the work in the kitchen and takes good care of the animals.

If Mama should die, I won't go to Grasse for the November 30 hearing, but if she's well enough for me to leave Monday evening, I'll take an evening train so as to be in Grasse on Tuesday. I'll spend Wednesday there, and that evening I'll leave again for here, so as to be back here Thursday, December 1.

My fondest regards from a very sad heart, dear Henri.

Devotedly yours,

Marthe

CHARLES DE CERILLEY
TO HENRI DE CERILLEY
Montpellier, November 27, 1898

Dear Henri,

Your aunt is better, as demonstrated by her pulse, her voice, her strength, and her fits of impatience. I can come back to Hyères tomorrow, Monday evening, at about nine o'clock. The doctor says she's curable but at the mercy of the slightest accident, which could kill her within twenty-four to forty-eight hours. That's the great danger, for we're moving into winter.

Your aunt has spoken to me a lot about her general intentions regarding you. She's concerned with the *costs of conveyance* and has the intention, if God gives her back a little health, of transferring a certain amount of capital to you directly to cover them. You would pay her the interest at a lower rate that the one she gets: 2 percent instead of 3 percent. But she doesn't tell me whether she's talking about two properties or just one. She instructs me to ask both you and Adèle not to put so much stress *on your filial feelings* and *her maternal feelings, so as not to alarm Marthe, who reads your letters addressed to her.*

Your aunt has noticed that since Éléonore's death, Marie (your sister) has suddenly started to write her again and again in the tenderest and most *meaningful* fashion. But your aunt, without telling me clearly that she isn't giving her anything, made this remark to me: "I'm very glad to make up in some measure for the losses Henri suffered at the hands of his parents-in-law." I reminded her that this loss was 200,000 francs.

So both of you keep in mind the very well-motivated and well-intended notice that your aunt is giving you.

With her permission, I've made a note of all the valuables that Éléonore left.

Today, after all the deaths are counted in, Marthe's fortune runs to around 400,000 francs, including half of her mother's, out of which, by law, she can dispose of over 250,000 francs. This is not at all precise, for in the liquidation there are many questions that cut across or offset one another, and sometimes create illusions. In short, today I know more about it than ever. Delicacy alone kept me from asking too many questions.

Marthe asked me to whom her mother was giving the Minster, because it makes such a convenient lodging. I responded with the truth: "I don't know." Your aunt hasn't talked about her intentions to Marthe any more than Marthe has talked about *hers* to her mother. Marthe tells me she wants to keep her secret. *Don't be surprised, then,* I remarked, *if your mother acts the same toward you.*

The doctor is just leaving. He authorizes me to leave tomorrow, and in case of danger he will have a wire sent to me. *He* wouldn't have had me summoned this time, but it's agreed that I won't budge except on a sign from him.

This is a letter that will interest you very much, I think.

We send our very fondest greetings to you all.

Your affectionate father,

Charles de Cerilley

CHARLES DE CERILLEY
TO HENRI DE CERILLEY
Montpellier, Thursday, December 1, 9:00 A.M.

Dear Henri,

I'm just back from Grasse, where at one o'clock yesterday I got an alarming wire from the doctor; we left that very evening at 7:34.

Your poor aunt is lost! The heart is affected, and the damage moves fast: a question of not many days, I fear. So I'm not stirring from here. Your aunt keeps everything in mind nonetheless, even to having 2,000 francs drawn from the Crédit Lyonnais. I'll wire you in case of need.

Your affectionate father,

Charles de Cerilley

TELEGRAM
CHARLES DE CERILLEY TO
HENRI DE CERILLEY

Aunt deceased 11:00. Funeral Monday.

De Cerilley

CHARLES DE CERILLEY
TO ADÈLE DE CERILLEY
Montpellier, December 2, 1898

Dear Adèle,

Maître Tassin, the notary whom your aunt consulted for her will and who had it opened by the presiding judge of the court, came yesterday evening to give us the reading of it. Well, Henri by himself inherits *half* of his aunt's fortune, beginning with the two properties she owned at Sangy. I don't want to delay the expression of your gratitude.

I'm very upset by this death, which was superb in its courage. I'll give Henri the details. Your aunt expired at eleven o'clock after taking communion one more time in front of us.

The body will leave tomorrow, Saturday, around eleven o'clock, and should arrive Sunday during the night. I've left the time of the funeral up to the curate.

Good-bye, dear daughter. I send a very tender embrace to you all, but with my heart quite shattered by this martyr's end.

Your affectionate father,

Charles de Cerilley

SOPHIE DE MONTBOURG
TO CHARLES DE CERILLEY
Sainte-Apolline, December 5, 1898

Dear Charles,

I want my letter to prove to you, and also to Marthe, how much our hearts are with you today—our hearts, our tears, and our fervent prayers! I'm quite sure our poor sister offered her life for Marthe. May she derive from that the conditions for salvation and relative happiness. Your little note of this morning tells me you were able to come back from Grasse in time, also that she had received all her sacraments with admirable resignation. I couldn't possibly express my profound regret. To pray beside her poor body, martyr to so many physical and moral sufferings, would for me have been the only possible consolation, and I know how much our poor sister Clémence shares my regrets. But we're praying so hard from afar that perhaps prayers and sacrifices will obtain more than our consolation.

I've picked out and sent the most beautiful and substantial wreath I could find here. You'll put it on the coffin of our beloved sister for me. It is to arrive Sunday evening at the Sangy station.

My poor brother, what a trip! And what a cruel day! I have no doubt that Marthe is with you. My fondest wishes to you all, including Henri.

Very tenderly and sadly, your sister who loves you,

Sophie

CLÉMENCE DE CERILLEY
TO HENRI DE CERILLEY
December 12, 1898

Dear Henri,

Your father wrote me the day after the very formal letter dated from Sangy, which I answered yesterday. He has devoted himself for so long to our poor sister that I understand perfectly the arrangements made in your favor. She saw in it a double act of well-earned gratitude and of confidence toward you, my dear boy, who are in a better position than anyone else to carry on your father's familial devotion. I congratulate you on this sign of friendship, esteem, and confidence from the aunt who was, alas, so sorely tried in this world here below!

I'm having Mass after Mass said, and am fully disposed to participate in a Gregorian trental, if we could reach agreement with the family to have it performed by taking *fixed and traditional dates.* I don't offer to pay for the whole trental, because our parish fees are *high.*

However, these days I'm having prayers offered more urgently on account of Marthe's dismal affairs. I've written my feelings to your father and also to Marthe. The *categorical* religious law is this: whoever takes the initiative in a request for breaking up a marriage is *absolutely* guilty. One may submit to it if the mob law of the state supports the request, but to *profit* by it is impossible without offense. All one can do is *protest,* and publicly if need be, against the request, since, wherever it comes from and whatever was the promise made to her dying mother, the only thing possible, without sin, is *judicial separation,* as severe as one wants, but leaving the door open to the return of better feelings and a reconstituted union.

I'm speaking to you in confidence, dear Henri, because I love you and respect your heart and your judgment.

I seasoned my letter to Marthe with tact and enough affection to get my advice across while *urging* her to make inquiries as to whether hers might not be one of the cases where the supreme religious authority in Rome accepts the marriage as null. I've known of at least *two* that ended up being sanctioned in Rome. So the parties were able to benefit from it without remorse and without moral dishonor.

I felt it my *duty* to sound this note before there is a *verdict* in criminal law. Unfortunately legal! What a thing the Maquet Law is!!!

My very fondest greetings to you. Share them with Adèle, but keep my severe observations for yourself alone and burn my letter. You must certainly judge matters as I do, being upright as I know you to be.

Your devoted aunt,

Clémence de Cerilley

SOPHIE DE MONTBOURG
TO HENRI DE CERILLEY
Sainte-Apolline, December 13, 1898

Thank you, dear Henri, for your long letter, so full of details that I was hoping for and that your father didn't have time to give me. With what despair your aunt closed her life! What could have been worse than Éléonore's death followed by Marthe's decision? Could a mother suffer more? I certainly suspected from her letters (which reflected a cynicism verging on mindlessness) that the heart and mind of the poor girl were very low. Nothing will astonish us as a consequence, and we understand her mother's will very well. Your uncle and I are very glad that your aunt chose you as heir of her disposable portion. Dear Henri, from every point of view you should have been the heir, and been so alone: for if your poor cousin should allow herself to be robbed in the milieu into which she is going to cast herself, one man alone could save her from dire poverty. In giving us her salon furniture, your poor aunt no doubt intended to give us some compensation for the part of the Montbourg fortune that is passing into your hands via her share of the inheritance of Émile and Éléonore; and we're grateful to her for it. We'll see, after the assessment of the value of these pieces, what is the least costly way to take them all the way to Normandy (a trip clear across France!). With the pictures it will be easier. When you have colored photographs made of the portrait of your aunt, would you be kind enough to ask the artist what he would charge for a second picture? If my means allow, I'll ask for one. This is only for information.

In exoneration of poor Marthe, I certainly believe her husband must have maltreated her and made her very unhappy, if not quite that he beat her brutally: she was attached to him all the same. She had said that to her mother, who wrote it to me. I think it's a case of the beaten slave who has gained his freedom. Alas! If you knew how little she has known of the charms of a distinguished, educated milieu, you'd be less astonished at her bent for the common people, who flattered her in her isolation.

Your poor aunt *suffered so much* for not listening to my advice and putting too much faith in her daughter! Let reproaches stop on our lips where she is concerned. As you say, there's nothing more to do for the poor child, and her peasant will still be better than the street. Oh, bring up your children otherwise! Let peace be the basis of their education, let their first communion be well prepared and made in a meditative atmosphere, pure and religious.

Would Robert d'Aillot have asked for a divorce if he had been able to foresee all the deaths? With the child dead, the shame would have disappeared and the fortune would have been left him, good riddance. What was he demanding in order not to make a scandal? Marthe wrote me that he would no longer submit to the conditions set by his uncle du Fermet, and that his lawyer was advising him to hold fast. I hope your father will give us some details after today's meeting at Grasse.

Good-bye, dear Henri. When shall we see each other again, and where? I wish it might be here and that your father might come with you.

Your very affectionate aunt,

Sophie de Montbourg

CHARLES DE CERILLEY
TO HENRI DE CERILLEY
Grasse, December 14, 1898

Dear Henri,

At three o'clock today the final legal attempt at reconciliation took place in the chambers of the presiding judge. Marthe, Maître Tassin, and I were there when suddenly Monsieur d'Aillot, contrary to his word, burst into the room like a cannonball without saying hello to me. Maître Tassin and I went out, and the meeting lasted for at least half an hour; then Monsieur d'Aillot emerged, letting Marthe pass ahead of him. He walked past me very fast without any greeting, and Marthe gave Maître Tassin and me the following account: Monsieur d'Aillot talked sentimentally even while persisting in his accusations, promising pardon and limitless devotion, which, moreover, he has also said in a two-page letter addressed yesterday to Marthe care of the Martins. This letter has been added to the dossier; Maître Tassin says it's precious and we must keep it as a model of play-acting.

The judge, according to the law, made every effort to sway Marthe, but she was very firm to the end, and rejected his last accusations without discussing them.

The judge is quite aware of everything and did nothing but play his part.

Monsieur d'Aillot told him that Marthe never had an idea of her own, to which she replied, "I've always done your will because you forced me, and because sometimes you've threatened me with your revolver."—"You see this woman, Your Honor," he went on, *"she has no education, she's even ignorant of certain expressions of the French language."* That's stupid, as was his remark to the judge: "There's something strange about the death of this child whom they take back from his nurse full of life and who dies two or three weeks afterward; then it's his aunt, then the grandmother!" Another peculiarity: he rambles and doesn't know what he's saying. In short, we have done everything we can here; it will take three months for the judgment to be handed down and become definitive.

The deed for the sale of Saint-Savin cannot be drawn up until after these delays; but they're going to propose to Monsieur d'Aillot that he give his proxy for the breaking of the seals and inventory and liquidation. Maître Tassin will be asked for a form. If Monsieur d'Aillot acquiesces in this, he'll be given an immediate supplementary present of 100 to 300 francs, for he must be starving—in fact, he has grown thinner! If he makes difficulties, he'll be taken to court and any kindness will be withdrawn. We'll keep him well in check.

Marthe is stirred up by this trial. I'm taking her to our place at Hyères to give her a rest for a few days.

The Martins seem to me to be playing a double game and to be jealous of the influence Louise may have. It's visible—they hide it very badly.

Good-bye, dear Henri. We send you our fondest wishes from the heart. Your affectionate father,

Charles de Cerilley

SOPHIE DE MONTBOURG
TO CHARLES DE CERILLEY
Sainte-Apolline, December 18, 1898

Dear Charles,

Thank you for your long letter, which fills all the gaps in our knowledge: Clémence needed to be brought up to date so as not to scatter her shot right and left, with the best intentions in the world! I answered her by presenting the final situation without the details.

Meanwhile, my dear, I marvel that d'A. contents himself with the sum of 19,000 francs, which will give him a very slender income. The legal proceedings have to keep him well in line! He must have put himself in a very sorry mess! I understand why his wife is not taking the risk of putting the yoke back on. The poor girl played her cards well in saying herself she was irresponsible—without thinking that irresponsibles get themselves locked up! Whatever she does, it would be well for you to tell her that this affirmation will make her the slave of anyone who wants to take advantage of her, *whoever he may be,* and that it would be smarter not to say it even to her legal husband. Alas, maybe it's already done! If it's the one named by d'A. . . .

I don't want you to think, dear Charles, that because we were waiting for Honoré's answer, we're sorry about Henri's good luck. No, indeed, no! And I wrote him our affectionate congratulations right away. *It's true that Émilie might have considered that a part of her children's inheritance would be leaving the Montbourgs, but she was absolutely free to dispose of it, even as Marthe is with her half of the Montbourg fortune;* no one has any claim to it. Your Henri should bless Providence on his knees, for that is what guided everything. The deaths had to happen in the order they happened for our sister to have made that will; love for the little Chinese children had replaced Éléonore's love of the family, and if she had survived her mother he might perhaps have had nothing at all.

Is cousin de Saint-René informed of the present situation? And of Marthe's intentions? Our poor cousin hasn't left his bed for a month and can't write any more. His eighty years make his illness serious. He now has a nun as nurse. She won't let him finish without sacraments: that's the important thing.

I couldn't invite Marthe to come to Sainte-Apolline, but merely told her she'd find an affectionate refuge with us if she felt the need for it (her story is too well known here among the people).

I can't wait to learn the result of your last trip to Grasse, and how things are going. Will there be any court appearance? *Did you also curb the local paper?* That's something not to forget. If the paper keeps silent, they won't know anything here. But all it would take is the tattling of one single Provençal woman to get it around.

Good-bye, my good brother. Sunday is Christmas. My most heartfelt prayers will be offered at the crèche for all the good things of body and soul for you and your dear ones. My most affectionate greetings.

Your sister who loves you,

Sophie

Hyères, December 23, 1898

Dear Henri,

Since Maître Tassin has some doubt about the coherence of Marthe's thinking and fears for the fee that's due him, which he sets at 3,000 francs for all consultation and the court appearance on January 9, plus 300 francs for his two trips to Grasse, he has written me about it hinting that I should advance it to him, unless I can charge it to the inheritance. Without formulating a refusal, I replied that I would inform my niece and tell her to go see him and reassure him: these gentlemen have too heavy a hand to run risks, and besides, in these circumstances, you can't discuss their figures, seeing that it's to their ability that we owe such a happy solution from the standpoint both of finances and of scandal held to a minimum.

Marthe stayed with us here four days, with Louise; both were delighted with this little visit. Marthe is very conscious of our kind attentions and advice, and seems disposed to follow our counsels—namely, first of all, to take care of her health, and to try to make herself an active and very independent life in a new area, which means trying *to do without him.* Now, since her health is often poor, she is haunted by the idea that she would not want to be stuck with a husband on whose devotion she could not count.

I've written to the notary in Normandy, *who didn't know of your aunt's death,* to bring him up to date and explain to him the reason for the delay imposed on the buyers of Saint-Savin, seeing that my niece's situation won't be settled until three months hence. But we should get busy to obtain from Monsieur d'Aillot a proxy in return for a present of 100 to 300 francs; should he refuse, Maître Tassin will take care of the formalities to gain court authorization to bypass him in every way; we'll try to be as active as possible, and Monsieur d'Aillot will have no interest in raising difficulties, for then we'd withdraw any agreement and would have him expropriated. The buyers of Saint-Savin, who are getting a superb deal, are making a pretense of threatening to give up the deal "if we dawdle too much."

I must tell you that Marthe wants to have the old chest from her mother's dining room. It's the best, you know. We are agreed that good taste should leave to her the choice of everything she'll want to include in her share. So much for principle; in practice I'll appeal to reciprocal proprieties. That way everyone will be content. I am eager that Marthe should feel touched by our efforts in her behalf, in her own present and future best interest. All this has not kept Monsieur d'Aillot from writing her (once via the Martins) that she was surrounded by ravishers of her fortune.

She has proved to me that the Martins are greedy and are make-believe friends playing Monsieur d'Aillot's game.

Your aunt Sophie certainly managed to make her point that your aunt might have considered that part of the Montbourg fortune would leave the family because the portion of the deceased children would devolve to your aunt. You see clearly that the cloven hoof nearly always shows.

Good-bye, my dear son.

Your affectionate father,

Charles de Cerilley

MARTHE CARON D'AILLOT
TO HENRI DE CERILLEY
Millau, December 29, 1898

Dear kind Henri,

I'm very touched by the feelings of affection that you express for me, and I beg you to believe likewise in mine. Thank you for the good New Year's wishes you offer me. Yes, let's hope that 1899 will be less painful for us all, and even though my heart is quite torn by the series of events that have just taken place, I thank you again for the kind words your letter holds.

You will no doubt be a little surprised to see my letter dated from Millau, but two days after we arrived in Montpellier, my hedgehog[50] was summoned by wire to be with her sick mother. I wasn't eager to stay alone with Marguerite, who is as deaf as a post, and I left with my hedgehog.

You see that our rest didn't last long. To jump from one railroad car into another this way is sometimes fun, but with illnesses you have to be ready for anything. Except for my hands, which hurt from gout, the rest of my person is well.

You're quite crazy to spoil me so—a thousand thanks for the goodies you're surrounding me with. I promise you I'll relish the candies in good conscience when we're quite reassured about the condition of Louise's mother. We'll be returning to Montpellier.

My very fondest wishes, dear Henri, and also to your wife and your dear children.

Devotedly yours,

Marthe

1899

MARTHE CARON D'AILLOT
TO CHARLES DE CERILLEY
Millau, January 4, 1899

Dear Uncle,

Maître Tassin has informed me that he received the proxy we had asked Monsieur d'Aillot for. I'll be in Montpellier Monday evening. I won't commit myself, for I badly want you to be present for this whole liquidation business, and I'll tell him so when I'm in his office.

I've written to Monsieur de Tourville asking him to send you the farm rents from Saint-Savin and authorizing him to place them in your hands until the liquidation of my mother's affairs is complete. Yes, I've looked into finding a place to stay in Millau. I have my eye on several, but I won't rent until I see one tomorrow that I think I'll like, for there's a big garden surrounded by walls and we'd be alone in the house. Tomorrow I'll go see the landlady and we'll inspect the apartments; the weather's too bad today to go and see them.

I like Millau very much. My health is good here, and you won't recognize me when you come to Montpellier, for I've come to look like a nun and have a face like a full moon.

My hedgehog, Louise, tells me to thank you for your good wishes; her mother will be well enough to let us go back on Monday. Maître Tassin has informed me that on Monday the decree of divorce was handed down. He's anxious to make it final and will speed things up.

Devotedly yours,

Marthe

Dear Henri,

At half past eleven I will have finished sorting the papers. Tomorrow I pack the pictures and, in the evening, sign the fees for the inventory.

In sifting through the papers, I found an amethyst brooch with pearls and gold that had been forgotten. It will be appraised at 30 to 40 francs. Plus a handsome watch with your aunt's initials with diamonds. It's her wedding watch, I think. Since there is no coat of arms, Marthe can perfectly well take it and wear it on special occasions, in spite of her countrified tastes.

You will do well to come by here during the days preceding Ash Wednesday, February 11–12, to come to an understanding with Marthe about certain details concerning the furniture: in two days you'll get more done than in a month from a distance.

There's nothing to deduct from *Marthe's* share except what's involved in all the consequences of her flight and her divorce, and outside of the chalet, the 8,000 francs of unpaid debts, the 1,800 francs' worth of bills, and all the trips taken *for her*. What her mother may have paid for Monsieur d'Aillot's discharge from bankruptcy is lost amid her maternal kindnesses above and beyond the terms of the dowry.

I assume that, *with everything paid,* you will have a net capital of more than 25,000 francs to invest. If you're given good securities, keep them as they are. That means so much less in brokerage fees.

In short, you're even more fortunate than we thought at first, and so much the better.

The statue of Christ is very pretty and in good condition; Mama will take it off your hands just as it is, even though the gilt is a little tarnished. The velvet is still acceptable, even for her, fastidious as she is.

No mirror for you, no dinner set, no linen. Your cousin needs all that to set up housekeeping. Your aunt sold a fair bit at Saint-Savin. I've found the particulars, which you'll see some day.

Marthe is ailing in mind and body, in several ways; as at sea, her nature is subject to stormy moments. If she were without any affection right around her, she'd surely fire some kind of broadside. Louise is her everything, someone to lean on, her daily counsel, her helper, her company, her moral support. I'm convinced that's fortunate.

We'll be at Millau Saturday or Monday evening to spend three days that are free for me. Marthe will expect you here around the 11th or the

12th of February. Her cook will stay here, and you'll always find her home.

Good-bye, I'm going to work. We both send fondest greetings to you all. Your very devoted father,

Charles de Cerilley

CHARLES DE CERILLEY
TO MARTHE CARON D'AILLOT
Hyères, February 11, 1899

Dear Marthe,

While your cousin is at your house, I want to be close to you both, at least by a letter. It will be as though we could see each other, and we can hear, through the thoughts of the heart, the voices of those who are no more. To think that it's in the plural that we must speak of them!

Have you begun your packing? Don't be in too much of a hurry to go to Millau. As for me, I wouldn't agree to go outside in any weather; oh, no.

I've finished sorting out the papers. Lord, what correspondence, throbbing with painful interest!!! And how important it is to preserve it well! That's your protection.

If you need money before the liquidation is completed, you know where to get some: Maître Tassin has in his hands over 500 francs for you. If Henri is short, tell him that I'm in a position to advance him 400 francs to settle his current bills.

If Montpellier were no farther away than Marseille, I would certainly join you; but I have to go there once more, and if I could time it with our departure, that would save me fatigue and money.

Good-bye, dear Marthe. We embrace you and your cousin from the bottom of our hearts. A cordial greeting to Louise.

Your affectionate uncle,

Charles de Cerilley

CHARLES DE CERILLEY
TO HENRI DE CERILLEY
Hyères, February 16, 1899

Dear Henri,

I received your letter of Tuesday after you left for Millau. I approve everything you've said and done. Here's a draft of a letter for Marthe. Tell me your opinion: I've smoothed off the edges of my thought all I could. I'm inwardly outraged at so much duplicity. What the devil, I'll agree that hysteria is an invincible passion; but it renders us oblivious to our acts only during *crises*, and in anticipation of such crises the honest soul appeals for protection. Did she? No. When she hasn't been cynical with her mother she has put on shows of every kind, lying out of self-interest or fear, shrewdly imitating candor half by nature and half by ruse to give herself credit. So I think with her you need a mixture, or, rather, an *alternation,* between feelings and *harsh truths* in the background.

If between now and August there is the slightest snag in the promise she gave you, I warn you that my door will be forbidden her at Sangy. Return to me the draft of my letter to that unhappy Marthe with your comments. You've seen and heard, you've conferred with Maître Tassin, you can be a good judge of this present moment that throbs with such sad interest.

I'm expecting Marthe's letter; if she delays too long, I'll write her along the lines of my enclosed draft.

You did well to repress your first thought, of sending her to us at Hyères—that idea is no good at all. She wouldn't have wanted to come, not being at ease with her aunt, and we'd have had to put her up at the hotel: think of the danger of a sordid episode, which we've seen happen before! Oh, no, never right under our noses. She will find protection when she needs it: that's our supreme and ultimate safeguard, if it please God, which I doubt. Yet it would be right: Providence should protect the insane and the mentally ill, though it doesn't. "Heaven helps those who help themselves" is the only true saying.

February 17, 1899

Adèle, whose letter I've just received, tells me that the advance of 400 francs will be useful to you at this moment. Instead of waiting for your answer, I'm passing them to you herewith.

That wretched Marthe sickens me beyond any expression. She is a repugnant sick woman rather than a vicious one. But it's that artful duplicity that irritates one. So when she puts on a show of frankness, one has to say to oneself, "Isn't she still lying?"

Do you think Victorin came *on his own* this last time, or was he called? I suspect that Louise favors him, so as to avert the danger of a return to the conjugal residence, which Marthe regrets not being able to go back to now that her health is good. No, it's the feeling of having been betrayed that gives her the strength to resist. If she sticks with or marries her V., she'll soon reduce everything to the simplest term, for there's no power that will stand up against a hysterical woman.

I foresee unhappy events that no one will be able to do anything about; you can't boss a woman of twenty-seven like a girl of fourteen or fifteen.

Good-bye, dear Henri. I'm in the dumps about this sad future.

Your affectionate father,

Charles de Cerilley

We've just this moment learned of the death of Monsieur de Saint-René, without any family at all. That's sad! To whom will his meager estate go?

LOUISE GALOURET
TO HENRI DE CERILLEY
Millau, February 19, 1899

Dear Sir,

I thought to please you and at the same time to fulfill toward you the duty I've taken on, to keep you posted on what might be happening, dear sir, to your dear Marthe, to whom you have shown so much attachment and sympathy.

Our trip went very well, although it was a bit sad, for Madame wept a good deal along the way. I did my best to reassure her, and at this point she's very well. Her health is good, we take walks, we divert ourselves as best we can, since that is the only way she'll be able to overcome her rather impulsive character. But right now, all is for the best, and if God comes to our aid, everything will turn out well. She still says she's ready to keep the promises she made you to have no further dealings either with that individual or with any other man.

However, dear sir, we haven't received any word from your father, so I'm worried about this silence and would be much obliged if you'd be good enough to send me a word in reply and simply tell me what Monsieur de Cerilley said to you about your letter informing him of this unfortunate affair, for you may be well persuaded, sir, that I'll do all that is required of me to keep things in their current good state, for it would be regrettable if your father were to act with violence or threats against Madame, which would destroy the good intentions she now has. Tomor-

row, Monday, I'm leaving to begin moving and would be happy to have news from you. During my brief absence, Madame is staying under the supervision of my family, who surround her with their care just as well as I do. So I beg you, dear sir, to be good enough to use much indulgence toward us, for we want to see a good result, which I hope will come about if nothing ruins it. Hoping to hear from you as soon as possible, I remain
Respectfully yours,

Louise Galouret

CHARLES DE CERILLEY
TO HENRI DE CERILLEY
Hyères, February 19, 1899

Dear Henri,

I was convinced of Marthe's guilt. They're having to dismiss Victorin, who has the nerve to try to get some blackmail. Monsieur d'Aillot's attempt failed. Let it be the same with the valet's. We're dealing with an unconscious hysteric who's also crazy and a liar. Once she knows that you've brought me up to date, I think my silence toward her will carry the meaning of all I've warned her about—that is, that I won't see her again, that she'll not set foot in Sangy any more, and that all I can do is administer her two legacies until further notice.

I noticed in Montpellier that Marthe and Louise often went into town and spent several hours there without ever indicating what they were doing. I had a suspicion of some shady rendezvous, but not with the ex-valet! Today all is clear. What filth! Ah, my poor sister, what martyrdom!

Louise would much prefer that Marthe get along without a male, but since the need is there, I suspect she still prefers Victorin to any other: they'll share the pie.

Whatever fortune Marthe has will become a prey to her entourage; that's sure, and if she lives long enough to see the end of it, her old age will be horrible. Your poor aunt had good instincts, but her mother's tongue often denied what her inmost instinct revealed to her. It doesn't help that Marthe fears me; she knows I'm a man of my word.

You did very well to act forcefully with Victorin and to threaten him with the police. I see nothing but turpitude on every side. There's a streak of madness. I see that unhappy girl at sea. Marthe will be known at Millau only by the name of Madame de Montbourg. Your Aunt Sophie would like her to take a pseudonym. But that's a matter of committing falsifications, and we don't need such new dangers.

You did well to approve those 100 francs that Marthe gave Victorin to get him out.

If these crazy, morbid vices are discovered some day in our milieu, all we have to do is call it a case of unconscious hysteria. That's the hunchback's hump.

Your long letter of Monday evening upset me more than it surprised me. I had so many suspicions. Now we have the dismal certainty. Let's keep it all between us, if possible.

Your affectionate father,

Charles de Cerilley

Did you bring back the twenty old coins, the gold piece of Murat as king, and the watch? Did you know that the characteristic of hysteria is that the desires can *never* attain true enjoyment or satisfaction? It's desire always present, with intermittent crises. What a terrible malady! When the condition is acute and permanent, it's more or less madness: we might be obliged to have her locked up some day. I'll bring this to Maître Tassin's attention.

CHARLES DE CERILLEY
TO HENRI DE CERILLEY
Hyères, February 20, 1899

Dear Henri,

I'm sending my letter to Marthe and I'm keeping a copy attached to your letters dealing with the same subject. She doesn't dare write me, and it's well for me to reassure her about my state of mind in regard to her. It's not good to carry severity to the point of untimely brutality. When it's necessary to break off clean—if the need arises, that is—I won't hesitate. Meanwhile, let's put off that extreme solution with all our might.

The best thing would be for you to allow her to live in your house in the Minster gratis, as if she were the owner, as long as she remains as she is, free, but without V. She would be comfortable there, much more so than at the château, where she would come to have her meals on Sundays and Thursdays when that suited her. That's what Mama instructed me to tell you. But it's up to you to take the initiative with Marthe. If she accepts, isn't that a very effective and practical protection? Still, she's got to want it.

I'd rather see her do that for the summer than see her buy a property in Aveyron. At Sangy, she'd have hunting for several months. Mama had the idea of giving you for your birthday a four-cup Russian coffeepot, if you don't already have one, for you can't get good coffee except by this method, practiced before your eyes. Let me know.

Anna spoke the naked truth; what I understand least is the 900 francs to Guillaume. She must have wanted not to create jealousy between the two. Victorin, for his part, was first paid in kind.

We'll see a lot more of this, I fear, and I'm making a big sacrifice to offer her the *modus vivendi* at Sangy, as I have explained to you above. I dread the scandal. She'll buy her amours, and her Norman past has made such an action very easy for her. At the first foolish act, we'll have to get her out, but it will be *too late* in terms of the local effect. So think well before furnishing her with the means and the time to form *guilty relationships under our eyes.* Aveyron is a long way from us all, and that's what I like about it. Let her come in vacation time—so be it, that's limited —but for too long it's dangerous.

Good-bye, dear Henri.

Your affectionate father,

Charles de Cerilley

P.S. Your poor aunt understood her daughter's position so strongly that she made no request to any of us to take in the unfortunate child. She left it up to our conscience, our wisdom, tacitly; it's certain that we owe more protection to Marthe than do all the other members of the family, by virtue of the generosity of which you are the object. But that protection must be *asked for and deserved.* We're making an offer, on condition of moral behavior; that's our duty and we're very much disposed to fulfill it. What I've done thus far is a sure guarantee of what we'll do in the future, *as long as it's made possible for us.*

Your aunt, whom I questioned on what to think of Monsieur Loubet,[51] gives me this answer: one-time monarchist; opportunism has made of him a very opportunistic, hence two-faced, republican. Madame Émile Loubet is a good Christian, and your aunt sees that as the source of all the successes of the family. In Paris, they think that the country's general opinion is not with the new president of the republic; he puts his more than average intelligence at the service of his duplicity. Your aunt sent a wire of congratulations to Monsieur Loubet, a native of Marsanne. Mother love, this is what you're capable of for the sake of your son's epaulets. Your uncle was on *tu* terms with him; in short, if we put ourselves in her place, we would have done the same. But it's funny all the same.

Your Aunt Clémence is upset by her rheumatism. She asks for a wee memento of her sister. I'll send her a photograph twenty years old but which will still recall her well, especially to Clémence, who hasn't seen her since 1868.

LOUISE GALOURET
TO HENRI DE CERILLEY
Montpellier, February 26, 1899

Dear Sir,

I can only thank you very much for being kind enough to answer my letter, and especially for being kind enough to take on the advocate's role with your father to obtain his indulgence toward Madame d'Aillot. Believe me, sir, I'll do all that is required of me to spare her from shattering herself against such reefs, to which she is so drawn, for I really believe that with God's help we'll suceed in mastering the reins a bit; that's what I'm trying to do in connection with her family and her unhappy lot, into which she would cast herself if she were to continue the path she has taken. She has written me from Millau, telling me she is in very good health and is waiting impatiently for me to rejoin her, which I'm going to do today, Monday, for I, too, am in a hurry to get back. I wanted to leave Saturday, but I couldn't. Anyway, it's over, thank God, and this evening I'll see my native region again.

I'm dispatching to you the case of books as you wished, postage due and to the address you gave. I forgot to tell you, sir, that Madame passed me a letter from your father, very affectionate and full of the best advice. I thank you for it very much, for it's because of you that Madame will find mercy at the hands of her uncle, who must be her sole support and her sole confidant.

In case you, sir, have something to tell me, I'm still at Millau staying with my sister, who would get letters to me without Madame d'Aillot's even suspecting.

Please be good enough to count on me for whatever I'm capable of that might be useful to you.

My very respectful regards,

Louise Galouret

Hyères, March 9, 1899

Dear Henri,

It's still raining today. Nothing better to do than chat with one's children. Now no letter from Marthe since the one in which she tells me that Louise's mother had an attack and that she can't go alone to Montpellier, where Maître Tassin has called her to sign a proxy for the sale of Saint-Savin. M. doesn't want to be known at Millau under the name of Madame d'Aillot, so she has to go to Montpellier, since Maître Tassin can't send her the document to sign: it has to be done in his presence. Hence a forced delay of at least a week.

Monsieur d'Aillot is being cruelly punished in the place where he has sinned. Yes, it's the jealousy he foolishly aroused with his carryings-on with Mademoiselle L.S. that made the fur fly. What crazy rashness on his part! But what abjection [of Marthe's] to love his valet! Your poor aunt failed in her mission because she lacked direction in the education of her daughter, who needed either the convent at a tender age or else an early marriage; the mother didn't understand it! She was blinded by the death of her first two children, from meningitis.

At Toulon, the day before yesterday, at seven o'clock in the evening, someone fired two revolver shots at a sentinel, who, flabbergasted, didn't think to fire back. He saw six individuals run away. Moreover, they found a pack of thirty dynamite cartridges near a powder magazine or barracks. All that indicates a connection with the Lagoubran catastrophe[52] and is linked with the great upheaval the Dreyfusards[53] have threatened if they're not given satisfaction.

At Sangy, my left-hand mare, broken-winded, worries me; she had a very sharp attack of breathlessness the other day; when the veterinarian came, he applied two hundred grams of mustard and prescribed putting her out in the meadow in good weather. I'm waiting for news of her. If I lose her, I won't change my team until next year. The hail in July 1898 cost me 3,500 francs.

Mama is well now: no blood, no mucus. A little weakness in the legs, a result of her nervous attack. How is Adèle? As for me, I'm wonderfully well.

The fund-raisers for the [Lagoubran] catastrophe are going around and collecting a lot. The Chamber [of Deputies] has voted 200,000 francs in relief. To think that the state owes nothing by law! But, then, what about humanity's law???

Good-bye, dear Henri.
Your affectionate father,

Charles de Cerilley

LOUISE GALOURET
TO HENRI DE CERILLEY
Le Monastère, April 5, 1899

Dear Sir,
I hasten to reply to your letter and reassure you about Madame's state of health. I've been a bit negligent, it's true, in giving you our news, but, having written to your father on March 28, I thought you would have been brought up to date on everything. Madame is pretty well now, although not very strong, for she had an abscess inside her left cheek that hurt horribly and she couldn't get a bit of rest until the doctor had lanced it. This left her very weak, for she hadn't been able to take any food during that time, her face being extremely swollen, and she was having difficulties even in swallowing a little milk. The doctor has had her take strengthening wines and good food, and now she's just about back to normal. She'll write you the first day she can, was very happy to get your news, and thanks you very much for the nice things you do for her. As for her temperament, you know, sir, that hardly changes all at once, but at present, since we moved into Le Monastère, she's been pretty calm, keeping busy with me in the house, taking walks with me, chatting—in short, leading a life that will, I hope, go very well if it continues as it is now. She likes it very much here, the weather is splendid, and if her health could improve a bit, I think everything would be for the best.
All my most respectful wishes.
Your wholly devoted,

Louise Galouret

MARTHE CARON D'AILLOT
TO HENRI DE CERILLEY
Le Monastère, April 10, 1899

Dear Henri,
I'm very late in answering your good letter, but I've been so tired in

a sad way that it's only today that I can apply myself to my correspondence.

I've bought a little mare along with her carriage and harness, the whole thing, whip in hand, for 500 francs. It's a pleasure for me to have this little carriage and horse: that way I spare my legs, which still hurt a little.

Don't give yourself the trouble of finding me a dog. I've bought one who is a little love, quite charming; you can tell me what you think of him when you see him.

My hand won't write any more, so be my very affectionate spokesman to your wife; I thank her with all my heart for her kind, hospitable offer to have me come, but this year I'm not stirring from home any more: I'm too much afraid of gout attacks.

Louise sends you all her affectionate respect.

Devotedly yours,

Marthe

LOUISE GALOURET
TO CHARLES DE CERILLEY
Le Monastère, April 26, 1899

Dear Sir,

I hasten to make known to you the news we've had concerning Monsieur d'Aillot. We received yesterday from Monsieur Martin the list of the objects that Monsieur d'Aillot is willing to hand over, a list much smaller than what is asked of him, for many things are missing, some rather important. One entire bed is missing—the one the cook slept in— plus the two sofas from the salon, the china service, all the lacework representing, it seems, a value of 1,250 francs, a little silverware, and lastly linen, even some of Madame's shifts.

Monsieur d'Aillot wrote in his own hand at the bottom of this list that he was holding for Madame all the objects to be found in his house that did not belong to him, but he says he has no responsibility for the missing objects, seeing that Madame's departure left the house open to strangers and he doesn't know what's become of everything. Madame willingly accepts what he is willing to offer, but she had me write to Monsieur Martin that she wanted to have her two sofas from the salon, as well as her china service, which came to her from her aunt. So we're going to wait for Monsieur Martin's answer, and, depending on what it is, we might leave immediately so that at least that would be finished. Madame is better: she's hardly coughing at all and her plasters are just about dry, but her hands still hurt from that wretched gout.

Please accept, sir, my most respectful wishes.

Louise Galouret

MARTHE CARON D'AILLOT
TO CHARLES DE CERILLEY
Le Monastère, May 3, 1899

Dear Uncle,

I'm sending you enclosed the copy of the letter that Monsieur Tubert has just written me. Please be kind enough to explain to me what this means. This gentleman tells me that I want 13,000 francs on account between the 15th and the 20th of May. I haven't written anything of the sort, but, while I'm willing to look after my affairs, I'd like you to keep me a little more in touch with the sale of the château, for that concerns me personally. Don't delay too much letting me know what I'm to write to Monsieur Tubert. But please, my dear uncle, keep me in touch a bit with my affairs.

As regards Monsieur d'Aillot and what he's holding back from me, I don't want to have any estimates made: let's bury this wretched affair as quickly as possible. As soon as I have Monsieur Martin's reply giving me the day when it will be possible to get the things moved out, Louise will leave with her brother-in-law. I don't want to have any more wranglings with my ex-husband at any price; you see, dear uncle, he doesn't have too much money, and the sooner he gets his 1,250 francs, the better he'll be able to get along; so let's not give him any trouble over that. May God go with him. I wish him much happiness. If he finds another woman as stupidly kind as I was, so much the better for him!

Thanks for being willing to look after the graves that remain alone at Sangy. For All Saints' Day I'll send some wreaths there. Alas, that won't bring them back to me.

Please, dear uncle, be my affectionate spokesman to my aunt and my cousins, whose writing I'd like very much to see more often.

Devotedly yours, dear uncle, from the bottom of my heart,

Marthe

MARTHE CARON D'AILLOT
TO HENRI DE CERILLEY[54]
Le Monastère, May 15, 1899

Dear Henri,

At last I've seen your handwriting reappear; I was very upset by your long silence. I'm glad to know you're in good health, as well as your dear family. It's very nice of you to offer me your two handsome bull terriers. I accept them with special pleasure because I'm fond of that breed, so you can send them to me when you wish. Let me know the day you'll send them, for I mean to go get them at the station myself. Tell me if these charming animals are used to soup, and also their names.

I thank you warmly for thinking of me on this occasion. Rest assured, they will be well cared for.

Adèle must be very displeased with me since I don't write her, but I admit to you frankly that she intimidates me a lot. She's very nice—yes, I believe it—but I don't dare write her, for my lack of style embarrasses me greatly. So, be my affectionate spokesman to her, and give your children a very tender hug and kiss for me.

I'm in pretty good health for the moment. The walks do me a great deal of good.

A very affectionate hug and kiss for you, dear Henri, and thanks again for your lovely dogs, for I'll be thrilled to have them in my house.

Devotedly yours,

Marthe

MARTHE DE MONTBOURG
TO CHARLES DE CERILLEY
Le Monastère, May 23, 1899

Dear Uncle,

I was waiting to write you till I had news to give you. I got a Cannes newspaper that was sent me by Monsieur Martin, and in it was a notice of my divorce (with Monsieur d'Aillot to blame for the wrongs and grievances), recorded perfectly at Cannes. So there is something finished at last, but I admit to you frankly that I'd prefer it if Monsieur d'Aillot hadn't given rise to such things. Anyway, the wine is poured, we have to drink it.

I had to go to Montpellier a few days ago to sign a paper useful to

Monsieur Martin, but as soon as I get the least bit tired, my legs swell up so, it's a shame. At any rate, I'm a bit better now.

I hate to leave you, my dear uncle, but my hand hurts so cruelly that I can't write any longer.

Marthe

G. VALLON, CURATE OF SAINT-SAVIN
TO CHARLES DE CERILLEY
Saint-Savin, May 24, 1899

Dear Sir,

I take the liberty of writing you about Madame de Montbourg's farmers at Saint-Savin. These poor people have confided to me their terrible situation, and since it's a very religious family and among my best parishioners, I think in conscience I'm obliged to take an interest in their sad lot, and I hope, sir, that you will see in this step I am taking toward you nothing but a feeling for equity.

I remember seeing you and speaking to you for a few moments at the time of Monsieur Émile's death, and this recollection leads me to attempt this step, which I take on my own.

The family of these farmers has for seventeen years had the use of the Saint-Savin farm. At the end of the first lease, these tenants, who had arrived on this farm richly equipped, were in arrears. The Baroness *made them sign* a new lease for 8,000 francs, saying they would manage. In the judgment of all the farmers in the region, it was much too expensive; it was impossible for them to make money on it; I could give you every reference on this subject. For seventeen years they've worked like real laborers at their task—father, mother, children—entertaining no one, and depriving themselves even of things that day laborers allow themselves. You know the price of butter, 1 franc 10 a pound; it's impossible to make 8,000 francs on that farm.

The new landlord is planning to rent it for only 5,000 francs. So you see the difference, and I wonder how they managed to pay what they had been paying up to then.

And these are Christian people, observing the law of the Sabbath, keeping up their house well, incurring no superfluous expense, working, I should say, like galley slaves, who are going to be reduced to absolutely nothing. I assure you, dear sir, my heart as a pastor and a priest bleeds at that thought. You will ask me why they took out a second lease.

Because they were bound by the first one, and a noose around the neck is quite hard to break. As for fault of theirs, there isn't any. I entreat you, dear sir, leave them their bread; for if they must pay you for the present year, they'll have nothing left, and less than nothing. That would be real reason to despair for our fine, decent farmers, who are respectful of God's law everywhere. Pardon me, dear sir, for writing you these things; but, once again, I believe I'm obliged in conscience to do so, remembering that I am a pastor and father, especially of those who set a good example.

In closing, I pray to God to grant my prayer to you. Deign to accept, Monsieur de Cerilley, my most respectful wishes.

G. Vallon

CHARLES DE CERILLEY
TO THE CURATE OF SAINT-SAVIN
Sangy, May 29, 1899

Dear Curate of Saint-Savin,

At the end of 1898 the farmer owed a round figure of 20,000 francs. He was let off half of it, on condition of payment next Michaelmas Day and a year's interest at 4 percent, plus the current farm rent. The eloquence of these figures will confront you with the enlightened charity we have practiced, which is better than the blind charity that should not bear the name of charity.

Yours truly,

Charles de Cerilley

MARTHE DE MONTBOURG
TO HENRI DE CERILLEY
Le Monastère, June 1, 1899

Dear Henri,

I'm sending you two letters that your father has sent me. One is from the curate of Saint-Savin, who takes up the cudgels for the farmer, so your father writes him very dryly. He does very well: the curate is an ugly fellow who's in cahoots with the farmer to annoy us. It's an encouragement to robbery. So much for the virtue of Curate Vallon; but if he's a Norman, so am I, and I'm onto their cunning. Don't let yourself be moved to pity by his letter and its mystical style, for he's a prick of the first water.

I'm sorry to give you so much trouble about your sending your dogs, and I thank you most affectionately for the gift you're making me of them. It's most gracious of you to give them collars with my name; that's a bit of thoughtfulness at which I was very touched. I think it would be better to have these two charming animals travel in a latticework case; when I was at Saint-Savin I was involved in selling dogs, and I always made out well sending them in a latticework case. You just have to put plenty to eat in their cases and write in large letters on the cases, "PLEASE FEED THE DOGS."

I would have written you sooner, dear Henri, but your letters found me in bed with a sort of inflammation of the lungs that quite tired me out. Finally, thanks to the devoted care of my dear Louise, I'm better and can get up now, which means that she's going to leave for Mougins, where she will be Wednesday to supervise the move. I won't be alone during that time, though, for her mother will come and keep me company.

I hate to leave you, but my hand is worn out.

Share my fond greetings with your entourage.

Devotedly yours,

Marthe

MARTHE DE MONTBOURG
TO HENRI DE CERILLEY
Le Monastère, June 14, 1899

Dear Henri,

Your two enchanting bow-wows arrived quite safely at Millau, and feel at home with us. Even my mare is giving them an affectionate welcome. I've enlarged my menagerie with a little all-white albino dog two months old,[55] this little animal answers to the name Boulette.[56]

The move out of Mougins has been carried out very well. Robert d'Aillot was quite nice: he himself helped pack up all the furniture and things, which we certainly weren't expecting. Everything was returned in good condition, but how painful, painful, this move was for me. I frankly admit to you that if the furniture hadn't been given to me by my mother, I would have left it all to him.

At last, all that is finished. My ex-husband is going to remarry next month. He's right to, for he can't remain alone. He's marrying an English-woman, a former governess whom I used to know a bit, but who's ten years older than he. This lady runs a restaurant in Nice. All that is very sad, dear Henri, but I assure you, I forgive him for everything he made me suffer; let him be happy with his new mate. As for me, I have no desire to get married again; I feel nice and calm in my hermit's life and I stay in it happily in the midst of my little pack of five dogs, whose harmonious voices charm me much more than the loveliest concerts you can find in the world. I'm not in very good health, for since last December, when I caught that chill in Sangy, I haven't stopped coughing. So I'm going to take stern measures to put an end to this state of affairs.

You'd do me a great favor if you would send me the dogs' pedigrees, for I plan to show them at Millau, where there will be a dog show soon. I'm sure they'll take first prize, and I'd be very flattered, though I have no ambition except for my animals.

My very fondest wishes to you, dear Henri, and I thank you again for your lovely gift.

Devotedly yours,

Marthe

LOUISE GALOURET
TO CHARLES DE CERILLEY
Le Monastère, June 29, 1899

Dear Sir,

Madame has asked me to step in and let you know her news, for the gout makes her hands hurt pretty badly. She's been spitting up a lot of blood, and the doctor is having her leave for the Mont-Dore (Puy-de-Dôme) to strengthen her lungs. It seems it's blood flowing into the chest, which could become dangerous, so we'll leave next Monday; as soon as we arrive, we'll send you our new address.

As regards the liquidation, I think it won't be finished very soon, for Maître Tassin says he must have all the accounts in hand to get anywhere. So Madame asks you to be good enough to send everything that's due us for inheritance, or for her share, to Maître Tassin, so that it can be finished, for it's been dragging pretty long. Madame has also received a letter from Monsieur Tubert telling her that he had only 38,000 francs left to pay out on the purchase of Saint-Savin, whereas Madame only knew about the sum of 50,000 that had been paid into Maître Tassin's hands; she doesn't know when the other sum was paid and to whom, which worries her a bit, for she claims that she should have been notified when

312

there was something new in her affairs, so she'd know where she stood. She can't make any reply at all to Monsieur Tubert, for she doesn't want to let him see how little anyone cares about keeping her up to date on her own affairs. I'm writing about this at the same time to Monsieur Tassin, and she thinks she'll soon know what to believe.

Monsieur and Madame, most respectfully yours,

Louise Galouret

MARTHE DE MONTBOURG
TO CHARLES DE CERILLEY
Mont-Dore, July 18, 1899

Dear Uncle,

My state of health is still the same, and four days ago I had a fit of choking that almost carried me off. I consulted a specialist in Clermont-Ferrand, who listened carefully to my chest and, after a serious examination, declared to me frankly that the condition was grave, but that with a serious treatment I might perhaps pull through. I'd be very pleased to have the liquidation not be completed until August, for I mean to follow my treatment here carefully—I care a lot about saving my skin.

Do be reassured, dear uncle. I'm well provided with warm clothes, and Louise is well outfitted, too. I'm sending you a box in the mail by this post. In it there's a bedjacket of local wool for my aunt, a pen holder in local stone also for her, and, for you, a pipe of local wood and a shaving brush set in local stone.

The dogs are in good keeping.

My fondest wishes to you both, dear uncle and aunt, with all my heart.

Marthe

MARTHE DE MONTBOURG
TO HENRI DE CERILLEY
Mont-Dore, July 22, 1899

Dear Henri,

We both thank you with all our hearts for your charming brooches, which gave us the greatest pleasure.

I thank you, too, for the photographs of the white dogs' ancestors and for their pedigree. It was nice of you to send the photographs of your kittens with the double paws. They look very nice, especially since they look a lot like you, which means they'll be as nice as you.

My hedgehog would have been willing to write you to thank you, but today she's indisposed because of a remedy that's supposed to do away with a tapeworm that's bothering her.

The waters[57] have done me a great deal of good, but no doubt I'll need several seasons here to be definitely back to normal.

Your father has written me that he got a sunburn in his eyes, and that he sees clearly that he'll have to take it easier (something he should have done long ago: at his age it's unwise for him to run himself ragged the way he does).

I leave you with regret to go drink my half-glass of water.
Devotedly yours,

Marthe

LOUISE GALOURET
TO HENRI DE CERILLEY
Mont-Dore, July 28, 1899

Dear Sir,

I hasten to give you our news and to thank you for the brooch you were kind enough to send me. I thank you for it with all my heart and am very touched by the nice souvenir you're kind enough to give me.

Last Saturday, when Madame wrote you, I was quite tired from a remedy I had taken to get rid of the tapeworm, which nevertheless didn't succeed in clearing it out of me. That means I stayed in bed all day Saturday, for that had quite exhausted me, so Madame went out for a bit alone in the afternoon. She was seized with acute discomfort outside and they brought her to me in the hotel in a carriage. I was helping get her undressed, and as soon as she was in bed she lost consciousness completely and had a bad fit of hysterics that lasted at least an hour, which gave me a terrible fright. The doctor attributes this to the tiring effect of the treatment, for it is very tiring, the more so because she is anemic and so her nerves overcome her more easily. It has finally got better since then, but from time to time during the night she had a few little spells of fever. Even yesterday she stayed in bed all day, and the doctor cut down the treatment that she should otherwise pursue, for if this malady can't be checked, she'd never be cured of it, which would be very unfortunate at her age. The doctors have made no secret of it and have urged her to take great precautions if she wants to have a chance to be cured, for it's the tip of the left lung that's affected. While I've been writing my letter, the doctor has come to see her. He thinks she's better than yesterday, and he's prescribing carriage rides for her, as long as she doesn't tire herself. But the lung is still so-so, and he has decided to try cauterization next Monday. He's a very good doctor, very gentle, and he comes to see her every other day, and more often when I come and get him.

With most respectful wishes,

Louise Galouret

MARTHE DE MONTBOURG
TO HENRI DE CERILLEY
Le Monastère, August 26, 1899

Dear Henri,

Although you're a bit of a lazybones about writing to us, I want just the same to give you our news, which is pretty good for the moment, although the gout often pays me a visit (something I could very well do without).

I think, dear Henri, that you're the proprietor of some good vine-yards. It would be very nice of you to sell me a little cask of fifty liters of white wine, for my Mont-Dore doctor ordered me to drink some with Vichy water. I know your wine won't be adulterated. So tell me your prices.

I think your father is staying with you. Please give him and your wife my affectionate greetings.

Devotedly yours,

Marthe

P.S. Be a dear and send me a number of *Le Chasseur Français.*

MARTHE DE MONTBOURG
TO CHARLES DE CERILLEY
Millau, August 27, 1899

Dear Uncle,

I'm enclosing Monsieur Tourville's answer; you'll see how this gentleman responds to my question. He claims he told everything to you as well as to Monsieur Tassin. It's really a shame that I, the proprietor of Saint-Savin, can't have serious details. Monsieur Tourville regards me as nothing, but I'll show him I'm something. I wrote him that it was absolutely ridiculous to give *you* more details than me. He refused to answer me.

My health, as Louise told you, has progressed very well with the waters of the Mont-Dore, as well as with the cauterizations, which I'll have to continue here. I've got my hunting permit, and my gouty legs are doing very well with the exercise. I'm sleeping well and eating to match.

Hoping to hear from you soon, I send my sincere affection.

Marthe

MARTHE DE MONTBOURG
TO HENRI DE CERILLEY
Le Monastère, October 28, 1899

Dear Henri,

Write to Monsieur Tourville for me. I don't want to write him any more: he won't give me any details, so I'm not spending my time corresponding with such a clam any longer.

Thank you very much for your offer of wine, which I accept with pleasure. You'll send that off to me in a few days? I'm getting along perfectly, thanks to the good care of my dear Louise, who tends me with all her heart.

I've had good news from your father, which pleases me considerably. Do share with your entourage all my affectionate greetings.

Devotedly yours,

Marthe

MARTHE DE MONTBOURG
TO HENRI DE CERILLEY
Sangy, November 5, 1899

Dear Henri,

Taking advantage of these fine days, I've come to Sangy to pay a pious visit to my dear deceased and at the same time to see you all, for I'll arrive Tuesday at 11:37 A.M. at the station. I'm planning on spending two days with you. Louise is with me, as always. Do be very nice and give me a room where she and I can be together, for with my sometimes sudden fatigues and the gout, I ought to have my faithful guardian always with me.

Yesterday my uncle had me make a detailed inspection of the four properties from the point of view of construction and repairs. He gave me all the details and showed me all the accounts of the inheritance. We're agreed on what he told me.

A big hug and kiss to you all.

Devotedly yours,

Marthe

MARTHE DE MONTBOURG
TO HENRI DE CERILLEY
Le Monastère, November 13, 1899

Dear Henri,

We arrived safe and sound at Millau, where all our company was very glad to see us back.

Let me thank you again with all my heart for the warm welcome you gave us. Your genuine affection consoled me for many disappointments. I don't know how to tell you how sympathetic to me your wife has been, so I tell you this in all truth, you're the only ones in the family that I love.

I've given orders for them to start making repairs on my house immediately, which means that in the space of two weeks to twenty days I'll be installed in my new premises. If the weather stays good, I'll resume hunting the fallow-finches and other birds; not having a dog, I can't aspire to bag hares.

We hope you'll write us often and give us news of your excellent wife and your dear little children. My hedgehog sends you both her best. And I, dear Henri, send you a very tender hug and kiss, also to Adèle, who by her tenderness has been able to acquire a friend who will always love her.

Nor do I forget your children in my endearments.

Devotedly yours,

Marthe

P.S. If the little photograph of Mama is ready, send it to me, and be at your photographer's when the big one is ready, for I'm dying to have it. In a few days I'll send you our portraits.

MARTHE DE MONTBOURG
TO HENRI DE CERILLEY
Le Monastère, November 27, 1899

Dear Henri,

I thank you for your kind letter, which I received this morning and which I am answering immediately. You don't tell me whether Monsieur Tassin has written you. He made no answer to me; a week ago now, you promised to hurry him, and I see you're not doing it. I don't want to wait till next year, for this gentleman has been saying the hell with us for too long. Write him, for I want everything to be finished up between now and December 15, when I'll go get my papers. I don't want any more dawdling.

I thank you for sending the wine you so kindly offered me. As soon as it arrives I'll write and let you know, but please, answer me right away whether Monsieur Tassin has written you. I don't know what creature it is that you call Morelle[58]—I don't know that animal. Is it some sort of wild duck, or another land bird?

I'm not writing you any more this time, for I'm just in from the hunt, where I killed nothing but a robin redbreast, and I'm tired.

Share among your family all my affectionate wishes, big kisses to the children.

Devotedly yours,

Marthe

1900

HENRI DE CERILLEY
TO CHARLES DE CERILLEY
Saint-Étienne, January 10, 1900

Dear Papa,

We've come here for the chore of inspections in spite of the strikes, which have been called off in part by the leader of the miners, who have resumed work. For the makers of trimmings, it'll be longer and more delicate, for they must consider, *on the side of the manufacturers,* that ribbon has hardly been in fashion for a long time, and that if they raise the price in this way they'll be at a disadvantage against the foreign competition; *on the side of the workers,* that it is widely recognized that the trimming makers don't earn a good enough living. Last week's brawls weren't the doing of the strikers but of a few anarchists who showed up for the occasion. The strikers' temperament is more mocking than destructive, judging by what I've seen today on the Place Marengo.[59]

For the three weeks that the trimming makers' strike has lasted, the administration has wrongly tolerated long processions of men and women with flags and music. In these long processions of sometimes five to six thousand people, they gaily sang a carmagnole[60] adapted to the local circumstances; no acts of violence; but following last Thursday's clash, a prefectoral decree prohibited the return of these demonstrations. Then, from that moment on, you've been seeing on the Place Marengo, black with people, the trimming makers, men and women, walking around in groups of four or five, sometimes two by two in lines of twenty persons, pretending to tell their beads, which they carry ostentatiously in their hands, others intoning anthems under their breath, others greeting a group with these dry sarcastic words: *"Pax vobiscum, mon frère. Et cum spiritu tuo.* Hey, Cathérine, aren't you coming? — Wait, I've another ten to say."[61] And during this time, the policemen move about placidly. However it may be with these peacefully satiric gestures, the situation is sad, and spirits can only be embittered by the wait, already too long, for a solution. All the troops are standing by; the garrison, already comprising three regiments, has been reinforced by cuirassiers from Lyon.

The munitions factories are under military guard. One waits, hoping for a solution that still does not appear, given the complex state of the opposing parties.

We send our fondest wishes, Papa and Mama, with all our hearts. Your affectionate son,

Henri

MARTHE DE MONTBOURG
TO HENRI DE CERILLEY
Le Monastère, January 18, 1900

Dear Henri,

I didn't answer your letter sooner, for I was waiting till I was back on my feet from a chill, caught while hunting on the riverbanks; I had to stay in bed three days, but rest easy, my indisposition left me only with a loss of voice. My hedgehog is making me keep warm and has placed an absolute ban on my returning to the hunt.

I find nothing better to do than follow her advice, for I'd rather do without hunting than get pneumonia. As regards Abbé Bosset, I completely agree with you: we must give him the time to comply without wringing his neck. He was very good to me when we were in Grasse.

As for the guest house, Mama didn't want it to serve as an inn, so before renting it to the first person who comes along, I want to have the offers examined. I think I'm fulfilling a sacred duty toward my mother's memory in writing you about this matter as I'm doing. We should sell it to a small farmer, if we find one. It will have bidders, for it's very pleasant.

The papers are still talking about the strike at Saint-Étienne, and saying that there is fear of grave accidents. Be careful and always take along with you your traveling companion.

Devotedly yours. A thousand fond wishes all around you.

Marthe

MARTHE DE MONTBOURG
TO HENRI DE CERILLEY
Villa Marthe,[62] *May 20, 1900*

Dear Henri,

We were very sorry that you couldn't come to Belgium with us. Frankly, you might well go there, for Belgium is a country to see. We've recognized that the Belgians are a hundred times more pleasant and welcoming than the French; we've been so splendidly treated everywhere in this country that we'll long retain the memory of their kindnesses. For my part, if I hadn't had to hurry back because of my house, I'd have gladly stayed there longer, so much did I enjoy myself in that lovely country.

From Belgium, we went back to Paris to see its monuments in greater detail, and the Exposition [World's Fair], which deserves a visit from every point of view. It's beautiful! It's magnificent to see! And it's well worth the trip. But the Swiss Village is the most charming pavilion to visit; it made me want to go see those beautiful mountains in reality, but I won't carry out that plan this year: I've traveled enough this time and I want to stay home a bit.

I'm delighted to learn that Paul has resumed his rank as army captain, for, frankly, a Cerilley was not in the right line practicing the profession of a traveling salesman. I didn't call on him in Paris, and as you can see, I was right, since I wouldn't have found him. Besides, I'm not at all eager to make new acquaintances. His wife is a magnificent doll who would be well placed in the Exposition, but who wouldn't get along with me, for I'm far from being one. It would be very nice of you, my nice Henri, to go to Grivolat's and order a gun from him; I'd like a .24-caliber, with safety catch, and at the price of 180 francs. That way I'd have my weapon for the opening of the season. You know I like a good weapon better than the loveliest jewelry in the world.

We brought back a Madagascan dog, perfect for a guard dog. You'll see him when you come. When do you plan to come?

Devotedly yours,

Marthe

MARTHE DE MONTBOURG
TO HENRI DE CERILLEY
Villa Marthe, August 2, 1900

Dear Henri,

I find on my return a letter from Bouchard,[63] requesting yet another delay. *I won't grant it to them.* They also ask me for a reply, which I won't give them. I put you in charge of everything. Write Monsieur Tourville to act in our names and do everything to see we are paid. These people are taking advantage, and we mustn't let ourselves be involved; they have had since 1887 to rid themselves of their debt.

I'm enclosing the letter from Bouchard, whose property you will do well to seize—they might skip out without a peep, as they often do in Normandy.

While awaiting the pleasure of hearing from you, I send my fondest wishes from the heart.

Marthe

MARTHE DE MONTBOURG
TO HENRI DE CERILLEY
Villa Marthe, August 31, 1900

Dear Henri,

I went and spent a few days in a country place in the neighborhood of Millau, and it was not until I got back home that I could cash the money order you sent me.

I think you acted for the best with Bouchard. Be on the watch to have him pay the rest next year.

We're glad to know that your son is rid of the ferocious carnivorous animal that had taken up residence in his stomach.

I've received a letter from Vincent asking me to lend him 8,000 francs to help him finish paying his debts. I'll try to help out with half of it, but I'd like to know if he's solvent. You who know your way around in business better than I do, advise me right away, so I can give him some kind of answer. I urge you not to talk to your father about it.

All my fondest wishes to your wife and to your kittens. My hedgehog sends all her best to you and your better half, and her pats for your little pussies.

Devotedly yours,

Marthe

Villa Marthe, December 15, 1900

Dear Henri,

I would have answered your affectionate letter sooner, for it did me much good, if I didn't have my hedgehog in bed with a heavy bronchial catarrh. This is seven days now that she's been in bed without getting up, except from time to time to make her bed. She's coughing a lot, so my doctor is tending her with much devotion and attention, coming to see her often—and, I've become a nurse. I have someone to do the cooking for me, so I can stay close to my beloved patient.

It's quite natural that I should devote myself to her, for she has *much devotion* for me. Louise is at the same time a sister and a mother, and I, who have no one left who's very close to me, no more home, I feel completely comforted by her tenderness and her indulgent kindness; I, who am far from being pious, thank God for giving me such a support. I entrust to you, my dear cousin, the care of the graves of my dear deceased, and I even go along with your advice to have black-gray marble, but I'm telling you, I don't want any imitation of any style whatever that's germinating in your father's brain, and I *want* wrought iron fencing, painted black and with the coats of arms as we've said, and it's *you alone* who are to look after it.

I thank your dear wife with all my heart for her kind letter, but it seemed only natural to me to offer her my house if she had intended to change climate for a while.

My very fond greetings.

Devotedly yours,

Marthe

P.S. The Montpellier doctor is dead, so I can't write him in the other world; besides, I'm better.

Since I don't frequent the ecclesiastical tribe, have them put down for Émile whatever you think best suits his loving and lofty character.

MARTHE DE MONTBOURG
TO ADÈLE DE CERILLEY
Villa Marthe, December 24, 1900

Dear Adèle,

I love you too much to let this year's end slip by without offering you my very sincere New Year's wishes. So I wish you a new year without sadness or illness. Take your dear heart in both hands and consider that soon perhaps you won't be living in Lyon, where the climate doesn't suit you. Take good care of yourself.

I wish we were into the good weather, to keep you in Aveyron. If you were to come and see me next year, it would be a real joy for me. Think about it, I entreat you, dear beloved cousin, and always rely on me to try to be agreeable to you, for in spite of my rough character, your adorable sweet smile won me completely.

My hedgehog is well into convalescence now, which makes me very joyful. She's so completely devoted to me that I've become deeply attached to her. What would become of me if I didn't see her any more? I think my life would be quite desolate, for it's very rare in our times to meet a real friend. I have a treasure, and I'm keeping it!

Devotedly yours, dear cousin and friend,

Marthe

1901

MARTHE DE MONTBOURG
TO HENRI DE CERILLEY
Villa Marthe, May 13, 1901

Dear Angora Cat,

You're showing yourself to be miserly with your letters, and for a long time I haven't had any news from you or your dear entourage.

I announce to you, my dear Angora cat, the first communion of Gabrielle, daughter of my hedgehog, on June 13. This child won't forget you in her prayers. My word, it's the finest day of her life, for afterward there aren't any finer times for a child. Certainly, if I could go back again to my earliest childhood, I'd do so gladly, especially knowing what I know today. I'd guard against all fine talk, for life has its thorns and they're tipped with steel.

We're very well, the weather is superb, and our mountains of Aveyron are covered with a magnificent carpet of greenery; the nightingale is pouring out harmonious notes, singing with all his might the beauty of nature. I'm very glad, my dear cat, to have organized my hermit's life this way (that is to say, not entertaining anyone); besides, I often take my carriage out into the countryside, I love to breathe in whole lungfuls of the pure air in the mountains, and I find myself very happy. I wouldn't for anything in the world give up the sweet and peaceful existence I have now, having had enough sorrows to have earned the sweet quietude whose beneficent dew I am now tasting.

A tender embrace to you, also to Adèle and your cats.

Fondly,

Marthe

MARTHE DE MONTBOURG
TO HENRI DE CERILLEY
Villa Marthe, May 25, 1901

Dear Angora Cat,

I thank you for your kind letter and for your lasting sentiments of friendship. I fully approve not giving up the Nun's House for less than 1,200 francs—it's worth that hands down. It will give me pleasure when you come and bring your camera. We'll have a good hunt, with my dog Zut [Shucks], and I'll do everything I can to be nice to you and make your stay with us as comfortable as possible without too much boredom for you, dear Angora cat.

I've had good news of Aunt Sophie, but Christian's oldest son broke his wrist doing some gymnastics. With those little monsters you always have to worry. I've retained an excellent memory of the welcome Aunt Sophie gave me at Sainte-Apolline, so we're rather often in affectionate correspondence. It seems that she was very touched by my coming at the time of poor Uncle Honoré's death.

While I'm waiting to hear from you again, I send my very tender embrace to you, also to your wife and kittens.

Fondly yours, darling cat,

Marthe

MARTHE DE MONTBOURG
TO HENRI DE CERILLEY
Villa Marthe, June 12, 1901

Dear Angora Cat,

We are very distressed to learn that you and your wife are suffering from that nasty grippe, and we keenly hope you will both soon be well again. Fortunately, your kittens aren't sick. What can you expect, my dear Henri? That's the way life is, it's an onion that you peel as you weep.

Your father has written to me about tombstones. Even though I gather from what he says that they're too expensive, it doesn't matter to me: these stones will cover people who were honest and full of goodness, and they certainly deserve it!

I thank you with all my heart for arguing my interests that way against your father. He's not easy, but I let him talk and do just as I please. You know, if my mother hadn't reported to me her brother's kind words I wouldn't have known about them, but he really is the worthy brother of Harpagon.[64] I've known it for a long time.

You did very well to write to Bouchard, for we mustn't show them mercy now, and if they still want to dawdle, we must have a provisional seizure made. *He* is honest, but his wife wears the pants and leads him around by the nose. As for the fencing around the tombstones, I agree with you on not having them set until next year, for this year is very filled up. I approve of everything you've done, my good cat, and thank you again for your affectionate zeal.

You'll excuse me if I don't write any longer: I have a frightful migraine and I'm tired.

Fondly yours, sweet Angora cat,

Marthe

MARTHE DE MONTBOURG
TO HENRI DE CERILLEY
Mont-Dore, August 3, 1901

My good Angora Cat,

We reached our destination safe and sound, so I hasten to write you right away and get news of you all as soon as possible. I'll write one of these days to Monsieur Tourville about the Nun's House, for we must get rid of that house, which, when you come right down to it, brings us in absolutely nothing. I'm convinced that I'm going to get completely well again with this good piney air and the water, which also does a lot of good. This doesn't keep it from being rather unpleasant to go for inhalations: shut up in a room with fifteen or twenty people, each one perspiring more than the next, it's frightful, but so what? As long as it cures, one certainly has to put up with it.

I've written to Abbé Bosset that we are forgiving him the rest of the money he owed us. That excellent man was greatly touched by it.

Give me news of you as soon as possible, dear Angora cat.

Fondly yours,

Marthe

Caen, November 5, 1901

Dear Sir,

I'm sending you 150 francs out of the 500 I still owe you. At this point I can't give you more. You see, sir, I ask nothing better than to pay you, but the fact is I'm not rich and I have a lot of trouble earning my living. I'll send you the rest as soon as possible, and I like to believe that you, sir, and your cousin won't make trouble for me.

I thank you, sir, in advance.

Your humble servant,

Bouchard

MARTHE DE MONTBOURG
TO HENRI DE CERILLEY
Villa Marthe, November 25, 1901

Dear Henri,

I'd certainly told you that the Bouchards didn't care a rap about us. We mustn't leave them in peace: we've waited long enough as it is, and even with too much patience.

If Bouchard doesn't come through by December 1, you'd do very well to have him followed up by a bailiff, and firmly. Of course he'll pay for all the official paper we'll have to spend to make him pay us what he owes.

My health is coming back now, so I am giving up the cauterizations. It's not for me to speak ill of this treatment, which did me the greatest good, but it seems that my catarrh didn't require it: I talked about it to my doctor, who replied that it wasn't necessary. He gave me an excellent potion to stop the cough that was shaking me like a plum tree, and I found myself very much improved for it.

We're very glad to know you're all in good health. The snow has made its appearance at Millau, and it's bitter cold. I have to light a fire in the apartments, or we'd freeze on the spot. So I don't go out any more, just stay by the fireside, like a little cat.

I've gone back to my painting, since my hand is hurting less from the gout. It's a pleasant pastime, and although I'm no artist, I'm pleased with my works.

A fond hug and kiss to you.
Devotedly yours,

Marthe

Dear Henri,

You've overwhelmed me by sending me that magnificent Baccarat cup. It's really much too beautiful for me, who haven't done anything extraordinary enough to get such fine nice things—the chocolates and other things contained in the cup are excellent. Ah! if I were near you, how I'd pull your mustache happily for spoiling me as you do—as does your dear wife, whom I also thank with all my heart.

So you'll all come this year, that is to say next year. We're so close to the new year, you might as well say we're there. What happiness to have you all under my roof! I love you all so, I do, and I thank you all a thousand times for the warm tenderness in which you're kind enough to enfold me.

Fondly yours and Adèle's, with all the strength of my heart.

Marthe

P.S. Do as you like about the quarter-cask of white wine you've had the kindness to offer me. You're a charming Angora.

1902

Dear Henri,

We're not pleased with you: you'd promised to give us your children during the Easter vacation, and you're going back on your given word. That's *very bad* of you, you're the meanest Angora cat on the face of the earth. I will long remember this action, not very nice for us and for me in particular.

Keep the pressure on Bouchard, for he procrastinates to suit himself and I don't intend to have him say the hell with us any longer.

Come when you can; it will always be a pleasure for us.

The hedgehog sends you and your dear entourage all best wishes. Devotedly yours,

Marthe

Condition unchanged no aggravation. Tomorrow consult with Grasset Montpellier. Will write today.

Galouret

CHARLES DE CERILLEY
TO HENRI DE CERILLEY
Sangy, May 24, 1902

Dear Henri,

Your aunt brings me your letter and Louise's wire to you. I'm sending
a wire to Louise with a request to reply immediately, and if there is danger
for poor Marthe, I'll leave right away. I'll keep you posted. I'm not eager
to have you make this trip at this point, when you're barely over the
grippe. As for me, I'm well, as well as possible for my age.

I'm worried about this grave bronchitis! Marthe has thick blood, and
in her, ailments can grow serious fast.

If you were to receive anything, I'm quite sure you'd use the tele-
graph. I warn you that I'm getting up steam and that unless you tell me
not to, I'm ready to leave at the first sign of real danger.

Your affectionate father,

Charles de Cerilley

TELEGRAM
LOUISE GALOURET TO
CHARLES DE CERILLEY
Saturday, May 24, 1902, 15:20

No aggravation or immediate danger. Still unchanged. Consult tomorrow
with Grasset at Montpellier.

Galouret

CHARLES DE CERILLEY
TO HENRI DE CERILLEY
Sangy, May 25, 1902
Sunday morning

Dear Henri,

Enclosed is the wire received this morning. So I'll wait for later word
and go to Millau at the first disturbing sign. I've weighed the words of
Louise's wire, and all of us here have seen in them no request to come,

only notification of the situation. The consultation with Monsieur Grasset clearly proves that it's serious.

My road is mapped out, whether by night or by day; in any event, I'm the one who'll take it, and not you.

I'm going to Mass and taking this letter to the mail.

Your affectionate father,

Charles de Cerilley

TELEGRAM
LOUISE GALOURET TO
HENRI DE CERILLEY
Saturday, May 24, 1902, 17:25

Madame more tired. Come right away.

Galouret

TELEGRAM
LOUISE GALOURET TO
HENRI DE CERILLEY
Sunday, May 25, 1902, 4:35

Madame deceased this morning two o'clock. Notify Monsieur Charles. No answer telegram.

Galouret

TELEGRAM
CHARLES DE CERILLEY TO
HENRI DE CERILLEY
Sunday, May 25, 1902, 14:00

I leave Lyon this evening 23:30 for Millau. I am telling Louise.

De Cerilley

Sunday, May 25, 1902, 20:25

Doctor and I beseech you take greatest precautions because diphtheria. Not sleep house if not all disinfected. Write precisely. Very worried. Be very careful.

Adèle

EDWIGE DE CERILLEY
TO HENRI DE CERILLEY
May 26, 1902

Dear Henri,

Louise's sad wire of yesterday reached me only this morning, because the post office is closed on Sunday.

I'm very saddened to think that you must have arrived too late and that the poor child died without any of the family at her bedside; it must have been the gout gone to the heart or the chest that took her away so quickly. Did they at least think of the comforts of religion? That worries me. If you can, give me a few details. Are you going to bring her body back to Sangy? If so, I'll do my best to attend the funeral; I hope I'll be better.

I hope to hear that Marthe continued for you what her mother began; she loved you very much. Just the same, it's sad to go so young, poor child! . . .

I embrace you with all my heart. Thank Louise for all her wires. Alas, at this distance everything gets too complicated.

Aunt Edwige

SOPHIE DE MONTBOURG
TO CHARLES DE CERILLEY
Sainte-Apolline, May 27, 1902

Dear Charles,

Alas! What lightning swiftness for our poor Marthe!

I got your letter only yesterday, Monday, and poor M. died Sunday, the day before. . . . That's what Louise replied to my wire. What horrible anxiety I have that poor Marthe did not have the last sacraments in time! I'm immensely anxious to find out. Had she wanted to be buried next to her mother at Sangy?

I'm going to have a Mass said here. I suppose that M. must have made arrangements and that you're going to stay a few days in Millau to carry them out.

Write me as soon as possible. I need reassurance on the religious question.

I send you a tender and sad embrace.

Your very affectionate sister,

Sophie

LÉON DE MONTBOURG
TO CHARLES DE CERILLEY
Lisieux, May 28, 1902

Dear Uncle,

I was badly upset by the telegram from my mother announcing the death of poor Marthe, and I keenly regret not being able to pay her my last respects, but, according to my calculation, I couldn't have arrived at Millau in time for the burial. Besides, I'm a bit ill, but don't say anything about it to my mother or she will worry needlessly. You must have been the only one of the family to attend the sad ceremony. Poor Marthe! I liked her, because I think she had an excellent heart, and she liked me. Please give me some details about her illness and her death. I didn't even know she was ill. But with a temperament like hers, everything had to be feared.

There's one whole side of the family snuffed out in a few years. It's frightfully sad. Will her body be put beside her mother's? Did she receive the last rites?

Good-bye, my dear uncle.

Your affectionate nephew,

Léon

AMÉLIE DE MONTBOURG
TO CHARLES DE CERILLEY
Caen, May 29, 1902

My dear Uncle,

I was bowled over by the death of poor Marthe. The good Lord certainly did well to take her out of this poor world where she had such an impossible life, but how sorry I am for the poor child, who deserved better by virtue of her good heart.

I'm glad to see the properties concentrated in Henri's serious hands. As for Louise, I hope that everything she has gained was gained honestly, and that she truly deserves this good luck. You see such horrible things that you could easily doubt the devotion and fidelity of even the best domestics, who have every interest in seeing their mistresses pass away —and really it would have been more just for this fortune to return to the Montbourgs with a reasonable legacy to the maid. Anyway, poor Émilie was sorely tried by her whole family, and now there's that entire household, that whole stock, disappeared. It was probably in God's plans, and we can only watch them being carried out with trust and faith.

Was she able to have the last rites, the poor thing? Did she suffer much? Did you arrive in time to speak to her? I'm going to pray for her with the firm hope that the good Lord will be very merciful to her and will make it up to her. How many mysteries and what lightning bolts are falling around us, my dear uncle. By burying your own, my dear uncle, you will deserve to have a *sweet and pious* end, but you must still pray for it, even while your nearest and dearest, of whom I am one, add their prayers that that end may be delayed as long as possible.

Tell me whether faith awoke in Marthe's heart when she saw herself in danger, poor child.

Tell Henri that I applaud the return into his hands of the properties at Sangy, my dear uncle, and let me embrace you very affectionately and respectfully, and my aunt also.

Amélie

SOPHIE DE MONTBOURG
TO CHARLES DE CERILLEY
Sainte-Apolline, May 31, 1902

Dear Charles,

Poor Marthe's last dispositions, made or remade two days before her death, hardly correspond to her last letter, so affectionate, which I still have; for in them the Montbourgs are completely forgotten. Louise, whom I asked for details of the illness, tells me that she was taken ill on the 11th, and Louise didn't wire Henri until the 24th (after the will was made)!! Marthe wrote two months ago asking me urgently to go and see her at Millau. I was in no condition to, and expressed to her all my regrets. Did she feel dependent? And did she want to be free of it? Poor woman!!! Since I've been a widow, I myself have felt the ruthlessness of servants. This is the second couple I'm putting out the door. They all wanted to put me away. I'm eager to receive your letter with details. Henri is bringing together Émilie's properties—there is that much saved, at least, for the family. I was certainly expecting her to give a good share to Louise, but *so much,* that's really a bit thick!

Good-bye, dear Charles.

Your poor, quite tottering sister,

Sophie

ADÈLE DE CERILLEY
TO CHARLES DE CERILLEY
Lyon, June 2, 1902

My dear Father,

You cannot imagine how dumbfounded I still am at all these events, so swift have they been. Poor Marthe, to die so young—why, that's frightful! For someone like me, who's been a wreck for so long, you can imagine how that strikes me. In the last week I had felt the need to see the doctor twice even though I didn't feel ill—that gives you an idea, you who know me well and also love me well, of the state I was in.

I'm glad that Henri has these two properties. That's superb, but so extraordinary, for, after all, having already shared with her half of her mother's fortune, here he is receiving a lot more, for she has now given Henri a very fine piece of land at Sangy. All that pleases me, for us all, but especially for the children. Really, I simply seethe with indignation to think that that tramp Louise has *taken everything* from the Montbourgs. You know, that's unworthy, but I have no words to convey what I feel. Ah, what a smart woman, how well she knew how to ensnare poor Marthe, so weak in character, at least with this Louise, who had managed to cajole her thoroughly. You were admirably restrained and proper with her. If I'd been there, I couldn't have held back, and she simply would have had to swallow what I would have had to tell her.

Henri hasn't had a letter from anybody. I think at times he will receive feeble congratulations, for people will be jealous, and yet these are properties of the Cerilleys coming back to a Cerilley, whereas for the Montbourgs it's all their own possessions disappearing and going to a servant whose devotion for *only four years* was very self-seeking. What a shrewd woman!

Thank you for the candied fruit. You gave me great pleasure by thinking of me, my dear father.

Your affectionate daughter,

Adèle

VALENTINE DE MONTBOURG[65]
TO CHARLES DE CERILLEY
Paris, June 3, 1902

Dear Sir,

I've learned of the premature death of poor Marthe from Christian, and the other details from Sophie, to whom you sent them. I hope that the poor child died a Christian death; the presence of the curate, as public witness of the will, would be one proof of it. In this connection, my grandchildren's notary, to whom I was speaking of this will while going to sign for my pension, as I do every three months, advised me to ask to see the will, that being the right of blood relatives. I've always assumed that Marthe would leave all she possesses to her chambermaid, and it's fortunate that she gave your son your properties at Sangy. I think that's just, for you've always been so devoted to your brothers and sisters.

I don't know the name of the notary in Millau and I wouldn't have taken this step. But my notary tells me that the children's parents want it and would reproach me for not taking it, so will you be good enough to tell me the name of the notary in Millau, to whom mine will write.

With warm regards to Madame de Cerilley, I remain faithfully yours,

V. de Montbourg

MAÎTRE TASSIN
TO HENRI DE CERILLEY
Montpellier, June 4, 1902

Dear Sir,

I've just this moment received your letter of the 3rd notifying me of

337

the decease of your cousin Marthe de Montbourg at Millau and of her testamentary arrangements.

I'm totally surprised at this news. I haven't been informed about anything, though this doesn't astonish me on the part of the good Louise, of whom I have my own opinion.

I was the depositary of a handwritten will of Madame Marthe, but after her move to Millau and prompting that you can understand, she took it back from me and waited until the very day of her death to make another.

That poor lady was not really aware of her social position or of her wealth. It's still very fortunate that she left you the properties. The remainder of her fortune must have taken another road before her decease.

One must feel sorry for this poor lady and her sad end.

Devotedly and affectionately yours,

Maître Tassin

HENRI DE CERILLEY
TO CHARLES DE CERILLEY
Lyon, June 4, 1902

Dear Papa,

I wrote at length to Léon and Aunt Sophie, expressing to them our distress at seeing that Louise had all the Montbourg fortune and expressing my regret that Marthe at heart had not returned to fairer feelings for that part of the family, in spite of her affectionate relations with Léon and her trip to Sainte-Apolline. The truth is that there was the appearance of a rapprochement, which I encouraged as best I could with all my heart, but time alone (which was lacking) would have consolidated it, so many impressions had Marthe inherited from her mother, who, for her part, would certainly have returned to the Montbourgs most of what came from them. My feeling, my conviction, is that Louise didn't *ensnare* her, strictly speaking: she was served by circumstances. She didn't envenom Marthe's intentions, but did nothing to bring them back to her family, either. Marthe made her will in all freedom and lucidity of mind, as the curate first and then the notary have told us. Ah, her affection for Louise was deep; it would be enough to convince anyone to read the things, all tender, that she would write on the subject of her "dear Louise." Louise was her *all,* as she kept telling me: "She's my companion, she's my nurse, she's my accountant, for, would you believe it," she would say to me, "I don't even know how to add; lastly, when needed, she's my secretary." Without Louise, Marthe would have become Victorin's wife. She told me so a number of times, and she was sincere. I've seen things from too close up to be able to doubt it.

Good-bye, dear Papa.

Your affectionate son,

Henri

LOUISE GALOURET
TO HENRI DE CERILLEY
Millau, June 5, 1902

Dear Sir,

Not having had any news of your trip yet, I assume that it went well. Next Monday and Tuesday they will have the novena service here for poor dear Madame: they'll hold ten Masses. So if that day, sir, you can attend a few Masses and pray for her, I'd be very grateful to you, and from the heights of heaven, where God has no doubt admitted her, she'll protect us for as long as it is granted us to live here below.

Be good enough, sir, to give me news of yourself and all your family. That will always give me the greatest pleasure. We'll talk often about the dear deceased, who will thus live among us in our thoughts; for, believe me, sir, although I'm surrounded by my family, I'm finding myself very sad and alone in this house. She was so good to me that I can never forget it and that I can't get used to the idea of being separated from her forever. I still see her everywhere here, and if my means had allowed it immediately, I would have left this house where I've been so happy and where a great unhappiness has come to trouble my happiness, since for me she was not a mistress but a sister, a sincere and devoted friend. The seals are not yet broken: the justice of the peace kept raising problems because of my husband. However, according to my marriage contract, an attorney wrote to the justice to have him break the seals, so I think that tomorrow or the day after I'll be able to clean up the house, which needs it. Then I'll send you a few little souvenirs of the one who loved you so, and also her dear photograph. As soon as you've made a draft of the death notices, be good enough, sir, to get me one, so I can have a few printed for the persons with whom Madame was in frequent correspondence, either here or elsewhere.

Please, dear sir, accept my family's condolences and my assurance of deep devotion.

Louise Galouret

CHARLES DE CERILLEY
TO ADÈLE DE CERILLEY
Sangy, June 6, 1902

Dear Adèle,

Your letter was most welcome, bringing us good news of you all. As for me, I'm paying for often getting overtired. I almost haven't slept at all for three nights now. Enclosed is a letter from Madame Valentine de Montbourg, asking me the name of the notary who received Marthe's will. It's the right of blood relatives to know the text of the will, but let them not ask me for my testimony, for Henri and I have too clearly in mind Marthe's very *precise* intent. That does not keep us from regretting the *deliberate* omission of the Montbourgs; apart from that, the legal freedom to make one's will is a *sacred* matter.

Mama has learned indirectly that our chambermaid is considering leaving us a month or two from now. Consequently, we have to look around. So try to find us a replacement within that space of time. Wages: 350 to 360 francs a year. I'm also looking elsewhere. What a nuisance this merry-go-round of domestics is; they are all discontented.

Everyone has applauded Henri's inheritance. Léon has written me and I've answered him. I'm keeping all the replies and making a dossier of them.

For a long time to come, I won't buy any French securities, so black is the political future. We're going to pass through a crisis, and the sooner the better. The people will have to see that they've been deceived for a long time by those who exploit their passions. For that, a *general* crisis is necessary. We're getting there. Let's prepare for it, so as to get through the trial as tolerably as possible, for it may perhaps be hard but not very long: in our time, everything goes very fast in every respect.

Our collectivist deputy has promised the farmers a decrease in their farm rents and so on down the line.

Good-bye, my dear daughter. We all send you a hug and a kiss.

Charles de Cerilley

SOPHIE DE MONTBOURG
TO HENRI DE CERILLEY
Sainte-Apolline, June 8, 1902

Dear Henri,

I've been in such pain these last few days that I haven't been able to answer your long letter full of details on poor Marthe's death. I begin by telling you that I'm fully convinced that neither your father nor you tried to deter Marthe from leaving to the Montbourgs that part of their fortune that had come to her from them. My sister-in-law has asked me for a copy of the will because she has a responsibility toward the children of the family and she will turn the will over to her notary. This will—made two days before Marthe's death, without the family's being notified of her illness, which dated from May 11—may indeed seem strange. At least the absolute omission of the paternal family comes out even more in light of her letters, shorter in the last two months but extremely affectionate, not only toward me but toward all her cousins.

Two months ago, she was asking me urgently to come to Millau— she wanted to talk to me. My health unfortunately made it impossible, and I didn't suspect she might need my presence. Louise did not notify me of the illness in any way. *I* had to wire *her* on receiving your father's letter, and her answer was "Madame deceased yesterday, have notified Monsieur Henri."

To my request for details, she replied that the illness began on the 11th, that Marthe made her confession and received extreme unction, but did not take communion. Not a word about the will, naturally. In short, all that is strange, very strange, truthfully. There is no reason she should not leave a nice share to Louise, even from her paternal fortune alone, to bolster her income. But in these difficult times, to make the whole fortune disappear entirely strikes me as a lack of conscience. Alas! I've already had enough experiences with the covetousness of inferiors since I've been a widow to suspect what happened between her and Louise when illness placed her in absolute moral and material dependence!

I don't doubt that all the precautions were well taken for the validity of the public will. The residual legatee had every interest in that. The only family consolation is that her life ended favorably and religiously, whereas she might have followed her original intention after divorce. Let's hope that her charities will open the gates of heaven to her. I've had a Mass said for her this week just the same.

I don't think I answered the question about your death notices. It's obviously preferable not to send any at all, and to tell one another so in the family.

I'm keeping your letter to have it read by your cousins when they come to see me here.

Give your children a kiss for me. This makes them good catches!

I send you yourself a very affectionate embrace. Your poor aunt,

Sophie de Montbourg

J. BOUCHARD, CARTER
TO HENRI DE CERILLEY
Caen, June 6, 1902

Sir,

I hasten to send you herewith, in the form of a money order, the balance, namely 200 francs, of the debt I contracted toward Madame de Montbourg, and now being quit of that, so as to avoid troubles with your cousin's estates, I ask you to send me my notes by return mail.

Please, sir, accept all my thanks.

J. Bouchard

CHARLES DE CERILLEY
TO HENRI DE CERILLEY
Sangy, June 10, 1902

I haven't received a letter from your Aunt Sophie since that of May 31.

I wrote yesterday to tell you that the Montbourgs strongly favor not sending any general notices and contenting themselves with handwritten letters to friends and intimates. We have nothing at all to gain by attracting the public's attention to Marthe, whose position was very false. What name would you use for her, since the Church does not recognize divorce? The simplest thing is to be silent about it toward the public. My opinion has also been approved by Paul in his letter this morning. So that's one thing settled. I've written to all the family and friends. Write to Abbé Bosset in Grasse.

Poor Marthe employed duplicity out of an instinctive need to make her peace with her paternal blood. She lied all her life; play-acting came naturally to her. I'm very glad your aunt Sophie is, in her disappointment, quite correct on every point, in content and in form.

I'm also telling Louise that there will be only handwritten death notices and that I have done them.

Good-bye. Again, a thousand fond wishes to you all.

Charles de Cerilley

LOUISE GALOURET
TO CHARLES DE CERILLEY
Millau, June 13, 1902

Dear Sir,

Your letter greatly distressed me, for I see that even after her death, poor Madame Marthe is not placed on the same level as the other members of the family, and I don't see why. Is it because her whole life, however short, was for her a martyrdom in one way or another, because she'd been married off to a bad character who made her suffer in a thousand ways, and there had to be a separation—is it for that that she must be excluded from the honors that are due her? Yes, she was *divorced;* nevertheless, she was esteemed and loved by all those who came near her, and in the eyes of God she may perhaps have been greater than many of those whose religion is so hypocritical. She was frank, loyal, and charitable, qualities that are rarely met with. So, sir, for my part, a mere stranger who devoted myself to her as she devoted herself to me, I shall always bless and respect her memory. I've been able to know her and appreciate her better than anyone. Well, I dare to predict that after the good death she made, her good works will open to her the gates of heaven, and the hope of meeting her again some day there is what softens my great sorrow a bit. She loved me so, and she always told me she had been the least well regarded of the family and that the day God took her away they would all be very glad. If God permits her to see what's happening on earth, she'll see that her ideas are coming true, since even after being kind and devoted to all her kinfolk, she still has no right to the same things as the other members of her family. It's true that that matters little to her, but for me it has been very distressing. I wouldn't want to offend you with this letter, sir, but I'm frank and I say what I think, for until the final day, I'll do what I can so that the memory of the one who was such a devoted friend to me may be respected.

Very devotedly yours,

Louise Galouret

LOUISE GALOURET
TO HENRI DE CERILLEY
Millau, June 13, 1902

Dear Sir,

Your letter has reached me safely, along with its contents, and I thank you very much for being kind enough to send it to me. At the same time, I've just received one from Monsieur Charles that greatly distressed me and which I'm answering right away. You were asking me the number of death notices I'd need, for which I thank you very much, while your father tells me he has agreed with the family not to send any general notices, since Madame was divorced. I don't see why, sir, even after her death she is denied; they don't do for her what they have done for all the other members of the family, for the persons to whom these notices were to be addressed all knew her situation, and she was nonetheless respected and esteemed. As for me, sir, ever will I venerate and respect her memory. God has stricken us very cruelly by parting us so abruptly, but I put my hope in Him who is merciful.

Believe me, sir, I'm very saddened to find myself alone now. She was everything to me, as I was everything to her. As soon as I'm a little stronger and can overcome my sorrow, I'll send you a few souvenirs, but I don't yet dare face the things that belonged to her: it pains me too much. I'll send you her little photograph as soon as I have it, but for the moment it is at the photographer's so I can get several prints—for here she was so much loved that everyone would like to have one.

The seals were broken a week ago today, my papers have gone off to Paris to the bank, and I'm awaiting their reply. I will have a marriage contract that is very favorable for me; everything is paraphernal,[66] which means that I can control what I will have without my husband's getting involved; he may be able to ask me for an allowance, but between now and then I'll see what I have to do and I'll be able to ask for a legal separation.

I close, sir, with my very best wishes.

Louise Galouret

EDWIGE DE CERILLEY
TO HENRI DE CERILLEY
June 16, 1902

Dear Henri,

Thank you for the details you've given me about Marthe; in spite of her weak points, I loved that child; she had such a good heart, and may perhaps not have been fully responsible for all her actions, given her temperament and her extraordinary upbringing.

I was very concerned to know whether she had died in a good frame of mind, and since she prepared herself well, I think that for her it's perhaps happier that she went, for she might have let herself go again or remarried.

She had promised to visit me over the summer, and I would have taken her in with pleasure. She told me that she wouldn't do anything for the Montbourgs and that there were only you and me that she really loved in her family, and I told your father here that you would surely get the Sangy properties. I'm very glad you're happy, for I sincerely love you.

I've been long in answering you, but I'm not yet strong. My head spins as soon as I write even a little, and, besides, I have a lot to do, both outdoors and in. Your father may have told you I've settled in alone in my father's apartment, and, being unable to pay for a domestic, I have only a cleaning woman who comes very seldom. So I'm obliged to do almost everything by myself, which is arduous at my age, particularly since I don't have the habit of it.

Never in my life, I think, have I found myself so hard up. If Marthe had lived, she would certainly have got me out of this squeeze, for she always told me to turn to her, which I hadn't yet done, but I admit that at the moment when she fell ill I was going to write to her. Her last letter to me was dated during early May, and I got sick the day I received it. If I had answered her, she might perhaps have left me a little assistance.

You would do me an immense favor if you could get me 300 francs. I'll pay you interest on it and give it back to you as soon as I've sold my wine. I have so much to pay for at the end of the month that I'm losing my mind. Please don't speak to anyone about what I'm confiding to you, but really I have nothing left to sell in the way of furniture or knickknacks except a very ancient iron strongbox that comes from the Abbey of Cluny. My father turned down 500 francs for it, but I'd let you have it for 400 francs if you liked it, and if it didn't suit you, you'd certainly find a buyer for it. The lock that holds the lower part of the cover has seven tumblers and is very curious, all in fine steel;

it's all old, even the paint on it. Do you want me to send it to you by freight?

You see, you can't imagine my dismal situation, and yet I don't spend even a franc a day on food; it's true that I have a right to the fruits and vegetables from the garden. Did your father tell you that I'd turned over to him some family papers that I found in that very strongbox? It occurred to me that it was really to you, as head of the family, that they should go.

Excuse my asking, dear Henri, and try to help me, I beseech you. You'd give me great pleasure if you'd come see me this summer, and you'd see that I know very well how to manage when I have a single guest.

Fondest greetings with all my heart, and all my best to Adèle.

Aunt Edwige

LOUISE GALOURET
TO HENRI DE CERILLEY
Millau, June 17, 1902

Dear Sir,

Your two letters reached me yesterday and I reply right away.

I thank you with all my heart for the sympathy you always showed to your dear and lamented cousin. You alone loved her sincerely; take my word for it, sir, all her other relatives took hardly any interest in her. Look at them all, sir. Did they even send her a plain wreath as a last tribute? No, and yet, for example, when we were at Sainte-Apolline, didn't she do that for her people, and didn't she go to some trouble for them? This is how she was rewarded for it. Fortunately, she didn't wait for human gratitude—God alone will have recompensed her for all her sufferings and all her sacrifices, and she will watch over us all, sir. May she obtain for us a good and saintly death, just as hers was; that's what I keep asking, and when we're all reunited in God's presence, then we'll be happy and will all forget the tears we're shedding today.

As for the general notices, their reasons are hardly admissible. Everyone here thinks it's very queer. I know it's none of your fault and that you would have taken her side against the others, but we must let it go—those things can't reach her any longer now, and that way she'll see who really loved her. You didn't quite understand about Victorin. He had written only once and Madame hadn't answered, so he was kept at a distance. As soon as you're back in Lyon, I'll send you a few little mementos of the one who was so dear to us all. My whole family will come and live with me as soon as everything has been put in order. Here I haven't got a thing, which is so distressing to me.

My contract is coming along well, but if I can't get at my funds to carry out what she urged me to do without my husband's signature, I'm going to request a legal separation, which would secure me against everything.

Respectfully yours,

Louise Galouret

SOPHIE DE MONTBOURG
TO CHARLES DE CERILLEY
Sainte-Apolline, June 20, 1902

Dear Charles,

I've received your letter containing Louise's. Louise's letter is not wholly to the point with regard to us, for she says that Marthe was good to all her kin. That is true solely for you and Henri. What would you have replied to her if, instead of inheriting virtually the entire maternal fortune, on which I personally had a claim by blood, you had been completely omitted, as we are? I think your letter is not completely objective.

As for the breaking of the seals, I believe it's not so simple as you seem to be telling Louise; unless there's a very recent law, a stranger cannot be put in possession of the property left him until a renunciation is signed by those having claims by blood.

Now, I don't suppose that Valentine would sign a renunciation before receiving the will and having it examined, and we can't do otherwise than she does.

As you say to me, three and a half years of service do not motivate such a considerable gift. I don't care a rap about the question of the child. His name was d'Aillot, following the acknowledgment involved in her marriage, and he has nothing to do with the will question. If Émilie had him buried under another name, that's a legal misrepresentation. Indeed, I don't think our poor dear sister would have acted like Marthe.

You might perhaps be making a mistake to speed up your settling of accounts with Louise too much. The question remains pending, as you see. Louise would have been smarter to make a few gifts to the Montbourgs, smarter also not to notify Henri *alone*. I still remember your predictions for the future, when Émilie had her three children living.

... That seemed crazy to me ... and the future has proved you completely right. Poor Émilie! She had a very painful life! Here she is now, reunited with all her loved ones. She must have seen from up there that I'd offered to leave Marthe the furniture from the salon at Saint-Savin. We couldn't do anything more, you will admit.

My fondest wishes.

Your affectionate sister,

Sophie

CHARLES DE CERILLEY
TO HENRI DE CERILLEY
Sangy, June 20, 1902

Dear Henri,

Louise is quite indignant at my decision, approved by the Montbourgs, not to send any general notice of poor Marthe's death. I answered her with firmness and dignity, in such a way as not to offend her, and even to honor her. What do you think of your Aunt Philomène's playing dumb about Marthe de Montbourg's name, and asking in her reply if that might be a daughter of my sister Sophie, or a daughter-in-law? She pretends not to understand anything about it. I'm not answering.

Louise wanted to put on airs with the family. That built her up. I tell her that her gratitude made it hard for her to appreciate the delicate social reasons militating in favor of relative and tasteful silence around the grave of our poor niece.

Her triumph after three and a half years of very self-seeking devotion has gone to her head and is making her say stupid things, as you'll see by her letter, which will be returned to me after your aunt has communicated it to her children. I've also sent a copy of my reply to Louise. I'll be much approved for the content and the form.

If your poor cousin had wanted to put on a squalid act for Sainte-Apolline, she couldn't have done it better. But as for us, we often told her she had heart, lots of heart; that flattered her, and besides, there was in her a natural instinct to draw as close to the family as possible, to go and weep with her people, *never* to refuse herself. She did it without sparing either her strength or her purse. Consequently, *not play-acting*. But *disappointed hope* can still see it there. On that score, it will be our duty to defend her memory. Still, to have disinherited all the Montbourgs, abso-

348

lutely, so as to reward beyond measure three and a half years of devotion, *that's insufferable.*

I think, as you do, that Louise must have to reckon with her husband, from whom she is separated only in fact. She may be forced to reach some compromise with him in order to be authorized to accept the inheritance. It's a bizarre situation.

Good-bye, dear Henri.

Your affectionate father,

Charles de Cerilley

CHARLES DE CERILLEY
TO SOPHIE DE MONTBOURG
Sangy, June 23, 1902

Dear Sophie,

If you consider my letter to Louise not objective enough, I neverthe-less did my best to be, above all, just. Justice consists in respecting all rights, even those that offend us morally. Now, the impression you make at the moment is far from that ideal, and I urge you to be very prudent in this matter of the inheritance. It seems impossible to me to say that Louise ensnared her. Do you want an irrefutable witness? There's Adrienne, saying to Marthe that she would do well some day to think of her paternal family, to which Marthe, with her well-known crudeness, replied, "Me, leave something to the Montbourgs? Why, I'd rather found a hospital for mad dogs!" You can't very well top that, can you? I'd rather not have repeated that dismal outburst to you, but you need to get over illusions that you might regret.

In the case in point, Marthe acted within her crude right as far as you are concerned, and, one must admit, she was more logical toward her mother's memory than her mother herself would have been if she had survived *all* her children. But I respect legal expressions of will, *and you do well to have the will gone over with a fine-tooth comb.*

I think it's free of any legal flaw, except perhaps from the direction of Louise's husband. That's what you will do well to look into. Louise's is an amicable separation, and her husband hasn't legally forfeited his rights as administrator. The law needs to clarify this special point, which might well concern those two alone.

One shadow on Marthe's memory is that in drawing closer, *through the needs of her heart,* to her family by going on her own to Sainte-Apolline, she gave the illusion of having benevolent intentions that would find expression in her will, and all that for *nothing.* No, there was no play-acting; a person doesn't expend her strength and her money on such trips in winter—hard for a woman—to enjoy the luxury of play-acting. It's just illogical, that's all.

I would have other considerations to put before you to prove to you the state of mind of poor Marthe and her mother. Let it suffice to remind you that at the time of M.'s unhappy delivery, your husband refused me his help in seeking a house of refuge in Paris, whereas Monsieur de Saint-René, your quite distant cousin, gave me his without reservation. Émilie and her daughters never forgot that. *There* is some logic that must be considered.

I beg you, consider well, and don't plunge in at random. I'm well documented, and that doesn't keep me from blaming sharply the crude but freely chosen solution adopted by poor Marthe. That's the general feeling here.

Your affectionate brother,

Charles de Cerilley

EDWIGE DE CERILLEY
TO HENRI DE CERILLEY
June 24, 1902

Dear Henri,

In the same mail this morning I receive your good letter and the envelope containing 300 francs of the National Treasury, receipt of which I write immediately to acknowledge.

I can't thank you enough for your kindness to me. I was so touched by it that it gave me a palpitation. I'm certainly going to offer a prayer for everything to come out well for you and for Adèle's health to be completely restored again.

It must be very hot for your races, but it's good weather for the hay and the vines, and up to now the weather has been pretty bad.

Thanks again, and my very affectionate kisses.

Aunt Edwige

Dear Henri,

Your Aunt Sophie is back in line, under the influence of my letter. So the matter will rest there. To be sure, there are two points that might be raised: (1) The moral obligation (according to your aunt) of the heir to manifest his gratitude through general notices. There is in that a drop of malice on their part. (2) Your aunt believes that I had the gift of foresight on the subject of the death of your Aunt Émilie's three children. Come now, at the time of Émile's death, it was the doctor who called my attention to his water on the brain, and Éléonore's lesser case of it. As for Marthe, he said to me that she was solidly built.

It's only in the last two years that I've feared violent ills for her. But your aunt puts malice into it and tries to make me out a self-seeking prophet. If her letter weren't so proper, I'd tell her that, like the other home truths.

You don't need to return to me all the letters sent you; just keep them for me, that's all.

Good-bye, dear Henri.

Your affectionate father,

Charles de Cerilley

I've just received, dear Charles, through one of the high notables of Millau, a letter full of curious details about Marthe, and also a printed death notice (prepared by Louise, evidently) in which I appear in full *as mother of the deceased and Valentine as sister!* . . . I'm absolutely revolted by this action and I can't put up with it. It's a falsehood, known to be so, since Louise knew Marthe's mother, and since this falsehood has as its aim to sow calumny on our branch as having abandoned an errant daughter—and this after getting my children disinherited!

That's really too much, and can't get by!

Marthe got chills and fever on leaving a socialist banquet over which she had presided! That's where Louise's influence had led her! The radical mayor was one of her friends, hence the firemen at her burial. She made socialist propaganda for the elections. The impression at Millau is that Louise did more than take advantage of the wind in her sails. You knew more than I did about Marthe's habits, and I won't repeat to you what comes back to me about them, but people thought her completely lower-class. Louise dominated her entirely, and not in the right direction, it seems. Here, the death notice had the effect of a bomb! Everyone who's known the family knows it's false. Others will read in it that Marthe was a bastard abandoned by her relatives—by me, her mother (?), at their head. So much for Henri and you, so much against us; that's a contrast, you will admit, in Louise's behavior.

Good-bye, my dear chap.

Your affectionate sister,

Sophie

CHARLES DE CERILLEY
TO HENRI DE CERILLEY
Sangy, July 5, 1902

Dear Henri,

Are these false notices the deliberate work of Louise, and with what purpose? Or was it jealousy in that social underworld that devised this inept stroke? You may be sure that there is plenty of jealousy of Louise. What is your opinion, and what is to be done in regard to her? I'll point out the fact to her first of all, and ask for an explanation at the same time as for a copy of these false notices.

I expect that Louise will deny any part in the act. Her defense is made easier by the errors about relationships that she can't fail to know. Then who did the trick?

Your aunt's letter lets her jealousy of you and me show through! I hope for her sake she doesn't say too much about it.

I have no trouble believing that Marthe played the woman of the people in Millau. But didn't those who wrote to your aunt exaggerate anything? The socialists don't have the habit of religious ceremonies such as we have seen. That was an outburst of popular vanity, a democratic ovation. So much for the public. Beneath these official flowers there may have slipped in some jealous serpents who have elaborated ignobly on a theme more or less vaguely known.

You can't absolve yourself of protesting on your part to Louise:

That's why I'm writing about it to your Aunt Sophie, whom I'm warning not to take me for Louise's advocate, which is offensive to me, and that it's time she stopped thinking like that. Reread her letter well and keep it for me.

I'm telling your aunt that we've never *known* anything of Marthe's habits at Millau. All suppositions are possible with hysteria. But we haven't had any proof.

Good-bye, dear chap. What a bomb that notice was! It's a lowdown, jealous trick, for sure. A thousand fond wishes.

Your affectionate father,

Charles de Cerilley

P.S. By examining the notice one can probably find out the name of the publisher and his address. Then I'll write him to find out who ordered these notices from him and how many. What do you say to that?

HENRI DE CERILLEY
TO CHARLES DE CERILLEY
Lyon, July 8, 1902

Dear Papa,

The high notable of Millau who informed Aunt Sophie so well must be a part of the society that cannot accept, and with some reason, the fact that Marthe was so eager for popularity. To understand it, you have to know the whole past. But I don't swallow the story of Marthe *presiding* over a socialist banquet. She may have taken part several times in plebeian love feasts, all right, but without any political purpose. When I saw Marthe at Millau last October, she used to tell me she saw almost no one. Aunt Sophie imagines that Louise has had her children disinherited! I won't stop repeating it: Louise simply took advantage of poor Marthe's personal ideas. If Marthe had asked my advice, I would have given it to her so that in spite of her obstinacy, her paternal family wasn't totally left out.

But that was a delicate subject on which I saw no reason to take an initiative, because she was very touchy. Louise probably thought better of offering me the diamond necklace, or else her family dissuaded her from getting rid of a valuable piece of jewelry. In a letter of last week, she announces that she's sending me "a few little mementos." Now, yesterday I received for the children two vermilion tablecloths marked with their monogram, for Adèle a brand-new mauve parasol, for me a tie pin, a cigarette holder, and a hunting game-bag—all pretty paltry things. But no necklace. Aunt Sophie lets her spite burst out too much and sometimes doesn't make sense.

Good-bye, dear Papa.

Your affectionate son,

Henri

SOPHIE DE MONTBOURG
TO CHARLES DE CERILLEY
Sainte-Apolline, July 8, 1902

Your letter, dear chap, gave me pleasure, for I don't like to suffer unreasonably from an act that may come from another hand than the one I thought. It may be that the death-notice trick comes from d'Aillot. But I wouldn't see the point of that, as you say, whereas from Louise the notice would explain to the public at the same time both our absence from the burial and the will in her favor. I didn't look on the death notice for the printer's name before sending it back. There is Millau, to be sure, but ordinarily the printer's name is in very fine print in the margin or at the edge on the bottom. Louise's husband wouldn't have had an old model of a family notice, since he was separated when Louise entered Émilie's service. Valentine has just told me she's seen the name and address of the Millau printer on the death notice, but she didn't copy it. So it exists. Yes, the whole family is on that notice, I as *mother,* Valentine as *sister,* then I don't remember the order—you're on it, Clémence is on it, and all my children.

The notary has finally made up his mind to send the copy Valentine asked for.

From the point of view of Marthe's Christian death, it's better that she shouldn't have remarried as a divorcée; but what about the name, which she had resumed? The result, brought into the open by the death notice, is disastrous, and I don't know how to conjure it away for my children. How can one not attribute it to Louise, after the furious letter from her that you sent to me and that my children have read? Would some jealous riffraff have paid the cost of it? Did that block the will and make them the heirs? Truly, no, so that's unacceptable on that score. Alas! I'd

354

like to doubt the cause of poor Marthe's illness and death, but *vox populi.* . . . It's sad—it all might have gone unperceived without that death notice.

My affectionate greetings, in which my children join me,

Sophie

[Note by Charles:]

It's the uncorrected notice of Éléonore's death that served as a very incorrect model for Marthe's death notice. So it's quite simple.

CHARLES DE CERILLEY
TO HENRI DE CERILLEY
Sangy, July 14, 1902

Dear Henri,

Your Aunt Sophie is at last satisfied about the quite involuntary cause of the mistakes in Louise's death notice, but how many wild theorizings it brought about! The notary sent to Valentine de Montbourg—or, rather, to her notary—the copy of the will. So now they're clear all along the line, and it's high time. I was tired of that correspondence, which was getting out of hand.

I'm going to ask you to do an errand at the Grandes Galeries:[67] on my last stay with you, I bought a coffeepot there that I thought was for at least five cups, and Mama wanted it for six cups, and it holds only four. It's untouched, hasn't been used at all, and is in its packing carton. The question is to find out whether they would take it back and give us one for six real cups—with us paying the difference of course. Let me know if they will, and I'll send you the article by parcel post to exchange.

I have a touch of eczema, a little on the left thigh, a little on the hands, and especially on the left eye; it made me very tired yesterday and last night gave me insomnia. It's getting better, and I hope it won't be bad for long. It's almost always in July that that happens to me, as a result of a few rather hard manual jobs in the sun.

Good-bye, my dear chap. Your affectionate father,

Charles de Cerilley

P.S. My eyesight is weakening, and that worries me a bit.

LOUISE GALOURET
TO HENRI DE CERILLEY
Millau, July 20, 1902

Dear Sir,

I was very glad to see that the little parcel reached you, for I would have been sorry if it had been lost. Here everything is working out; my husband, having been notified that he was wanted here, arrived this week. He gave me the authorization I needed to accept the inheritance. I think now it will all be finished soon, for which I'm waiting eagerly, especially to carry out her last wishes. The first thing for me is to do what she ordered me to, the biggest thing of all. Did you find the photograph suitable for reproducing? It seems to me it's not bad, except that the way she has her hair isn't the same as these last few years. Your father wrote me about the erroneous death notices that were sent to Sainte-Apolline and that angered the family. I was the one who made these mistakes, by giving as a model a notice that had served for Mademoiselle Éléonore, and since I had a lot on my mind, I didn't think to correct it; but I only had some sent out in Millau to invite people to the funeral, which doesn't explain how some managed to reach the family.

If you stop by here, we can revisit in her last resting place the one whom we so mourn. She'll be so happy to see you so near her, sir, for rest assured that you'll always be at home here. Everything is at your disposal. You loved her so, too, you who were able to understand her and sympathize with all her suffering, which explains, sir, why I would always be so happy to talk with you about her. All Millau misses her, especially in this quarter, where everyone had come to appreciate her. What consoles me and should assuage some of the sorrow of this great loss is that she died as a good Christian. That's the only consolation, and I hope some day to be reunited with her, never to leave her again, her and all her noble family, who were all so good to me.

Most respectfully yours,

Louise Galouret

LOUISE GALOURET
TO HENRI DE CERILLEY
Millau, August 7, 1902

Dear Sir,

I'm enclosing a photograph of our dear and late-lamented Madame de Montbourg. I think it's not too bad. The printer again made a mistake in the name, but I couldn't send them back once they were finished, and I don't think that can make anybody angry, for it's just to recall her to the memory of those who knew and loved her. I'd address one to your father, but since the spelling of the name is incorrect, that might perhaps annoy him. So be good enough, sir, to tell him that if he'd like one, I'll keep it for him till you're good enough to let me know. Since the whole family took offense about the death notice, I don't want the same thing to happen with these pictures: I never had any idea of giving the slightest distress to anyone, but unfortunately the sad circumstances caused this mistake.

Devotedly yours,

Louise Galouret

LOUISE GALOURET
TO HENRI DE CERILLEY
Millau, November 3, 1902

Dear Sir,

Here I am back home again for a few days now, after accomplishing a very painful task. I can't express to you my sorrow when, at Montpellier, I saw once again the house where I was so happy, a time cut short when three beloved people were taken from me. Once again I saw, at the cemetery, the little coffin containing the remains of a little angel. It is true that today he is no longer to be pitied; he's happy and has escaped all human miseries. Yet I loved him very much, too, the little darling, and then there was greater pain when I saw again the sarcophagus that forever encloses the body of the one who was everything for me. Oh, how sad that was for me, for now there is nothing more here of that good family, nothing but their memory, which will last as long as my life. Oh, how painful it is, sir, to see pass away, one after the other, those who are so good. The cross is very heavy, and yet God asks us to bow beneath the hand that strikes us, and we must obey. How I bless Him still for giving a gentle death to all those I've seen cross the threshold of Eternity, in which they were able to receive all the comforts of our religion. Today, All Souls' Day, after Mass I went to their tomb and prayed for them all, for in the same recollection they are all reunited. They were all so good to me that I would be the most ignoble of creatures if ever their memory were erased from my heart. I couldn't set up any memorial, not having been able to get the money soon enough, and now that winter is coming, I can't risk having stones that the frost could ruin. I'm going to order it and in the spring have it set up. For now, I was in a hurry to get the vault in order to bring them together at least, and that's what I've done; I'm very happy that at least they're there, now and forever. Here everyone is pretty well, I'm not very strong myself, for the grief is killing me, but as long as you can drag yourself around, that's everything.

I don't think I told you that my husband has come back to me. He's repented and I've forgiven: life is so short that it's no use living on meanness, and at his age he was unhappy, and I was sorry for him. I've forgotten everything, and I hope God will grant us a few more good days, for up to now I've been very unhappy.

Please, sir, present all my respects to Madame de Cerilley and a fond caress to the little ones if they'd like it. I might send them a few postcards, as they had told the dear deceased they would like to have some. My whole family joins me, sir, in renewing to you my assurance of our feelings of respect and devotion always.

Louise Galouret

Translator's Notes

1. Marthe's reasons for using this name are unclear.
2. Still husband-to-be as the letters begin, before he and Marthe had met.
3. Homestead of the Montbourg family, owned by Émilie, who lived in it with her daughters, near or in the village of Saint-Savin; here usually called "Saint-Savin" or "le Moutier" ("the Minster," an old term for "monastery"). It may once have been a monastery.
4. Émilie's term for the nuns who ran the home or asylum where Marthe was confined, on Rue Saint-Jacques (Paris 6e, Left Bank), between the Sorbonne and the Jardins du Luxembourg. She was confined as an unwed mother-to-be suffering from hysteria, leucorrhea, and other ailments apparently traceable to the syphilis her father had contracted and given her mother (letter from Robert Caron d'Aillot to Charles de Cerilley of November 25, 1895, and *passim*). The home was one of many known as "Saint-Raphaël"'s, named after the archangel.
5. The "good curate" of the village of Tourette near Grasse, friend to Marthe and her family.
6. The director of the Saint-Raphaël where Marthe was a "boarder."
7. Evidently one of several homes so named, more rigorous than Marthe's Saint-Raphaël.
8. The Jardin des Plantes, on the Left Bank near the Salpêtrière and the Gare d'Austerlitz, includes a small zoo.
9. Another cleric and family friend, less close than the curate but higher in rank.
10. Location of the office of a doctor much consulted (by mail only) by Émilie; he was helped in his practice by his wife, a clairvoyant, known here as *la somnambule de Bordeaux.*
11. See note 3.
12. The Virgin Mary as patron goddess of war; a sculpture of her is on the Arc de Triomphe de l'Étoile (Paris), which was built between 1806 and 1836 by order of Napoleon to commemorate his victories.
13. The French *collège*— religious, municipal, or private in support (in contrast to the state's *lycée)*— is more like a U.S. high school (though more advanced) than like a U.S. college.
14. September 22, 1792, the day after the republic was proclaimed, was the first day of the Revolutionary Calendar.
15. Sainte-Apolline, home of Honoré and Sophie de Montbourg, was renowned for its pears, generally rated the finest in France.

16. Not otherwise identified; nor is the "surrogate guardian" *(le subrogé tuteur)* referred to just below and often in later letters.
17. First anniversary of the death of her much-lamented only son, Émile, which, though stressed earlier, is curiously not mentioned here.
18. "French Huntsman" (or "Hunter"), a favorite magazine of huntress Marthe.
19. Supporters of Don Carlos de Borbón (1788–1855), then his son Don Carlos de Montemolín, against Napoleon and later French successors in occupation and rule; generally ultraconservative and devoutly Catholic.
20. Drug used to provide relief from fevers and rheumatism.
21. As brought out by Robert d'Aillot in a letter to Charles de Cerilley of November 25, 1895, before Marthe was conceived, her father had contracted syphilis and passed it to Émilie, his wife; Émilie passed it down to Marthe, who has presumably passed it on down to wee Georges.
22. A great French financial and political scandal in 1892, arising from the building of the Panama Canal.
23. Little round gingerbread cakes originally made in convents.
24. Also called the Hôtel des Ventes Mobilières, this was a great Paris auction house on Rue Drouot and Boulevard Haussmann.
25. Cap de Bonne-Espérance or Cap des Tempêtes, noted for fierce storms and thus a critical point in sailing around Africa.
26. Adèle de Cerilley, wife of Charles's son Henri.
27. Apparently the Tourette stationmaster mentioned earlier in this letter.
28. Edwige de Cerilley, sister-in-law of Émilie and Charles.
29. Not otherwise identified; another matchmaker eying Marthe's money and prospects.
30. Marie-François Sadi Carnot (1837–94), president of the republic from 1887, assassinated by an Italian anarchist.
31. Jean Casimir-Périer (1847–1907), president as of June 27, 1894, resigned January 15, 1895.
32. Word unknown.
33. According to Webster, "a high-swung pleasure vehicle carrying six or more passengers, driver, and footman."
34. *Paysan du Danube sans esprit* was taken, no doubt rightly, as an insult; but the original, in a fable by Jean de La Fontaine (1621–95), was a Silenus figure, outwardly repulsive but in reality a keen-witted "noble savage."
35. From the comic novel *Tartarin de Tarascon* (1872) and its sequels, by Alphonse Daudet (1840–97), caricaturing the swagger and heroics of Daudet's fellow southerners.

36. *Ratote,* clearly a term of endearment formed from *rat* (rat).
37. Meaning not clear: possibly something like Bovril.
38. Tidbits of crusty bread.
39. *J'ai peu mangé un blanc:* a puzzler, translated here as if a double misspelling by Marthe for *"j'ai pu manger un blanc."*
40. Cannibalistic intent seems unlikely here. Possibly the meaning is "slander her" or "squander her money."
41. Émilie seems to be assuming here that beardlessness implies sexual impotence.
42. Here the plural, not of Dumas's hero *(Three Musketeers)* but of a breed of hens named after him.
43. The leading, most prestigious and advantageous professional schools, such as the École Normale Supérieure, École Navale, École des Sciences Politiques, École Polytechnique, etc.
44. Presumably motorcycles with sidecars, then used in racing.
45. Félix Faure (1841–99) was president of the republic from 1895 to 1899.
46. From context, apparently a daughter-in-law of Charles's making her debut in the correspondence here.
47. Priests and nuns of the Order of Saint François de Sales (1587–1622), dedicated to the education of young working-class men and women.
48. Presiding judge of a law court.
49. A preposterously heinous theft, equivalent to our "selling the Brooklyn Bridge." In Rabelais's *Gargantua* (1534), the young giant takes the bells of Notre-Dame to hang on his mare's neck.
50. Marthe's unexplained pet name for her beloved nurse-companion-friend, Louise Galouret.
51. Émile Loubet (1838–1929), president of the republic from 1899 to 1906.
52. During the night of March 4–5, a naval powder magazine in the Lagoubran quarter of Toulon exploded, with extensive loss of life and property.
53. Defenders (generally liberal) of Alfred Dreyfus in the Dreyfus Affair, which split France bitterly in two in the late 1890s.
54. This is the first letter seeming to hint at Marthe's coming affair with Henri, apparent later.
55. The French is *albanais,* which means Albanian, not "albino"; but since this seems to make no sense, and the dogs are all-white, I suspect a slip on Marthe's part.
56. Little ball, or sphere, or globe; a *boule* is a large ball, as for the game of bowls. This name might be rendered as "Rolypoly."

57. The curative waters (arsenical and silicate) for which the Mont-Dore is renowned.

58. The common noun *morelle* means the plant nightshade. The proper name Morelle (feminine of *moreau,* "Moorish," hence dark, black) might be given to a black mare.

59. A principal square (named for a Napoleonic victory) in Saint-Étienne, a busy industrial city of 225,000 or more, central to coal, steel, and textile manufacture. A strike that began in Saint-Étienne in late 1899 among the weavers and makers of trimmings for clothing seems to have become general by January 1900, when Henri de Cerilley is writing.

60. A dance and song of the French Revolution.

61. From time immemorial the Catholic Church in France has been allied with the aristocrats, the moneyed, and the managers, against the democratic workers, usually anticlerical and often antireligious. Therefore these strikers have shrewdly adopted as passwords Christian, clerical Latin formulas; Henri can merely note their phoniness (repetition, colloquial context, etc.).

62. A year and a half after her mother's death, Marthe has now taken over and rechristened her villa in Grasse.

63. A carter from Caen still owing Marthe a debt once owed to her mother; see more about this later.

64. Protagonist of Molière's grim comedy *L'Avare* (The Miser). His name, from the Greek *harpazō, harpagē,* means "grasping" and suggests rapine. Since 1668, when the play was written, it has represented the embodiment of avarice for the French and is thus not a nice term for the addressee's father.

65. Apparently the wife of Christian de Montbourg, another cousin.

66. Belonging to the wife and unrelated to the dowry.

67. The big Paris department stores, such as Louvre, Printemps, Bon Marché, and Galerie Lafayette.